# Developer, Advocate!

Conversations on turning a passion for talking
about tech into a career

**Geertjan Wielenga**

BIRMINGHAM - MUMBAI

# Developer, Advocate!

**Acquisition Editors**: Dominic Shakeshaft, Jonathan Malysiak
**Project Editor**: Kishor Rit
**Development Editor**: Joanne Lovell
**Technical Editor**: Saby D'silva
**Proofreader**: Safis Editing
**Indexer**: Pratik Shirodkar
**Production Coordinator**: Sandip Tadge

First published: September 2019

Production reference: 1270919

Published by Packt Publishing Ltd.
Livery Place
35 Livery Street
Birmingham B3 2PB, UK.

ISBN 978-1-78913-874-0

www.packt.com

*"I dedicate this book to Bob Gembey and Rick Tersmette, who started my journey in the technology industry, in 1996, when I had no idea what I was getting into and no way of knowing how interesting it was going to be."*

# Contents

**Geertjan Wielenga** was born in the Netherlands and moved with his family at an early age to South Africa. That was because, ironically, his father was appointed by his church as an evangelist in South Africa, just as his son was to become an evangelist, though of a very different kind, over the course of his career in the software industry.

After completing his university studies, which were focused on political science and legal studies, Geertjan left South Africa in 1996 with the intention to travel for a year before resuming his direction in the legal domain. However, he soon found that he needed financial resources to sustain his travels and found himself editing and proofreading technical software manuals in the Netherlands from May 1996 onwards. A series of technical writing stints followed, in a variety of software organizations in the Netherlands, followed by several years in the same domain in Austria and the Czech Republic.

In Prague, he worked for Sun Microsystems from 2004 until its acquisition in 2010 by Oracle. He wrote documentation for NetBeans IDE, while writing and delivering training courses on the NetBeans APIs. He traveled all over the world introducing large organizations to the benefits of building their enterprise software on top of the NetBeans Platform. With the takeover by Oracle, he became a product manager focused on the enterprise JavaScript ecosystem and increasingly specialized in Oracle JET, which is Oracle's free and open-source JavaScript toolkit for frontend user interface development.

His enthusiasms in the software domain have concentrated themselves around the open-source ecosystem and in unlocking the resources that large vendors have for supporting education and open-source ecosystems.

Over the years, he's also informally engaged a number of developer advocates around the world in conversations around their profession, which has led to this book, which he hopes you, the reader, will benefit from and that it will inspire new developers to broaden their perspective on interesting and fulfilling ways of working in the information technology industry.

# Introduction: how to become and how to be

For years, I've been walking around with a growing set of questions to ask the many friends I keep running into on the stages of tech conferences around the world. An example is "How did you get started on the journey that brought you here?"

Inevitably, that journey can only have been uniquely inspiring, since the people you see on the stages of tech conferences, or hear about working behind the scenes to create content to share technical knowledge of various kinds, can't have taken a degree or followed a developer advocate course, because those degrees and courses don't exist or to the extent to which they exist today, they didn't exist at the time these journeys began.

Developer advocacy, broadly referred to as "developer relations" today, is new. Those who practice it have fallen into it in one way or another. And, just as the processes and theories in the world of programming have evolved over several years as programming itself has become a more generally accessible profession, so too the ideas underpinning developer advocacy have come to the surface gradually over time.

This has been as a result of the work that developer advocates have been doing out in the wild using their own initiatives.

Aside from exploring these areas, I've also had a range of questions up my sleeve around the day-to-day existence of people who find themselves in this role. In the modern world, the concept of getting up at a set time and going to an office where work is done until a set time is increasingly less common.

That is even more the case for the inherent itinerancy of the developer advocate's lifestyle, which is frequently precisely the reason for choosing it or for sticking with it in cases where the choice was not so explicitly made. For those interested in or even less aware of this profession, the various ways in which a life can be lived is also something that I wanted to explore.

A third set of concerns I've had for years, and that I've bothered many with over beers at conferences around the world, relate to the ethical dilemmas of the developer advocate role. Though every role inevitably has its own dilemmas, those connected to developer relations are particularly specific, since the role itself is not so clearly defined. Where does your allegiance lie? Clearly somewhere between a community and a company, but where exactly? If the answer is that it shifts from case to case, how can the humble developer advocate understand the path to take? At the same time, many developer advocates don't have this dilemma or intentionally eschew it by working independently, which brings its own set of challenges.

I've been collecting questions around these themes and when I met Dominic Shakeshaft from Packt, who told me about a series of books being put together around interviews in the tech domain, it was clear that I finally had a channel through which these themes could be developed.

The book you're holding is the outcome of a lengthy process of working out questions, discussing them with Dominic and his team at Packt, sounding out developer advocates around the world, and finally, recording interviews with them. The team at Packt, and in particular Joanne Lovell, worked the interview transcripts into coherent discussions, while Kishor Rit managed the process and Jonathan Malysiak rounded off the work and helped to guide the project to its release.

To be perfectly honest, I worked on this book simply to answer questions for myself and to find out how others in this domain struggle with the questions that I've personally been struggling with. Just like the vast majority of those I interviewed, I kind of stumbled into developer advocacy by chance and have wondered where it is that I've stumbled into and how to understand the world in which I've been working since the mid-'90s. In that sense, this book is not a collection of interviews at all; rather, it is a collection of conversations with myself, with each conversation bouncing off a different developer advocate, in some shape or form, while I reflect on a set of questions that are of concern to me at the time of the conversation.

There was a time, not all that long ago, when you would choose a profession in your teens or early 20s, study in that direction, and then work in that domain, in one way or another, all your working life.

In today's economy, that is far less the case and millennials have no problem switching from one domain to the next, or from one service platform to the next, without much concern for what they'll be doing next year or in the next decade.

Flexibility is becoming, to the extent that it hasn't been already, the norm. In this sense, the role of developer advocate is interesting in that those working in this field have already been working in the flexible-millennial way over the last few decades. One could argue that it is a profession whose time has come. It is a profession for our time, for now, while those engaged in it come from a generation slightly previous to that.

Underpinning each conversation that I've had in the context of this book is passion and enthusiasm. A framing that was suggested initially by the publisher was that of "spin doctors," that is, the central questions to be dealt with in this book would have been "Who are these people? How honest are they really? Are they pretending to be one thing while actually being another thing?"

I fought quite hard against this framing, since in my experience, everyone involved in developer advocacy is genuinely authentic and simply wants to share their enthusiasm and the hard-fought knowledge that they've acquired around a tech domain. The questions for me, increasingly, became "How can these people be so passionate? Where does that come from? How do they sustain that? Isn't it amazing that knowledge sharing can be turned into a profession?"

Somewhere underneath the conversations in this book, everyone appears to be asking themselves, in wonder, how it can be that they're being paid to have fun and to share that fun experience with others.

It is enthusiasm that drives all of them, whether they're working independently or for a company of one form or another. They're mostly a little bit concerned that when their employer, if they have one, discovers how fun their working life is, they might be given other less enjoyable work to do. Essentially, everyone in this book is a child-like explorer of a tech domain. Many domains in tech are not explored or are badly explored.

The people in this book are tinkering on the edges of new worlds, expanding them, documenting them, sharing them, and generally enthusing about them.

Another aspect is that of communities. Rather than working in isolation when exploring and extending a tech domain, the people in this book derive and sustain a large degree of their enthusiasm from working together with others, in many cases even being involved in establishing or leading developer communities. That enables all kinds of people, with every imaginable personality trait, to find a valid place in this world.

An interesting discovery for me has been that a lot of developer advocates consider themselves to be introverts. If you're regularly standing on a stage in front of hundreds of people, how can you possibly be an introvert? Well, consider that a stage with a lectern to stand behind, and all the people at a safe distance, simply interested in listening to something that you're passionate about, can be a very inviting place to be for an introvert. Also, of course, developer advocacy is far more than standing on stages—many involved in this field write blogs, articles, and technical tips and tricks, while also holding communities together through behind-the-scenes networking and interactions.

I'd like to thank everyone involved with this project at Packt and all those who took the time to engage in the conversations that make up this book. Several others could also have been included, of course, and hopefully there'll be more books around these themes where those not involved here can be included.

For example, there could be a book of conversations with the people who set up tech conferences. Why do they do it? How did they get started? What are some helpful tips and tricks? Another interesting angle could be people involved in driving open-source projects. What's the current state of open source? What has worked? What hasn't? How do you engage new people and keep them engaged?

Books of conversations can add new layers of authenticity to a topic. Reading the actual words about the experiences of those who live them brings unique insights and has the potential of conveying more deeply what it is that moves people to do the things they do and live the lives that they live.

With this background, I hope the conversations that follow will explain and inspire and maybe entice the reader to in one way or another get started or deepen their involvement in authentically sharing knowledge in general, though in particular around tech, which is so central to our lives today and inevitably will be in the future too.

## 01

> *Advocacy is something that you feel compelled to do.*

# Scott Davis

# Introducing Scott Davis

Scott Davis is a web architect and principal engineer with ThoughtWorks, where he focuses on innovative and non-traditional aspects of web development. He was also the founder of ThirstyHead, a Denver-based training and software development consultancy, where he became convinced that having the freedom to be honest about a product was the only way to speak about it with real enthusiasm. Scott has written a number of articles and books about web development and over the past 10 years has built a reputation as a hugely engaging keynote speaker on developer advocacy. Find Scott on Twitter: `@scottdavis99`

---

**Geertjan Wielenga**: To begin with, do you consider yourself to be a tech evangelist or a developer advocate, or something along those lines?

## The advocacy versus evangelism debate

**Scott Davis**: We could spend our entire conversation simply unpacking the politics behind those two phrases. I prefer "advocacy" over "evangelism" because it implies a more measured, thoughtful, and nuanced discussion. But I can appreciate the passion behind evangelism, and my speaking style has been compared favorably to a "pastor in the pulpit" more than once.

For most of my professional career, as an author, teacher, and speaker at software conferences, I've tried to focus on advocating free and open-source tech.

I like lending my voice and passion to projects that may not have large corporations behind them.

**Geertjan Wielenga**: But wouldn't you say that in the term "evangelism" there is something about enthusiasm that "advocacy" might be missing?

**Scott Davis**: Since I'm not being paid by a corporation to talk about its products, I definitely have an honest, heartfelt fire in the belly for what I choose to talk about.

The first time I spoke at the Great Indian Developer Summit in Bangalore, India, one of the attendees went up to the conference organizer after my talk and said, "I don't remember his name, but be sure to invite back the speaker who has hair like a lion!" I love that! Admittedly, I do roar about standards-based development and open-source solutions quite a bit; it's an apt comparison.

On a related note, it's interesting that what works well on stage (having an outsized personality and a booming speaking voice) works less well for pair programming. You don't want someone who is boisterous and loud as a partner; you want the power dynamic to be far more balanced. Ideally, you want to pair up with someone who listens more than they talk.

**Geertjan Wielenga**: Would you consider the term "spin doctor" to be applicable to you at all?

**Scott Davis**: We're really drawing a fine line here. I think developers, generally speaking, tend to be averse to that kind of marketing spiel. "Marketecture" is the unflattering portmanteau of "marketing" and "architecture" that we use to describe disingenuous tech solutions.

We've all heard stories about key architectural decisions being made between a sales rep and a vice president or chief technology officer (CTO), out on the golf course. True or not, when a tech stack isn't the right solution for the problem at hand, it simply doesn't smell right, and no amount of persuasion will convince you otherwise. It's not the job of the sales rep to point out a product's shortcomings.

> *"Once you lose that authenticity, it's really hard to win it back."*
>
> —*Scott Davis*

I think that, for developers, authenticity is really crucial to the message. I'm a long-time Apple fan, but I'm not an apologist. There was a recent scandal where Apple was accused of intentionally slowing down older legacy phones. The technologist in me can say, "Oh, so Apple is slowing down phones to protect against aging battery issues? That sounds plausible." The suspicious skeptic in me says, "No, Apple is slowing down older phones to make the latest model seem more appealing." The truth is probably some combination of the two, but once you lose that authenticity, it's really hard to win it back.

**Geertjan Wielenga**: Have you ever actually worked for a company and promoted its tech?

**Scott Davis**: I haven't. I've interviewed a number of times with a number of different companies for roles like that. I've had lots of opportunities to be a "product evangelist," to use that phrase.

One of the things I bring up in those interviews is "hey, are you okay with me saying good things about the competition? Are you okay with me talking about rough spots in our API or our product?" I think those questions are crucial to my credibility as an advocate.

Mostly, the response is "are you kidding me? No, you can't say nice things about the competition! No, you can't point out the shortcomings of our product!"

Not being able to speak honestly about a product would mean that I was failing as an advocate. Here's a hypothetical example: if I was a product evangelist for MongoDB, I would want to be able to say, "I really like MongoDB. I've been through the training. The software is good. It has great professional services and support, but it's purely a server-side solution. There isn't a solution if I want to keep some or all of the data local, like in a browser, or if I want to synchronize between multiple instances. It doesn't seem to have an "offline" story. In that case, I'd look to something like PouchDB or CouchDB. Now, if you don't need local synchronization, then MongoDB is a solid option. Let me show you some of the cool things it can do."

That, to me, doesn't feel like I'm being hard on MongoDB. I mean, if it's a feature that the software simply doesn't have, I feel it's important to address it and offer alternatives.

**Geertjan Wielenga**: What would you say are the advantages or disadvantages of being a developer advocate working for a company versus working for yourself?

**Scott Davis**: I ran ThirstyHead—my own software consultancy—for a decade before joining ThoughtWorks. What I enjoyed about working for myself was the freedom to talk authentically about the tech that was really exciting to me.

Thankfully, ThoughtWorks encourages me to continue talking about what I'm most passionate about. It doesn't exert any editorial control at all over what I say on stage or in my writing.

> *"The upsides to working for a large organization in a product advocacy role are that you get a steady paycheck and deep insider knowledge."*
>
> —*Scott Davis*

The upsides to working for a large organization in a product advocacy role are that you get a steady paycheck and deep insider knowledge. You can talk about the cool, new, upcoming features that no one else knows about.

**Geertjan Wielenga**: How did this all begin for you? If you go right back to the very beginning, was there anything in your family life or in your past that led you to where you are now?

## Scott's path to advocacy

**Scott Davis**: Yes, absolutely. My parents met at IBM in the 1960s. My dad was a software engineer and my mother was an IBM Selectric (an early programmable typewriter) consultant.

I literally grew up surrounded by tech in the house—the first IBM PC came out while I was still in elementary school. My dad taught me how to put together spreadsheets, and my mother showed me how to crack open the computer case to add more RAM. I'm not sure that I could've ended up anywhere else than where I am right now, given the parents that I had.

**Geertjan Wielenga**: Initially, were you purely into programming?

**Scott Davis**: I actually started out studying architecture at the University of Nebraska. I was doing fine except for all of my architecture classes, so I dropped out for a year to figure out what I wanted to study next.

I got a job answering phones at a call center for a long-distance phone company. On my own, I put together a spreadsheet that had the names of the operators down one column and the days of the week across the top. I used this magical @sum function to total up the number of calls each operator answered every day. I showed it to my boss and it blew her away. I got into software development very quickly after that.

What I was doing at work wasn't sophisticated, but it was a real game changer in terms of what my boss had to do. Having software take those mundane, repetitive tasks out of your life really adds value.

When I went back to school, I ended up with a degree in Information Systems and Quantitative Analysis (ISQA)—half statistics and half software development.

**Geertjan Wielenga**: How did your career progress from there?

**Scott Davis**: My first job out of college was teaching software classes to business professionals. I started out teaching DOS classes—things like Lotus 1-2-3, WordPerfect, dBase, and Harvard Graphics. Not too long afterward, I started teaching classes for brand new Microsoft products like Windows 3.1, Word, Excel, PowerPoint, and Access.

As we installed networking in the classrooms, I got certified in Novell NetWare 3.11 and began teaching those classes. Over the next couple of years, I ended up with 15 Microsoft certifications in Windows NT 3.51 and 4.0, Exchange, SQL, TCP/IP, and Internet Information Server (IIS), the web server included with the operating system. That was in the early- to mid-1990s, when the first web browsers like Mosaic, Netscape Navigator, and Internet Explorer were introduced to the general public.

What teaching allowed me to do was take a deep dive into different, competing software packages in the same category. Each of those applications was stronger in certain areas and weaker in others. It gave me a more democratic view of software in general—there isn't "one ring to rule them all" when it comes to software. There isn't one true way to do things. There isn't one true programming language, or one true web framework, or even one true operating system.

Tech really is a world of strengths and weaknesses. Advocacy, I think, is where you honestly say, "If we balance out the pluses and the minuses, I'm going to send you down the path where there are more strengths than weaknesses. But I also want to make sure that you are aware of the sharp, pointy edges that might nick you along the way."

I spent eight years in the classroom as a software instructor and that has really informed my entire career. It's one thing to sit down and kind of understand how something works when you're cowboy coding on your own. It's another thing altogether when you're standing up in front of an audience of tens, or hundreds, or thousands of people.

**Geertjan Wielenga**: How did you get from that classroom setting where you were teaching Windows and DOS to being on these public stages?

**Scott Davis**: My mother, in addition to working for IBM, was also in theater. Thanks to her, I've been on the stage since I was five or six years old, so I've always had that confidence that comes from being a performer.

> *"I know my lines and the audience doesn't; it's not a fair fight."*
>
> *—Scott Davis*

It boils down to this: I know my lines and the audience doesn't; it's not a fair fight. They aren't going to know when I make a mistake unless I stumble. The audience is there for the performance, not for a line check of every last word and syllable. Honestly, they want you to succeed—they want to be entertained and informed.

A great stepping stone on your way to presenting on the "big stage" at professional software conferences is giving a talk at a local meetup or user group. I've spent over 20 years in the user group community.

I was the president of the Denver Java Users Group in the early 2000s, and after that I ran the Boulder Java Users Group for years. I just wrapped up the HTML5 Denver Meetup after running it for over a decade.

If you don't feel ready to give a 60-minute talk on a topic, look for lightning talks. They are typically only 10 minutes and 10 (or so) slides. It is literally just long enough to say, "Hey, have you heard of this framework? Here's how you install it, and here's a quick 'Hello, World!' example." But in that quick 10 minutes, you still have the basic elements of an effective 60 minute talk: introduce the topic, pique the audience's curiosity, and give them enough to explore it further after the talk.

**Geertjan Wielenga**: How did you get to an international stage? What was that process?

**Scott Davis**: It was through the Denver Java Users Group. I started attending that and then thought, "There are a lot of really great advanced talks here, but could we have a series of talks that would be a gentler introduction to Java?"

Starting a "Basic Concepts" series of talks at the Denver Java Users Group led to a writing opportunity—my first book, *JBoss at Work*. Then, as an author, you start getting invited to local and regional software conferences. From there, it grew to national conferences within the U.S., and later, I was able to broaden out to the international stage.

**Geertjan Wielenga**: Developer advocacy isn't a common career path. Why is this?

## Getting up on stage

**Scott Davis**: Public speaking continues to be one of the number one fears that many people have. There's that common nightmare where you're standing up in front of your classmates at school giving a report and, all of a sudden, you're naked or you've forgotten what you wanted to say next. It takes a real act of courage to stand up and present yourself as an authority, especially to a group of your peers.

On the flip side, I really try to be mindful about not appearing arrogant. I try to turn each presentation about software into a personal journey—a "hero's journey" if you're familiar with the literary concept. I don't want to stand up and say, "I know this and you don't, so why don't you sit back and listen to me talk about how much I know." I like standing up and saying, "Hey, I'm a Java developer and I just discovered this new language, Groovy. Let me show you what I've learned so far."

> *"No one can call you a liar for sharing your personal experience."*
>
> —*Scott Davis*

It's fantastic being able to come from a very personal place to say, "This appeals to me and let me tell you why." It's the best cure for imposter syndrome I know of because you're talking about your journey and your experience with the software. No one can call you a liar for sharing your personal experience.

Even if being on the stage holds no appeal for you, you can still contribute to the conversation through writing blog posts or an article series; starting a podcast or screencasts; or even posting code to a public Git repository. These are all low- or no-cost ways for you to find your voice and share it with the public. You don't need to ask permission—just do it!

**Geertjan Wielenga**: Would you say that you need to be a complete expert on a particular tech or on a topic before you can be a speaker or author in this developer advocacy domain?

**Scott Davis**: Getting back to that voice of authenticity, I tend to enjoy blog entries and articles where people are very honest about what they struggle with. In that way, the writer says, "This is a concept that really didn't make sense to me at first, but here was my breakthrough moment."

I had an experience like that most recently when dealing with RxJS, a reactive library for JavaScript. It wasn't the syntax that I was struggling with: it was the underlying concepts, the reactive/declarative mindset, and the worldview, if you will. I've been dipped in imperative programming my whole life, so I was really struggling to get into that reactive mindset. But once it happened, that lightbulb went on and I thought, "Oh, now I get it!" It was like staring at that duck/rabbit optical illusion and finally being able to see the rabbit.

Now when I'm giving presentations on RxJS (or reactive programming in general), I always tell that story. It humanizes me and more than a few people in the audience are probably fighting that very same battle.

I give an imperative example and then a declarative one right afterward: "See how the declarative example is doing the same thing in far less code? That's the rabbit I was telling you about!" That's the "hero's journey" in a nutshell right there. It's not the solution alone that's important: it's the journey leading up to the solution as well.

**Geertjan Wielenga**: What are some things that you wish you had known at the start of your career, especially as an advocate?

**Scott Davis**: My little brother also went into software as a career. Just as he was getting ready to graduate from college, one of his professors said, "There's a good chance that you're never going to use the programming languages that you learned here in class out in the real world."

It's true! I had two semesters of COBOL in school and never once got a paying gig writing COBOL after graduation. The idea that you can learn a single language that will carry you through to the end of your career is probably setting you up for a lot of heartache and disappointment. You have to be prepared to be constantly learning, constantly adjusting, and constantly evolving over time. You need to be prepared to be a polyglot programmer, which is Greek for "many tongues" or many languages.

When I call a plumber, they don't show up with a single wrench in hand and ask, "Okay, where's the leak?" They show up with a whole truck full of tools, some of which might only be used once or twice a year. But when the job calls for a specific tool, that plumber is prepared to use the best tool for the job.

**Geertjan Wielenga**: What have you been advocating recently? I've seen you talking about conversational user interfaces (UIs) and responsive progressive web apps. How do you choose which tech to advocate?

## Scott's hot topics

**Scott Davis**: The iPhone is now over a decade old. I vividly remember when it came out thinking, "Wow, this is a game-changer: a full-fidelity web browser in my pocket!" That was before the App Store was even a glimmer in Apple's eye.

That was also the timeframe when Google Maps was first released. I was working on a pre-release version of Google Maps for a satellite imaging company, and I could viscerally feel how AJAX-based websites changed the whole user experience for the better. The iPhone and Google Maps forever changed the way we do web development.

> *"You can actually use your voice to communicate with the device in your hand in a meaningful way."*
>
> —*Scott Davis*

I'm feeling that same way right now about conversational UIs. We're hearing devices actually speak to us in realistic voices, not like the primitive chatbots of the past that used robotic speech synthesis like Stephen Hawking or in the movie *WarGames*. You can actually use your voice to communicate with the device in your hand in a meaningful way. We're seeing this show up on our smartphones, on our watches, and even on our television remote controls.

I used to laboriously tap out *Breaking Bad* one letter at a time on an onscreen keyboard using the left/right/up/down arrows on the remote. Now I hold up my remote control and say, "Breaking Bad."

I really feel that conversational UIs have got to the place now where the software, hardware, and bandwidth are all there. It's that perfect storm where it's all come together. This idea of talking to computers is really breaking down barriers once again. There's something very natural about walking in and talking to a computer. I'm really fascinated by that.

Where this really shines is when we start talking about accessibility. I walk into the kitchen in the morning and say, "Hey Alexa, play some Bob Marley." It's a novelty for me, but imagine if I had low vision or full blindness. All of a sudden, it's not a novelty—it's my whole user experience.

In both the U.S. and worldwide, the literacy rate is only about 85%. For 15% of the world, a conversational UI is their whole user experience. If you have dyslexia or another cognitive impairment that makes reading hard, conversational UIs can help. If English is your second language, perhaps it's easier to hear it than read it. Heck, if you're driving or have a baby in your arms, a conversational UI can make your life easier.

We're on the cusp of the "next big thing" with conversational UIs, and I'm having a blast exploring all of the possibilities.

**Geertjan Wielenga**: How do you stay up to date and in touch with the latest tech developments?

**Scott Davis**: I read incessantly. I think the biggest sources for me are my Twitter feed and going on websites like *Ars Technica*, *A List Apart*, *Wired*, *TechCrunch*, and the like.

When you visit those different sites and see the same story told from different perspectives, you really begin to see the trends emerge.

You have to have a love of learning. I get itchy and do everything I can to not get bored from a tech perspective. I'm like a shark that has to keep swimming to stay alive. Much of that motivation has to come from within.

> *"Find a job that lets you do what you love."*
>
> —*Scott Davis*

What can make that hard is when the tech that interests you is not what you're working with for your day job. So, in an ideal world, you have to find a tech that you love and then find a job that lets you do what you love. I think that's the perfect model.

## Moving away from pure programming

**Geertjan Wielenga**: What would you say is the advantage of developer advocacy over spending your life being a pure computer programmer?

**Scott Davis**: Look, not everyone needs to be an advocate. I've got lots of friends whose real passion is rock climbing or snowboarding. For them, programming is an interesting, exciting, and innovative job, but more importantly, it's a well-paying job; it's something they do as a means to an end.

For me, I've got Alexa at home in several rooms. My family members all have iPads and iPhones. My advocacy, once again, comes from a place of authenticity—this is how we live; we live these digital lives.

My iPad is the first thing I see when I wake up in the morning and it's the last thing I see when I go to bed at night. A device, to me, is not just a computer that you sit down at and walk away from—it's something that you develop a kind of relationship with.

In terms of advocacy, it should be personal. You should be talking about something that you're passionate about. Advocacy is something that you feel compelled to do. You're almost not choosing the tech: the tech is choosing you and you can't help talking about it. If you can find something like that, then it's easy because you're doing what you love.

**Geertjan Wielenga**: You travel frequently and you come across developer advocates everywhere. What would you say are some commonalities among them?

**Scott Davis**: What I love most about going to software conferences is meeting the other speakers. I love sitting down at the end of the day and having a drink with them or waking up in the morning and having coffee and a masala dosa with them.

There is something about being a conference speaker that draws us all together, regardless of the language we speak, the company we're working for, or our platform of choice. I love hearing iPhone developers talk passionately about Objective-C and Swift, and I love hearing Android developers talk passionately about Java and Kotlin.

> *"I'm attracted to passion. Honestly, the particular focus of that passion is less important to me."*
>
> —*Scott Davis*

I'm attracted to passion. Honestly, the particular focus of that passion is less important to me. I just love hearing someone else be really passionate about something they love; it makes for great conversation.

**Geertjan Wielenga**: Have you been in situations where your audience or a client was more knowledgeable? How did you handle that?

**Scott Davis**: You just described the life of a consultant! I find myself in that situation all the time, whether it's in the classroom or on a new software project. I try to establish some ground rules early on to help to nip it in the bud.

For example, if I come into a pharmaceutical company, I say, "Hey, you know much more about pharmaceuticals than I do, but I know a thing or two about software development. Let's sit down together. You have an idea of what you want the app to do. I have the software skills to help translate your vision into running software and make it come to life." So, rather than setting up an adversarial relationship from the start, I try to respect and acknowledge their strengths. In turn, hopefully, I give them a way to respect my strengths as well.

**Geertjan Wielenga**: In the life of a conference speaker, technical glitches happen all the time up on stage. How can they be avoided and how do you react to these situations?

## When technical glitches hit

**Scott Davis**: Resiliency is something we always talk about in software. I think resiliency is something you have to strive for as an instructor or as a conference speaker.

It's not avoiding technical glitches that makes you a pro: it's the grace and humor you use in reacting to the glitches when they inevitably happen. I've had a number of people come up to me after a talk that went badly and say, "I'm sorry that you had trouble up there on stage, but I probably learned more from watching you debug it in real time than if everything had gone right in the first place."

Nowadays, I take a screenshot of every website that I'm going to mention in my presentation and put it in my slides with a hyperlink. If I'm at a conference with good Wi-Fi, then I can click on the screenshot and seamlessly scroll around the live website as I talk about it.

If, on the other hand, I end up in a hotel conference room in the basement with crummy Wi-Fi, then I just discuss the static screenshots in my slide deck. I never apologize for not having a live Internet connection—that's part of the theater experience. You silently adapt to the presence or absence of good bandwidth, and the audience never knows the difference.

I love to give live coding examples in my presentations, but I always have a working, finished copy of the example saved in a parallel directory. If I get stage-blind and can't find the bug while I'm live coding, I don't spin my wheels for too long. I say, "Okay, let me show you what I was trying to demonstrate here." I then pull up the working code and make some trivial edit, like changing "Denver" to "Frankfurt" or "Oslo" (wherever I happen to be at the time), which gives the illusion of live coding.

I might then take that working code and purposely insert a syntax error to illustrate a point: "See how easy it is to miss a semicolon here? Let's look at the error message so that when you find yourself in a similar situation back at the office, it won't be nearly as scary."

**Geertjan Wielenga**: What about the laptop-not-connecting-to-the-projector scenario? What then?

**Scott Davis**: Years ago, I did all of my presentations in PowerPoint. Later, I graduated to Keynote. PowerPoint was, for better or worse, the least common denominator. It was something you could assume would be available if your personal laptop wouldn't work with the audio/visual setup at the conference.

Sadly, most of my legacy presentations are now trapped in an outdated, proprietary nut that is harder to crack than you might think. Apple and Microsoft are far less concerned about backward compatibility and legacy support than I am, apparently.

What I've started doing now is writing all of my slides in HTML and posting them on the web. I call it "Talk-o-Vision." It's pure HTML5, CSS, and JavaScript, with zero external dependencies. Just as every Jedi must build their own light saber, as a professional presenter, I take great pride in building my own slide decks from standards-based tech that should stand the test of time.

As a result, if I get into a conference situation where my laptop won't connect, I know that any device with a browser and an Internet connection will allow me to pull up my slides and proceed.

If the overhead projector isn't working, that's an entirely different kind of problem. You can laugh about it and offer to do an interpretive dance in lieu of your prepared slides!

Not having a projector is a more difficult challenge to overcome, but if your slides are publicly available on the web, everyone in the session could still potentially pull them up on their own device and you could proceed with the presentation.

**Geertjan Wielenga**: How do you deal with the whole area of jet lag, missed flights, and the typical problems of the world traveler?

## Travel management tips

**Scott Davis**: I optimize less. I used to be really aggressive about it, saying, "Alright, my first talk is Monday morning at 9 a.m. I'm going to get in on Sunday at midnight because that is the least amount of time I need."

Unfortunately, that strategy doesn't leave any margin for error, as all professional travelers learn. Nowadays, I try to give myself a full 24 hour buffer coming in.

When traveling to India from the U.S., that 24 hour buffer is almost a requirement. There's a 12 and a half hour time difference between the two countries and around 18 hours of flight time depending on how many hops it takes to get there. At that point, night is day, left is right, and up is down. That kind of time shift can be brutal if you don't anticipate it and make accommodations.

> *"Trying to live in one time zone while being physically located in another is a recipe for disaster."*
>
> —*Scott Davis*

Whether I'm traveling across the world or just to one of the coasts in the U.S., what helps me best adjust to the new time zone is simply eating breakfast when the clock on the wall tells me I should, instead of when my internal clock tells me I should. Trying to live in one time zone while being physically located in another is a recipe for disaster. If I can get one solid "wake up when the sun comes up, go to bed when the sun goes down" cycle in, that's typically enough to get me through the next day of presentations.

**Geertjan Wielenga**: With these topics we're discussing now, coupled with the passion of this profession, do you think that there's a risk of burnout?

**Scott Davis**: Sustainability is a really important topic that we don't often talk about. Here's one way to think about it: an introvert is someone who can interact with other people— and maybe even enjoy it—but it drains their battery. It's crucial that they get some quiet/alone time to recharge.

I know a number of conference speakers who have this great, outgoing stage persona, but they self-identify as introverts. They are absolutely wrecked once they get off the stage and need time to recuperate.

I'm an extrovert, so I find that being on stage is what actually charges my battery. If I haven't been on stage in a while, if I'm not giving presentations, wildly gesticulating with my hands, or talking loudly and passionately about something, that drains my battery. I almost always come off the stage with more energy than when I started.

Whichever camp you fall into, be sure that you take care of yourself. It's far too easy to plan for your presentation and forget to plan for your recovery.

**Geertjan Wielenga**: When you're at a party or speaking to people who are not at all in the tech field, how do you explain what you do?

**Scott Davis**: Rather than saying, "I do responsive web design," "I write progressive web apps," or "I'm really into offline-first web development," I say, "I make sure that websites look good on your iPhone or Android."

I might also ask, "Have you heard of Alexa? Have you heard of Siri? Cortana? That's what I do: I do conversational UIs. I do my best to make sure that your devices make sense when they talk to you."

> *"Put yourself in the shoes of your end users."*
>
> —Scott Davis

I think that it's far too easy for us to focus on the tools we use rather than the people who use our apps. Step one in design thinking is "empathy"—put yourself in the shoes of your end users for a moment and view your app through their eyes. I'm fairly sure that if you ask a typical software developer what step one is, they'll say, "Download a framework or set up a code repository."

Mozart wrote symphonies. If you asked him what he did for a living, I doubt that he would have said, "I write notes on a musical staff with a quill pen."

Many times, when I'm talking to a customs agent or someone in passport control, saying that I'm an author helps. I'll say, "I'm speaking at a software conference about this book that I've written." It establishes what you do in a common language that everyone understands.

**Geertjan Wielenga**: What talks are you working on right now?

**Scott Davis**: I'm working on a keynote called "The Ship of Theseus." It's an ancient Greek paradox about a wooden ship that belonged to one of the first kings of Athens.

Theseus sailed over to the island of Crete and killed a vicious monster called the Minotaur. When he returned, the citizens of Athens preserved his ship out in the harbor as a memorial to this momentous victory. Every year, they'd take Theseus' ship out for a victory lap to commemorate the event. According to the story, this went on for centuries after Theseus' death.

Here's the paradox: as you'd expect, various wooden parts of the ship rotted away over years. The citizens of Athens dutifully kept the ship in working order, replacing all of the parts necessary to keep the vessel seaworthy. Therein lies the question: since the ship was no longer made up of the original wood from Theseus' time, was it still truly Theseus' ship? If not, when did it cease being Theseus' ship? Is there a specific percentage, threshold, or milestone that we can point to and say, "There! Right there! That's when this thing technically stopped being the Ship of Theseus."?

Isn't that a lovely thought experiment? It really forces you to consider what the true essence of something is versus the raw materials used to build it. What a perfect metaphor for web development!

If you did an archeological dig on my website, you'd find 30 years of then-current, now-abandoned web technologies: ASP pages; JSP pages; Prototype and Scriptaculous; Groovy and Grails; jQuery; Backbone; Angular; Node.js; and Express. And yet, despite all of that churn, not once have I ever considered it anything other than "my website."

When you ask a typical web developer what they do, they'll often say, "I'm a React developer. I'm an Angular developer. I'm a VueJS developer." As far as I'm concerned, that's like saying, "I'm a spoon chef," or "I'm a hammer carpenter."

These tools that feel so important to us right now—that define us—are, in fact, ephemeral. The average lifespan of a website's design is typically less than two or three years. So, all of our efforts are spent on the surface of the water, being buffeted by the waves and dodging the flotsam and jetsam of last year's "gotta-have-it" framework.

Did you know that the original web page that Tim Berners-Lee published is still available on the web today? It still renders in 100% of modern browsers. Talk about the Ship of Theseus, right?

This is why I'm really focusing my efforts these days on standards-based techs like HTML, CSS, and JavaScript. Their longevity is measured in decades, not years or months. The deeper you go into the water, the slower the currents run, and the longer you can reap the benefits of your return on investment.

**Geertjan Wielenga**: We've established that you're not a traditional developer advocate, but you do promote particular techs. There's a whole range of people who one year are promoting tech A and then a couple of years later are promoting tech B. How do you feel about that? Should we look kindly upon that and be forgiving or be harsh and questioning?

## Changing your mind about tech

**Scott Davis**: I think that it's important to be able to change your mind professionally. You have to ensure that you never get so dug into a position that you can't back out or make an opposing argument later.

One thing that I try to do, whenever I'm advocating a tech, is point out its shortcomings as well as its strengths. That kind of balanced approach is what I look for in conference speakers too. If they aren't able to say one nice thing about another tech, or one bad thing about their own, that's when I get suspicious and my spidey senses start tingling.

Neal Ford popularized the "Suck/Rock Dichotomy." This is when people say, "This framework is the best thing ever! That framework is the worst thing ever! Mine rocks! Yours sucks!"

> *"Since we're programmers, it's easy to slip into a purely binary mindset: 1 or 0, true or false, black or white, good or bad, and so on."*
>
> —*Scott Davis*

Since we're programmers, it's easy to slip into a purely binary mindset: 1 or 0, true or false, black or white, good or bad, and so on.

The real world, of course, is a wee bit more nuanced than that. I like reminding developers who use the binary argument as a rhetorical crutch that it takes 8 bits to make a byte. Every single character that you type on the screen is a healthy mix of 1s and 0s.

**Geertjan Wielenga**: Thank you, Scott Davis.

"The pleasure is momentary, the position ridiculous, and the expense damnable."

—Lord Chesterfield (1694–1773)

## 02

> *If you're in developer relations and you think that you get to create the message entirely absent from anybody else's influence, you're fooling yourself.*

# Ted Neward

# Introducing Ted Neward

Ted Neward's career has spanned close to three decades, and in that time, he's keynoted at conferences, written books and many articles, and built out a developer relations team from scratch at Smartsheet (where he worked at the time of this interview). He's now started a new role running a platform strategy team at Quicken Loans, the world's largest mortgage lender. Over the years, he's accumulated dozens of laptops, dozens of smartphones and tablets, a working knowledge of at least 10 programming languages and platforms, and a passing knowledge of close to 100 more. Find Ted on Twitter: @tedneward.

---

**Geertjan Wielenga**: There's this whole debate that we have about whether we are tech evangelists or developer advocates, which is a topic in itself. How should we describe ourselves?

**Ted Neward**: The term "evangelist" has always left a little bad taste in my mouth. So often we use the term in a negative fashion. An evangelist is seen as a zealot. Frankly, it's all of that connotation of religion.

Personally, I don't evangelize anything. A company might come to me and say, "Hey, we've got this problem and we'd like to know if Smartsheet can help." If I looked at the problem and there was really no way that my company could help, I wouldn't try to sell our particular brand of religion, because it's not a religion. There are lots of interesting tools in the world. I'd rather point companies toward a better one so that when I do recommend Smartsheet, they'll believe me.

Evangelists go around preaching and there's not that level of nuance or that intellectual authenticity. So, for that reason, we choose to use the term "developer advocate" in my company, from the standpoint that we advocate for developers not only inside the company but from the outside world. That's why we have the term "developer relations," because we're talking about how developers relate.

Developer relations is going to explode in many respects over the next decade or so. On the one hand, when you look at companies like Oracle or Microsoft, what we call "developer relations" is really just sales and marketing for them; their target markets are developers. You have to know how to talk to developers and how to meet them halfway.

Every time you go to a conference and you get a surge in downloads for your particular product, there's a very causal relationship between developer relations activity and results. Similarly, when you're a consulting company—if you're ThoughtWorks or Arthur Andersen, for example—developer relations is more of a sales activity. You're going in and you're literally proving to people that you're really smart and that they should hire your team.

For companies like Smartsheet, Netflix, Ford, and just about every other company that's out there in the world that doesn't sell to developers, they don't have that causal relationship. For Smartsheet, for example, our target user is generally a non-technical user; we don't sell to developers. Our chief executive officer (CEO) literally goes around and talks about Smartsheet as a no-code utility.

**Geertjan Wielenga**: How do you get the budget to go to developer conferences and why do you go to them if you don't have that direct connection?

## The value of attending conferences

**Ted Neward**: In some sense, it's the same as asking, "How does marketing get their budget?" People understand intuitively that brand recognition is an important thing.

As a non-developer-product company, we have an API, but we don't have that direct connection. Coca-Cola is considered to be the number one most recognized brand in the world and yet it spends billions of dollars every year to stay that way. Part of it is this notion of locality of reference inside your brain. If you've just seen a Coca-Cola commercial, you say, "Oh, yeah! Coca-Cola! I want one of those!" It's that idea of keeping it fresh.

For Smartsheet in particular (and I think this is true of Netflix, Ford, and, again, all of these other companies that are being told repeatedly that they need to go and build APIs), we have to justify internally why we need to create these APIs. The CEO, the chief financial officer (CFO), and the vice president (VP) of marketing don't see why we need to build APIs.

Why does Netflix have such a huge open-source presence? Why is Netflix putting all this effort into open source? Yeah, it gets some bug fixes, but at the same time, developers recognize Netflix as being number one. It becomes a place where the cool kids hang out, so that nets the company a lot of developer mojo.

Any other business that wants to integrate with Netflix already knows a great deal about it. If Netflix wanted to go and cut a deal with, say, Domino's Pizza, then when you fire up Netflix, you could also get a message saying, "Hey! Do you want to order a Domino's pizza? As a special deal, we'll deliver it straight to your house." Netflix knows where you live and Domino's knows what kind of pizza you want.

> *"As each company builds an API, they not only need people to maintain it, but also people to promote it and tell people how to use it."*
>
> —*Ted Neward*

That ecosystem doesn't happen unless developers are involved, but that doesn't happen unless there are people from Netflix going out to the developers and saying, "Do you want to do this? Here's all these reasons why you should and here's all these resources that enable that." That is the natural progression. As each company builds an API, they not only need people to maintain it, but also people to promote it and tell people how to use it.

**Geertjan Wielenga**: But what's the reason that you see such a strong distinction between developer advocates who come from organizations that are talking about code and tech versus those that are talking about APIs?

**Ted Neward**: Oh, it's not so much a distinction between the individuals doing it as much as it is about the companies at which it's done.

If you want to use the API for Smartsheet, you actually don't have to download the product; we're all cloud-based to begin with. We have software development kits (SDKs), but they just wrap our API endpoints, so there is nothing, as a developer, that you need to download.

More importantly, our success isn't in getting developers to use Smartsheet: our success is when my VP of enterprise sales walks into Oracle and says, "Hey! You guys really want to buy some Smartsheet."

The Oracle CEO then says, "This looks good. We should buy some of this."

Next, the VP of IT says, "Wait a minute. I've seen too many of these no-code tools where data just goes to die. I have no faith." The alternative is that the VP of IT goes, "Some of my guys have been talking about how they keep seeing these Smartsheet guys at conferences, so I have some faith." There's that brand recognition.

My target audience, in some respects, isn't where I'm aiming: I'm aiming at the developers of these IT companies. I'm not aiming at the actual person who's writing the check, because there's a connection that needs to happen. That's really what a lot of this non-developer company developer relations stuff is about.

Imagine, for a moment, if we convinced Domino's to spin up APIs. Domino's doesn't even realize what a huge market it could have if it created a partnership with Meetup. Every time you wanted to schedule a meetup, you could automatically enable a web-hook automation to have pizza delivered to the meetup building.

But the developer who would build that is not the direct consumer of Meetup and they're not the direct consumer of Domino's, except that they happen to be a human being that will occasionally consume both.

That's what I mean when I say that when you're Oracle or when you're ThoughtWorks, your developer advocates are marketing directly to the people who buy your stuff; there's a causal link. When you're Smartsheet, or many of these other companies, it's more this indirect mechanism, which means, unfortunately, that it's hard to prove your success.

There's a certain amount of faith that has to happen on the part of the company. When I came in a year and a half ago, Smartsheet had no developer relations department. I had to meet with the VP of technology and the chief technology officer (CTO). I had to meet with a number of people across the company to convince them. I had to say, "No, really, you guys need this."

## Being headhunted

**Geertjan Wielenga**: How did that connection start if they weren't aware that they needed such a function? Why did you pick that particular organization to do this at?

**Ted Neward**: Well, actually, it came about rather accidentally. I met the principal technical recruiter for Smartsheet at a HackerX hiring mixer about two and a half years ago. I also met with the VP of engineering and we just had a nice chat. It was purely random.

Then, about five months later, one of my students from my university classes was interning at Smartsheet.

He emailed me to say, "By the way, thanks for the class. It really helped me to get ready for this internship."

I said, "Oh, Smartsheet, I know those guys. Tell them I said hi." That brought me back to the top of the cache, so to speak. They said that they wanted to talk to me.

> *"I said, 'I won't be a developer advocate, but I will build the department for you.'"*
>
> —*Ted Neward*

Brian, the VP of engineering, said, "Well, we don't really have any place in engineering for somebody who talks as much as you do, but we don't have anybody who talks as much as you do! Would you be interested in doing that for us?"

I said, "I won't be a developer advocate, but I will build the department for you."

I think the larger message is that Domino's doesn't know that it needs a developer advocate. There are so many companies that you can start rattling off; that's the realization. If every organization is an IT organization and if we are telling these IT organizations that they need to build APIs in order to enable public integration with all these other companies, then they need somebody who can go around and talk about why you would want to integrate with them as opposed to somebody else.

In some respects, my boss, Andy, who is the senior VP of technology, admitted right out of the gate that a third of what Smartsheet wants developer relations for is to use it as a recruiting function, which, again, is brand recognition.

We're saying, "This is where the cool kids are and we're working on some interesting ideas."

For those companies that think that they have all the developers they could possibly need (which you and I both know isn't true), developer relations is not just a recruiting function: it's also that sense of creating those technical partnerships. So, for example, if Smartsheet decides to do some sort of partnership with Meetup, who's going to have some of those initial discussions? If we want to start doing some cross-branding on the blog or if we want to do some partnerships at hackathons, then there's this ecosystem of developer relations. You're literally acting as an advocate not to consumers but to potential partners.

Developers spend all of their time writing code, except maybe for a small sliver of time doing meetings, but with developer advocates, it's much more of a split. You're coding, but you're typically coding samples. You're not actually writing production code; instead, you're writing prose and so forth. You're writing articles for the blog, if not articles for some publication. You're presenting at conferences or doing customer visits. You're helping the sales team to sell.

**Geertjan Wielenga**: Let's move on to talking about what makes this so interesting for you. What are the key points that make this position so valuable and relevant for you?

**Ted Neward**: I think part of what makes it interesting on a personal level is that just from one day to the next, I'm never doing the exact same thing.

> *"This is not a job for people who want to hide."*
>
> —*Ted Neward*

One day I'm working on a blog post; the next day I'm working on the sample code for that blog post; the day after that I'm working on some slides for a presentation; and the day after that, I'm flying to Amsterdam to go and deliver a talk on this topic. So, in many respects, if you're one of those individuals who loves the idea of walking into your space and putting on your headphones and just writing code all day, this is not the job for you. This is not a job for people who want to hide.

As much as we like to say that developers are just code monkeys, most people actually have a desire to change it up every so often. So, the idea is that you can actually make use of some of your other soft skills in terms of communicating with other people. I do think that developers, as a whole, are required to communicate more with their peers than 10 or 15 years ago. I think that that's going to make the developer relations position more attractive to a larger number of people.

One of the things that I'm finding is that developer relations is very attractive to people who come from non-traditional CS backgrounds. As a matter of fact, in my developer relations team one guy is a former sports writer for soccer. He then got into tech and was working on code. He's thriving. The other guy on my team spent a fair amount of time working in event management for wealth management seminars. He writes the best talk abstracts. So, we've got two people who many other companies would just completely give a pass on.

**Geertjan Wielenga**: But what's your story? How did you end up being a developer advocate in the first place?

**Ted Neward**: I didn't ever hold the title of "developer advocate" until I became the director of developer relations at Smartsheet.

I spoke on the *No Fluff Just Stuff* tour and I've written a number of books. I've done that consulting style of developer relations because I had to go to places and convince people that they had a problem that I could help them to solve, which, again, was some of that sales and marketing stuff.

If you're an independent developer or if you want to build your own consulting company, you have to do those sorts of things. Whether you see that as developer relations or sales and marketing, there's a fair amount of overlap. Quite frankly, there's so much overlap between being an independent speaker and being a developer advocate that they're almost synonymous in many ways.

**Geertjan Wielenga**: How did you get to where you are now? It's obviously been a long journey with many twists and turns.

**Ted's advocacy journey**

**Ted Neward**: I'd always been interested in programming, ever since my dad brought home an Apple II Plus in 1978, but I never really thought of it as a career path until college.

I was scouring the paper looking for jobs and I found one company that was looking for a programmer. My roommate basically double dog dared me to interview for this position. I said, "You've got to be kidding me!"

He said, "What's the worst that could happen?"

So, I interviewed and actually almost got the job, which really surprised me because out of 35 candidates, I was one of four finalists and I didn't have a CS degree. I had been working in C++ for a couple of years at that point. That was really where the light flipped on in my head. I realized that I could do this professionally. I could, in fact, make a career out of this. That was something that I had never really thought was possible. I'd always assumed that I had to be a CS major and have a deep love of all of these algorithms, which I find tremendously boring.

The next step was working for Mike Cohn. He was the first certified Scrum Master trainer in the world. The phrase I'd like to use is that I "worked for Mike before either of us was famous!" He was working on a book, with a couple of other people from the company, so I knew somebody who was writing a book. When Manning Publications approached me about writing a book I said, "Why not? A book is just a really long paper. So, sure, let's go after this."

That's what got me into the book world. From there, I ended up teaching for DevelopMentor and doing corporate training, largely based on having done a Java book. Now I stand in front of rooms and teach on a weekly basis. So, from 1995, when I started working on the book, to 1999, when I went to work for DevelopMentor, to 2002, when I was invited to my first conference, I went from just coding in the background all the way up to standing in front of people and talking about this stuff.

**Geertjan Wielenga**: Few people know about this profession. Why do you think that's the case?

**Ted Neward**: It's new from the standpoint that previously, developer relations was limited to those companies that were marketing to developers. Oracle, Microsoft, and Google have had these roles for 10, 15, or 20 years.

Unless you wanted to work for one of those big companies, you'd never really heard of the term and there was really no chance of you doing anything outside of those companies. Plus, you had those developer-facing companies that just called the role "sales or marketing," as I mentioned. But the turning point, I think, was the proliferation of API culture: when APIs stopped being something that only developers used. APIs are now becoming more consumer-facing. Even if we have to dress them up and put them into a big blue box, they can stack together.

As APIs have become more prevalent, they have begun moving out of the tech-only sphere and into every company. If every company is an IT company and every company wants to talk to other IT companies, then, by definition, every company is going to become an API company. Who's going to talk about that? Who's going to own that story? That very naturally falls on the shoulders of those who can write code, write about code, and talk about code.

**Geertjan Wielenga**: Let's say that you're an IT student or someone in a completely different profession and you want to make a switch to this interesting role. What would you need to do? How do you get started in this?

**Ted Neward**: I think the starting point for most people would be learning to code. You really have to have that technical knowledge.

Otherwise, if it's just writing and speaking, you're in the marketing department. It's that knowledge of code that's going to make the difference between somebody in marketing or sales and somebody being a developer advocate.

## Finding a developer relations job

**Geertjan Wielenga**: Once you have programming skills, how do you find these developer relations positions?

**Ted Neward**: In the same way that you find any other position. On the one hand, yes, there are the job sites that have keyword searches and so forth, but on the other hand, much of it is word of mouth still.

Finding a programming position is not that hard, but some of these companies don't know that they need a developer relations team. So, certainly, there's a challenge there from the standpoint that if you want to work for company Z and it doesn't have a developer relations team, you may have to go and convince people. The hard part is, obviously, that you have to convince people that they're wrong and that they do need this thing. But I think that that is going to become easier as more and more companies do this.

If you're Zeeks Pizza, which is a local pizza chain here in the Washington State area, and you have APIs, then when Domino's looks around and realizes that it is losing a whole bunch of business to this competitor that has APIs, it will say, "Well, we'll stand up APIs."

Then Domino's will realize that it's still losing business, so it will say, "What's the difference?

Somebody from Zeeks is going out and talking at all these places about how to use the Zeeks API here in the Washington State area. Who is that person? That person does developer relations. Well, we need one of those people!"

The more that companies start doing this, the more it's going to create competitive pressure on their peers and the more this industry will start to steamroll. Ford wants to put APIs on cars. As we start talking about autonomous drivers and all these other things, that's going to require APIs and that's going to require somebody to talk about that and build that ecosystem.

> *"Remember, this is a three-headed horse: you have to have the coding skills, the writing skills, and the presentation skills."*
>
> —*Ted Neward*

If you want to get a job as a programmer at a company that makes an open-source product, then contribute pull requests. If you want to get a job in developer relations, don't just contribute pull requests: go out and talk about the product. Remember, this is a three-headed horse: you have to have the coding skills, the writing skills, and the presentation skills.

If you're looking to define a developer relations story at a company, then I think, in some respects, the goal is to go in with that story. The notion of Smartsheet is that it's a tool that can serve at the center of a larger IT strategy. Somebody needs to talk about that story. Somebody needs to revisit that story and sell it to other people and other companies.

That is the story that my management chain carried to the rest of the company to say, "This is why we need to create this department."

What developer relations does is help to support the sales cycle by creating a narrative arc. So, if you want to convince a company that it needs a developer relations department, your first job is to create that narrative arc.

**Geertjan Wielenga**: Is there one specific thing that you like least about the developer relations role?

## The downside to developer relations

**Ted Neward**: Probably the fact that, as we said earlier, it's not well known yet, so I spend as much time talking about what it is as I do about strategies within it. But that will correct itself over time.

That's not something that I can educate my boss about and suddenly everything will correct itself. My boss actually has a fairly good idea about what developer relations is and for the most part, he leaves it to me to define the rest.

Technically, I'm not even a developer advocate: I'm in management. So, it's about making my team successful and not about what I do. My job is basically meetings and emails. Scott, the former sports writer, told me that the thing that he really likes about the job is that on any given day he walks in and says, "Do I feel like writing code today? Then I'll work on a sample. Do I feel like writing an article today? Then I'll work on a blog post."

**Geertjan Wielenga**: With the diversity of the role and how interesting it is, why on earth would someone not want to be involved in developer relations?

**Ted Neward**: Some people don't like it. Let's recognize that our personalities are similar, but let's also not make the mistake of assuming that everybody's personality is similar.

My wife, for example, prefers to know what the boundaries are. If she's supposed to do a job, she likes to have boundaries in which she operates. If you were to present her with a very open-ended task to make people aware of a company, she could do that, but that's not what she likes to do. What she likes is to know exactly what her responsibilities are so she can carry those out and go home at the end of the day.

In the CS world, they teach developers that there's one right answer. Every time somebody up on stage says the words "best practices," we reinforce that notion that there's one right answer. There just isn't. You and I have been trained from our university education to see things not as black or white but as this long shade of gray. But there are people who don't want to deal with that.

We could also ask, "Why isn't everybody a start-up founder? Well, because a lot of people don't like taking those risks. They don't like being in a position where they're responsible for other people's livelihoods.

## The dilemma of authenticity

**Geertjan Wielenga**: What do you do when the direction of the company that you work for conflicts with your own vision and, of course, your whole career is about being authentic?

**Ted Neward**: There are easy answers at the edge of the continuum. Your company is breaking the law; what do you do? That's the same for any job; that's not a developer relations thing.

If you're not comfortable with being on stage and taking uncomfortable questions, then you need to question whether or not you want to be in this position. If your company's doing something illegal, and if you're in the news because you're a developer advocate, there's a certain amount of needing to say, "Okay, that's above my pay grade. I don't know what's going on there. I'm just as baffled as you are." There's always that answer as an option. If you're the press secretary for the President of the United States, you're expected to convey his message. Even if you don't personally believe it, you're expected to convey it.

**Geertjan Wielenga**: At what point should you say that you don't want to be involved anymore?

**Ted Neward**: That's entirely a personal decision. We don't know where our particular lines are because we haven't explored that, but I guarantee you that they are in different places.

The bigger question is: do you know where your line is? More importantly, the question of illegality is really not the right one to ask. The question is more along the lines of managing a difference of opinion. Mark Mader, our CEO, goes around and tells everybody that Smartsheet is a no-code tool, which, quite frankly, I think is a terrible thing to say.

To give another example, I had been at the company for one week and we were having an engineering leadership meeting.

Mark was saying that we had just had this report in from Gartner or Forrester that used the term "citizen developer." He was very contemptuous of that term. He asked, "Who here knows a citizen developer?"

> *"Was right there in the meeting, in front of everybody, the point in time to tell my brand-new CEO that he was wrong?"*
>
> —*Ted Neward*

He was not asking the question; he was making a point. But I know a citizen developer: my dad. He's done a lot of what I would consider to be citizen developer kind of things. Scott Davis also started out as a citizen developer and wrote Excel macros. There are lots of citizen developers in the world. Was right there in the meeting, in front of everybody, the point in time to tell my brand-new CEO that he was wrong?

What I want Mark to do is steal a little bit from the Python community and say, "This is no-code required and, as the Python guys say, it's batteries included. We have all this extensibility out there, but, in fact, if you just want to take it as it is out of the box, it can still be useful."

Now, do I go up on stage and say, "Our CEO is an idiot. He totally doesn't understand the thing that we have built. Listen to me; I'm the smart one." No, you don't undercut the CEO. There are ways to carry your opinion forward without visibly undercutting your CEO and without visibly doing your company harm.

**Geertjan Wielenga**: What are those ways?

**Ted Neward**: It begins by socializing the message internally. I want Mark to eventually realize that he's wrong about what he's saying and that there needs to be a nuance there, but I can't publicly put him in an awkward place.

So, I will begin by talking to other people who will socialize that message to him in passing, until at some point he and I will sit down and I will say, "Oh, by the way Mark, I wanted to talk to you about something."

He will then say, "I totally get that and this is what I'm thinking we should do."

Then it's his idea and not mine, which is great because it means he'll own it and it means that I still get my way, even if I don't get the credit, which is also fine because I don't need the credit. If I want the credit, I can go public, but then I may not have a job! This is part of working inside a corporation; it's a living, breathing entity. You can't just go rogue or you may not have a job.

A bigger question in some respects is: if somebody's considering a position in developer relations, how comfortable are they with the sublimation of their own opinions to that of the company as a whole? Frankly, I don't care what company you're at or even if it's your own company, at some point, you and somebody else inside the company are going to differ. You have to have the internal fortitude to be able to say, "You might be right. Let's talk about this. Maybe I don't have the right answer in terms of how to think about this. Let's talk about this further. Let me hear your vision."

I'm pretty sure that I'm right about this no-code thing and I'm pretty sure that Mark also knows that, and that he's using the no-code thing because that's what the board is trying to sell.

If I go to Mark, I think that he'll say that he agrees with me, but whether or not he can change his public messaging is another story, because he's got a different set of concerns than I have.

If you're in developer relations and you think that you get to create the message entirely absent from anybody else's influence, you're fooling yourself. You are very much part of a team and that vision will be something that, in the ideal world, you'll agree 80-90% with. What matters is that you're all pulling in the same direction.

**Geertjan Wielenga**: What do you do when you're doing a presentation and someone asks a question that you don't know the answer to?

## Being put on the spot

**Ted Neward**: You never bullshit. You admit that you don't know the answer and then say, "But I think I can find out and I'll get back to you if you want to know more." I also think that it's worthwhile to take a guess and say, "Based on what I do know, I believe that the answer will be this and if you'd like to, we can do a little research and see if we can figure it out."

In that way, you actually have a new contact in your network, whereas if you knew the answer, you probably would have given the answer and would never have spoken to that person again. Truthfully, nine times out of 10, when somebody at a conference asks you a question, it's because they're speculating. They're not looking for the answer; they're just trying to see how it fits within their mental model.

If they get the answer they expect, even if it's not guaranteed to be accurate, it helps to solidify the mental model in their head. Now, there will be the occasional person for whom this is a really critical thing and the people who want to follow up with you will come up afterward. You can either do the research right there and then or exchange contact information. It depends on them at that point.

**Geertjan Wielenga**: One topic that I'd like to talk about is issues of jet lag and travel. What are your feelings on those of aspects?

**Ted Neward**: I've had situations where I've woken up in a hotel room and I've looked around and thought, "Where the hell am I?" Sometimes I have to physically get up and walk over to my phone to see that I'm eight hours from home.

> *"We're not martyrs here; we're merely people who follow in a long line."*
>
> —*Ted Neward*

There are many positions that involve travel and this is just one of them. There are people who travel far more than we do. There are salespeople who do this all the time. We're not martyrs here; we're merely people who follow in a long line. There are consultants who do the same thing.

**Geertjan Wielenga**: Is burnout a risk in this profession and if so, how do you prevent or deal with it?

**Ted Neward**: It's most definitely a risk, particularly when coupled with the travel. It's very easy to experience burnout if you travel too much, especially if you have a family at home.

There are people who get divorced because one of the partners is traveling too much, not at home enough, feeling disconnected, and so on. The way to avoid that is to recognize that burnout is a risk and make sure that you're taking steps to combat it.

The diversity of the developer advocate role can actually accelerate burnout. It's a question of how well you know yourself and how well you can recognize the signs. Do you work for an organization that recognizes burnout as a real problem and is taking active steps to prevent it? For example, my developer relations team never travel more than 50% of the time.

As a manager, it's up to you to help your team to avoid burnout, particularly because people can experience burnout through a variety of different avenues. It's important to recognize that there is a difference between work and progress. You can be doing a ton of work, but if you're not making any progress, that's going to be the key thing that will lead to burnout.

The other point, though, is the realization that we all need to recharge. We all need the opportunity to get away and work on other things. We all need hobbies. Exercise is one of the key things that helps to keep people sharp. When you're exercising, there's literally nothing you can do but think. Everybody needs an opportunity to disconnect and engage in some sort of meditative state. For me, sometimes that's just taking a long, hot shower. I can't hold my phone in the shower. God help me if I ever get one of those waterproof Samsungs!

I don't get as much exercise now as I would like, but on an airplane, I don't pull out my laptop anymore; I actually just sit and watch a movie and let my mind wander for a while. Everybody needs to know how to do that. That's not just a developer relations concern, because I know developers, salespeople, and managers who experience burnout. Everybody has to have a notion of what works for them.

**Geertjan Wielenga**: Thank you, Ted Neward.

## 03

> *I believe this human side of tech, and the purpose behind what we're building, has never been more important.*

# Sally Eaves

# Introducing Sally Eaves

Sally Eaves' career has spanned working as a chief technology officer (CTO) and becoming an award-winning thought leader in innovation, digital transformation, and emergent tech, including blockchain, artificial intelligence (AI), machine learning, and robotics. A member of the Forbes Technology Council, Sally is an accomplished author and makes regular contributions to leading business, tech, and academic publications. She is an international keynote speaker and respected online influencer. Sally strongly believes in tech being an enabler for social good, which is reflected in her active roles as an ambassador, trustee, and mentor. Find Sally on Twitter: @sallyeaves.

---

**Geertjan Wielenga**: Could you start by explaining what you do and where you fit into the industry?

## Sally's advocacy work

**Sally Eaves**: I have come from a CTO background. I started my career with hands-on coding and then increasingly split my time across the management of tech, including the key aspects of people, values, and culture.

Application, for me, is massively important, but I also have a strong education and research background. So, today, as both a global tech advisor and a professor in emergent tech, I specialize in disciplines such as blockchain, AI, 5G, skills development, and business/IT alignment.

I care deeply about how we can apply tech and harness it for sustainable social impact at scale.

I work with organizations like the United Nations (UN), seeing where and how we can bring about business change and social impact change in tandem. I have also developed an international EdTech program called Aspirational Futures to open up access to opportunities. The program is focused on enhancing inclusion and diversity, alongside scaling up "tech for good" projects across the world.

**Geertjan Wielenga**: What do you see as being emergent tech?

**Sally Eaves**: Tech that breaks boundaries would be my core classification. Some of these techs have existed for many years, but critically, it is only now that the context is right that they can be applied and/or integrated.

AI is an example. With advances in computing power, alongside the cloud, the conditions became right for AI. We're in the era of implementation beyond the lab in specific fields. I have just been at the UN discussing how AI can contribute to progressing Sustainable Development Goals (SDGs). Transformation at scale is key to what I do.

**Geertjan Wielenga**: How did you get involved in the blockchain world?

**Sally Eaves**: A combination of education and practice. It was at a time when I had completed my MSc in tech and management and then was researching toward a PhD. At the same time, my day job was being a CTO. As part of this, I was looking at foresight horizon planning and what would be happening next, centered on the future of tech in transactions and beyond.

I became very excited by the idea of being able to prove identity and could see a real leapfrog opportunity there for under-represented groups from the unbanked to refugees. Everybody seemed to be talking about the cryptocurrency side, whereas, for me, it's always started from the underpinning tech and all the different applications that can come from that.

**Geertjan Wielenga**: In a nutshell, what does blockchain mean to you?

**Sally Eaves**: Blockchain is all about the secure, unchangeable, and transparent exchange of value, identity management, and the embedding of digitalized trust. Given the global trust deficit that is impacting all sectors, this is an imperative. Take DNA data, which is the most sensitive data that we all have. Although at an early stage, I think developments here offer a great demonstration of how we can use blockchain, AI, and machine learning together.

Blockchain can provide the security for DNA data sharing and gives the end user control and ownership. You can decide who you want to share your data with. In the past, particularly before the General Data Protection Regulation (GDPR), there were examples of users effectively signing off their data to be used by multiple third parties and often without full awareness of the implications, meaning they no longer had control over where it had gone and what use it was being put to.

In the near future, you will be able to decide if you want to monetize your DNA (and indeed other forms of data) or equally, give it for free to a research trial of your choosing.

This can be a change maker for health studies, especially for groups such as ethnic minorities, where we simply do not have sufficient volumes of quality data to work with. Unless a disease or condition gets significant funding (for example, heart disease and specific forms of cancer), there just isn't that depth of quality data that can be mined with AI and machine learning to gain new insights and help more people. Applications of blockchain and tech integrations with such a high human impact potential really appeal to me.

**Geertjan Wielenga**: What is it about the world right now that has brought forth blockchain? Why wasn't blockchain around five or 10 years ago?

**Sally Eaves**: I think the advance and increased attention very much fits into a quest for democratization. For me, this especially relates to financial inclusion. We have five times more people in the world with a phone than a bank account, which I think is quite a staggering statistic. 1.7 billion people remain unbanked or underbanked. I recently attended the World Mobile Congress in Barcelona and opening up access to financial services was a key focus.

There is a fantastic opportunity to combine the prevalence of mobile phone availability, blockchain for identity, and AI to mine unstructured data to create a novel form of credit history. The rollout of 5G and simply improving connectivity and access more broadly is also key—this infrastructure imperative is often not talked about enough. For me, this is all about integration and cross-sector partnerships, which I'm very active in building and scaling.

Blockchain is a big part of it, but not all of it. I'm always looking for the gaps, whether that's mobile access, legacy systems, or education and awareness needs.

> *"The media typically highlights and headlines stories on the darker side of tech."*
>
> —*Sally Eaves*

Our trust in systems and institutions is at an all-time global low, as I mentioned. This lack of trust is even affecting charities and social enterprise. It is touching every area of our lives and blockchain can help to embed that trust back. The media typically highlights and headlines stories on the darker side of tech by focusing on what tech might take away, especially around the future of work. This understandably creates fear and not trust. As advocates, we can help to provide some balance so that people can make informed choices. We can give a more holistic narrative on opportunities and challenges and talk about what tech can bring to home, work, and society.

**Geertjan Wielenga**: You've brought up the word "advocate" here. Do you see yourself as an advocate of something?

**Sally Eaves**: Yes, I consider myself to be an advocate of positive change, with tech being a core enabler for that to happen and critically, for that to happen sustainably and at scale. I'm not saying that people can't make a profit—of course, that is important—but we can also create, sustain, and scale social impact alongside it. In fact, I believe this is the future of good business.

**Geertjan Wielenga**: You mentioned refugees earlier. What's the connection between blockchain and refugees?

## The power of blockchain

**Sally Eaves**: We have a crisis and a new surge in refugees across the world, more than at any time since World War II. People can be held in a frightening and frustrating limbo, whether that's at a refugee camp or in transit trying to move to a new country. Many of these refugees are stateless and have scattered, inadequate, or no documentation at all, so there can be acute difficulties in establishing or proving who they are.

Where a paper ledger could be stolen, lost, or worse still, manipulated, identities verified on the blockchain are time stamped and can't be changed or faked. Identity opens the door to access to opportunities, so this is critical. Using a blockchain solution, governments could begin to issue digitally authenticated identification documentation, which would change so many lives, providing the pathway to financial services and work, while enabling better collaboration and transparency for all involved. The UN World Food Programme has also used the Ethereum blockchain to support refugees, providing cryptocurrency-based vouchers for redemption in food markets.

Beyond this, I work a lot with supply chains, which is probably the most natural use case for the use of blockchain tech. One nascent project in Malaysia and Thailand has looked at ethical and fair-trade opportunities.

Oud, as one example, is a commodity that we hear less about in Europe, apart from in perfumes and cosmetics, but in the Middle East, it is very prominent and meaningful from a cultural perspective. The problem is that 10 to 20 billion dollars a year of the oud trade is illegal and everybody across the supply chain is missing out. Governments lose tax revenue, trees are destroyed by not using best practices for extraction, product quality may not be clear to purchasers, and the farmer typically receives a small fraction of the end value. With new tech extraction processes supported by science, alongside radio-frequency identification (RFID) tagging and blockchain to track and trace, you can bring all of this together, from field to retailers, with everybody getting value. I'm excited to see where this goes.

**Geertjan Wielenga**: Would you say that it's the combination of different techs that is special? You have mobile, AI, blockchain, and so on. All of these different newish techs are coming together and filling in the gaps in these scenarios that you describe.

**Sally Eaves**: Absolutely, it is only when you get true integration that scale and sustainability start happening. We're at a tipping point right now. But it is also the people who are coming together that is important alongside the tech.

I work with all sorts of different stakeholders, from bleeding-edge start-ups to large traditional and transitioning organizations. I also research, speak, and engage in university environments and advise government and professional bodies.

I was at South by Southwest (SXSW) in Austin recently running a workshop on "tech for good," talking to young people, and looking at how we can do things differently, for example, by bringing transparency and accountability to the supply chain.

We need to be engaging in more than one community and this broadening of awareness is key. I have different types of audiences and sometimes they effectively use different languages, which can often be a barrier for knowledge sharing. There is so much jargon or buzzwords that aren't properly understood unless you're embedded in that specific community. The very word "blockchain" is a great example of this! We need to have more metaphors, I think, to help people to relate, alongside more tangible real-world examples that make the tech meaningful and relevant to everyday lives and experiences.

We need to make tech more accessible to people. I'm currently writing a book and supporting education and awareness is a big part of what motivated me to do that. I want to provide good-quality, non-biased information, but also for it to be accessible, relevant, and to spark curiosity about what can be achieved. It can be hard for people to find content with that balance and often, people just don't know where to go for informed and trusted content. I've just built some courses on blockchain and AI. I'm trying to make them very accessible for different types of groups.

**Geertjan Wielenga**: Tangibility, as you say, is often what is missing with all of these different terms and buzzwords. What can we do, as advocates, to make all these terms meaningful?

# Making tech solutions relatable

**Sally Eaves**: My example is always that people know about the phone in their pocket because phones are such an implicit part of our everyday existence. We need to find ways to make complicated subjects relatable so people feel that they matter and are relevant to them.

I often take people on a journey in my talks and ask the audience about how food ends up on their plate, and what tech might have been involved in that specific journey. I ask the audience to think about what could have made that process better. I think that is a good way of making it tangible, with food being a great example because it's something we all share as an activity. Taking these familiar contexts and using them for tech awareness is a useful tool for advocacy. A recent lost suitcase experience of mine also provided a great real-life example to show the benefit of applying blockchain tech!

The more we can personally and publicly share pilot successes, or tangible case study examples, the better, especially with blockchain, as a lot of content has been more conceptual than actualized. That's my focus with the keynotes that I do.

> *"I travel so much because you need to be out there."*
>
> —*Sally Eaves*

I travel so much because you need to be out there spending time with people, being open to questions, and learning yourself from the different views people have about the tech and change.

Online is a fantastic channel, but if we bring that together with face-to-face time, it becomes the perfect combination and builds community.

**Geertjan Wielenga**: You mentioned that you're passionate about education. Quite a few people come to tech from languages or creative disciplines. What's the connection between those areas and IT, AI, and all of these tech topics? Traditionally, those are completely separate worlds.

**Sally Eaves**: They are often treated as separate worlds. I'm a very big believer, though, in creative imagination and I feel that diversity of perspective and experience is incredibly important in all we do. If we can harness that creative confidence with the ability to build things for the future using tech, that becomes a very powerful combination.

I very much advocate for science, tech, engineering, arts, and mathematics (STEAM) learning. In many schools, from a UK perspective, I fear the arts are being squeezed out and I also see this internationally too. You can only access certain opportunities, like music lessons, for example, if you can pay for them, whereas they used to be embedded in the curriculum. I'm so concerned that we are going to have a lost generation to the arts if we don't address this now.

With curriculums, it tends to be a 10-year cycle with changes in focus and the time it takes to make changes if agreed. This is one of the reasons that I founded Aspirational Futures and have set up community-based hubs where people can go and learn about tech like blockchain, AI, and robotics, but equally, they can go and play an instrument, paint, or sew.

I think we need that fusion of different experiences to learn from and to socialize at the same time.

I wrote a piece recently about the beauty of algebra. Rather than saying someone is good at mathematics and they're not so good at something else, we should be more open. I think sometimes we put people into prescriptive "boxes" too early and we take away the vital time for experimentation and keeping options open.

We have to be able to imagine what the potential future can be. We need teams that are made up of people with different skills and backgrounds to achieve the best results and maximum innovation. We have some major global challenges to address collectively. Through my work with the UN and integration with the SDGs, I see this fusion as a critical way of designing, developing, and delivering the change that we need.

**Geertjan Wielenga**: You've mentioned a few times your involvement with the UN. How did you get involved there and what is your role?

**Sally Eaves**: I became involved quite naturally over time through the type of shared value projects that I focus on, alongside my charity activities. I believe wholeheartedly that frontier tech, such as blockchain and AI, has a key role to play in meeting the SDG targets and I'm very active in their application.

I also look at social impact project funding and measurement, which is another critical area. Look out for some exciting announcements related to this at the UN Assembly later this year! Within this area, there is a big focus on how blockchain can support inclusion and diversity too.

**Geertjan Wielenga**: Something from your story that is quite interesting is that in the past, people were programmers, testers, architects, and so on. Everyone had a specific role. But what you are is a whole range of different things at the same time. What kind of personality fits this very diverse role best?

**Sally Eaves**: I know that I have a very active, holistic, and always "on" mind. I also like to explore purposeful tangents! So, I'm always thinking, especially about how things can fit together—I love seeing the connection possibilities and then putting that into action. I think this agility of thought and willingness to experiment, iterate, and actualize is key.

I also believe that you need drive, determination, and a degree of pragmatism too. Advocates must be willing to share and want to amplify messages rather than keeping them in a closed circle. You often need to be prepared to go on a stage in front of different types of audiences and be willing to interact both on and offline.

All these roles are continually evolving. There are no fixed boundaries anymore. I think there are going to be more and more diverse but integrated roles like this in the tech industry and beyond it too. This is why being comfortable with agility is vital and this is reflected in the type of education experience we cultivate with Aspirational Futures.

**Geertjan Wielenga**: How would you describe yourself to somebody who is not technical?

**Sally Eaves**: Someone described me a couple of days ago, actually, and I really loved what they said.

They called me a "torchbearer for ethical tech." I thought that was lovely and it meant such a lot to me. If I was to be known for that, it would make me very happy because that is what I believe in as my core ethos.

**Geertjan Wielenga**: As advocates, would you say that we are all torchbearers?

**Sally Eaves**: Absolutely. We are helping people's voices to be heard, ensuring that people feel that their views matter, and critically, bringing these voices together. Many people have fantastic ideas. They want to get involved, but they simply don't know how to. And often they can feel alone. I think we can make a powerful difference in this area.

**Geertjan Wielenga**: Whose voices in particular do you think are not being heard as well as they could be?

**Sally Eaves**: There remains under-representation. Take blockchain as an example. I believe around six percent of the industry is female. AI development and cybersecurity also reflect this gender disparity. With AI, when we're designing and developing this tech, we must be careful of algorithmic bias, which could, in fact, be completely unconscious, but it is an issue.

> *"It's about bringing together people with different experiences and different ways of thinking."*
>
> —*Sally Eaves*

Decisions informed by AI must be fair and the criteria transparent and explainable. We need to have teams that are truly diverse to support this. Again, this goes far beyond a question of gender. It's about bringing together people with different experiences and different ways of thinking. If we don't have diversity embedded now, these gaps are only going to get wider.

**Geertjan Wielenga**: Advocates working for companies tend to represent the tech that those companies provide, whereas those working for themselves can really be authentic. Where do you find yourself in that range?

## Sally's views on authenticity

**Sally Eaves**: Authenticity is key, absolutely. You can, of course, still work for a specific organization and be very authentic, but I do like being able to offer a broader view of the tech industry, experience from a deep cross-sector network, and independent thought leadership.

This can help and guide companies for the dynamic future of work and bring together research and practice in cutting-edge tech, skills development, and impact. I really enjoy working with organizations on a range of exciting projects, especially bringing together digital transformation and societal transformation opportunities. I believe this is the authentic future of good business.

**Geertjan Wielenga**: Could you say a little more about your foundation?

**Sally Eaves**: Yes, with pleasure! Aspirational Futures brings together eight years of different projects around the world. Our three core pillars for change are STEAM learning, social impact at scale, and "tech for good."

We're truly international in approach but it's important to note that even in our own hometowns, there can often be such disparities in equality and access to opportunities. We're aiming for 5,000 hubs in three years and I'm looking for ambassadors across the world. This is so close to my heart. If you're reading this and want to be involved, just shout!

**Geertjan Wielenga**: As you travel a lot with your work, do you have any tips for dealing with that?

**Sally Eaves**: To be honest, by now I should be able to sleep on planes, but I've never mastered that! Many of my friends maximize the time for sleeping, but I typically use flying time as writing time. It's amazing how much you can get done in the air and by resisting connecting to in-flight Wi-Fi. I recommend that digital-switch-off time for thinking, writing, music, and so on—whatever is your passion.

**Geertjan Wielenga**: Do you ever encounter any technical issues when you're speaking in another country?

**Sally Eaves**: It has never really been an issue. In some countries, language translation tools are part of a session, so you need to take extra care with delivery speed. Of course, I do use decks to support presentations, but they are very much a backdrop and not a necessity if the connection was to drop, for example.

I am a passionate speaker and expressive on stage—I really want an audience to feel part of it all. So, yes, ironically, for a tech person, I don't rely on the tech! I'm less about slides and more about the engagement and the experience. I like to make topics accessible, encourage curiosity, give tangible examples, and showcase the "why." I believe this human side of tech, and the purpose behind what we're building, has never been more important.

**Geertjan Wielenga**: Thank you, Sally Eaves.

## 04

> *If you want to be accepted by developers, you have to be a person who they respect.*

# Kirk Pepperdine

# Introducing Kirk Pepperdine

Kirk Pepperdine has been performance tuning Java applications as an independent consultant for about 20 years. He was named a Java Champion in 2006, has been a JavaOne Rockstar numerous times, and can be found at Java User Groups (JUGs) and conferences worldwide. The author of the original Java performance tuning workshop, Kirk continues to be an ardent supporter of the Java community as the cofounder of JCrete, a Java unconference, and helps to establish other unconferences across the globe. Find Kirk on Twitter: @javaperftuning.

**Geertjan Wielenga**: Being a developer advocate is all about promoting tech; would you agree?

**Kirk Pepperdine**: I think we're all about promoting ourselves, but you can't really do that directly. So, you have to promote tech. As a side effect, you get promotion.

What I think happens is that people go to promote a certain tech, for one reason or another, and then they end up being the person that people go to when they have a question. Then they tell their friends about it and it goes from there. If you're helpful, then I think people tend to seek you out and if you're not, then you're less successful advocating the tech that you're trying to advocate!

**Geertjan Wielenga**: What kind of personality traits make one suited to this role?

## People who are suited to advocacy

**Kirk Pepperdine**: When I look at the good tech advocates today, such as Josh Long, Simon Ritter, or Heinz Kabutz as Java Champions, they're Java Champions because they're good advocates of the tech.

What makes them good advocates is that they're first and foremost entertaining, and that's part of the job that I don't think people recognize. They're entertaining in how they present the information that they want to deliver to the audience, so it's not just a matter of delivering the information.

First, you have to have good content. I think you have to deliver that in a way that's consumable by the audience, and keeping their interest is important. If you're a dull, boring speaker, I think there's a certain percentage of your audience that will tolerate the boring bit just to get the information, but you won't bring new people in. You'll probably lose them very quickly. The people who are engaging and have a deep understanding of the tech are the people who are going to be successful at advocating their particular tech stacks.

**Geertjan Wielenga**: Would you say that developer advocacy really lends itself to extroverted people?

**Kirk Pepperdine**: Surprisingly enough, I think that some of the people that are very good at this are more introverted than extroverted. Without giving names, I would say that some of the better advocates I know are rather introverted.

Those people are just able to set that aside somehow and focus on delivering the message.

They don't think about the audience in the sense that they're there and you actually have to talk to them. Some people are just able to do that. Introverts will be nervous before going up on stage and afterwards, they will need to be alone for a while to wind down.

I'll talk to people and they'll say, "How do you do an all-day event? After a one-hour talk, I'm basically finished." I find that after a one-hour talk, I'm finished too, but there's a different energy level that's required in a one-hour talk compared to when you're doing an all-day seminar workshop. The one-hour talk is like a sprint and the workshop is more like a marathon, so you just pace yourself differently.

In a one-hour talk, you're trying to pack a message into it and that requires a lot of energy. With a workshop, you never feel that pressure to draw the audience in and get them engaged with whatever it is that you're speaking about.

**Geertjan Wielenga:** There's more to developer advocacy than purely standing on a stage at a conference, right?

**Kirk Pepperdine:** Yes, you're right. There's plenty of behind-the-scenes work that goes on. I think the interesting part is that the good advocates will spend time making sure that they're just working with the tech.

The better ones are very enthusiastic about what they're doing and that enthusiasm certainly comes off in the talks. They're saying, "Look at this really cool thing that I'm able to do! Here are some ideas for how you might be able to use this and it should hopefully make your life better."

> *"You call me a developer advocate, but I've never thought of myself as one."*
>
> —*Kirk Pepperdine*

The talks become a byproduct of the process. You call me a developer advocate, but I've never thought of myself as one: I'm just doing stuff. I'm seeing people struggling and I'm helping them to make their life easier. It's not that I'm advocating anything: I'm just sitting looking at developers saying, "Dudes, you guys are struggling here and I can help."

**Geertjan Wielenga**: How, then, would you identify yourself and where does developer advocacy fit into what you do?

## Kirk's style of advocacy

**Kirk Pepperdine**: I don't know if I'm really that different from many of the developer advocacy guys that I know, in the sense that they're just out there doing a job and they're getting paid. They're still deep into the tech.

I think one of the differences is that I actually engage in a lot of research on a particular topic. I know that there are other advocates that are like me. They don't get paid for it and it's not their job title, but they do research. I might do research for two weeks and then something interesting will come up and I'll say, "Ah, that's something cool to talk about!" as a side effect.

I might look at something for a year and be playing with it and poking it. Then, finally, something will come out of it.

For me, it's not like someone says, "I need you to talk about our product X." I don't have to scramble to learn, sort, figure out, and throw together a talk. That's where the difference is: the talk is the endgame. I'm doing the research to help my clients and a talk coming out of that is a byproduct of the entire process.

**Geertjan Wielenga**: What kind of work do you actually do? What does your day look like? What is your job if it's not directly developer advocacy?

**Kirk Pepperdine**: My job is to know as much about the space I work in as I possibly can. I work in the computing space, building large software systems and deploying them. That's specialized down into Java and specialized down into making sure that everything runs smoothly. It's performance tuning, if you want to make it less abstract; that's my job.

I spend every morning reading for about an hour. Sometimes it's tech and sometimes it's not. Most of the time, it's going to be some technical-related thing that I'm interested in knowing more about. After that, the days vary, but if I'm not on an engagement then I'm going to be pulling out a problem that I know exists and seeing what I can do in terms of researching it more.

There are a few open-source projects that I've been tinkering with, so I might do something with them or it might be just product development: writing code.

If I'm on an engagement, then, of course, my time belongs to my client. If I'm engaged in a workshop, then that's a pretty clear process where you're just in a room with a bunch of people, working with them to try to improve their understanding of how to efficiently and effectively performance tune a system.

**Geertjan Wielenga**: In addition to that, you're also really involved with the conference scene, the community, and various conferences like JCrete. How did you get involved with all that?

**Kirk Pepperdine**: The same way everybody else does: I just showed up. You find like-minded people and you discuss tech.

**Geertjan Wielenga**: Why don't you simply do your work and go home at the end of the day? Why are you involved in the community at all?

**Kirk Pepperdine**: The people who I have a shared common interest with are showing up in the community. For me, this isn't a job; it's not really work. I can actually get paid to do this, which is quite amazing. It's a dream. How many people can say that they really enjoy what they're doing?

There are all kinds of really good things about this industry. I'm sitting here right now in Sydney looking at one of the harbors. Before we started talking, I was just looking out the window and developing software. I was thinking, "This is wonderful because next week I'll be in Atlanta and I'll be able to meet up with a whole bunch of different people, who are essentially friends."

We're all in the tech space and it's just great. For me, a conference is a chance to meet up with people, meet new people, and just talk about tech. Basically, I use giving a talk as a means to actually attend a conference.

On this trip, I'll be speaking at a JUG. I'm going to meet these people here in Sydney and it's wonderful.

I like to turn my talks into discussions and if that works, we'll have a great time. I'll get to meet a whole bunch of interesting people here in Sydney, which is fun.

JCrete started around 12 years ago. Heinz and I were talking about having a conference where we could get like-minded people together in the same place and create a fun environment. Life gets in the way sometimes and it wasn't until about five years later that we really started putting the whole thing together with the pushing of John Kostaras. We built a JCrete community and everything is open. We want to make sure that everything is shareable under Creative Commons and it's non-commercial.

> *"The only time I use the speakers' room is if I'm looking for someone."*
>
> —*Kirk Pepperdine*

Nobody there is directly trying to sell you something. There are no vendor booths. We've had people say they would like to sponsor the conference and we've turned them away. Everybody in the conference is on an equal footing. When you go to other conferences, you get the speakers' room and all this other stuff. I can tell you now that the only time I use the speakers' room is if I'm looking for someone. I generally don't stay in there because I want to be out where things are happening.

## The increase in conferences

**Geertjan Wielenga:** Don't you also get the feeling that maybe five years ago, even, there weren't as many conferences as there are now?

**Kirk Pepperdine**: Yes, I think a few more have popped up. If you look at what's going on in Poland, that's pretty amazing. Poland seems to have a very active community and there are a lot of conferences. There are a couple of conferences that are back to back in Krakow. They both draw 3,000 people. I can't spend my entire time speaking because I need to pay the bills and speaking, unfortunately, doesn't really pay the bills.

**Geertjan Wielenga**: Do you find that as a result of being at conferences and networking, it helps your business?

**Kirk Pepperdine**: I haven't been able to correlate attendance at a conference with my business. Now, I know there's a correlation but nothing is ever immediate. Everyone thinks that you go to a conference and you walk away with 10 new clients. That doesn't happen.

You might walk away with one client or two clients, but you won't get that one client or two clients until maybe a year and a half after you've attended the conference. There's a huge lag, especially for what I do, between speaking at a conference and someone seeing you and saying, "Hey, we might like this guy to come into our company."

They have to wait for a budget cycle and the right conditions. All of a sudden, they'll call you and you'll get an engagement out of it. Meanwhile, you might have just spoken to 600 people, maybe more. I had one customer who said, "Oh, we saw you speak three years ago." They decided to call me because of the talk. That is a crazy long time to remember somebody!

**Geertjan Wielenga**: You mainly focus on performance tuning. So, when somebody calls you up, do they basically have an application that's dead on the table and it has to be released tomorrow, for example?

**Kirk Pepperdine**: It actually gets worse than that. I've been called in to projects that had already been cancelled and this was the last-ditch effort to see if I could revive them or get them uncanceled.

It's quite a strange situation because I'm just a goofy guy walking into a company. The company's about to tank, or has already tanked, the project and everybody's highly stressed. I just come in and I'm in beach surf vacation mode. You're really in this juxtaposed mood condition.

When I said that I don't always read about tech, I meant that you have to read about the other things. You have to recognize that most of the time, the problem isn't tech. Yes, there's a technical problem there that needs to be solved, but there's also this human problem that needs to be looked after.

> *"I'm supposed to come in and change the world in three or four days."*
>
> —Kirk Pepperdine

A company has had their best people looking at this problem for months and I'm supposed to come in and change the world in three or four days. I know nothing about what they're doing when I walk through the door.

Somebody's had to go through a hard sell to say, "Let's get someone who's completely clueless about what we do and just call them in randomly and they're magically going to make our problem go away."

There's this human aspect of the problem that you actually have to manage, as I say, and that becomes more important than the tech in some sense. One time, we had members of the board wandering around the developer pit. We had the phones completely ringing off the hook. The system they had deployed was just falling over very badly.

These guys were really good developers, but they had made one mistake. Before I could find it, I had to somehow calm everybody down. I used this technique I use to implement some tactical hack: I had to go off and start killing things in the system.

It did mean that the people who were doing the important work at the time could work uninterrupted and the phones stopped ringing. The board members all went back to their offices to look at something else. You could just feel the tension completely drain out of the room when the phones stopped ringing. Then, everybody's brain turned on.

After that, I could say, "Okay, what did you guys do here?" These guys explained the problem to me and all I had to do was tell them what they told me. Then they knew what the problem was and they went off and fixed it. I didn't do anything; I just found a pressure relief valve.

**Geertjan Wielenga**: You're like a psychologist more than anything else, then?

## Using psychology to solve problems

**Kirk Pepperdine**: Yes, I find a lot of performance issues are a reflection of some dysfunctionality within the organization and not really a problem with the people who deployed the tech.

Something has gone wrong at an organizational level and it creeps out somehow into the systems. You actually have to deal with the psychology of the situation.

Sometimes, people get fired, which is never nice. In a couple of cases, I've actually managed to keep people from being fired because I knew they did the right thing, but they just messed up in one really small way. They actually had taken their company three or four steps forwards but their one small mistake took them back one step. Everybody was looking at the one step backwards and not at the fact that they took the company four steps forwards in the process.

**Geertjan Wielenga**: These are really interesting insights that you have gained from your engagements. How do you feed them into your conference topics as a speaker?

**Kirk Pepperdine**: I used to talk about the psychology of certain situations, but I stopped because developers are never really interested in that. I talk about tactical hacks and the effect that they can have on the psychology of the situation instead.

The funniest story is one tactical hack I put in. The CEO was talking to me afterwards and asked what I had done. I said, "Well, I have put 13 lines of code in the application to do this really bad thing to the system that makes it run smoothly."

He was shaking his head and he said, "Wow, that's the most expensive 13 lines of code I've ever paid for!" I didn't say anything at the time, but actually the other lines of code that were causing the problem were more expensive!

**Geertjan Wielenga**: Java performance is what you get engaged in and also what you talk about, but what are some of the specific topics?

**Kirk Pepperdine**: Garbage collection is the topic that many people are interested in. I keep talking about it all over the place. What makes garbage collection interesting is that it can have a really huge impact on the performance of your application. Just to give you a hint, with one of my clients that I'm currently working with, all I've been doing is tuning garbage collectors. With the first set of tuning that I did, I took the service-level agreement (SLA) violation rate down from 6% to 1% and it was just by tuning the garbage collector.

**Geertjan Wielenga**: Have you written books or guidelines that collect all these insights about garbage collection, or performance in general, together?

**Kirk Pepperdine**: I never have. The problem is that the space changes at such a rate that by the time you write anything more than an article, what you've written is obsolete.

## The advantages of being independent

**Geertjan Wielenga**: Going back into the general developer advocate discussion, since you don't work directly for a company, does that means that you can be 100% honest about everything and just speak from the heart?

**Kirk Pepperdine**: That's what I do. I generally speak true to my experiences. There have been some really funny situations.

Heinz and myself were the first non-Sun Microsystems people invited to speak at Sun Developer Days. The most embarrassing thing was that Simon Ritter, who was working for Sun Microsystems at that time, had something like 19 people at his talk. Heinz and I were looking at each other saying, "Okay, that's crazy because Simon Ritter is an absolutely fantastic speaker. He just nails it every time."

I actually really enjoy going to see his talks and I attend them regularly because he's really good. But he had 19 people at his talk and at my talk, I had 385. I remember the number because I remember the distinct gap between what the official advocates were getting and what I was getting and what Heinz was getting.

I was trying to figure out why this was. Was it because I'm a better speaker than Simon? No way. The problem was that people thought they were going to get product pitches from Simon. They weren't interested in the product pitches. I know, for sure, that Simon was not delivering product pitches, so these people missed out on a really good talk.

> *"I think that it gives us a little bit of a boost not working for anyone."*
>
> *—Kirk Pepperdine*

There were obviously enough people at the conference, but what it came down to was that we didn't work for Sun Microsystems, so we had some street cred. I have always thought that was crazy. I think that it gives us a little bit of a boost not working for anyone. People look at us and say, "Okay, you don't have an agenda."

I look at Cameron Purdy as the person I really learned a lot from. He's another amazing speaker. Cameron gave a pure tech talk, always. Everybody knew that he did the Coherence product. Everybody knew that he was a VIP at Oracle. But that didn't matter, because it didn't change Cameron's style.

I think marketing at Oracle was a little upset with him at times. They wanted to preview his talks because he got into a bit of trouble with them. The marketing people couldn't do anything to him, though, because he was the person in Oracle who was attracting everybody. Everybody wanted to see his talks because they were entertaining and highly informative.

He didn't do product pitches but everybody knew where he was from and everybody knew what he was working on. He didn't have to get up there and say that: they knew. It was because of that that people came to see him. From my perspective, that is a much better way of marketing things than what the traditional marketing people want you to do.

**Geertjan Wielenga**: How do you feel about developer advocates who advocate one tech and then a year or so later advocate the competing tech?

**Kirk Pepperdine**: I'll go back to what Cameron did. Cameron looked at the problem that he was trying to solve and he brought the problem down to first principles.

He never really talked about the product because he was sometimes actually pointing people to competitors.

Cameron did have a level of freedom because he wasn't a person who marketing could control. They wanted a more corporate message from him.

Cameron recognized that no one listens to the corporate messages. Since he was getting results by doing it his way, the marketing people had to relent in the end. They had to just let him go off and do what he was doing because it was working.

I think many developer advocates say, "Look, if you don't let us speak to developers the way we need to speak to developers, then you're just not going to get the audience. You're going to spend all of this money, time, and effort, and you're going to be giving not necessarily a bad message, but a message to the wrong audience." That's not to say that the Oracle marketing message isn't a useful message for somebody; it's just not a message that developers are willing to listen to.

Cameron and Simon, to just pick on those two, are authentic. They live, breathe, and eat what they're talking about. They're not really coming in and delivering a talk: they're telling you what they're doing. I would like to think that I do the same thing.

One talk that I put together a number of years ago, I keep doing over and over again because people just like it. It's entertaining and it's engaging. I would say it's close to a good magic trick. I give a performance problem to the audience and I say, "You solve it: here are the rules of the game." The people in the audience are engaged because they're trying to figure out what's going on. People are shouting out suggestions and they're directing the demo.

**Geertjan Wielenga**: Technical glitches happen all the time, so what are some horror stories that you've encountered?

## Kirk's experience of technical glitches

**Kirk Pepperdine**: I had one failure where I just couldn't get the screen to work on my laptop and I had all my demos set up on it. It was a very demo-heavy talk, so it was a real problem.

We had a late start and then things just went downhill from there, and there was nothing I could do about it at that point. It was just a case of apologizing to the audience. That was a bad one. I had another one where we just couldn't get the projector to recognize my laptop. I had no slides and they were working really hard trying to fix it. I said, "Okay, I'm just not going to have enough time for this talk if it keeps going this way."

> *"Everyone was sort of upset when the projector started working and I could return to slides!"*
>
> —*Kirk Pepperdine*

I talked without the slides. I was hand-waving and making shapes. I actually got a lot of positive feedback on that one. Everyone was sort of upset when the projector started working and I could return to slides! They said the explanations were clear because I wasn't relying on the slides at that point in time.

**Geertjan Wielenga**: Imagine that you're a student at a college or university and you find this whole developer advocacy story interesting. How would you get started in this?

**Kirk Pepperdine**: If you want to be an advocate towards developers, the first thing you have to do is be a developer. If you want to be accepted by developers, you have to be a person who they respect. You have to be someone who has put the miles in.

You need to contribute, whether it's contributing to open source or not. Apache NetBeans is a great project. There are a lot of advocates around the Apache NetBeans platform, but they're putting the miles in in terms of helping the project to move forwards.

I guess, to be authentic, you want to be talking about what you do because that's what's going to make you accepted. That's how you're going to get your message across most effectively. Again, you need to develop street cred. You can't be a marketing person and be accepted by this particular group of people.

**Geertjan Wielenga**: Do you travel a lot? What are the pros and cons of that? How do you deal with the side effects of that?

## Juggling family life

**Kirk Pepperdine**: I tend to travel in stretches. I'm not home for certain events when they happen. On the flip side, when I am home, I'm there for all of these events.

When my kids were in school, I was often the only father showing up at events. I've missed a few because I was away, but when I was there, it was really no issue for me to go and see whatever school events were happening. I just know that other fathers never got the chance because their jobs never allowed them to do something like that. You're away frequently but when you're around, it's actually advantageous. Plus, sometimes it's fun. You can bring some of the family or the entire family with you.

Going back to JCrete, we don't want to set up another event where you're away from your family. We made it so that families can attend and they do. We get the kids involved and I think a lot of the spouses really enjoy the experience. They're quite surprised by it.

**Geertjan Wielenga**: Is burnout a risk and how do you deal with it?

**Kirk Pepperdine**: Is it a risk? Yes. How do you deal with it? If it's happened, go away on vacation. If you recognize that it's happening, at that point you just have to learn how to say no.

We talk about the travel issues at JCrete and we try to do our best to come to some balance with them. When you start mixing in time zones, then it can get really brutal. I had a close to 24-hour trip getting here. Next week, as soon as I get back from here, I'm going to Atlanta. I've immediately taken my calendar and put a big black X through the following week. In other words, I have no intention of going anywhere!

You've just got to look at the schedule and say, "Well, I know I can tolerate that if it's within one or two time zones that are close together." After a certain volume, you just look at it and say, "Okay, I have to black that week out; it's gone."

Then you hopefully will have a supportive employer. When I was working for a company just as a consultant, my employer was very aware of consultant burnout and say, for example, something at home happened, you were out of there and on a plane home, because that's where you needed to be. That was more important to them than the engagement. That employer was absolutely fantastic and I was exceptionally happy working there.

On the other hand, I've seen speakers who have basically almost fallen over on a couple of occasions. I was really disappointed in their employers. In both cases, the people involved were not in a position to make solid decisions for themselves, so someone had to step in and make the hard decision for them, and go to their employer on their behalf.

I think if your employer doesn't support you when you're in that type of situation, then it's probably not a position you want to keep anyway. It's a two-way street: the employer and the employee both have to benefit.

We get this argument about business class seats for frequent fliers because they're so much more expensive for engagements. My position on that is that I fly often enough that when I do long-haul flights, that's how I fly.

An employer should see the entire picture of what you're doing, but as an individual consultant, you don't have someone who's in this umbrella position and looking out for your long-term health. Your clients don't care. They want you to come in and fix their problem. Then you go away, which is really cool.

You also have to, on a personal level, look at this from the long-term aspect and ask, "Okay, if I'm doing these long-haul flights quite frequently, what is that doing to me and what can I do to minimize the effects of these long-haul flights?"

> *"You really are responsible for yourself if you're an independent."*
>
> —*Kirk Pepperdine*

Business class is just one of those things that minimizes the long-term effects of flying from here to there and everywhere. If you fly once a year on vacation, it's not going to matter, but if you're flying long haul, maybe once a month or maybe more frequently, then you need to start worrying about these things. If you experience burnout, then you're no good to anybody. At that point, you really are responsible for yourself if you're an independent.

## Suffering from burnout

**Geertjan Wielenga**: There's an argument that because there's so much variation in what we do, the possibility of getting burnout is smaller. Some people say that burnout is mostly from doing the same thing under high stress over and over again. Is that true?

**Kirk Pepperdine**: Not necessarily. There's a repetitive stress thing happening if you think about it. If I'm flying from one engagement to the next, then I'm doing the same thing repetitively, it's just not for the same employer or client. Yes, the scenery will change, but the rhythm is still the same. You can still suffer burnout from just exhausting yourself. If you get to a point where you're too exhausted, then you're not going to be effective anymore.

This morning I did my reading and I clocked in a 6 km walk. It's really important to do that and I think walking is, for me, the best thing to do. If you're on the road, you can just throw on comfortable shoes and out the door you go.

I just went through 10 time zones, so that really helped me to adapt to this particular time zone. Now I can be productive here.

**Geertjan Wielenga**: Thank you, Kirk Pepperdine.

## 05

> *Many people still see conference speakers as better developers who are at a level that they will probably never reach. I try to give them a different view about that.*

# Rabea Gransberger

# Introducing Rabea Gransberger

Rabea Gransberger is a software engineer and co-leads the software development department at MEKOS. She is also a well-known speaker at Java conferences and user groups around the world. Rabea is a Java Champion and started the Bremen Java User Group in 2012. She doesn't necessarily see herself as a developer advocate, rather her main focus is on keeping the code base clean and educating her team, and developers around the world, to write better code. Find Rabea on Twitter: @rgransberger.

---

**Geertjan Wielenga**: Can you explain who you are and what you do?

**Rabea Gransberger**: I'm from Germany and I work in Bremen as a software developer, department lead, and project manager. So, it's a bit of everything.

In my team, we mainly get our tasks from our customers and we are in the nice position of having two major customers that allow us to work in an agile way. They give us some tasks, we prioritize the tasks together, and then we can pick the tasks that have high priority, along with some smaller ones, which are good for filling up the sprint.

We have a team of five developers and I'm responsible for architectural design and educating the team, as well as completing tasks from the sprint. I'm trying to educate the team by doing code reviews and hands-on labs. For example, when Java 8 came out, we had internal training sessions where we solved some streams and lambda exercises to get some practical experience with the new APIs.

**Geertjan Wielenga**: At conferences, you often talked about code reviews. What started that?

## Rabea's ideas for talks

**Rabea Gransberger**: The idea to give a talk about code reviews was inspired by my daily work. Sometimes, I also get ideas for topics when I'm attending conferences.

For example, one of my talks was called "Effective IDE Usage." I've seen many people at conferences struggling to get the code to work correctly during their talks because they didn't use any of the content assist in the integrated development environment (IDE), so that is how I got the idea there.

When I did the functional libraries talk for Java 8, I just submitted the idea for the talk because I was interested in the topic myself. I wanted to find out if there were any nice libraries out there that my team could use in our company. When the talk was accepted, I was already doing all the preparational stuff and investigating the libraries.

**Geertjan Wielenga**: What were the main points in your talk about code reviews?

**Rabea Gransberger**: I made the point that every company should start doing code reviews. It's okay if you just start when you feel the need to do a code review. For example, if you have a change in a very critical component, you might think that somebody else should do a code review.

If you start like that, I think you get better results. Some companies say, "Every piece of code that we're writing has to have a review." I think people are driven away by the additional effort.

**Geertjan Wielenga**: What does a code review consist of?

**Rabea Gransberger**: A code review, for me, is just a very informal review: having a look at the code and writing down comments, and giving them back to the author of the code so he or she can improve the code.

**Geertjan Wielenga**: What kind of person should be the one doing the review?

**Rabea Gransberger**: The person doing the review should also be a person who has plenty of knowledge in the domain. So, for an optimal result from the code review, they should be part of the same team because this also gives the benefit that more than one person in the team knows the code. If some issues come up later, then there will be more than one person who can fix the code.

**Geertjan Wielenga**: What led you to go down this career path?

**Rabea Gransberger**: When I was still at university, I registered for a German forum where people would ask questions. It was just a general IT forum. I tried to answer the Java questions myself, even the things that I didn't understand at first. I usually tried to create a little test for myself and read up on things to see if I could actually solve the problem.

Then, in 2004, I got my first job as a Java developer when I was still a student. So, this was also how I got better at programming Java. After one year, somebody on the job told me that there's a debugger.

Nobody at university would ever tell you that there's a debugger! I was always fiddling around with `System.out.println` statements and my colleague asked, "Why are you using those? Just use the debugger." For me, it was kind of embarrassing. I was also angry that nobody at university ever told me about the debugger!

**Geertjan Wielenga**: How did you build on these experiences?

**Rabea Gransberger**: When I started at my current company in 2009, I had to learn a lot because the mineral oil/petrol station business domain, which is the focus of our work, is very specialized.

After two years, I was bored. There was nobody left to teach me anything about programming. I always wanted to become better at Java programming, so I was looking for other ideas.

I was reading *The Java Specialists' Newsletter* from Heinz Kabutz at the time and he had a special offer for participants of his regular online courses to attend his masterclass on the island of Crete. So, I flew there and did this four-day course. I was a junior Java developer at that time and the course was very challenging. I couldn't solve all of the exercises, but, apparently, I was good enough that Heinz kept in touch with me!

## Attending conferences

**Geertjan Wielenga**: Was your introduction to traveling to conferences via Heinz's JCrete unconference?

**Rabea Gransberger**: Yes, in 2011 I was invited by Heinz and did travel to the first JCrete unconference.

There I got in touch with other developers who traveled to conferences. They were always asking, "Why don't you go to conferences as well and give a talk?"

I would reply, "But I don't have any ideas for talks because what I do at work is in a very specialized domain."

I didn't think that a talk that I gave would be interesting for the outside world. When you completely understand what you're doing, you feel that it's very boring and nobody else could possibly be interested.

My first talk was at EclipseCon Europe in 2012, which I did with a coworker of mine. That came about because we attended one of the Eclipse demo camps that are held when some new Eclipse version is released.

One evening, we were traveling to Hamburg to the demo camp and we were talking outside in a smoking area. There was another guy there and he was asking what we did for work. We said, "We're developing products based on the Eclipse Rich Client Platform and we're using the Eclipse Remote Application Platform to have the same code base for the desktop application and the web application. We're also investigating how to use Tabris."

At the time, Tabris was a platform that was bringing the same code base from the desktop to mobile devices, so it had a special way of "converting" the code to Android or iOS.

The stranger said, "That's very interesting because there's a lot of theory about using a single code base for having those three different user interfaces, but not many people are actually doing that. Would you be interested in giving a talk at EclipseCon Europe?"

> *"We realized that nobody was doing what we were doing, so we gave our first talk."*
>
> —*Rabea Gransberger*

That guy was Ralph Mueller, who was one of the chairpersons for the EclipseCon conferences at that time. We realized that nobody was doing what we were doing, so we gave our first talk.

That year, I started the Java User Group in Bremen. I had been looking for a Java User Group in Bremen for some time. I would go searching for it every couple of years, but there was no such group. So, I finally decided to create my own. It does still exist. I'm not the lead anymore because so much time goes into organizing that kind of stuff. Now we have an organization team with three other people involved.

**Geertjan Wielenga**: That's the best thing! The next phase is to hand it on to somebody else. Isn't that the perfect cycle?

# Running a user group

**Rabea Gransberger**: Yes! It's also great because I'm not good at motivating people. I'm good at teaching people who are already motivated, but I'm not good at motivating people.

We initially had very low attendance at the Java User Group, but I think that was more due to the platform that we chose. In the beginning, we chose to create all the notifications for the meetings on the German XING platform, which is like the LinkedIn platform, and XING is just not good at sending out a meeting invitation.

You only get an email that you have a new message. Then you have to log in to actually be able to read it. I, myself, would never read a message sent via XING, unless the topic was very interesting.

We had 200 people who were registered to that group, but only five people were showing up for the meetings. Due to the low attendance, it was hard to convince speakers to come to Bremen. Peter Neubauer, a founder of Neo4j, for example, came down from Sweden and there were only around six or seven people attending. I felt very sorry for him because of the long travel, but I was very grateful he came and I was able to show him the city. I would always warn the speakers, saying, "Don't expect more than 10 people to come!"

After a while, it didn't feel right to me anymore to ask people to drive such a long way for just a small group of people. So, when I was reading emails from Simon Maple, who was organizing the Virtual Java User Group at the time, I was thinking, "Oh, he's so good at motivating people and I'm just not good at it."

I decided that somebody else would do a better job and I gave the position of the Java User Group lead to somebody else. We also changed the platform to Meetup, which is very good at reminding people about meetings and informing new local users with an interest in Java about the group. Now we have around 50 people attending the meetings, which is much better.

**Geertjan Wielenga**: How did you start speaking at conferences on a regular basis?

**Rabea Gransberger**: I was at Devoxx and I got to know some people. They told me about the inaugural Devoxx UK conference, so I submitted a talk and that worked out. In 2013, I gave my first conference talk alone in London.

> *"It was a whole different world to see normal developers giving talks at conferences."*
>
> —*Rabea Gransberger*

What is very interesting is that before I went to the Java masterclass in Crete, I didn't even know that there were conferences about Java! So, for me, it was a whole different world to see normal developers giving talks at conferences and I really liked that because the people were very friendly. You would meet some other passionate people, you could talk about what you were doing, and you could learn from others. I stayed with the conference scene after that.

**Geertjan Wielenga**: One of the last times that I saw you, you were actually helping to run JCrete. Are you still doing that?

**Rabea Gransberger**: Yes, I'm in the "unorganizers" team for JCrete! I've been doing that since 2014. I mainly help with the event and with the setting up, and I make sure that everything runs smoothly when I'm there.

I was also part of the JavaLand program committee for three years, but I'm not doing that anymore because I just don't have the time for it.

**Geertjan Wielenga**: Do you also write articles or books, or anything like that?

**Rabea Gransberger**: I did write one article for the German *iX Developer* magazine, which was published last year. The article was about Java 9 modules and I did answer some interview questions for another German online magazine.

I don't do that much because writing articles just takes time. Currently, I don't feel that I need to write any articles. I also started my own blog, but the only blog post was about creating the blog!

**Geertjan Wielenga**: Since you're doing all of these different activities, how do you find the time to be involved in the community?

**Rabea Gransberger**: Currently, it's hard for me. When I was younger, until I was probably 30, I would enjoy writing some code in the evenings after I got home from work. I would sit at home and read something about Java or do some coding, and so on. But for the past few years, I haven't found the time anymore to do that. Now I need time to relax in the evenings!

Sometimes, when I have a longer vacation, I feel like I need to write some code. I'm also doing some open-source work, like helping to solve some of the Eclipse bugs.

With conferences, it's usually one week before I have to give a talk, then it turns up on my calendar and I think, "Oh, I should probably start creating the talk or rehearsing an older talk again." It consumes so much time. It takes one whole weekend until I have the basic structure and slides for a talk if it's a 45-minute talk.

**Geertjan Wielenga**: When do you decide that you've had enough of a talk and you want to do something new?

## Knowing when to retire a talk

**Rabea Gransberger**: It's just a feeling for me. Usually, I've been submitting a talk for around two years, then, at some point, I just stop because I don't want to hear it again myself or the topic is out of date.

Eventually, the "Java 9 Modules" talk will be out of date, when everybody knows how to create Java modules, and then I will have to stop it. But with the code reviews talk, for example, it's funny because I think that it was in a very good state when I gave it for the last time. It was a very good feeling. Before that, I always had the feeling that I didn't like the talk myself. I got very good feedback about the talk from the conference rating systems and so on, so I continued to give the talk, but I was never really satisfied with the talk myself.

**Geertjan Wielenga**: If you were to describe yourself at a party, what would you say that you do?

**Rabea Gransberger**: That's really difficult. Probably, nowadays, I would say that I'm a software developer and consultant because at my company, it's mostly consulting work that we do for our customers.

Half a year ago, I would have told people that I was just a software developer, but when I got to work with other companies on customer projects, I found out that what we do is mostly consultancy work. Usually, a software developer just gets a task and solves it, but they aren't thinking about processes and trying to extract tasks from the processes that the customer needs.

**Geertjan Wielenga**: You're not a developer advocate who goes to a conference to talk about a particular product. You're not representing your company: you're representing yourself. Is that correct?

**Rabea Gransberger**: Yes, at my company we don't have a project that is open source and we don't have a product that can be used by other developers as well. I'm not in the position to advocate for a framework or product, but I do mention parts of my work during my talks.

When I gave the "Java 9 Modules" talk, I was also referring to Open Services Gateway initiative (OSGi), for example, which I use in my daily work. There were several times when a developer advocate position was offered to me by other companies, but I don't think that's what I would like to do, actually.

**Geertjan Wielenga**: Interesting. Will this be a developer advocate book with somebody saying that they don't want to be a developer advocate?!

## Freedom at work

**Rabea Gransberger**: Yes! I have the same feelings about other software development positions, as well, because in my current position, I can just do what I like and also decide on the future for my team.

> *"If I took that kind of job, the company would send me to conferences and I wouldn't have the freedom to decide to go to a conference."*
>
> *—Rabea Gransberger*

With many other positions out there at well-known companies, which regularly sponsor conferences, there will always be a booth at a conference and those people will have to do some booth duty. I wouldn't want to do that. If I took that kind of job, the company would send me to conferences and I wouldn't have the freedom to decide to go to a conference. It's actually my decision now.

When I talk to other developers at a conference, many of them say that they were sent there and they don't really enjoy what they're doing. They could be developer advocates or just developers who go to conferences and have to do some booth duty.

**Geertjan Wielenga**: Are there any other reasons for avoiding "advocacy" work?

**Rabea Gransberger**: Yes, I also enjoy working with customers, by which I mean not only software developers as customers but people outside of IT. I enjoy translating what they are saying into development tasks and trying to optimize their processes, and also learning about their domain.

Customers call us and ask, "How can we solve this topic with your software product?" Sometimes, it's a very domain-specific question. It's mainly asking, "How can I optimize this process that is part of my daily work?"

In my job, I'm in a position where I have learned enough about the role that the customer is working in that I can actually help them. That is what I enjoy the most. I wouldn't like it if people took away that freedom from me. I want to make my own choice about what I'm doing.

For example, today is a home office day, which I enjoy. I can usually choose whether I want to work from home or from the office. I normally go to the office because I just like to see my coworkers.

**Geertjan Wielenga**: Since you don't work for a company that sends you somewhere, does your company pay you to go to these places?

**Rabea Gransberger**: Yes, now my company does pay parts of my travel. In the beginning, I was taking vacation to go to conferences. I paid for the flights, I paid for the conferences, and I paid for the hotels. I paid for everything.

**Geertjan Wielenga**: Why? What motivated you in this scene in the first place?

**Rabea Gransberger**: It probably was about reaching a goal because I need goals in my life. I get all my motivation from having a goal that I can actually reach.

**Geertjan Wielenga**: What was the goal?

**Rabea Gransberger**: My goal was becoming a Java Champion, which I became last year. I'm always calling Java Champions "Java Marketing Champions." Many people think that a Java Champion is a very good Java developer, but it's not about being a good Java developer. It's about developer advocates who are going out there and advocating for Java as a great language, and selling Java without getting paid for it.

I wasn't too interested in becoming a Java Champion in that way, but still, it sounded appealing.

I wanted to become a well-known speaker and to be invited to conferences in the first place. Last year, I was very happy when people started to invite me to conferences, pay for my travel, or pay for hotels, because it was a recognition of the hours and hours that I put into preparing my talks.

**Geertjan Wielenga**: Do you mean that even without sending in an abstract, these conferences contacted you and asked, "Do you want to come and speak?"

**Rabea Gransberger**: Yes! I think it's easier for me, though, because I'm a woman and people are always looking for women speakers at conferences. If you're not really bad at giving talks as a woman, then I think you're invited to conferences at some point. You have to fail a lot before you're not invited back to a conference.

I'm actually constantly trying to improve my talks. People have very different opinions about what a good talk at a conference should look like. Many people are now saying that a talk should be without slides and mainly free, with just notes.

> *"It just has to be a well-delivered talk."*
>
> *—Rabea Gransberger*

Two years ago, I was sitting at a conference thinking, "Okay, what are the reasons that I like a talk myself? Is it because it's given freely or are there some other factors?" I decided that it just has to be a well-delivered talk. People can give a talk with slides. Some people just hold onto the desk and don't walk around on stage. I found that these aspects don't really matter to me.

**Geertjan Wielenga**: What is a well-delivered talk to you? What does that mean?

## The qualities of a good talk

**Rabea Gransberger**: It means that the speaker is very knowledgeable and that he or she has a well-prepared talk, and they don't skip some of the answers that I would actually expect to have given to me.

A great talk should also match the abstract. Plenty of speakers give talks that don't match their abstract at all because they don't read it again. They submit something for a conference, half a year before the conference, and when they prepare the talk, they have a different idea for the talk in their mind because it developed over that half year.

If a talk doesn't match the abstract anymore, then it's not good for the audience. The audience is at the talk because they expect something that they read in the abstract. Sometimes, some of the points that were raised in the abstract are not addressed in the talk.

What I had to work on, after giving my first talk, was that I was very nervous at the beginning. When I'm very nervous, I tend to talk too fast. When I talk too fast, I can't breathe anymore. So, at some points, I had to struggle between talking and actually breathing.

I think that now I'm more relaxed. For example, last autumn I had five talks in six weeks and it was always the same talk. At the end of that period, I wasn't nervous anymore because I had been giving the talk all the time and it was very easy for me. It's a nice experience to be very fluent in giving one of your talks.

It feels great to not be nervous anymore, walk freely on the stage, and describe some of the aspects of the talk.

I'm trying to improve. I know that I will never be like Venkat Subramaniam, for example, but that also comes with experience. I will never, ever, give as many talks as Venkat! If you give a talk every couple of days, then you have a very different experience level compared to other people.

**Geertjan Wielenga**: Is it purely a question of speaking frequently, would you say?

**Rabea Gransberger**: No, it's also that you have to be willing to improve yourself. What I still can't do is actually watch my own talks. I just can't do that. It's still embarrassing to see myself giving a talk. But I try to learn from the feedback that I get from other people.

Another reason that I give talks is that they have helped in growing my self-confidence. I used to be a very shy person, so before I started going to conferences, I could never have imagined myself traveling the world alone and going to different places.

I used to travel with my parents as a kid, so traveling was nothing new for me. I knew how to get around and I knew airports, and how everything works, so that was a big advantage for me. But I could never have imagined actually going out myself, into a city that I didn't know before, and getting some dinner alone.

That was a big barrier in the beginning, but now I think my confidence has improved a lot. I'm not that shy anymore. I think just going on stage is a good thing for shy people.

Now it's normal for me at conferences, when I see nobody that I know for lunch, for example, to ask people if I can share the table with them, and just talk to them. It's a very big step forward from a personal perspective!

> *"I don't have a problem with sharing my personal mistakes on stage."*
>
> —*Rabea Gransberger*

Sometimes, during my talks, I also refer to personal mistakes as well. I don't have a problem with sharing my personal mistakes on stage because I think people have to learn from that. Many people still see conference speakers as better developers who are at a level that they will probably never reach. I try to give them a different view about that. I just say that I have made my own mistakes as well and that I'm not perfect.

**Geertjan Wielenga**: Have you been in situations where you've known that the people in the room, or you suspect that the people in the room, know more than you do about the topic that you're talking about? How do you deal with that?

## Receiving feedback on your talk

**Rabea Gransberger**: Did I ever have somebody attending one of my talks who made me feel uncomfortable? I don't think so, but I like to hear some criticism about my talks as well, so that would be fine for me.

What I think is sad is that you usually only get the good feedback about your talks and you rarely hear why people didn't like your talks.

For me, it was very nice when Heinz was sitting in one of my "Effective IDE Usage" talks because I learned many of the things that I was showing from him.

With the "Java 9 Modules" talks that I was doing, I don't think anybody was there from Oracle, but I did talk to one of the guys from Oracle at Devoxx in Antwerp, and he said that he liked my talk from a recording he had seen.

I had this one moment when a talk was rejected and I actually got feedback about why. It wasn't useful because the feedback was just questions. The organizers had questions but because they couldn't contact me and ask those questions, they rejected the talk. I would have felt better had I just had a simple rejection, without any explanation, in that case. That's something that I have to work on myself. I always like it when I get some critical feedback, but it's also hard to actually read it.

**Geertjan Wielenga**: If you're at a conference and you're doing a talk, and someone asks a question that you don't know the answer to, how do you deal with that?

**Rabea Gransberger**: I'll say that I don't know the answer, or I'll ask the audience if they know the answer. This has worked out well, even in a big room.

I was giving a talk in Stuttgart and I had a very big room with 500 people attending. I offered back the question, which was related to code reviews, to the audience. At that conference, they had people walking around with a microphone, so it was possible for somebody else to answer the question.

For me, it's completely fine if speakers say, "Come to me afterward and we'll talk about it," in cases when the answer is longer or the question is too specific for the whole audience.

There was a very funny aspect about my code reviews talk because most of the questions that I got after giving the talk were about teams that didn't talk to each other. They did code reviews, but they only talked through the comments of the code reviews and they didn't talk to each other. The team would try to solve social problems during the code reviews, which wouldn't work. So, the main answer was to just talk to each other in person.

**Geertjan Wielenga**: Let's discuss technical glitches: when you're at a conference, it often happens, right?

# Dealing with technical glitches

**Rabea Gransberger**: Once, I was at a conference and I was on the stage preparing to give a talk, but after the previous talk, some of the pins of the VGA adapter were not straight anymore. I couldn't fit them into my port and so there was a technician coming, and so on. It was probably only one minute before my talk that we actually got this fixed.

This incident didn't make me nervous: it actually made me more relaxed because I had something to focus on. I had to focus on the technical problem and not focus on being nervous about my talk and what to say. So, for me, it was a good experience because after that, I became much more relaxed before my talks.

**Geertjan Wielenga**: Have you ever had an experience at a conference that really did make you nervous?

**Rabea Gransberger**: The only experience I had where I was really anxious was at Devoxx Morocco.

I had a new laptop and I didn't know if my adapter would work because there were some scary stories online about the adapter that I had to use.

When I did the setup before my talk, I couldn't get a connection to the projector. I was worried because I wanted to do some live coding and I also needed my slides. At some point, one guy from the audience pointed out that the other end of the cable wasn't connected to the projector. I was very happy that he did because I didn't check that!

At a conference last year, they had many technical issues because they were using very long cables and half of the signal would be lost before it reached the projector. I was doing some live coding, which was an integral part of the talk, and whenever I moved the mouse, you would only see black-and-green lines on the projected screen. So, it didn't work at all.

In the end, I had to point people to a video recording of the talk, so they could actually watch that at home. That was kind of sad, but I think nobody was really angry because they did know that it wasn't my fault and there were many technical problems throughout the conference.

**Geertjan Wielenga**: Is burnout something that you have experienced?

**Rabea Gransberger**: Usually, when I'm coding, I forget about time. I tend to work too much. I think the most I did was two weeks in a row with more than 80 hours per week. After that, I was really exhausted.

> *"Whenever I get some of the symptoms that show that I'm very overworked, I try to have a day to actually relax."*
>
> —*Rabea Gransberger*

Now I know the symptoms that I have when I work too much and I usually try to monitor them. Whenever I get some of the symptoms that show that I'm very overworked, I try to have a day to actually relax and not do that much work. There's no point in working so much because you will get slower and slower in actually getting your work done.

**Geertjan Wielenga**: What are some of the symptoms of burnout?

**Rabea Gransberger**: For me, when I work too much, I struggle to find my words and when I speak, it sounds terrible.

I find that I'm not able to remember things that easily, which I'm usually very good at. For example, I forget my lunch and leave it at home in the fridge. Then, I'm sitting in the office and don't have my lunch. Sometimes, I try to make some coffee in the office and forget to turn on the coffee machine, or I just brew some hot water because I forget to put in the coffee powder. All kinds of funny things happen!

I know how to monitor myself now, but three years ago, it was really bad. I had one day where I couldn't get up.

I was only staying at home and I couldn't get up because I was just so exhausted that my body refused to work. I made an appointment with a traditional healer and he found out that every muscle in my whole body was so tense that he couldn't do any of the tests he was trying to do.

The healer showed me some exercises to shake off the stress in the evening. Actually, you should do it three times a day. If you watch a dog, for example, after a dog has experienced a stressful situation, it shakes because it releases the tension of its muscles. Humans have forgotten how to do this. Shaking out stress used to be in our genes, but it became socially unacceptable and this is why we don't do it anymore. So, shake like a dog! It looks funny but it helps, so I'm trying to do that.

This is also one of the reasons that I'm not coding in the evenings anymore when I come home. I just need to take the time to recharge overnight to be able to work the next day.

**Geertjan Wielenga**: If you go to a conference and you attend a number of sessions, how much do you learn from that?

## Knowledge gained from conferences

**Rabea Gransberger**: In the beginning, I learned a lot about core Java and about performance in Java. Learning about the future of Java helped me because I knew more than other people and could pass this knowledge on to them in conversations.

The main thing is just the broad knowledge that you get at conferences. You get a very early look at some new tools that are coming out, like Testcontainers, for example.

I did hear about that a year ago at the GeekOUT conference and now it's gaining an even bigger audience. So, I think it's good to be one of the first people to know about a certain tech.

I invest a great deal of time in researching a topic for my talks. It's not always that I know everything about the topic myself. For example, with code reviews, I had my own impression of them. I also read papers about code reviews to actually create the talk and to get some more knowledge.

I put articles that I find on my reading list. When I go to conferences, I try to catch up with where software development is heading. I try to get these ideas back into my company as well.

I usually read Twitter, where I get plenty of ideas. You get people tweeting new and cool stuff from conferences, even if you're not at the conferences. Almost all the people I know from conferences are on Twitter. If you're following those people on social media, then you get something out of that as well. I've been to too many unconferences that got me into bad habits. So, nowadays, I tend to hop between talks, even at normal conferences.

**Geertjan Wielenga**: Can you talk more about unconferences?

**Rabea Gransberger**: The official name of an unconference is an Open Space Technology conference and it's a conference with no fixed schedule at the beginning. You just go there, then everybody is asked to propose a topic.

You try to cluster similar topics and put them into a preliminary schedule.

The interesting thing is, you don't have to have any prior knowledge of the topic. At the unconferences I've attended, I mostly just went to discussions where everybody could have a say. I think this is a more intense learning experience for me. I tend to learn more at unconferences than I do at conferences.

**Geertjan Wielenga**: What are some things that you've learned, maybe over the past year, that you didn't know before?

**Rabea Gransberger**: There's a reason that I'm always taking pictures at conferences and that I like to take pictures with my phone: sometimes the year moves by so fast that I enjoy browsing through the pictures. I like to review the year and see what I've done throughout it.

> *"I learned to actually enjoy talking to people who have a different opinion."*
>
> —*Rabea Gransberger*

I think one special thing that I learned at conferences is to enjoy talking to people, even if they have very different ideas on the topics. Usually, when you're in your personal environment, you try to find people who have a similar opinion and you become friends. But at conferences, it's somehow different. I learned to actually enjoy talking to people who have a different opinion, which broadens my point of view as well.

What I also like about conferences is learning from people who come from different parts of the world. I always had this feeling that there's a certain truth about some aspects of the world.

I thought that everybody has to have the same feeling that something is right or that something is wrong, but it's just not the case. Everybody's so influenced by how they grew up that they have a very different view on what is right and what is wrong. I think that's something I really enjoy about conferences: hearing about how other people are living in their own countries and their own cultures.

## Rabea's view of developer advocates

**Geertjan Wielenga**: As you don't have "developer advocate" on your business card, when you go to conferences, how do you view the developer advocates? Do you see a difference between the way that official developer advocates present their content versus people who are not official?

**Rabea Gransberger**: I'm not sure that I would actually notice the difference if I didn't know that they were official developer advocates. It's pretty much the same.

It might only be different for people who go into new roles. I never feel that the developer advocates are presenting their material like some of the speakers of sponsored talks. They always try to sell their product, but developer advocates don't do that too much.

**Geertjan Wielenga**: Could you explain a little bit about sponsored talks at conferences to draw out that distinction?

**Rabea Gransberger**: I usually never go to sponsored talks because I think much of it is just marketing. Many of the speakers are not honestly presenting the product: they have a lot of marketing stuff in their slides.

The speakers present things that probably do not even work today, but they *might* work in the future. I think people get disappointed if they go to the sponsored talks and then go and try out the materials, and find that they don't work as expected. The speakers don't honestly answer any questions from the audience either. I don't like that.

**Geertjan Wielenga**: Let's go back to you saying that developer advocates working for companies are hard to distinguish from speakers who are not working as official developer advocates. What's the reason for that?

**Rabea Gransberger**: No, that's not what I'm saying; I'm saying that I don't see a difference in the way that they present the talks. I'm sure that there's a difference in what they do for daily work, but I don't see a difference in how they present talks in comparison to other speakers who are not in the developer advocate role.

I think that they are very passionate in delivering what their job allows them to deliver. One of the differences between sponsored talks and developer advocate talks is that many sponsored speakers don't seem to be people who are very passionate about the topic.

**Geertjan Wielenga**: Since you're not a developer advocate, how do you see your career developing from here?

**Rabea Gransberger**: I'm not sure what my career will look like in the future because when I was still in university, I would always have some goals to work toward and achieve.

My goals for the future are not particularly related to work or my career anymore. I'm pretty happy with my role now. I don't want to go down the management career path, like other people have. I'm already partly in management, but I don't want to go into full-time management. I want to do some more open source to actually be able to learn from others through the code reviews.

**Geertjan Wielenga**: Are there people in your team who you talk to about going to conferences? Do you mention that this is something that they could add to their working life?

## Encouraging more people to attend conferences

**Rabea Gransberger**: Yes, I do. There's a small local conference called the Java Forum Nord in Hanover, which is just one hour away by train. I always ask coworkers if they want to go there because it's a good conference for people who haven't been to a conference before.

> *"Some people are intimidated by the atmosphere at conferences."*
>
> —*Rabea Gransberger*

Many people don't like the idea of going to conferences. It's just a different way of learning and I think everybody's very different in how they learn. Some people are intimidated by the atmosphere at conferences.

If you're going alone, for example, and you don't have anybody to talk with, I think it can be very overwhelming to see all those people running in different directions. Then at lunchtime, you're standing there alone. So, I think conferences aren't a good way for everybody to learn.

**Geertjan Wielenga**: What are some topics that you're currently beginning to explore?

**Rabea Gransberger**: I think that security-related topics are very important nowadays and I'm still busy implementing some stuff related to the General Data Protection Regulation (GDPR) in our applications. This is probably the main topic right now that I have to read up on. It's a huge amount of effort to actually implement, but I still think it's a good idea to give people back the power over the data that they're sharing.

**Geertjan Wielenga**: What does it mean to implement that in an application?

**Rabea Gransberger**: If you have a product and you're storing personal-related data, you have to have a report that says, "Okay, this is the personal-related data that we store about you."

You also have to say if you're sharing the data with any other companies. If the person wants their data to be deleted, you have to comply with that. In some parts of our application, we have to change the data structures we use to store the data in to be able to create reports more easily.

**Geertjan Wielenga**: When was the last time that you bought a tech book?

**Rabea Gransberger**: The last time I bought a tech book was last year. I bought the book from Paul Bakker and Sander Mak: *Java 9 Modularity*. But I don't buy that many books.

For me, I don't think it makes any sense to have a very deep knowledge, which I get from books, about things that I'm probably not going to use in the near future. I only read books about things that I'm trying to use as I'm starting to use them or if I want to learn more about the things I enjoyed using previously. Other than that, it's important for me to have a broad basic knowledge to be able to choose the areas I want to learn about in more detail.

**Geertjan Wielenga**: What would the younger version of yourself think about what you do now?

**Rabea Gransberger**: I would never have thought that I would be leading a team because I've always had problems talking to people. I'm proud of what I'm doing today and what I've achieved over the last few years. I've not only learned about software development, but also how to deal with people and how to talk with people. I think that's very important. I'm dealing with people and not with resources, so I can't only see them as work resources.

I've met many people who started to study psychology and then changed to computer science. This seems to be a pattern, at least in Germany.

**Geertjan Wielenga**: What's the connection between the two?

**Rabea Gransberger**: I think that, often, computer science people don't feel like they fit in with today's society.

They're probably trying to find out why they're different, so they go into psychology.

Through their studies, they learn that they should just do what they love to do and find other people who have the same thoughts. They meet them and then they build up their own micro-society of people.

**Geertjan Wielenga**: Thank you, Rabea Gransberger.

## 06

> *If you come with honesty and talk with technical authority, instead of being just a corporate mouthpiece, smart developers will see that.*

# Laurence Moroney

# Introducing Laurence Moroney

Laurence Moroney has been a developer advocate for over a decade and currently works at Google. Laurence is especially an advocate for TensorFlow and the possibilities of artificial intelligence (AI), and finds himself speaking to the non-tech world about AI every bit as much as the developer community. His YouTube interview show *Coffee with a Googler* helps developers and fans alike to put a human face on the roles inside a big tech company, and his many published works include *The Definitive Guide to Firebase*. Find Laurence on Twitter: @lmoroney.

---

**Geertjan Wielenga**: Could you provide some background about where you're from and what you do?

**Laurence Moroney**: I'm based in the Seattle area of the U.S. and I'm a developer advocate at Google. I work for Google AI (Google Brain) as a developer advocate for TensorFlow. My background is that I'm actually European. I grew up between Wales and Ireland, and I emigrated to the U.S. 23 years ago.

I discovered the role of developer advocacy while I was here in the U.S. I've worked as a developer advocate for three companies. The first company was a start-up called Mainsoft, the second was Microsoft, and the third is now Google.

How I landed in the developer advocacy field was that I worked for the chief technology officer (CTO) at Reuters and our job was building prototypes. We were kicking the tires of new tech and then advocating that inside the enterprise. That turned into a full career in advocacy.

With the official title "advocate" I've been doing this since about 2005, so, 14 years. I think I was one of the early ones.

**Geertjan Wielenga**: Let's first talk evangelism versus advocacy. Do you think this is a relevant discussion? Is there a difference?

## The importance of job titles

**Laurence Moroney**: I don't think, ultimately, there is a difference, unless you really think about semantics. I'll give two reasons why I prefer using "advocate" over "evangelist." Firstly, evangelism gives the impression that it's a one-way street. You're saying, "I'm here to tell you the good news." That's literally the definition.

To be the best evangelist or the best advocate, there needs to be a two-way street. I advocate our tech to developers and I advocate developers' needs to our engineering people and to our product managers. As a result, I think "advocate" is a much better description.

The second reason is that Microsoft, when I worked there, used to call the role "evangelist." Nowadays, the role is called "advocate" at Microsoft. One of the things that I did at Microsoft was I trained and equipped what we called "field evangelists." I was based in the headquarters in Seattle, but we had different people in different parts of the world who were evangelists for Microsoft.

There was one young man in Southern Asia who I was helping to train as an evangelist and he traveled to a Muslim country.

When asked at the border what his job was, he said he was an evangelist and he got detained! I got a call from the border security at this country asking to verify that he really meant he talked about tech and not religion. I think that was one of the signals to maybe change the title!

**Geertjan Wielenga**: How do you train evangelists?

**Laurence Moroney**: I can talk about what I did in the past and what I do now. In a big company like Microsoft, people work in the field in regional offices, such as Singapore, Tokyo, or London. The evangelism had to be multidisciplinary for those people; they had to be able to evangelize multiple types of tech, whereas the people in corporate were able to specialize.

I worked as the main evangelist for a tech called Silverlight. I wrote a bunch of books on Silverlight and I drove what the messaging around it should be. When it came to people in the field who were evangelists, they would have to know Silverlight, Windows, Office, and many other topics. My job was to equip them with what they needed to be able to evangelize Silverlight to partners and customers.

At Google, it's similar. Part of my job with TensorFlow and with AI is to equip our people in the field. I make sure that they have the most up-to-date messaging, decks, and demos. If they want to run an event or visit a partner and be able to brief them on a particular tech, then I help them with that.

**Geertjan Wielenga**: TensorFlow and AI are what you're really known for nowadays. What enthuses you most about those areas?

**Laurence Moroney**: Firstly, I'm excited by the positive changes that AI is bringing to the industry. Secondly, I work with some of the smartest people on the planet and going shoulder to shoulder with them to build a product and communicate a product is really exciting. Finally, I enjoy being a spokesperson for AI.

**Geertjan Wielenga**: Could you not say the same things about any tech that you find interesting? What is unique about AI and TensorFlow?

**Laurence Moroney**: I think the level of enthusiasm in the outside world that I'm responding to is unique. I've worked with tech that people absolutely adored but not to the same level as this and not to the same level among non-technical people. A lot of business people understand that they need to know about AI and they're excited about the opportunities. Many politicians want to hear about the opportunities too. AI goes beyond just developers and that's one thing that's super unique about it.

**Geertjan Wielenga**: What are some of the upcoming developments in AI that you see happening?

## How AI is developing

**Laurence Moroney**: For us, at Google, we're working on TensorFlow 2 and we're getting ready to release that. We have a number of events where we're going to be talking about that. Next week, we have a TensorFlow Developer Summit, where we'll be talking about some of the newest and greatest things.

The week after that, Google is hosting something called Cloud Next. I'll be speaking at that in San Francisco. The month after that, there's Google I/O. I'm doing talks about AI, machine learning, and deep learning.

My personal passion, and what I'm trying to drive within Google, is bringing AI out of the research and academic space to become a tool that any developer can use. I want AI to be the same as Java, widgets, or anything else that just became another tool in a developer's toolbox.

> *"I've been working with some of the biggest names in AI on developer-oriented training."*
>
> —*Laurence Moroney*

To that end, some of the advances that you'll be seeing in 2019 include making the APIs much more straightforward for the typical developer to use. I've been working with some of the biggest names in AI on developer-oriented training.

In addition, we're focusing on different runtimes. For example, it's all very well for you to be able to understand how to train a state-of-the-art model (for example, something like image recognition), but how do you get it into people's hands? The two biggest trends in development, of course, are mobile and web. I've been working with a tech called TensorFlow Lite, where the idea is that that's a runtime that will work on mobile devices like Android and iOS, as well as embedded systems.

You can start building your models on your development workstation and then deploy those models to a Lite runtime that works on embedded systems or mobile devices.

This also works when it's disconnected. You can do smart things using deep learned models too. For example, on an edge device, you can have a camera that might recognize a door opening or a door closing without round trips to the server.

Lastly, we've been working on something called TensorFlow.js, which is a JavaScript library that not only will allow you to run inference and models in the browser but will also allow you to train models in the browser. You can train a model to recognize you looking up, down, left, and right. Then you can control a Pac-Man game with that. That's one of my favorite demos that I like to show and that involves doing all of the training to recognize those images for computer vision directly in the browser, as well as executing that model in the browser.

**Geertjan Wielenga**: What is it, do you think, that makes AI and machine learning such hot topics today?

**Laurence Moroney**: I think it's the potential. Everybody wants a piece of that pie. That opportunity makes things exciting. From a developer's perspective, if I don't think about the dollars, I'm always excited by new things that open up new scenarios that weren't previously possible.

I'm old enough to remember that you used to build software that you'd burn onto a CD. Somebody would have to go to a shop and buy that CD and install it and hope that it had matching drivers. Then, the web came along and it opened up whole new possibilities for applications. The same thing happened when mobile devices came along. Now, you have this thing in your pocket that has web connectivity and a whole bunch of sensors. Would Uber have been possible if it wasn't for mobile devices? Would Instagram have been possible?

That's one of the things with AI that I always like to talk about from a developer perspective: there are problems that it's very difficult for you to solve as a developer writing traditional code. Think about activity recognition. If you're building a device like a fitness device, how do you detect if a person is walking? How do you detect if they're running or biking?

You might have a signal from the device for speed. You could say that if the speed is less than four, the user is probably walking. If it's greater than four and less than 12, then they're probably running. If it's greater than 12, they're probably biking. But that's a really naive algorithm and it really doesn't work. If you want to detect golfing, for example, those rules get thrown out of the window.

With AI and machine learning, the paradigm is shifted. I can gather data from a device when somebody is walking and be able to say that's what walking looks like or what running or biking looks like. A computer can be very good at spotting the patterns that distinguish these activities from each other. When it spots those patterns, it's actually coming up with the rules for walking, running, and biking, instead of me as a programmer trying to figure out the rules. Now, a whole new set of scenarios has opened up and become tools in my toolbox that weren't previously available. As an innovator, I think, "There's this problem that I want to solve. I couldn't solve it before, but maybe I can solve it now."

**Geertjan Wielenga**: What is available now to make those developments possible?

**Laurence Moroney**: In some ways, a lot of the techniques have been around since the '50s. This includes things like neural networks, the math behind neural networks, and gradient descents. I think there are two key differences now. The first difference is the availability of data. To go back to my earlier example, you can get data for what walking looks like, and so on.

The second difference is compute power. The rise of things like graphics processing units (GPUs) has made the ability to train systems fast feasible. You could potentially, in the '50s, have written something like a neural network that could have done training, but to train it to do the simplest possible scenario might have taken months or years. Now that this takes hours or even minutes, we've reached that critical point where training becomes feasible to do.

**Geertjan Wielenga**: One interesting aspect about your work is that you're not actually a TensorFlow developer advocate in the sense of being a tech advocate: it's more a conceptual thing and TensorFlow is a way to implement that. Would you agree that you are able to be a thought leader in the machine learning/AI area because of your developer advocacy work with TensorFlow?

**Laurence Moroney**: Yes, exactly; it becomes like a circular relationship. It obviously depends on the audience, but mostly when I speak with an audience, many of them are only familiar in passing with the concepts of AI, machine learning, and deep learning. I will explain how Google thinks about these things.

The industry is quite immature still. I read a statistic the other day that there are somewhere between 25 and 30 million software developers in the world but only 300,000 AI practitioners. Most of the time, I'm talking to the 24.7 million developers who are not AI practitioners.

Can you name any other tech that's been the subject of science fiction books since the dawn of science fiction in a negative way? Many people say that the very first science fiction novel was *Frankenstein* by Mary Shelley. When you think about it, that's AI. Dr. Frankenstein created this artificial life, which then ended up going wrong.

## Fear of AI

**Geertjan Wielenga**: The other aspect of this is that in the '50s and '60s, there were many books and movies about how robots would take over our lives. Robots were understood to be large, clunky devices or externalized aliens. Now, we have washing machines, refrigerators, and comparable devices, which are all actually robots. Robots have taken over our lives, but in a good way. Do you think the fear comes from worrying about a loss of control?

**Laurence Moroney**: Yes, but also people generally are afraid of things that they don't know. Much of the job of an advocate is helping people to know. You need to be able to communicate to people that there's not a button that you press and suddenly there's a living creature in there. AI is just the new paradigm for programming that kind of emulates the way humans do things.

I often joke that sometimes, the way we name the tech kind of oversells it. We talk about something being a neural network, which makes people think that maybe this is emulating the human brain. The truth is it's only emulating it on the most basic of layers. Neurons in a neural network aren't the same as neurons in your brain. Training a neural network is not the same as how your brain trains. Setting those expectations is a big part of the job.

> *"Ultimately, it's my job to make you disillusioned!"*
>
> *—Laurence Moroney*

The company Gartner had this hype curve where there's a tech trigger and then there's a peak of inflated expectations, which falls into the trough of disillusionment. After the trough of disillusionment, there's a rise in productivity. AI is really interesting because there's this massive peak of inflated expectations and also a peak of paranoid expectations. My job is to tunnel people through to the trough of disillusionment so that they can start being productive. Ultimately, it's my job to make you disillusioned! If you look at any tech, it goes through a curve. When people get really productive and do great things, they start from the trough of disillusionment and not the peak of inflated expectations.

**Geertjan Wielenga**: Is this like going back to basics with tech?

**Laurence Moroney**: Yes. Let's take the smartphone as an example. When Steve Jobs went on stage and introduced the iPhone, the world went into a peak of inflated expectations. We could throw away our desktops and laptops. Then, we fell into the trough of disillusionment and we realized there are problems like battery life and tiny screens. Now, people have started getting productive. I see the same thing with AI, so I start my talks by saying, "Hey, I'm going to disillusion you today!"

**Geertjan Wielenga**: There are people who are independent developer advocates going to conferences who are not connected to any company. They can be completely authentic in the sense that they're not representing anybody. As I'm listening to you, it's clear that being tied to a vendor means that you can be an integral part of the developments that you're talking about. Does being right there in the engine room, where these things are happening, give you an advantage?

**Laurence Moroney**: I think there is still room for independent developer advocates, particularly in the open-source world. If you're an independent developer advocate not tied to a particular company, you can drive whatever the product is that you're advocating. If that product is open source, then you can be part of the engine room for that, too. But it's hard to be a fully effective independent advocate for a closed-source project because you don't have the ability to change the product directly.

**Geertjan Wielenga**: No matter how generic you make your pitch, ultimately, you're from a particular vendor; you're representing that particular perspective. Would you say that there's no getting away from that?

**Laurence Moroney**: There is no getting away from that, yes, but I will say that it's not an impenetrable barrier. I think the best companies that hire developer advocates always encourage them to be as independent as possible and let their authority speak for itself.

I'm lucky because one of our philosophies in TensorFlow and with Google AI is to try to be vendor-agnostic as much as possible. I'm under no pressure from my company to pitch Google Cloud as the best way of running these things, Android as the best operating system, or Chrome as the best browser. But when I do use a particular product, I will use it because of the merits of that product and I will talk through the merits of the product from my own experience.

Often, I'll use an iPhone for doing demos, for example, instead of an Android. If I'm doing the demos on a small form factor, I prefer Android. If I'm doing the demos on a large form factor, I don't know any Android tablets that I like as much as my iPad. I'm given that freedom.

> *"While developers may not trust you 100%, they won't trust you 0% either."*
>
> —*Laurence Moroney*

Not every developer advocate who works with a vendor has that freedom; I agree with you on that. But what I've found from experience when working for vendors is that when the person can talk with authority about the tech and just focus on the tech, the barrier tends to dissolve a little bit. If you come with honesty and talk with technical authority, instead of being just a corporate mouthpiece, smart developers will see that. While developers may not trust you 100%, they won't trust you 0% either.

**Geertjan Wielenga**: If you're at conferences, there's always an interest in independent developer advocates for their unaligned voices, but there's also always an interest in what companies such as Google, Microsoft, and Oracle are doing. Would you agree that people do want to hear the official pitch from the official developer advocates working for an official vendor?

**Laurence Moroney**: Absolutely, and I think most developers are smart enough to see through corporate speak and to see through marketing speak. If a developer advocate only does corporate speak and marketing speak, they will get marginalized.

# Working for a large company

**Geertjan Wielenga**: Also, people who are not working for vendors often forget that developer advocates coming from the large vendors often have a choice on which tech they want to work with. Couldn't you be working on something totally different from TensorFlow at Google?

**Laurence Moroney**: It's funny because I joined Google as a cloud advocate because that was what I was hired to do. I really enjoyed that, but I preferred mobile. So, when the opportunity came to jump ship to mobile, I think I became a better advocate because that was something that I was passionate about.

That ended up morphing into me becoming an advocate for Firebase and a little over a year ago, I was working on a tech in Firebase called Firebase Predictions, which uses AI around your analytics to help you to determine customer churn and customer spend. That uses machine learning under the hood and it helped me to drive a lot of feedback to the AI group within Google.

Part of my feedback was around the developer experience because I'm a developer and not an AI researcher. The AI group asked, "Why don't you come and join us?" My natural passion just bubbled to the top. I think that makes me a better developer advocate because this is something I love doing.

**Geertjan Wielenga**: This again illustrates the benefits of working for a large vendor: you can make that transition from one product to another versus if you're working for some small start-up with one specific tech. Do you see one of the appealing aspects of Google, Microsoft, Oracle, and others being that these large organizations have such a range of tools?

**Laurence Moroney**: Yes, but if you don't work for those organizations, then many of them have developer networks. At Google, we've got two groups: one is called Google Developer Groups (GDGs) and the other one is called Google Developer Experts (GDEs). Instead of just leaving these groups to go and do their own thing, we help them, but we don't control them.

We give them places to host meetups and provide them with information, swag, and stickers. People who don't work for us tend to rise up and become independent advocates and often, the ones that become the experts have access to a network of resources, as well as the ability to give feedback. They almost become light versions of the developer advocates who work for the company. They can also go between different tech stacks based on their passion.

Big companies can help people to explore their passions for developer advocacy, even if they don't work for them. That often helps people in their career so that they get hired as developer advocates later, maybe by that company or maybe by another company. They get the best of both worlds in some ways. They are that independent voice that you were talking about earlier, but they're an independent voice that has been validated by the vendor. They can go on stage and say, "Google says I'm an expert, but I'm an independent, so I don't work for Google. Here's my opinion." That can be very powerful.

**Geertjan Wielenga**: A dilemma that often can arise with developer advocacy is when you're enthusiastic about a particular direction your company is going in and then the company changes its direction. Have you been in that situation and how do you deal with that?

**Laurence Moroney**: I've been in that situation, yes. A good advocate will prepare their developer community for change, without actually leaking that that's going to happen. It's a fine line that you have to walk along.

I think if you are passionate in the space that you work in, you can see the trends and if your company is beginning to take a right-hand turn, then you can start preparing people for those trends. But that's the toughest part of the job.

**Geertjan Wielenga**: It can be difficult if you are very emotionally involved with a particular tech and you've been promoting it. Have you experienced any problems with that?

## Empathy when advocating

**Laurence Moroney**: I have had death threats on social media from people who felt like they had been left high and dry. I think it was an emotional reaction in that case, but it did help me to realize that I have to be careful to have empathy for the people that I'm advocating to and not just be very salesy about my job. I have to help developers to navigate through things and as a result, be more authentic as I'm advocating tech.

**Geertjan Wielenga**: One part of the message could be that this is something that we recommend right now, but who knows where we will be 35 years from now. However, there's a strong possibility that someone listening to that might decide to stick with whatever they're doing right now and skip this particular thing, and five years from now pick up whatever is there at that point. Is that a valid response?

**Laurence Moroney**: It is a valid response, but that risks missing the boat for five years. You've got to make sure that you're not throwing the baby out with the bathwater. Sometimes, people think they've got to throw out the tech and start again.

I've never encountered a situation with a person having to start again from step zero.

When Java 2 Platform, Enterprise Edition (J2EE) was at fever pitch, a lot of people designed their architectural systems to work with it. But when I was working as a Microsoft advocate and helping them to move to ASP.NET, it wasn't a complete rip and replace. They'd made all these architectural decisions, designed databases, and designed authentication systems. Much of that thinking was still valid. When you look at the software development life cycle, that's probably 80% of the work. People often have a knee-jerk reaction when there's a tech change.

**Geertjan Wielenga**: What I've picked up from listening to you is the diversity of activities that you're involved in. How do you manage all that?

**Laurence Moroney**: Have you ever been really hungry at a buffet? That's what it's like. There are so many ways that you can advocate. Do you go to meetups? Do you speak at conferences? Do you write blogs? Do you write books? Do you make videos? Do you brief customers? The answer is all of the above.

The question then becomes, which tasks are best for Google? Which tasks are best for me? Which tasks are best for my audience? It becomes a balancing act between those. Fortunately, in a big company, there are different people with different skills. There are some people who are much better at writing and there are some people who are much better at speaking. Every one of those gaps is going to get filled; I don't have to fill all of them at any moment in time.

If I broke my time into slices, I'd say I'm probably spending 30% of my time making videos because they scale really well. We have a channel on YouTube that I run. If I'm not making the videos myself, I'm guiding other people in making them and I'm scripting them. 20% of my time is spent focusing on the product itself and understanding how it works, as well as trying to drive and shape how it works. Giving feedback is the final 50% of my time or speaking at meetups and conferences.

At Google, we've got two types of advocates: scalable advocates and partner advocates. A scalable advocate goes outbound with their message at scale. That means working with hundreds or thousands of people. A partner advocate is the one who goes into depth. I'm a scalable advocate. When I'm talking about slicing my time, it's really about the scalable things.

At the TensorFlow Developer Summit next week, we have 20 people speaking at the conference, many of whom are not advocates or speakers: they're product managers or engineers. It's my job to craft how they speak to the public, what their decks look like, and what their demos look like so that it can be less ivory tower and more developer-friendly. Guiding others to be part-time advocates is how I look at that side of my role.

**Geertjan Wielenga**: Is there a danger of burnout with all of these different activities?

**Laurence Moroney**: I think everybody's different in this space. When you're working as a developer advocate, you're generally passionate about what you're advocating. I tend to work extremely hard and my managers will always come to me concerned about burnout.

Hard work has never burned me out, though. If you're pushing me into things that are pointless or if I'm doing something for political reasons, then that could lead to burnout.

I have suffered burnout at times and almost every time it was because of some internal political issues. I think that applies to most developer advocates. Fortunately, the company I work for now is not very political. It's very technically oriented and if you focus on your tech, you can tune everything else out. I really love that. That hasn't been the same everywhere I've worked.

**Geertjan Wielenga**: Let's say you travel to a conference somewhere far away and then your laptop doesn't connect or there's some technical glitch; do you have some horror stories of that kind?

**Laurence Moroney**: Not quite as dramatic as that, but whenever I would go to another country, I used to learn a child's nursery rhyme or song from that country. I would tell people before I did a complex demo that if that demo failed, I was going to sing the song. That became a win-win situation. There were always people in the audience who were waiting for the demo to fail so they could hear me sing! I've sung nursery rhymes in Hebrew, Chinese, Japanese, and some other languages.

I have had a catastrophic failure where I required a network connection to be able to do my demo on my talk and no network connection existed. The authentic thing to do was to be vulnerable. If you're good at your tech and you know what you're working on, then you can talk about it, without slides.

## Tips for new starters

**Geertjan Wielenga**: Anyone reading this interview is inevitably going to want to know how to be just like you. What tips would you give somebody who wants to enter into this field?

**Laurence Moroney**: The number one thing that you need is passion. I think developer advocacy has to be something that you really love. It's not the kind of thing that means you can sit down and think that you will earn so much money if you do this or that. With that mindset, you just won't be good at it and you won't enjoy it.

Beyond passion, you need to be knowledgeable. You need to really understand the tech in depth. Finally, you need to be compassionate. You need to be able to walk a mile in someone's shoes so you can understand where they're coming from.

In practical terms, if you're not working for a big company, then get involved in tech communities and become a star in those communities. If you have those three attributes, that will just happen. When you're a star in those communities, you'll either be that independent advocate or you'll be giving yourself the ammunition to be able to join a company as an advocate.

> *"I was a massive Microsoft fanboy."*
>
> —*Laurence Moroney*

I was a physicist at college but there was no work for physicists. I was a massive Microsoft fanboy. I thought that Microsoft built great tools and operating systems, so I learned Visual Basic and I built a career as a computer programmer.

I developed my career as a software engineer, then a software architect, and then a Microsoft specialist.

I mentioned earlier that my first advocacy job was for a start-up called Mainsoft. The irony was that what Mainsoft was doing was helping people to transition from Microsoft to Linux. There was a cross-compiler that allowed you to cross-compile ASP.NET into J2EE. Then, with your logic and stuff that was built in ASP.NET, you could compile those as Enterprise JavaBeans (EJBs) and run that. I joined as a Microsoft expert and I ended up becoming a bit of a star in the community around interoperability between Microsoft and J2EE. I spoke at JavaOne in 2004 and that got me noticed by Microsoft. At that point, I'd written a few books as well. When Microsoft was hiring for this thing called WPF/E, which later became Silverlight, it needed an evangelist for that.

People can grow in a way that isn't really possible in other industries. If you're madly in love with TensorFlow, Firebase, or Windows 10, you've got the opportunity to become that community's superstar. If you want to go and join the big boys, the opportunity to do so is there. If you want to stay independent, then the opportunity is there too. Developer advocacy is not something that you can study; it's just something that you do.

**Geertjan Wielenga**: Thank you, Laurence Moroney.

## 07

> *How can you not be excited about software right now? What a time to be alive!*

# Scott Hanselman

# Introducing Scott Hanselman

Scott Hanselman is a programmer, teacher, and speaker who works on open source at Microsoft. His blog at `hanselman.com` has been running for over 15 years. In addition to writing a number of books, Scott hosts several podcasts, including *Hanselminutes*, which recently published its 700th episode. Scott talks about code, tech, culture, gadgets, diversity, code, and the open web. An avid presenter, Scott has spoken in person about code and coding to over half a million developers worldwide. Find Scott on Twitter: `@shanselman`.

---

**Geertjan Wielenga**: Do you see yourself as a developer advocate?

**Scott Hanselman**: Perhaps, but for some there's a generational gap with developer advocates. You have people in their early 20s who treat the role differently. I've made software for over 20 years and even now, I'm still not 100% comfortable saying, "I'm a developer advocate," because some people feel that developer advocates aren't doing any work; they're just running around giving talks at conferences.

**Geertjan Wielenga**: That is work, isn't it?

**Scott Hanselman**: The problem is that there are a lot of young people who have never built anything. How can you advocate for developers if you've never built anything? I tend to disappear for several months, ship something, and then talk about it.

We, as advocates, should seek to find a balance between building and talking—in that middle space we can find advocacy.

What I worry about is people in their early 20s who have never shipped anything working as developer advocates. They might get to 30 or 40 years old without building software. What are they talking about at conferences? Are they simply marketing people with charm?

I'm a big fan of the Kelsey Hightowers of the world: people who build stuff and then talk about it. I try to follow that. Should developer advocates give talks professionally 100% of the time? They also need to take [customer] feedback to their team, so you really need to dissect the word "advocacy."

If Oracle does something wrong and doesn't hear my voice, I can call you. Microsoft has 130,000 employees and I've got followers on Twitter. I need those followers to be able to say, "I've got a buddy who works at Microsoft. Hanselman will help us." I'm not their buddy in real life, but they do know that I will advocate on their behalf.

**Geertjan Wielenga**: What do you focus on building?

**Scott Hanselman**: My main goal is to open source .NET, which means making sure that we're doing the right thing in the entire stack. .NET historically wasn't open source and there were patent issues. Our larger team is currently working to merge .NET, Mono, and .NET Framework, and make sure that our licenses and codes of conduct are solid.

I need to be able to hear all voices. Someone wanted to do something on Linux on a container a couple of weeks ago. The license wasn't right, so we fixed it.

**Geertjan Wielenga**: What led you to Microsoft in the first place?

## Scott's path to Microsoft

**Scott Hanselman**: I was the chief architect at a company called Corillian that did retail online banking. I reported to the chief technology officer (CTO) and shipped a bunch of software called Voyager that ran about a quarter of America's retail online banking.

I built a big distributed system that was like Kubernetes, except that it was written in C++ and ran on Windows. I also wrote the .NET software development kit (SDK) wrappers around it, so I was in the open-source .NET community early on.

Then I helped to introduce open source to banks, which was challenging because large banks don't usually like open source. I had to deal with the General Public License (GPL) and others. This was in the early 2000s, so people were really tense about free and open-source software (FOSS) versus open-source software (OSS). We'd go to a bank and hear, "No, we don't want to have open source here because we're afraid that you'll have to make the whole bank open source." We would work through those problems. We didn't have pull requests at the time, so it was all Concurrent Versions System (CVS) and Subversion (SVN), but we'd do diffs and patches to log4net and so on.

I happened to be at an O'Reilly conference called Foo Camp and I saw two Microsoft people: Steven Sinofsky, who was getting ready to do Windows 8, and Scott Guthrie. I talked to them both and Guthrie was looking at Ruby on Rails. He was thinking about doing a Model-View-Controller (MVC).

I said, "Hey, this is exciting. I've been doing web forms and open source. Let's see if we can make .NET on Nails." That's what I wanted to call it, but it ended up with the name ASP.NET MVC. We started by making a web framework open source and then other things open source like the C# compiler. We slowly peeled the onion layers away until we eventually open sourced everything and today we have .NET Core, which runs basically anywhere.

**Geertjan Wielenga**: Did you go to conferences and talk about those developments?

**Scott Hanselman**: Yes, I had already been talking at local user groups. I'm a big fan of developer advocates doing the same thing that stand-up comedians do: you work at a small bar, you do some open mics, and you move your way up to the big rooms. That's often how it's done.

I think that people should come to developer advocacy in the same way. It's amazing, by the way, if you can go from never speaking before to speaking at a large conference like Velocity, but not everyone can do that. So, perhaps speak at your company, then at a code camp, then at a regional code camp, and then at a large international conference.

I was enthusiastic. I don't think of myself as an advocate as much as a professional enthusiast. I'm just really stoked about software. Even sitting here, within hand's reach I have a robot that I'm working on and a microcontroller that runs .NET. There's also a Raspberry Pi Kubernetes cluster on my desk. This isn't advocacy work; this is just geekery.

You've got to be a huge dork to care about this stuff. I've got half a dozen laptops on my desk and two 3D printers. How can you not be excited about software right now? What a time to be alive! I'm overflowing with enthusiasm about software. I'm not paid to go and do any of this. My job is to own the .NET Foundation and to make sure that we do open source right. Speaking is basically a side gig. Microsoft also does have a group called the Cloud Developer Advocates; they're like our main conference speakers.

**Geertjan Wielenga**: What's your relationship with them?

**Scott Hanselman**: I work with them and coach them, but I'm not one of them. I was here early on, so I encourage them to engage with the community in an authentic way. We had a conversation recently about whether or not someone should do paid talks. I don't know how it works with your advocacy, but I don't do Microsoft talks and get paid for them. It's not appropriate or ethical. If you're a consultant, you can do paid talks and that's great, but an employee shouldn't be doing that.

**Geertjan Wielenga**: You're working for this large vendor and going up on stage, so one way of looking at it is that you're a shill for the company or a spin doctor. What's your take on that?

**Scott Hanselman**: I've actually got "Microsoft Shill" on a couple of my slides. I then try to show the audience that I'm not a shill by doing the opposite of what they expect.

**Geertjan Wielenga**: Would you agree that once you're seen as just a marketing person, you're done?

**Scott Hanselman**: Yes, in the past I had a lot of impostor syndrome. In the last three or four years, I've finally become comfortable in my skin. I can say with a little bit of ego that I'm good at this. I definitely have street credibility because people know what I won't talk about.

> *"If I say something is cool, it's probably because it's cool and not because Microsoft is paying me to say that."*
>
> —Scott Hanselman

There are certain things that I've just stayed away from and in dodging those things, I've gained some credibility. If I say something is cool, it's probably because it's cool and not because Microsoft is paying me to say that. I don't think I've ever gone on stage and talked about anything that I didn't think was important; that's just not my style.

**Geertjan Wielenga**: People often don't realize that developer advocates at the large vendors have a choice of multiple different projects that they could be working on. You may be hearing the company line, but it's most likely something that that particular person has chosen because they're enthusiastic about it. Would you agree?

**Scott Hanselman**: Yes, and I think people forget how big these companies are. Right now, we have a political issue because one person at Microsoft wrote some dumb stuff and it's all over the news. 130,000 people work for Microsoft, as I mentioned. Statistically, that will include some racist and sexist people.

There are definitely assholes at this company, but there are assholes at every company.

**Geertjan Wielenga**: If you're on stage on a Monday morning and during the previous week the company that you're representing did something damaging or questionable, you're still the ambassador. Have you had experience of that?

**Scott Hanselman**: Yes, think about how it felt before Satya Nadella joined Microsoft. Even today, someone can do something stupid before you get on stage and suddenly it's your fault. We're doing great stuff with open source, but when someone does something stupid with Android patents, we get asked about it. It's got nothing to do with any of us, but it becomes a challenge. That's extremely frustrating.

## Handling the bad headlines

**Geertjan Wielenga**: What do you say on stage when the predictable questions are asked about something in the news?

**Scott Hanselman**: I do the best I can to be super straight with people. I say, "Listen, there are jerks at every company. Microsoft does some dumb stuff but we, as a whole, are always trying to do the right thing."

I also point out that we're not nearly as organized as we would need to be to be as evil as some people think we are. I've been at Microsoft for over 11 years and no one has ever been in a meeting and twirled their mustache and made a diabolical speech! We sometimes do dumb stuff but we're not evil; there's a difference. I just tell the audience that "incompetent isn't evil."

**Geertjan Wielenga**: There's this perception that large vendors are seamless monolithic wholes where everyone is aligned. Typically, the employees at large vendors have no clue what the people in the next room are doing. Is this true in your experience?

**Scott Hanselman**: Yes, to give an example, there's a Twitter account called @msdev that's very popular. Apparently, it's not even run by one of us; it's run by a vendor. The vendor tweeted a joke after the Mueller Report came out.

The tweet was a picture of a Visual Studio Code theme that would automatically redact all of your code and make it all just black lines. It was funny, but it came at a sensitive political time. I direct messaged that account and said, "Hey, this is probably not a good look."

That started an internal thread and someone said, "Oh, that's so-and-so. He's usually funny but no one double-checked his work." That's a perfect example of us not being organized in the way people think we are. The post was pulled down within an hour.

We're always playing whack-a-mole because things are popping up and we have to whack them back down. I'm constantly doing that, whether I'm dealing with licensing issues, foolish pull requests, or even leaks. Sometimes there's a secret that another organization has. That secret will come out in a pull request or a public discussion. Of course, our solution is to do everything in the open.

My goal is to push this open-source snowball up the hill and if I can get it high enough, it'll roll back down the other side of the hill and then Microsoft can't stop it.

I'm just going to keep open sourcing stuff until they kick me out. A couple of times a quarter, I think, "Do I get fired over this? Do I quit over this? Is this the thing?"

> *"It's easy to quit, but, at the same time, there's a privilege in being able to quit."*
>
> —*Scott Hanselman*

If I'm going to quit, I can only do it once. It will be big news, so I've got to pick a good reason. Ethics are important and I'll have to quit if we do something stupid. On the other hand, as a senior leader, arguably I need to stick around because that's the hardest thing to do. I need to fix whatever is wrong. Nowadays, I think, "Maybe I need to become a vice president or someone with power so I can keep these things from happening in the first place." It's easy to quit, but, at the same time, there's a privilege in being able to quit. You hear about many advocates quitting because of bad environments, but you've got to fix the environment.

**Geertjan Wielenga**: If you quit, the impact of that will only last for a few weeks. Then there'll be a new cycle and you'll be completely stranded somewhere outside of the tent. You'll have no impact and you won't get back in again because you're not going to be forgiven any time this century. Have you seen that happen?

**Scott Hanselman**: Yes, that's a big problem. There are some people who were instrumental early on in Microsoft who are gone. I don't know what they're doing now.

**Geertjan Wielenga**: Would you agree that people can get overwrought about things?

**Scott Hanselman**: Yes, why don't people fix things that they're upset about? The drama in the open-source community can largely be fixed by simply talking human to human.

I wrote a blog post called "Software and Saving Babies" (https://www.hanselman.com/blog/SoftwareAndSaving-Babies.aspx). When you're writing software, you have to ask, "Are we saving babies here?" If you're writing software that is actually helping babies to survive, then you should take your software really seriously. But if you're just making a shopping cart, you should turn it down a notch and take a breather.

People worry that something's going to get onto Reddit or Hacker News but ultimately, that's only going to be seen by a couple of thousand people, or maybe a couple of hundred thousand. There are eight billion people in the world who really don't care about your software. Unless you're Facebook, take a breath.

**Geertjan Wielenga**: I've been working on not taking things too seriously in terms of internal politics in particular and thinking, "The impact of this is going to be much smaller than it seems at first. Six months down the line, I'll be doing exactly what I was doing before." What's your view on that?

**Scott Hanselman**: That's interesting because people talk about how they want to be a senior engineer in five years, but it took many of us 10 or 15 years before we had a title like that. I look at many people's LinkedIn pages and I see that they spent one year or nine months at a company. What can you do in nine months other than get your email set up?

This might be controversial, but I feel that organizational change doesn't happen in nine months.

You've got to stick it out. I've always believed in spending three to five years at a company whenever possible. I spent nine years building banking software. I think three versions came out in three years. Windows itself is an 18-month to two-year cycle. You can't spend three to six months on Windows and say you shipped it.

Think about the people who worked on Windows 7; that was a high point. Windows 8 was a low point and now Windows 10 is a high point again. To have lived through all three of those Windows must be something amazing. Those people who are still there must have learned so much.

**Geertjan Wielenga**: What qualities do you need to advocate tech successfully?

**Scott Hanselman**: I've found myself in this position because I care deeply. I'm constantly triaging issues. There's little stuff like spelling mistakes or 404 links that I fix. People ask, "Why do you care?" I care because I want Microsoft to be successful. If you care, you can be a successful advocate.

## Achieving a work-life balance

**Geertjan Wielenga**: Is there a danger of taking these problems home with you?

**Scott Hanselman**: It's a balance. You have to know exactly when to stop. My wife's a nurse and she has to turn her brain off after work. You can't care about everybody or save them all. I would say that I'm pretty good at stopping.

There was a person on my team who was stressed out about stuff and they needed a day to focus on their mental health. They didn't want to take the time off, but I said, "Listen, it's not that big of a deal. The work will still be there on Monday."

> *"Remote workers can be paranoid that people are thinking that they don't do anything."*
>
> *—Scott Hanselman*

My dad used to say, "You're no good to me dead." It's a silly and morbid way to say it, but you need to take a couple of days off. Go to bed. You just have to or you'll go nuts. If I want to go and hang out with my wife, that's okay. I have things I could be doing for work, but I need to not do them at that moment. Remote workers can be paranoid that people are thinking that they don't do anything, so they work extra hard.

**Geertjan Wielenga**: Do you travel frequently?

**Scott Hanselman**: Yes, I would say maybe for a week every month. It depends; there are busy times, but I get in and out of a country fast. I'm very aggressive about that. I spend five days away and then come home for dinner on a Friday. I don't spend 10 days going around Europe because I'd rather be at home.

**Geertjan Wielenga**: What are your tips and tricks for jet lag?

**Scott Hanselman**: I use melatonin. It works for me. Also, the second I get on an airplane, I switch to local time. That way, I've got time to get acclimated. Most people see a plane as no man's land; they don't know what time it is.

They only start thinking about the time when they land. Get on the plane and spend 11 hours getting ready. It's a psychological trick, but it matters.

**Geertjan Wielenga**: Let's say that you've traveled to some faraway destination and a technical glitch hits; how do you handle that?

**Scott Hanselman**: I'm known for not having things go wrong on stage and that comes from a great deal of preparation, as well as knowing what could go wrong. When things do go wrong, assuming it's not my fault, I usually take that opportunity to show the audience how to fix them.

I'm pretty good on stage. You don't usually catch me saying, "Gosh, I don't know what's going on here. I'm just going to give up." That comes from experience. I know what could go wrong. I'm trying to think of the last time something broke and I had no idea why. It's been a long time. I'm not trying to toot my own horn, but if you've run through something many times, you should have already seen it break.

I'm going to go and give a keynote at Microsoft Build in a couple of weeks. We're going to sit down and figure out all the possible things that could go wrong. I want to see things break. It's almost like security risk analysis: "What could go wrong? The network could go down, the disk could go bad, the code could not compile, and so on."

**Geertjan Wielenga**: How honest are you when you know that there are bugs in the tech that you're talking about in demos? Do you skirt around things? Do you mention them? What's the right approach to that?

**Scott Hanselman**: If there's a *bug* bug, you have to be honest. If I'm demoing a beta but I know that a bug has been found and is being worked on, then I can work around the bug. The only "lies" that I've ever told are what I call "sequences have been shortened."

In America, Julia Child was our famous baker. She would make the pie and then she'd put it into the bottom oven. Next, she'd go to the top oven and pull out a cooked pie. I do Julia Child's pie maneuvers occasionally, but that's part of being prepared. That's not a lie and I think the audience knows that.

**Geertjan Wielenga**: What are you excited about right now in tech?

## Scott's areas of interest

**Scott Hanselman**: TypeScript is demonstrably important and it happens to be from Microsoft. It was a risk to talk about TypeScript before it was deemed important, but, clearly, it is. The trick is to use your gut.

Another example is WebAssembly. We have a thing called Blazor that lets you compile ASP.NET pages to WebAssembly. Part of it is from Microsoft. I think it's cool and it will change things. Blazor might not become the next Ruby on Rails, but it is important.

WebAssembly is the foundation. Saying, "Here's a library and it's built on JavaScript," is different from saying, "Here's an entirely new language you've never heard of." JavaScript gets you the interview; it's your way in. Another example is getting C# to run on the Java virtual machine (JVM). You can use one thing like a bridge to the other thing.

Remember all that time that we spent trying to get virtual machines running in browsers? Little squares, Java applets, Flash, and Silverlight were all different ways that people were working around the internet itself. HTML didn't do what we needed and JavaScript was immature. We needed real tools. Java made Java applets, C# went with Silverlight, and Flash was for animations and then YouTube. Flash pushed us forward in the context of video codecs, Silverlight gave us really great graphics, and Java gave us Java applets in the browser.

We all did physics demos, but then everyone was asking, "Why did Microsoft kill Silverlight?" No one killed any of those plugins. The Internet itself killed those plugins and now we have a virtual machine in the browser: JavaScript. Rather than remoting user interfaces, we're now remoting code, which is not VT100 terminals or HTML terminals: it's now bytecode terminals and JavaScript is the bytecode. WebAssembly or binary WebAssembly is going to be the bytecode.

If someone has spent 15 or 20 years in the business writing C#, they will say, "I don't want to learn JavaScript. I've got all this C# code."

If we came out and said, "Here's some secret sauce that runs inside of WebAssembly," or, "Here's a plugin," which is what we did with Silverlight, "and it's all secret and closed source," that would be one thing, but there's not a non-open-source thing in the entire stack. Having an entirely open-source stack becomes compelling.

Blazor lets you go and manipulate the Document Object Model (DOM) and write full-on single-page applications (SPAs) in C#, and take existing 15-year-old dynamic link libraries (DLLs) and repurpose them, and run them in the browser. That's got to be important.

Tiny devices also interest me. The device that I held up earlier is not a Raspberry Pi, which is a microcomputer; this is actually a microcontroller. It has 5 or 6 MB of RAM and can run .NET. Imagine running a .NET application on a microcontroller and talking to sensors and the Internet of Things (IoT), and having the battery last for weeks instead of hours.

Microcontrollers aren't microcomputers; that's significant. If I can have something this big run .NET, then I can run it in 64K on a tiny device or in 64 GB, and I can run it on Apache Spark or something like that. This proves that .NET scales.

**Geertjan Wielenga**: Do you talk about these topics when you go to conferences?

**Scott Hanselman**: Yes, absolutely.

**Geertjan Wielenga**: What other talks have you given recently?

**Scott Hanselman**: I was in the Netherlands a couple of weeks ago. I went to Breda and then 's-Hertogenbosch. I called a couple of buddies of mine and said that I was in town. They rented a cinema in 's-Hertogenbosch and they put the word out. We combined three user groups and about 750 people turned up.

I believe that the talk was called ".NET Everywhere: Is It Possible and Is It Cool?" That was just me on stage for two and a half hours straight talking about Raspberry Pis. I showed Docker in the web on Windows and Linux on Mac; it was a tour of the .NET ecosystem, and it was designed to challenge assumptions.

I provide edutainment, which is education and entertainment. Putting on a show is easy, but I like to edutain. The fact that I could make that many people happy and sell out a movie theater is pretty cool. That's the culmination of my job, but it's not about me. People think it's about me. They say, "Hanselman is in town. Let's go and see him at the movie theater," but when you go to church, you don't go to see the preacher: you go for the community. My goal is to bring people together.

> *"I'm maybe the people's programmer, but we're all members of the same community."*
>
> —*Scott Hanselman*

When you go to the circus, you don't go to see the ringleader: you go to see the elephants. I'm a ringleader of the .NET community. I'm maybe the people's programmer, but we're all members of the same community. If the audience leaves saying, "Man, there's such great stuff happening in .NET right now," then I've been successful. Do you see the difference? That's the ideal advocate in my opinion.

## Not knowing an answer

**Geertjan Wielenga**: For anyone wanting to do this job, do you need to know everything to be up on stage?

**Scott Hanselman**: I was in Switzerland a couple of weeks ago. I was teasing people about the Swiss Army knife. I asked, "We live in fear of the Swiss Army because of this knife? What's so great about the Swiss Army knife?"

It's not a great knife, scissors, or pair of tweezers, but it does all those things pretty well together. You have to be a Swiss Army knife. You have to know lots of stuff 85%—you don't have to be an expert.

I'm speaking from a place of privilege because I recognize that I'm privileged in being able to receive a question on stage and reply, "I don't know." If I was a woman or a person of color early in their career, it would be difficult to go on stage and say, "I don't know the answer to that, but I'll go and ask." Because everyone knows me in the community and I've been around for 20 years, I can say, "I don't know."

The older I get, the more I have a network on which I can rely to answer these questions. Recently, I was talking to this group of architects; it was me and 50 of them. It was very stressful because I didn't want to embarrass myself. However, I was able to use a chat application to talk to people at work in real time when I said that I needed to ask someone else about an answer. I was only able to do this because of my network.

**Geertjan Wielenga:** What would you say are some of the disadvantages of developer advocacy?

**Scott Hanselman:** My wife doesn't always appreciate that I'm plugged in a lot. She has begun to say, "Get off Twitter. You're on Twitter all the time." I'm not actually only on Twitter; I'm doing my job in many communities, but it can be challenging. Not everyone shares my excitement about using social media as a way to connect with the community.

**Geertjan Wielenga:** What would the 20-year-old you think about the you of today?

**Scott Hanselman**: I thought that I would be an actor when I grew up. I kind of am; I go on stage. I'm doing theater but with computers. I think I'm an enthusiastic professor; I'm a teacher with showmanship.

**Geertjan Wielenga**: Thank you, Scott Hanselman.

## 08

> *With so much going on in the community, you have to engage.*

# Heather VanCura

# Introducing Heather VanCura

Heather VanCura is the director and chair of the Java Community Process (JCP) program, an international keynote speaker and presenter, a leader of global Java adoption programs in conjunction with Java User Group (JUG) leaders, expert-in-residence for MedicMobile at Rippleworks, and the organizer of developer hack days (Hackergartens) all around the world. She is passionate about community building, raising the profile of women and all unrepresented people in tech, and meaningful STEM education for students across the globe. Heather has over 15 years' experience in Java tech leadership, engagement, and community development. Find Heather on Twitter: @heathervc.

---

**Geertjan Wielenga**: Could you start by describing what you do?

**Heather VanCura**: I'm the chairperson of the JCP at Oracle. That's a broad role because there are many different things involved. The JCP acts as the standards organization for Java. The JCP oversees everything that goes into the Java platform and the evolution of the platform itself.

I have an internal group that I manage, which oversees the JCP, the website, and the coordination of all the Java specification requests. I also work with JUGs, trying to increase the adoption of Java tech and their participation in the evolution of Java tech. That's where the international speaking and developer advocacy aspect comes in. I work with the Java development community around the world.

**Geertjan Wielenga**: What is it specifically about Java that you're passionate about?

**Heather VanCura**: When I first got started, I felt that the way Java was developed was really unique, and that was intriguing to me. I was interested in the community and the human behavior aspect of it. Java is used literally everywhere. All of the different ways that Java is used are really compelling stories and we don't hear them enough.

## Heather's path in tech

**Geertjan Wielenga**: What's your background and how did you get into the software industry in the first place?

**Heather VanCura**: I was interested in software development in college, but I was swayed away from it by my guidance counselor. I majored in business and focused on marketing administration, but I took modules in statistics and quantitative methods. I thought I would get into market research or even something to do with human behavior and observing how people interact.

When I got out of college, though, I knew I wanted to focus on tech. I did my internship at a company called Triad Systems. After that, I got jobs working on high tech accounts in advertising agencies, including Microsoft accounts. Eventually, I decided that I didn't like being in advertising. I wanted to get into the customer side, which is where the more interesting work happens at tech companies.

I found a job at Santa Cruz Operation, in market development, until, in 2000, I saw a job opening at Sun Microsystems, which I thought was really interesting because it involved working on Java.

**Geertjan Wielenga**: What was the job that you applied for at Sun Microsystems?

**Heather VanCura**: It was a marketing program manager role for the JCP, which had just started at that point. The program only had 100 members and the Executive Committee had just formed.

The job was to grow the membership, so one of the first things I did was build a different website. I thought we should have annual membership events, so that's how the annual JCP party started. I was also responsible for implementing the elections process.

**Geertjan Wielenga**: Many people would identify you as an advocate or an evangelist of some kind. Would you agree with that? It sounds like you were the original Java evangelist!

**Heather VanCura**: Yes, essentially, much of my work involves developer advocacy. Being the chairperson of the JCP is a prestigious role in the Java community. It comes with inherent respect and I definitely am seen as an advocate.

Part of the role is to bring the community into the development of Java, so it's very community-focused. I advocate Java, so, of course, many different topics and questions come to me, including on the health of the overall ecosystem.

I've started to speak on topics such as what types of skills you need to succeed as a developer and what types of projects you should work on to succeed. I often take part in panels, or host interviews at conferences, since I know many people in the community.

> *"I want to see more women attending conferences and women speakers at conferences."*
>
> —*Heather VanCura*

I'm also very involved in promoting diversity. Being one of the few women in the industry, which was especially the case back when I started in 2000, I want to see more women attending conferences and women speakers at conferences. For a long time, I was often one of the only women speakers, so I started to get questions about how we could get more women into tech, especially as the Java developer community got a bit older and started having children of their own.

Developers would look around and say, "There's no one like my daughter here at these conferences." They wanted to know how they could make a difference. Over the last five years, that's become more of a common theme. Often, I will give a talk about how we can change that ratio and make a shift in the community.

## Connotations of "evangelist"

**Geertjan Wielenga**: There's some debate over whether the word "evangelist" is too political to use. Is it all one and the same to you?

**Heather VanCura**: The word "evangelist" condenses down to the same thing as the word "advocate." But I think that both can be seen as being politically charged in some way.

"Evangelical" has a religious aspect for some people and "advocacy" can relate to politics. I don't really have a preference. Obviously, both titles are related to being passionate and speaking on behalf of a constituency. I'm passionate about the Java developer community and I definitely see my role as bringing the community in and ensuring that it's heard within the JCP. Both terms would apply to me.

**Geertjan Wielenga**: Do you see yourself as having been a spin doctor at Sun Microsystems and now at Oracle?

**Heather VanCura**: No, I don't see it that way. I think the intentions of the JCP were always good. The JCP was a formalization of the process that Sun Microsystems used from the very beginning to bring in that real-world developer feedback, so I think that's always been the intent. My job was more to explain it than to spin it.

The majority of developers don't understand how Java has developed. It's just one of those things that some developers don't care about or see as unnecessary. We tend to see a certain percentage of developers all around the world who do care passionately and know all the intricate details of how Java has developed. The majority of the 12 million Java developers don't fall into this category, however. Part of what I still do, even 18 years later, is explain how Java developed and how people can participate.

There is a need to reach more developers. Much of the time, you can be more effective with that within JUGs themselves versus the conferences.

At the conferences, you will often see the same people coming again and again, but with JUGs, you reach more developers and get a broader base of developers.

**Geertjan Wielenga**: Oracle is not an uncontroversial organization. How do you deal with a situation where you want to be authentic, but you may not agree with decisions made by your colleagues?

**Heather VanCura**: I've struggled with many of the same issues as I did at Sun Microsystems. Fortunately, I'm in a position where I'm not charged with representing my company. It's expected that I balance the needs of the community.

> *"Being a developer advocate can be like walking on a tightrope."*
>
> —*Heather VanCura*

Being a developer advocate can be like walking on a tightrope. At Oracle, it helps that I'm in the standards organization, so I can take a broader view. I may not always agree with everything that's being done and, if that's the case, I'll convey it in a more factual way. I'll say, "I didn't make this decision. I'm not saying whether I think it's the right decision or not, but this is the decision, so what can we do to move forwards?"

The acquisition of Sun Microsystems by Oracle has been complete now for eight years, but in the early days, people would ask me all the time what I thought about that acquisition. It was challenging for me, but in the end, it was a good thing for Java.

Oracle becoming the steward of Java was a good thing in terms of reinvigoration. Oracle hadn't done much work with developers in the past, but it was willing to learn.

In some ways, advocacy requires some cognitive dissonance and being flexible mentally. That's often a skill people don't have or they don't feel comfortable with. You have to keep it all in perspective: what your role is, what influence you have, and how to use it to the best advantage for the community.

**Geertjan Wielenga**: What would the 20-year-old you think of the person you are today and the work that you do?

## Heather's ambitions as a young person

**Heather VanCura**: I definitely always saw myself as succeeding and I was a very driven person. You could say that I've been successful in my career, so I think I would be pleased.

One of the things that I always wanted was a global role and responsibility with impact. Some people would see that as intimidating or something they wouldn't want, but I always saw it as something that I aspired to. I wanted a global perspective and I definitely have that in my role. Travel was appealing to me from a young age too.

I'm a keen observer, but I never saw myself as a public speaker until this role. That's a hurdle I had to overcome. I had something to share, so I needed to get over being uncomfortable to share that information.

**Geertjan Wielenga**: Are you saying that, even if you don't see yourself doing public speaking, you can grow into becoming a speaker?

**Heather VanCura**: Yes! While communication is key, now there's social media, blogs, and written articles to create as well. You could even do audio interviews and podcasts, where you're not presenting in front of an audience in person. Having said that, you probably would need to get over that hurdle of public speaking eventually because it's a great skill to have. I'm happy that I embraced that as part of my job.

**Geertjan Wielenga**: Can you talk a bit more about overcoming the anxiety of public speaking?

**Heather VanCura**: It's a little bit intimidating the first time you give a talk at a conference. I think my first talk was at JavaOne, which was a big conference; at that time, there were approximately 15,000 people coming to it.

I took courses and shifted my thinking to realizing that I had information that people needed to know. Over time, I've continued to practice and take courses. I've even worked with a communications coach.

**Geertjan Wielenga**: What are the key takeaways that you carry with you from those courses?

**Heather VanCura**: The first takeaway is that mental shift I talked about in terms of seeing yourself as educating others. Secondly, you should try to condense your presentation into the main points that you want to convey and organize them in that way so it makes sense and people understand it. You should use visuals instead of a lot of text on slides, which is difficult when you have something to explain like the JCP, which has many details surrounding it.

Another important point is modifying the presentation based on the audience and the type of conference. I always tweak my presentation for the audience and I try to get some interaction in to engage people. Even asking a couple of questions at the beginning, with a show of hands, can help you to gauge where the audience is in terms of their knowledge.

**Geertjan Wielenga**: The way you describe what you do is very varied. Do you enjoy that?

## Variation in the role

**Heather VanCura**: Yes, I like to do different things because I get bored easily. I like that there's a technical challenge to this job. I don't have a technical background, but I understand and have learned about tech at a high level. I've had to learn that. There's always something new to learn from people and the way they use Java around the world.

There are many different jobs that one can have within this industry. Often, people think that tech is not for them because they don't see themselves as being a programmer. There are many different roles and being a developer advocate is one of them. There are different official job descriptions for that position, as we've discussed. You wouldn't necessarily say that the chairperson of the JCP is an advocate, but that's definitely part of my job.

**Geertjan Wielenga**: Earlier, you mentioned women in software development. Could you talk about that further?

**Heather VanCura**: Part of my role is speaking with women and sharing my advice for working in tech.

I've noticed that women appreciate that conversation, especially women who are newer in the field or maybe want to take the next step in their career.

People tend to gravitate toward people like themselves, so women often think they need advice from a woman. What I tell them is that I never had a female mentor. You can do this role without having any other women around you.

There's this pervasive belief that tech is a meritocracy, so it doesn't matter who you are or what you are; if you just do your work and get it done, the belief is that it will be recognized. I think that's a fallacy. You do have to be excellent at your job, get your work done, and work hard to succeed, but that really is just the baseline for keeping your job.

If you want to thrive in tech, you also need to set aside time to grow your network. You need other people. You need to increase your visibility and you can't do that if you're just doing your job and not thinking about anything else. You also need to look at ways to expand your influence. If you're just putting your head down and doing your job, and then going home, you're limiting your ability to be successful in your career. I think that applies to a man or a woman.

**Geertjan Wielenga**: Are you saying that working hard won't help you to be successful?

**Heather VanCura**: No, you do need to work really hard, but that's not enough. There are certain things that you need to do, which tend to be things that a lot of women that I've spoken to don't enjoy doing, such as self-promotion and negotiation. Those things are not explicitly stated, but I believe you have to do them.

You also need sponsors, mentors, and allies. You need to take the time to do some out-of-the-office activities, such as going to lunch with people. Take the time to get to know them, especially people who are different from you.

> *"You have to negotiate for high-profile projects and assignments."*
>
> —*Heather VanCura*

Self-promotion is not just talking about how great you are, but looking at ways to make sure that the work you're doing is actually being seen and recognized. You have to negotiate for high-profile projects and assignments. You can't just take whatever comes your way. You need to take the time to look up and assess the situation. What does your manager care about? What does your vice president (VP) care about? What is the whole direction of your company? Are the projects that you're being assigned things that are going to contribute to that?

Negotiating can also be applied to asking for a promotion. It's not necessarily always going to be given to you if you don't ask. You can't expect that you're going to get a raise or that you're going to be paid well just because you're working really hard. People who ask are more likely to get what they want!

**Geertjan Wielenga**: What do you think about the idea that women may not be so well represented in tech because they simply are not that interested in tech versus other career choices?

## Challenges faced by women in tech

**Heather VanCura**: I think many women are interested in tech but often don't stay in it. I think the ratio is that over 40% of women who work in tech quit within 10 years, whereas 16% of men do. That's almost triple the rate of women leaving versus men leaving.

What women say is that they're not given the prime assignments, they don't feel welcome, and they face sexist behavior. Those are the top three reasons given for women leaving tech.

**Geertjan Wielenga**: I've seen you do a presentation that addresses men: "Top 10 Ways to Ally for Women in Tech." Can you talk a bit about that and what those 10 ways are in a nutshell?

**Heather VanCura**: This form of advocacy isn't part of my job, but I want to talk about this and change it. Everyone talks about the concept of diversity, but if we want things to change, we have to do something.

My original idea was to give men 10 ways that they can help. If we want to change the environment, we need participation from men also. The first step is the way you think about women in tech. Rather than saying, "I'm an ally," try to think of it as a verb: a thing that you actually do.

Secondly, you need to listen more than you talk, especially when you talk to women about this topic. Ask questions, acknowledge that you might not always get it right, and be open-minded.

Assignment distribution is the third point. That's thinking about how different people on your team are assigned projects. Are the men getting the prime assignments? Are they the ones taking all the ownership of the code, or are you distributing that across different people on your team?

One way to think about that is housework versus real work. There are always some housekeeping tasks: cleanup, reviewing the slides, and so on. Make sure that you're rotating those things. You can also watch out for housework in an office environment. Make sure that you're not always relying on women to clean up the kitchen or clean up the meeting room afterward. I've observed that happening many times.

> *"Women often leave tech because they don't feel comfortable."*
>
> *—Heather VanCura*

Creating a friendly environment is the fourth point. This addresses the problem of women leaving the tech field. Women often leave tech because they don't feel comfortable. Look at your job descriptions and the values that you're putting out there. Often, you'll see a culture that isn't as welcoming to people with different needs and interests. Rather than putting women into a mental grouping in your mind, try to relate to every person as an individual.

I don't get this often, but if you meet a woman at a conference, don't assume that she's in marketing or there with her partner.

If you're talking to a woman, don't ask, "Who takes care of your kids when you're at a conference? How do you balance it all?" This tends to send the message that she should be somewhere else right now.

The fifth tip is speaking up. When a woman is talking, one of the common things I've seen is that she will get interrupted. Women get interrupted three times more often than men do. Speak up in those situations. You could say, "I don't think she was finished yet."

The sixth point may seem obvious but it isn't always done. When you see something inappropriate happening, intervene. If you can see someone is uncomfortable, you should be stepping in. It's not enough to just be silent—you need to actively participate. In these types of situations, you need to speak up.

Being aware of character trait assignments is number seven. These are the types of traits that tend to be attributed to women when they're behaving a certain way, for example, abrasive, aggressive, or bossy. Filter that out and think, "If a man was behaving in the same way, would I call him abrasive?" It tends to be a word that we don't really use for men. Often, if a man is behaving in that same way, he will be called a strong leader.

The eighth point returns to the idea of self-promotion and negotiation. Be willing to encourage women if you get an initial reaction of resistance and self-doubt.

Number nine is about unconscious bias. You have to recognize that everyone has bias, men and women. One of the best ways to identify bias is by mentoring someone different from you.

If you're a woman, you don't have to mentor a woman and if you're a man, you don't have to mentor a man. You're actually going to learn more from each other through your differences.

The final point is inviting women to attend and speak at conferences or other speaking opportunities. Suggest women. Invite and encourage women to participate in panels. Often, people say, "This conference is open to everyone, but I don't see any women submitting talks."

I reply, "Maybe you need to specifically invite women, just to get them started." It could be that once you get through that initial resistance, there is progress from there. Once you start speaking at one conference, another conference will want you. Before you know it, you're speaking at many conferences and booking travel!

## The fear of not knowing enough

**Geertjan Wielenga**: I think many people, and maybe especially women, as you indicate, have the feeling that they need to know absolutely everything, whether it's about public speaking or a particular tech, before they can give a talk or submit an abstract to a conference. What would you say to that?

**Heather VanCura**: That was exactly the topic of the breakfast I hosted for the Women Who Code group in Atlanta last week at DevNexus. The topic was submitting a talk for a conference. The women attending felt that they didn't know enough yet and worried about what they would say if someone challenged their knowledge.

It's going to happen that you don't know the answer to everything and you must be open and willing to acknowledge it, whether you're a man or a woman. There are lots of different ways to deal with a situation where you don't have an answer. You can say, "I don't know the answer to that. I can go back and find an answer for you." You can also ask if anyone in the audience has anything to share on that topic. That's a way to get more interactive. Speaking on a panel is another option.

> *"User groups or small environments can be great places to share your first presentation."*
>
> *—Heather VanCura*

User groups or small environments can be great places to share your first presentation. Do a lunchtime session with your user group team, then smaller regional conferences, and then work your way up to a larger audience.

**Geertjan Wielenga**: Have you been traveling to many overseas conferences recently?

**Heather VanCura**: I just got back from the first Oracle Code day in L.A. It seems like I've been traveling most of the year already. I haven't had the chance to settle and do some deep thinking about anything; I've just been traveling from one event to the next. I've been to India, Australia, Japan, Kenya, and Bulgaria. I've been doing too much travel, but it's ideal to be able to tie that travel to a community conference. With so much going on in the community, you have to engage.

**Geertjan Wielenga**: Can you explain more about the difficult life of a global traveler in the sense of jet lag and missed flights?

**Heather VanCura**: I've learned through trial and error. I do enjoy traveling, but I have some tips. I try to only take carry-on luggage. I've found this helpful in terms of getting around when I'm there but also for reducing the time spent in airports. I've got my carry-on luggage and then my backpack on top, and I wheel it, so I don't have to lug around heavy things when I'm traveling.

Some people say, "Oh, just stay up all night and get your work done the night before a flight because you can sleep on the plane." I don't recommend that: it doesn't work. I try to keep my regular sleep routine. As soon as I get on the flight, I do whatever I think I should be doing at that time. If it's the middle of the day and it's my nighttime back at home, I force myself to stay awake and get on that local time.

Exercise, too, is really important. I try to get a workout in, even if it's brisk walking to get my blood flowing. I also try not to eat the food on the airplane. Obviously, water is your friend. Hydrating is essential when traveling.

**Geertjan Wielenga**: Is burnout a risk? How do you know you have it and how can you avoid it?

**The pressures of the job**

**Heather VanCura**: Burnout is always a risk with any job, especially in tech. There's constant pressure to keep doing more. I try to be conscious of my stress levels because your body will tend to give you signals that you're doing too much.

You should also listen to your support system. If you're hearing that you look really tired, you need to listen. I've never been at the point where I can't function, but I've heard of that happening to others.

You should look at what's really essential and peel away all the extra things because, as an advocate especially, you can be tempted to say yes to everyone. In reality, you just can't do that. Be conscious of how much you can actually do as one person. Part of being in a community is asking people for help.

I hardly ever take vacation. Most of my vacation time is spent visiting family, but it's nice to be at home sometimes. I'm planning on spending some time at home this summer. We'll see how that works out because there's always something coming up! I may be compelled to say yes depending on the activity.

**Geertjan Wielenga**: When you finally get to a conference on the other side of the world, how do you deal with unexpected technical situations when you're actually in the conference room?

**Heather VanCura**: Inevitably those happen, so I try to be prepared. I try to have all my connectors and multiple ones as spares. You can obviously borrow from the hotel or ask the conference organizers when you get there. If you end up at a conference and a technical glitch happens, there's usually someone there in the room who can help you out, so don't be afraid to ask for help.

To share a funny story, last year, in the Ivory Coast, I was giving an impromptu keynote talk. It wasn't something I had traveled to the Ivory Coast to do, but all of a sudden, I was at this boot camp for women coders.

There were 300 women there. I thought I was going to visit a school, but it turned out they wanted me to give a keynote presentation!

I did a variation of a past talk, but the power went out, so that meant that there wasn't any air conditioning. I didn't have my slides and the audience didn't necessarily understand English, as they actually wanted the talk in French. I don't speak French!

> *"They were just overjoyed that I was there and had shared what I know."*
>
> —*Heather VanCura*

I was sweating profusely in a climate I'm not accustomed to, so I had to be willing to adapt in that situation. At the end of the talk, I've never been so overwhelmed with requests for selfies. They basically rushed me and they all wanted selfies with me. They were just overjoyed that I was there and had shared what I know.

**Geertjan Wielenga**: In your experience, are there particular cultures where interaction from a stage works especially well and others where it definitely shouldn't even be tried?

**Heather VanCura**: I think throughout Europe speaking from a stage works well and also in the U.S. Audiences tend to come forward with questions throughout and interact.

It's more challenging in places like Japan and India, where it's difficult to get any questions at all. Although, last time I was in Japan, I did get some questions after my talk.

I had allowed time for questions. Some people also came up after the talk, even if they didn't say anything during the talk. I noticed a change, which was nice.

**Geertjan Wielenga**: What changed? Was it the culture or was it you?

**Heather VanCura**: I try different things to encourage questions, but there have been Java Days in Tokyo for several years. They get some Western speakers and I think it's a pretty common thing now to ask for questions, so people might have just got over that barrier.

**Geertjan Wielenga**: You're traveling a lot, but what does your typical day look like?

**Heather VanCura**: I don't really have a typical day. I'm traveling about 20-25% of the time. Otherwise, I'm doing events, meeting people, writing, and doing interviews. When I'm not on the road, I usually have one or two days a week where I go into an office and have meetings. This could be either in Santa Clara, where many of the Java development team are based, or in Redwood City.

I go and meet the VP one or two days a week. For the remaining days, I actually work from home. Those days are really when I get my actual work done, not that those other things aren't my work!

If I have meetings with people in other parts of the world, where I don't need to be face to face, I do that from home, early in the morning usually. Talking to people in Europe, Brazil, or Asia can mean an early start.

Apart from that, I will be developing materials, presentations, or abstracts, or working on JCP activities, like minutes or materials from meetings. I have several working groups that I run, as well as the Executive Committee board meetings. There is also the time spent responding to emails and communicating on social media is constant.

**Geertjan Wielenga**: How do you use social media in your role?

## Connecting through social media

**Heather VanCura**: I used to use many different kinds of social media, but that can quickly start to take up all of your time. I decided to figure out where the concentration of developers is that I'm working with around the world.

They're primarily on Twitter. There is some variation in some parts of Africa, where they're mostly using Facebook right now. Largely, I try to put my efforts into Twitter as a social media vehicle and some LinkedIn.

I experiment with Instagram and Snapchat, and Slack for talking with people. I feel I can only do so much, though, so I think concentrating on the Twitter platform has been the most effective use of my time in terms of getting feedback and sharing news and things that are happening. I would like to do a little bit more with social media, but at the same time, I've got out of the cycle of feeling compelled to post multiple times each day.

**Geertjan Wielenga**: How do you see other developer advocates? What do you like about presentations when you see someone up on stage doing a talk?

**Heather VanCura**: I always like it when people move a little bit away from their specific topic. Usually, there's the core topic, but looking at ways you can apply that in the world around you always makes it interesting and sparks different ideas or thoughts. I admire any developer advocate who doesn't have to use a script. Having a true interaction with the audience takes a lot of practice.

**Geertjan Wielenga**: Do you see yourself doing exactly this for the rest of your life? What is the career trajectory of a developer advocate?

**Heather VanCura**: I probably won't do this for the rest of my life; although, it's stayed interesting for a tremendously long time. As this role has become more common, I've definitely started to get more messages from recruiters. I think as developer advocacy becomes more valuable, it will translate into other things, including higher leadership roles within companies.

**Geertjan Wielenga**: Do you see the demand for this kind of role increasing, then?

**Heather VanCura**: Yes, I see the demand for this type of experience increasing. I definitely could see myself going into a chief experience officer (CXO) position or similar, but not immediately.

**Geertjan Wielenga**: What could be done to carry on raising the profile of this profession?

**Heather VanCura**: I hardly ever hear developer advocacy being spoken about, other than in the circle of people I know. Sometimes, as developer advocates, we don't think that our job is interesting to other people. I think many advocates are unique individuals, with different character traits that aren't necessarily the norm.

It might be the case that people don't like to talk about that other side of tech because they feel we don't have enough people getting into development work, and they want to encourage that by only talking about hard tech skills and jobs. The truth is that developer advocacy is a great job and I love it.

**Geertjan Wielenga**: Thank you, Heather VanCura.

## 09

> *People would tell me that
> I had so much knowledge,
> but I had only learned it
> the week before!*

# Matt
# Raible

# Introducing Matt Raible

Matt Raible is a developer advocate at Okta, speaking regularly at development events, and he has a reputation as a must-see conference speaker. Matt's been the lead user interface (UI) architect for LinkedIn and the chief architect of web development for Time Warner Cable. He's worked on the JHipster project and regularly writes technical blog posts for the Okta Developer Blog. One of the most experienced global presenters in developer advocacy, Matt's been building the collaborative developer community with his blogs for more than 20 years. Find Matt on Twitter: @mraible.

**Geertjan Wielenga**: Could you start by talking about who you are and what you do?

**Matt Raible**: I'm a developer advocate for Okta, which means that I'm tasked with writing a few blog posts per month and speaking at some sort of developer event once per month. I'm paid to do that.

The biggest pro is that I get to create my own job. I'm the one who decides what I work on every week. Around 25% of my time is spent doing maintenance work on blog posts or past presentations I've done.

For the most part, I create a plan every six weeks and decide what blog posts I'm going to write. The blog posts usually require an example app. I have to actually code for a day or two and make things work before I can write about them. I'm constantly learning new tech, new frameworks, and new ways to do things in order to talk about that.

If all I ever blogged about was Spring Boot and Angular, then there wouldn't be that many blog posts. If I need to write 50 blog posts a year, there's a lot to learn.

My company is the leading identity provider for cloud. The product that I focus on is APIs. Much of my work centers around authentication, but I do like to vary blog posts so that people know how to make two techs work together. Mainly, as developer advocates at Okta, we just try to help developers to learn tech and if they happen to have a need for our tech too, then that's great.

**Geertjan Wielenga**: Do you prefer the term "developer advocate" or "tech evangelist" to describe what you do?

## Choosing a job title

**Matt Raible**: At my previous company, Stormpath, and when I first started at Okta, I had the title of "developer evangelist." I went to Devoxx US one year and Arun Gupta said, "Don't use evangelist." Many other people in the room agreed because it has religious connotations. That doesn't work in some countries. You won't be allowed to speak if you say you're an evangelist. They immediately advised that I change my title, and I did. We call our group "developer relations" but we don't say we are evangelists—we say we are advocates.

**Geertjan Wielenga**: How did you end up being a developer advocate in the first place?

**Matt Raible**: I was an independent consultant for 20 years. I did do advocacy as a side hobby.

I started a blog in 2002 and wrote about Java a lot. This was before Stack Overflow, so I used Struts and Java Platform, Enterprise Edition (Java EE).

I posted my questions, which you would now post on Stack Overflow, on that blog with stack traces, and people would find them and help. It was a collaborative community. I've always done speaking at conferences on the side too.

I started working for Stormpath two years ago, as a part-time contractor, and I was working at Computer Associates at the same time. I was doing Java in the morning at Stormpath and JavaScript in the afternoon at Computer Associates. I really liked the people I was working with at Stormpath and they tried to hire me full-time. I told them to make me an offer that I couldn't refuse and they said, "We don't know what that is!"

> *"I spent a month coming up with my dream job."*
>
> —*Matt Raible*

I wanted to be able to blog and speak at conferences, so I spent a month coming up with my dream job. Stormpath wanted me to be its Java lead. The problem was that I like Java, but it's not my favorite thing. I tend to do more UI work.

The opportunity went away for a month and then I said, "There's a way to make this work! Can I do Java and JavaScript?" Stormpath agreed that instead of being more of a technical leader and owning the Java software development kit (SDK), I could be one of its advocates. There were a few other people on board in the advocacy team.

Six months later, Stormpath got bought out by Okta. As an independent consultant, I was used to switching jobs every six months, but I didn't expect that to happen once I went full-time. That's how I ended up at Okta!

**Geertjan Wielenga**: What would the 20 year old you think about your life today in terms of your professional development and what you're doing?

**Matt's career path**

**Matt Raible**: First of all, I would be pissed off that I have a Volkswagen Bus instead of a Lamborghini! When I was in my 20s, I wanted to be a Russian stockbroker. If you think about it, that's probably the most stressful job possible! I kind of am an international businessman with developer advocacy.

I studied Russian, international business, and Japanese, but I had student loans and I needed to get paid well as soon as I graduated. I had friends who were doing computer science and they were getting really good job offers. I started auditing computer programming classes and teaching myself.

I wasn't doing anything like real programming, but I ended up getting a job doing Year 2000 (Y2K) consulting. Then I got into HTML and Java and really enjoyed it. When I'm coding and I'm solving a problem or developing something new, I just love it. Back then, I would have thought that it's awesome that I actually get paid now to just write blog posts and example apps.

**Geertjan Wielenga**: What happens if you're in a situation, as an advocate, where a competing product works better in a particular context or you find a bug? Are you completely honest there?

**Matt Raible**: It's not really a dilemma that I have because I was an independent consultant for years before this and I always believed that my feelings toward software tech were true and right.

> *"I think it helps in the long run to expose flaws in tech."*
>
> —*Matt Raible*

I'm a developer in the sense that if something doesn't work and it's painful to use, then I'm going to tell people about it. That's not really hard for me to do. It's hard for my employer because I put bugs in blog posts, and the company doesn't like it, but it's part of my personality and who I am. I often fight to keep those bugs in my posts and then they do get fixed. I think it helps in the long run to expose flaws in tech.

It does hurt me because, for example, I wrote a whole bunch of blogs last year before many of our SDKs were ready for 1.0. I've spent a tremendous amount of time going back and updating the blog posts. If a title pertains to a specific tech or a specific version, then the chances are that, because of search engine optimization (SEO), we should write a new one. It's a necessity because we change things so often. It's become a huge maintenance burden, but as long as I'm writing cutting-edge posts on Angular and React, I'm going to have to update things.

**Geertjan Wielenga**: Do you see yourself in any way as a spin doctor?

**Matt Raible**: No, because, as I say, when I find bugs, I tell people. I think it's part of my authenticity and shows that I'm not trying to hide anything.

I've had some conversations internally, for instance, about using Keycloak with JHipster. People have asked, "What's the difference between Okta and Keycloak?"

Usually, I say, "Keycloak you can download and install locally. Okta has support and you can use it in the cloud."

People have then asked, "Why should we tell developers to use Okta over Keycloak?"

I've replied, "You shouldn't if they're using something that makes life easier for them. Eventually, they're going to get to a point where they're managing Keycloak in the cloud and think it's a pain, and they should then just use Okta." I try to advocate for whatever makes the developers' lives easiest.

## The qualities needed for advocacy

**Geertjan Wielenga**: What kind of qualities would be ideal for a person doing what you do?

**Matt Raible**: You really have to like to create content. That seems to be the most valuable asset. I'm one of those people who likes to write tutorials. I can whip out a tutorial over three days.

**Geertjan Wielenga**: When you write a blog, is it a more extensive process than just writing something and publishing it?

**Matt Raible**: Yes, it goes through a number of steps. First of all, there's the actual ideation: figuring out what to write about. I always know what I'm going to write about each week ahead of time.

I've got to write the example app, make it work, write a blog post, and then it has to go through quality assurance (QA). Typically, what I do is delete the app and use my blog post to write it from scratch again. Then I see what changed and check it into GitHub.

Once I'm done, someone with a really good sense of what writing should look like does a copy edit. From there, the blog goes into a pull request and then someone has to peer review it. Only after that is the post published.

**Geertjan Wielenga**: As you're far more focused on the blogging and on the writing side, does that leave the developer advocate job description open for more introverted people?

**Matt Raible**: Yes, and what I find, personally, is that I'm very introverted on some days and very extroverted on others. Today, we have the Denver Java Users Group, so I will switch on this afternoon to being my extroverted self because I'm one of the leaders there, and I will be socializing with everyone.

The rest of the time, when I'm blogging or writing example apps, I'm very introverted. I do have the ability to switch between them. Most programmers have somewhat of an introverted side and they just learn that they can be extroverted as well.

Many people think that a developer advocate is someone who travels and speaks all the time. If you look at Josh Long, or someone like that, he is speaking five times a week. I did do that last year. I was on the road for 140 days, but it's just not a requirement.

> *"If developer advocates want to travel, they can, but it's not a requirement."*
>
> —*Matt Raible*

We don't see a schedule like that as valuable at Okta, in the sense that when speaking, you only hit 100 people. You write a blog post and you hit 1,000 or 10,000 people. I think if developer advocates want to travel, they can, but it's not a requirement. I love going to an exotic location, but when I have two other trips right around it, I think, "Why did I plan all this?"

**Geertjan Wielenga**: Have you experienced any symptoms of burnout and how did you overcome them?

**Matt Raible**: I've experienced burnout twice in my career. Once was in 2006, when I was migrating AppFuse from Ant to Maven, and I was spending 60 hours a week trying to do it, and I had a 40 hours a week job.

That time, I experienced it physically. Every time I stood up, I would get really dizzy. I wasn't sleeping much. At that time, I actually went to the hospital because I thought I had mono or something similar. The hospital never really figured out a diagnosis but I figured it out myself: I was working too much.

In 2017, I experienced burnout as well. I had a couple of presentations that depended on me finishing code before I could even talk. I just remember getting back to the U.S. and being on vacation with my wife and being so tired. It took me a couple of days to realize that I was doing too much.

In my team, we all collectively decided this year to try to stick to one speaking engagement each month. If we can make that speaking engagement in our hometown, then great. I try to travel less and write more, so I don't approach that burnout stage.

## The social side of conferences

**Geertjan Wielenga**: There's also a social aspect to all the travel and the developer advocacy. Do you have some stories around favorite places you go to, favorite conferences, and the things you experience there?

**Matt Raible**: Yes, my favorite is Devoxx because it's in Antwerp, which is the home of excellent beers. I certainly enjoy that!

I think that's also something you have to be careful of. If you go to a conference for four days and you're out drinking every night and socializing with everyone, you're probably going to get sick.

One of the things I started doing a few years ago is monitoring my health. I do try to be conscious when I'm on the road to exercise and not drink too much, but it probably doesn't work when I'm with friends at a conference!

I feel a little guilt when I'm doing overseas conferences because there's a certain sense of my wife being at home with the children, when I'm off gallivanting in another country. I've realized that it's not the be-all and end-all to travel. If I was younger and I was single then I would go to all of these conferences, and that would be great, but that's not the way my life is now.

**Geertjan Wielenga**: It seems to me that this whole profession is completely unknown for many young people. What do you think the reason for that is?

**Matt Raible**: I think it's because there's a certain expectation right now that you must have proven yourself as a developer and I don't know if that happens before someone's out of college.

The best developer advocates are already well known before they become developer advocates. They've written books and are active in the open-source community, so they have got their names out there. It can be difficult to be a developer advocate without that profile being established, but at the same time, I do see it happening.

> *"It took me 10 years to become well known, so you might as well start when you're younger."*
>
> —*Matt Raible*

I've seen people who are recent college graduates becoming developer advocates and I think it's great. There's nothing wrong with getting followers or getting your word out there; we all did it at one point. It took me 10 years to become well known, so you might as well start when you're younger and have it as one of your main goals.

**Geertjan Wielenga**: If you're coming from a different profession, or you're a student, what should you do to be in a position where you could be hired by an organization to work full-time as a developer advocate?

**Matt Raible**: Just because of the general perception, you're going to have to be good at public speaking. If you're in the U.S., there's the Toastmasters club that you can join if you need some help getting over your nervousness of public speaking.

That's the most important skill and then the second skill is writing. You don't actually have to be a good writer if you work for a company that has editors, because they can restructure everything, as I mentioned earlier. I've learned a ton in the last year and a half just from the editor who I work with all the time. I've been writing for 20 years, so I think that goes to show that anyone can improve.

**Geertjan Wielenga**: That leads to another question: do you need to know everything about the topic that you're talking about in order to be an effective advocate? Should you wait to know everything before you start blogging, writing, and going to conferences?

## Not being confident enough

**Matt Raible**: No, one of the misconceptions when you're speaking on a topic is that you need to know everything. You're afraid that the founder of the open-source project you're talking about is going to be in the audience and they're going to call you out if you're wrong. That never happens. It's rare that someone who knows the topic better than you will sit in your talk because they will go to other talks.

The best time to blog about something is when you're learning it because that's when you find all the different nuances that other developers are going to find. If you know the tech because you wrote it, or just know it well, then you're not going to know those little things that people stumble upon. I think the best conference speakers are people who just learned the topic a few months before, because they know all the pain that they went through.

**Geertjan Wielenga**: If you're standing in front of a big crowd and you get a question that you have no answer to, how do you respond to that?

**Matt Raible**: I say, "I don't know." I've become better about it. That scenario is something that my team certainly struggled with when we first came on board with Okta. We knew Stormpath's API well, but we really didn't know Okta's API well.

We started a new developer forum and we had silence on there for the longest time. People would be asking questions, but we didn't know the answers. We had to learn them ourselves.

Our team had to become Okta certified and learn the whole suite of products, which meant we could speak to customers and help people.

In a conference setting, what I try to do now is to tell people that I'm an example programmer, because I'm putting stuff in production, but it's not for a company. It's for myself that I do outside projects.

I often tell people to contact me after a talk if they'd like more information because I can find people that know the answer. I struggled with impostor syndrome back in 2004 and 2005, when I wrote a book on Spring, just because I was learning it as I was writing it. People would tell me that I had so much knowledge, but I had only learned it the week before!

Now that I've been doing this for 20 years, I know that there's still stuff I learned last week and it's okay. Most developers can have impostor syndrome, even the greatest ones.

I actually attended one talk last week where the speaker was very entertaining. The talk had animated GIFs that made you laugh, and it showed a lot of code, but the speaker didn't write much code. Typically, I like to see people write code because then there's the suspense that it might fail! Some people live code the whole time and others don't, but audiences leave similarly happy.

**Geertjan Wielenga**: What, to your mind, is the advantage of doing live coding in a conference session?

**Matt Raible**: It engages the audience if you pull it off, or if you have failures, then that increases the tension, just like a movie. It is risky.

The best strategy is if you have backup videos that you can play, but I've also seen those videos be really grainy and hard to see on some conference screens, so that doesn't always work.

**Geertjan Wielenga**: We're in the area of technical glitches now. Do you have some horror stories of equipment exploding, people not finding the room, or you traveling to the end of the earth and finding three people waiting for you?

## Technical difficulties during a talk

**Matt Raible**: I've had a total of one person attend before and I just said, "You should go to another session!"

I think the biggest problem that I've had was laptop difficulties in 2005. I was just comparing web frameworks, but I was using a Mac, and the Macs weren't on Intel yet and were so slow. Things just beach-balled so much that I was apologizing to the audience. That started 30 minutes in. What came next was two more hours of me fumbling around and even trying a different laptop because I did have a backup, knowing that this might be a problem.

That was the ultimate crash and burn. It wasn't all over Twitter because Twitter didn't exist, but there was plenty of talk about it. It sucked, but that was probably my worst experience.

I'm doing a bunch of JHipster stuff tomorrow at the Utah Java Users Group, and what I've learned to do is just bring swag, such as t-shirts and books. If I know that it's going to take five or 10 minutes for some processes, I talk to the audience then and maybe mention that this is going to take a while, so let's have some questions.

My failure rate is probably 50% of the time on demos. I do tend to fail often. I think that it's part of our product at Okta, in the sense that it might take seven steps to integrate something, instead of one or two, so we have been trying to fix that. Anyone should be able to demo if they did it the day before, instead of having to memorize all these steps. I've failed enough that I'm used to talking my way out of it.

**Geertjan Wielenga**: Are you very hung up about your reputation? If things go wrong, do you worry that you're not going to get asked back or people are going to tweet negatively?

**Matt Raible**: No, for the most part you can recover from a bad performance. I love it when people tweet about my talks. There are certain conferences that a ton of people tweet at. If there's criticism, usually I can address it. I can post that the demo failed but here's a screencast that I did that shows that it does work. There are ways to work around that.

**Geertjan Wielenga**: You seem to have a very substantial Twitter following. Did you do something to build that?

**Matt Raible**: I think much of it is just due to my blog. When I got Twitter, many of my blog followers then followed me onto Twitter. I've tried, ever since I became a developer advocate at Stormpath and now at Okta, to increase my following. It hasn't increased much.

**Geertjan Wielenga**: Is there competition between you and other developer advocates out there? Is there anyone you aspire to be like?

**Matt Raible**: I think there absolutely is, but in the sense of being inspired by them. I look at Josh Long and Venkat Subramaniam as inspiration, more than anything else. Those guys are really good when they present, but in terms of how much they travel, that's not what I want to do. They're not inspiring in that way.

I actually have a colleague who has a large programmer following. We have an internal competition on who can get more views on posts. It can be a great way to motivate you to try harder and do better.

**Geertjan Wielenga**: Do you have any tips for coming up with talk titles and content?

**Matt Raible**: What I've learned is that it depends on the conference. For some conferences, you give a list of talks and they'll have you do all those talks.

That's not a great experience because it's a lot of work. So, because of that, depending on the conference, I'll just submit one or two talks, and I'll know that I'm going to end up doing one or both.

For other conferences, like JavaOne (now Oracle Code One), you're lucky to get one talk in if it's not a core Java topic. I'll submit around five talks. I make sure they're high quality talks and that I've given them several times before.

## Successful talk titles

**Geertjan Wielenga**: Do you try to make your titles and your content as broad as possible, to attract as many people as possible, or do you try to attract a few people who are going to be really focused on that particular topic?

**Matt Raible**: I certainly go with keywords. I've noticed that conference talks are very similar to blog post titles for SEO. You get more readers if you have the words "Angular" and "Spring Boot" in the title.

For conference talks, if you put the word "JHipster" in there without "Angular" and "Spring Boot," you're not going to get that many people coming. Keywords definitely attract people differently.

I might reuse a blog post. That's what I've been doing lately. I'll take a blog post as the main driver of the content, turn it into a presentation, and do the tutorial as a live coding exercise.

**Geertjan Wielenga**: How do you decide that you've done a session enough and should retire it?

**Matt Raible**: I've noticed that it's just a feeling I have. I decide that a talk wasn't great and I need to restructure it. I can still use the slides and put them into a new talk, but if I don't get good feedback, then that's the time to retire it.

> *"Creating new presentations all the time puts stress on you."*
>
> —*Matt Raible*

Something that I discovered last year, because it was my first full-time year doing it, was that creating new presentations all the time puts stress on you. If you have a set of five talks that you do over and over, the chances are that they will get better and you'll lose that anxiety.

**Geertjan Wielenga**: You were always the go-to guy for getting an overview of Java server frameworks. What was so relevant about that particular topic that you could carry on doing talks for 10 years?

**Matt Raible**: Developers just wanted to know which framework they could use. That was a time when Java was very popular. Many people were doing server-side Model-View-Controller (MVC). I had similar experiences to those developers, in the sense that I started with Struts and then picked up Spring MVC.

People were talking about how JavaServer Faces (JSF), Tapestry, or Wicket had a better component model. I picked those up and learned them, then gave my opinion on which was most productive and what you could write code the fastest in.

**Geertjan Wielenga**: What were the key points in that particular presentation?

**Matt Raible**: It started out with an overview of the frameworks, then showed the developer experience and how the code looked. Next, I got into the pros and cons.

That's what really fired people up. I did take quite a bit of heat from fans of any of the frameworks that I didn't like. I had to respond to them on blogs and comments, but I always did it with a nice attitude. I never got flamed too hard or made anyone too angry.

**Geertjan Wielenga**: Now you're doing the same thing but with JavaScript frameworks and libraries, right?

**Matt Raible**: I did one talk with JavaScript frameworks, back in 2014, at SpringOne. It was about React, AngularJS, and Ember.

I did a pretty thorough analysis, but at the end, someone in the audience asked, "Have you put all these frameworks into production?" That caught me off guard and because my answer was no, that shut down the whole Q&A session. It immediately, in the sense of the talk, discredited me.

I decided that I needed more real-world experience with these frameworks before doing that talk again. I've been learning the main three: Angular, React, and Vue, so I will have more authority to speak about them based on that experience.

## Matt's stage outfits

**Geertjan Wielenga**: I've seen you wearing a suit and drinking whiskey while presenting a session, which was a unique combination. What was the value-add of that?

**Matt Raible**: That was an idea I came up with for JHipster. I was really intrigued by JHipster because it was basically what I was doing for clients.

I was either doing Angular frontends or Spring Boot backends. I could never quite get any clients to sign up for me doing both. I really wanted to promote myself because I was an independent consultant at the time and I wanted to write a book on JHipster.

I was added to the project as a committer. Then, when I was first doing a talk, I was thinking, "Well, they have the word 'hipster' in there, so I'll do that: get hip with JHipster."

> *"By the end, I was a hip JHipster developer drinking whatever beer was hip in the country I was in!"*
>
> —*Matt Raible*

I decided I should be an old-fashioned Java developer and become a hipster throughout the talk. That's where the suit came in and the whiskey. I was an old-fashioned Java developer drinking scotch to begin with. By the end, I was a hip JHipster developer drinking whatever beer was hip in the country I was in!

**Geertjan Wielenga**: Have you ever worked for JHipster, though?

**Matt Raible**: JHipster is an open-source project, so I was always just a committer on the project. I certainly didn't invent JHipster, but people thought I did.

By the end of my talk, I would end up looking like the JHipster mascot. The logo had existed for years before I even got interested in the project, but I had a colleague tell me a couple of weeks ago that he thought I had founded the project for the first year that he knew me!

**Geertjan Wielenga**: How do you select what's relevant to spend time on?

**Matt Raible**: When I was a consultant, it was Spring Boot, Java, JavaScript, and AngularJS. I found it easy to just concentrate on those and write tutorials on my personal blog about them.

Beyond that, it was what I was interested in and much of that was conference-driven development, where I would submit a talk about techs, and then I'd have to learn them so I didn't look like a fool on stage.

My interests now are focused on gauging what's popular in the market and then trying to write about it. At the same time, because of the maintenance required for old blog posts, I'm actually forced to figure out how to do things again six months later.

**Geertjan Wielenga**: What are the new hot topics that are popping up at conferences or elsewhere?

**Matt Raible**: I think Progressive Web Apps are still a big thing, especially now that Safari has support and Microsoft is on board too.

I think Reactive will get perched in the mainstream, just because of Spring Boot and the fact that Spring is supporting it. I think there'll be a lot of cool things coming from Java EE and Jakarta Enterprise Edition (EE). The innovation can happen in the open-source community because we aren't held back by meetings or processes. There's also exciting stuff in the Java virtual machine (JVM), JavaScript, and TypeScript ecosystem.

**Geertjan Wielenga**: The very first time I came across you was through the blogger system I was using at Sun Microsystems. That was you, wasn't it?

**Matt Raible**: Yes! Dave Johnson invented Roller. It really appealed to me because it's written in Java. I wanted to build a new website and have a blogging system or CMS system.

I downloaded Roller, installed it, came up with a new theme, and contributed it back to the project. I became the third committer on the project.

> *"Back then, if you had a blog, you had a community."*
>
> —Matt Raible

We made some cool things happen in a short amount of time and many Java people used Roller. Back then, if you had a blog, you had a community, especially with Java. I got to know the leading Java people, so that was a great experience for me.

**Geertjan Wielenga**: If there was one thing that you could change about your professional life, what would it be?

### Knowing when to stop

**Matt Raible**: I wish I didn't have to work Fridays! Otherwise, last week, I found this rabbit hole of one blog post that spawned six others. I was thinking, "Oh my God! I've got to update them all!"

I did spend a day doing it and I only did a couple. I decided that I had to leave the rest because no one is really going to notice if they've been updated or not. I do get things like that that crop up and I feel that I need to work that night, but then I tell myself that I don't need to. No one cares: only I care. My team doesn't care and my company doesn't care.

One of the things that I've started doing is not even opening my emails. On Mondays and Tuesdays, I tend to do blackout periods where I shut off email and Slack, so there's no way for people to get in touch with me. I put my phone in another room and that's how I get stuff done. If I can have those two productive days at the beginning of the week, then the rest of the week is easier.

**Geertjan Wielenga**: Do you see yourself doing something with developer advocacy for the rest of your professional life or at some point doing something completely different?

**Matt Raible**: It has been interesting because now that I'm a developer advocate, I do get companies trying to hire me for that position. I don't know that this was ever a goal of mine. I do enjoy advocacy, but I also feel more stressed than I ever did as an independent consultant! As an independent consultant, it was 40 hours a week and it was easy to quit. You would stay up late on a Tuesday night, but you would only work up to noon on a Friday.

If Okta doesn't work out, then I'll probably go back to independent consulting before I try to get a developer advocate job somewhere else, and that's because of the stress.

At my company, we have a way to create goals, then define metrics that show that we've met those goals, and track them.

I had a goal a couple of months ago to be one of the top developer advocates in the world. My boss said, "If that's what you want to do, we support you, but there are also other things you could do."

I think there are certainly other opportunities at my current company, but I really like doing the developer advocate role because it allows me to play with all this new tech you hear about and live on the bleeding edge, even though it can be painful when things don't work.

**Geertjan Wielenga**: You mentioned that you aspire to be one of the top developer advocates in the world, but what would that entail? What are the measurables for that?

**Matt Raible**: To be able to give presentations without slides and to just be really comfortable speaking and writing. It's kind of a catch-22. If I really want to be known as one of the top developer advocates, then traveling all the time helps. I don't want to do that. I just want to be recognized as one of the best. I have that reputation now, so I'm in a good spot.

**Geertjan Wielenga**: Thank you, Matt Raible.

## 10

> *If a company doesn't have a developer relations team in place, and is trying to get into a market, we can help it to do that.*

# Tracy Lee

# Introducing Tracy Lee

Tracy Lee is a Google Developer Expert, JavaScript developer, and the cofounder of This Dot Labs, an agency that helps to mentor teams building ambitious apps. An entrepreneur who's been featured in media ranging from The Huffington Post to Food Network, Tracy discovered JavaScript after the acquisition of her last start-up, Dishcrawl. She now spends her time exploring code and building the JavaScript community with workshops, podcasts, and online events. Find Tracy on Twitter: @ladyleet.

---

**Geertjan Wielenga**: Could you start by explaining what you do?

**Tracy Lee**: I'm the cofounder of a company called This Dot. I started the company a few years ago. We do developer relations as a service and consulting on JavaScript. Typically, what we do is help brands that are looking to get started, or help them to integrate with the development community. To use JavaScript as an example, companies may ask, "What's the best way to enter the JavaScript industry? What are the best conferences? How should we build our brand? How should we build our social presence?"

**Geertjan Wielenga**: Do you see this as marketing?

**Tracy Lee**: Yes, it is marketing; that's what developer relations is. Developer relations is just an extension of marketing, but it's different when you market to developers because they don't like being marketed to.

The best developer relationships are genuine and authentic. When you look at marketing, most traditional marketing teams think, "Hey, here are these people and they're in this cohort. We need to market to them, and we're going to do X, Y, and Z to do this." Whereas marketing in the developer world has become more one-to-one. You're often marketing services by just saying, "I know this person who does this thing."

Even if you look at social marketing, like Instagram, it has become about one-to-one relationships. In the developer ecosystem, it's much more about word-of-mouth communication and about who's using what.

**Geertjan Wielenga**: Does a company that is involved in software in some way come to your organization and say, "We want a strategy to bring this tech to developers"?

## Helping companies

**Tracy Lee**: Yes, and then we do things to support that. A lot of enterprise companies, for example, will come to us and say, "We want to open source our project." But the company may only know that it wants to open source something because the term "open source" has become buzzword-y, so we'll talk through that. Many enterprise companies don't understand the idea of open source, so their ultimate goal, especially in marketing and sales, is determining how to generate revenue or how to immediately sell.

A lot of developer relations teams also work on developer experience. They ask, "How do we actually onboard somebody? What's our open-source strategy? Does it actually work? Is it going to be effective long term? Does it seem too corporate? Does it sit well with developers?"

There are certain things you can do. You can reach out to influencers and get them to spread the word, but nobody's going to listen to you if you just say, "Hey, promote my product!" You have to build an authentic presence.

A good example is we're currently helping this one company that has a really nice enterprise product and is trying to get into open source. The question is, who's going to use this product? You can't just go to open-source maintainers and say, "Hey, integrate my product because it's going to be super awesome."

The whole idea with developer relations, or marketing in the developer market in general, is that you have to give back before you ask. You can't just tell people to buy your product. What we focus on is saying, "You want to get into the JavaScript market, so here are the things that you can do to give back to the JavaScript market in general." This could be developing a series of blogs, interviewing key people for a podcast, or speaking at conferences.

There is a question about the degree to which developer relations teams should be concerned with sales if their primary function is marketing. Companies often ask, "What value does developer relations actually bring? How does it translate into sales?" Developer advocacy is not fully removed from sales, but developer advocates aren't trying to hit a specific sales quota. That's necessary, because if you're trying to make people chase sales and that's part of their job, then they're going to approach most of their interactions with sales in mind. That makes their developer advocacy less authentic, and, as a result, less effective.

Companies have to think about how to authentically position themselves in the market. In some cases, this means just realizing that this is human marketing. The more "human" we can make companies, the easier it will be for them to actually market to developers.

**Geertjan Wielenga**: Why do companies need to be shown how to relate to people? Why is authenticity such a critical thing in developer relations? Was it not a critical issue in the marketing world before developer relations emerged?

**Tracy Lee**: It could be down to all of the added competition, due to the rise of software-as-a-service-type companies. Another factor could be the rise in the number of conferences, which are now such a major component of the industry.

If you take the Angular world, for example, there was NG-Conf. It was the only Angular conference in the U.S. Then, you had London's AngularConnect. Suddenly, you had another conference to go to, then you had eight new conferences to go to, and so on. I think as our world begins to feel smaller, we become more global.

If you think about development generally, it was centered in very specific areas for a long time—Silicon Valley in the U.S., for example. Now with the rise of platforms like Twitter, companies are realizing that people in, say, Malaysia, are holding conferences, and there are tech centers in areas all around the world. All of a sudden, companies are starting to think, "We're catering to Europe and the U.S., but we can physically see these gigantic conferences in other countries. Wow, maybe we should be marketing to those people too."

There are huge tech communities in Africa, for example, that Twitter is now revealing to companies.

As the world gets more educated, and generally has more access to social media, companies need to focus their marketing efforts on different things. How do they do that effectively? This is where developer relations comes in. You need to hire somebody in Malaysia, you need to hire somebody in India, and you need to hire somebody in Africa who understands those markets. This is why being able to relate to people is important.

Many developer relations teams say, "Our job is to bring feedback from our markets to the people building the products." How do they do that? I think contemporary developer relations strategies have emerged because people have been getting smarter about not only targeting the U.S. or Western Europe. At the same time, you can't just fly somebody from the U.S. to Africa and expect them to understand what's going on in those markets. You really need to hire people who live in those communities.

**Geertjan Wielenga**: Do you work with organizations with existing developer advocates, or do the enterprises coming to you typically use you as a service?

## Developer relations as a service

**Tracy Lee**: We offer support in so many different ways. If a company doesn't have a developer relations team in place, and is trying to get into a market, we can help it to do that. It's hard to get into the cloud market, for example, if you don't know anybody.

We create good relationships for companies and offer genuine entry into a market.

Once the company is established in the market, it may ask, "Who would be a good representation of our brand?" In such a case, we might recommend different developer advocates who we believe to be well liked and well connected within that particular market.

When companies we work with already have a developer relations strategy, a marketing strategy, and/or a strong PR firm on board, we offer to augment and support their programs. We take organizations in their current states, and we try to figure out how we can triple the impact of everything that they're doing.

> *"If a developer advocate walks into a room, they should be known already."*
>
> *—Tracy Lee*

With conferences, you can go to a conference, you can speak there, and you can meet certain people. However, if you bring us in, we will find all the influencers that you should meet and build relationships with. If a developer advocate walks into the room, they should be known already. You can't just say, "I got to speak at a conference, so I'm doing developer relations." Developer relations is being able to say, "I was able to walk into a conference room and everybody recognized my brand, and everybody knew who I was already." That's the real impact that I feel developer advocates should have when they attend conferences.

**Geertjan Wielenga**: That takes a lot of work; it's not something that you can just get out of a box. Being known at conferences means years of authentic engagement and involvement. How can you package that and give it to somebody? Is it not something that develops organically over decades?

**Tracy Lee**: No, I completely disagree. Even if I've had nothing to do with Amazon, if I do enough research before a conference, and build enough relationships online, I can walk into the conference and people will already know who I am and the company I work for. They've seen me online engaging with their community, so now they're curious.

I would say that being known in an industry is not something that needs to be built up over 10 years. Most companies just need to be taught how to achieve that. On the other hand, you can't turn somebody who is solely focused on sales into somebody authentic. A lot of companies think that they just need to hire *somebody*, but there is a disconnect between traditional marketing and marketing to developers, as I mentioned.

If you go to a conference, there's a big difference between somebody at a booth trying to sell you something and somebody at a booth who is trying to educate you about something. Developer relations is about making developers become more aware about what your company is doing in a way that's not telling them to buy your product, but explaining what your product is.

**Geertjan Wielenga**: Do you need to have a developer background to be successful in this role?

**Tracy Lee**: I believe that developer advocates can come from different backgrounds.

I see many developer relations teams that include one person who doesn't go out at all and just writes. They get so much traction online and that's amazing. I also see developer relations representatives who go to conferences and speak directly with others, and they make their impact that way.

I'm a really effective developer advocate because of my personability and my desire to learn, teach, and connect with people. I love building brands and getting active in the community. I started doing development about three or four years ago. I was a beginner developer, and I had a Silicon Valley start-up until I sold it.

> *"I'm still a junior developer. I'm never going to be a senior developer, nor do I really want to be."*
>
> —*Tracy Lee*

I love learning new tech, so I was always working on things that were super obscure or not ready for production yet. I liked teaching people about things that were coming up, because that's what I got excited about. During my little break after selling my start-up, I decided to take a three-week JavaScript class. I wouldn't want to code for 40 hours a week, because that doesn't interest me. I'm still a junior developer. I'm never going to be a senior developer, nor do I really want to be.

**Geertjan Wielenga**: You mentioned that you go to conferences and present; what topics do you talk about?

## Tracy's conference topics

**Tracy Lee**: I'm on the Reactive Extensions for JavaScript (RxJS) core team, and I'm also a Google Developer Expert for Angular, and the web, among other topics. So, most of the time, when I speak at conferences, I talk about RxJS and reactive programming. I could be speaking about Angular, React, Ember, or React Native; all things JavaScript, basically.

Last year, I spoke about reactive programming in general. Reactive programming isn't a new thing, but it seems that many people still need a lot of education around it. Often, I need to educate people about what reactive programming actually is. I help people to understand, at a higher level, what reactive programming means. I also talk about easy ways to use reactive programming paradigms within your application.

**Geertjan Wielenga**: What are some of those ways?

**Tracy Lee**: It's very specific, so usually, when I talk about reactive programming, I talk about how to do it in a particular language. I often talk about reactive programming in the sense of dealing with sets of events over time and having this implicit propagation of change versus having a very explicit way to write your code.

I help people understand what a stream is and walk them through a simple Excel example by asking, "What would it look like if I programmed this and it was implicit versus it being very explicit?"

I talk about reactive programming in the different standard bodies, so looking at TC39 and the different proposals that are out there. It's also about educating people on how to get involved and showing people code examples of how reactive programming makes development easier. If you use abstractions (for example, RxJS), I'll typically show you a drag-and-drop example. Drag and drop on the web is usually not the easiest thing to solve, so I show how it can be accomplished in very few lines of code.

**Geertjan Wielenga**: Is there anything that you are particularly interested in at the moment?

**Tracy Lee**: Right now, my theme is diversity and inclusion. I talk about inclusive architecture and the idea of building a team that includes everybody. This could be including designers, junior developers, a project manager, and so on. I talk about the right way to do that.

**Geertjan Wielenga**: What are the key ideas for setting up an inclusive and diverse team?

**Tracy Lee**: Many companies feel that their projects can't support juniors. They think that the code or the application is too critical, the use case is too complicated, or the tech is too obscure. They give many reasons why juniors can't do the work.

I want to teach companies how to remove complexity by doing things like giving people the ability to use a simplified interface, which then allows them to be productive even if they're not senior.

I also educate people on mentorship, design reviews, code reviews, and having good architectural documentation that communicates intent clearly, so that people who aren't experienced can get up to speed on a project.

Creating a culture of mentorship means that you don't have to worry as much about turnover. It's about showing companies different tools, as well as how to incorporate different people, and then talking about how using things like frameworks, such as Angular View or Accelerated Mobile Pages (AMP), can make it so much easier to hire people.

> *"If you only hire senior people, that can be really expensive over time."*
>
> —*Tracy Lee*

There are many companies that say, "We only hire seniors because we do X, Y, and Z, and somebody really needs to know what they're doing." But, if you only hire senior people, that can be really expensive over time. If you use frameworks, have mentorship schemes, generate documentation, or create abstractions, your development costs less and can include more people.

**Geertjan Wielenga**: This also relates to developer advocacy, because normally, when I see developer advocates, they're pretty senior people, and the expectation is often that if you're involved in developer relations, or if you're a developer advocate on a stage, then you should know absolutely everything about a particular topic. Would you say that it's difficult for junior people to enter this domain?

**Tracy Lee**: I've seen a lot of juniors being developer advocates, so I definitely don't think you need to be a senior person to be a developer advocate.

**Geertjan Wielenga**: What are the basic personality traits or skills you need to have to be a developer advocate?

**Tracy Lee**: I think you have to want to talk to people. You have to want to teach people. There are plenty of developer relations people who are just really good writers, as I mentioned earlier. If you really know how to build your own social presence online, you don't necessarily have to be at conferences all the time. However, typically, the most visible developer relations people are at conferences.

**Geertjan Wielenga**: At This Dot, are there many different developer advocates? What's the size of this operation?

**Tracy Lee**: You can't have 100 developer advocates running around. At my company, we have about 50 people employed and most of them do high-level architecture consulting. We're a framework-agnostic JavaScript consultancy, and we offer services like staff augmentation, mentoring, and pairing on the development side. Then we have another side of our organization that does developer relations.

We pick select people to work with who are authentic and genuine. Much of that you can't automate. On the developer advocacy team, we have about 10 people working on different activities. We do things like community relations for the Node.js Foundation, and then we also pick very specific products to work on.

Right now, we're working with Google on creating AMP courses to try to educate people, for example. The thing I love about Google's AMP project is that it just allows a lower barrier to entry for development in general. That very much fits in with our vision.

Under our brand, we do work for the JavaScript community too. People know about This Dot because of the fact that we are, in essence, a media company as well. We have This Dot Labs, which is all the consulting stuff that we do, and then we have This Dot Media, where we bring together the greater JavaScript ecosystem. This involves talking about key things that are important, highlighting influencers who matter within the ecosystem, creating events, creating white papers, and creating articles. We do all this simply because we believe in doing it.

# The rise of developer relations

**Geertjan Wielenga**: The whole world is now so different, as you mentioned earlier. Developer relations as a service is really a sign of the times. Would you agree that companies understand developer relations more now?

**Tracy Lee**: It's interesting because when I talk to traditional marketing people, it's typically because a founder or chief technology officer (CTO) said, "We need a developer relations person." Suddenly, the marketing team wants to spend some budget on advocacy, but they don't really get it; they don't really know what developer relations is.

Eventually, they think, "Oh, you're just like our PR firm. You do the things that our PR people do, but you do them for developers."

I've never thought about it that way because we're obviously not a PR firm, but often, that's the way companies find they can relate to us. That's an interesting way to look at it. You could see developer relations as just an extension of PR, which all companies know they need and value. I think if you said that to a developer advocate, though, they wouldn't like it at all!

**Geertjan Wielenga**: You travel frequently, so do you have some war stories surrounding that?

**Tracy Lee**: Whenever anybody joins our company, they always say, "Oh, I see you traveling all the time. It sounds so awesome; that's what I want to do." They don't see what my life is like when I'm not at a conference! Sometimes I have meetings into the early hours of the morning.

The problem with conferences is that I still have a full-time job; it's not my job to go to conferences. I guess it could be my job if I wanted it to be, but it's not. Developer relations seems so amazing, but many people also deal with loneliness. It's cool and fun to travel for a while, but then what about your family? What about your home? People don't think about that at first.

Obviously, I have status, like most of us in this industry do. But if you've traveled enough to get that status, you probably don't care about it because you're so burned out. It's funny the way that works.

**Geertjan Wielenga**: What keeps you motivated in this job, then?

**Tracy Lee**: I like helping people. I believe in giving back to the community and this whole idea that if you do good in life and you're genuine, then things will just work out for you.

**Geertjan Wielenga**: Thank you, Tracy Lee.

## 11

> *We do need to get new blood into the presenting game.*

# Simon Ritter

# Introducing Simon Ritter

Simon Ritter is the deputy chief technology officer (CTO) at Azul and was previously the manager of Java tech evangelism at Oracle Corporation. He has spent 20 years presenting Java tech and is passionate about getting new faces and voices into the world of developer advocacy. Simon now focuses on the core Java platform and Java virtual machine (JVM) performance. He is a Java Champion and represents Azul on the Java Community Process (JCP) Executive Committee and in the Java Platform, Standard Edition (Java SE) Java Specification Request (JSR) Expert Groups. Find Simon on Twitter: @speakjava.

---

**Geertjan Wielenga**: It seems that this is a very hidden profession and a hard profession to get into. Would you agree with that?

## Getting into developer advocacy

**Simon Ritter**: It seems that it's harder to get into this kind of role than it used to be. I remember back in the day, when I started out, there weren't that many people who were doing this. There were less conferences, but also less people on the circuit talking about software-development-related subjects. It was easier to get into the role because it was easier to find gaps.

It does seem to be getting harder because there are a lot more people doing this. Both you and I know that when you go to conferences, you will bump into the same people who've been doing presentations for a long time now, which means that there's this hardcore group of people who tend to get picked for conferences.

They're the ones conference organizers want to get to present at their conferences.

Venkat Subramaniam is a great example of that because he's a fantastic speaker. I absolutely love Venkat but, obviously, if you're going up against Venkat in terms of trying to put together a presentation, and trying to get in at a conference, you're just not going to win. However, on the whole, if I submit a conference paper to a session, there's a reasonable chance it'll get accepted. I still get bounced from a number of conferences, but organizers tend to approach me now, rather than me having to approach them. That has certainly changed.

**Geertjan Wielenga**: What's the reason for this change?

**Simon Ritter**: I think it's because the whole idea of conferences, and spreading information in that way, has grown. If you think about the number of conferences that you see nowadays, there are far more than when I started out doing evangelism at Sun Microsystems. That was way back in 2000/01.

Most of the time, the events were being organized by Sun Microsystems. There weren't that many third-party events. That has gradually changed over time. We've seen things like JavaPolis becoming Devoxx. That's turned into a whole brand, with four or five different Devoxxes. You also have the Voxxed one-day events, which are in smaller venues. Conferences like Jfokus, JavaZone, and DevNexus have also grown.

I did QCon in London recently and that's a very cross-tech conference. There aren't just the conferences highlighting a specific tech: there are also the general ones.

**Geertjan Wielenga**: Would you not expect there to be an increased demand for speakers then, making it easier for more people to get into developer advocacy?

**Simon Ritter**: You would, but this is the whole chicken or the egg dilemma. What the organizers of these conferences want is people with a proven track record, so that they can attract people to come to their conferences.

Most of the time, they're going to charge money for a conference. The idea is that you need a track record in order to get accepted at a conference as a speaker. But, of course, in order to get a track record, you need to get accepted at a conference! As I say, it's the chicken or the egg problem.

It is hard. What seems to be a good way of getting into this field is coming up with some interesting ideas for different subjects to talk about. You can begin with lightning talks and things that aren't full conference sessions. Devoxx is the classic example because getting accepted at Devoxx is quite a challenge. So, if you're a new speaker, it's going to be very difficult to get a session there unless you've got something really interesting to talk about, versus doing something like a lightning talk, which is an easier starting point.

> *"The people who are doing the presentations are just getting older!"*
>
> *—Simon Ritter*

You need to gradually build up a track record of doing presentations and getting results with that. We do need to get new blood into the presenting game because at the moment, you look around and you see that the people who are doing the presentations are just getting older!

# Competition in the advocacy sphere

**Geertjan Wielenga**: What about the other developer advocates in your orbit? You come across them on Twitter and then you see them at conferences, but what is your relationship with them? Is the word "rivalry" of any relevance?

**Simon Ritter**: No, I think "rivalry" is the wrong term. If I was going to use that word then it would be "friendly rivalry."

Most of the time, the kind of subject matter that I cover (the JVM and Java SE) is not something that many other people tend to target. The majority of people, when I go to conferences, deal with frameworks like Spring, the enterprise side of things, microservices, embedded, and all sorts of other things. So, they tend to come at speaking from a slightly different angle. The people who you would expect me to see as competitors at conferences are the people from Oracle. Clearly, they're also presenting on Java SE, but Oracle has reduced the number of people in that role.

For the bigger conferences, like Devoxx, you get people like Stuart Marks and Brian Goetz turning up. Obviously, if they're going to be presenting on the future of Java, they will get the slot rather than me. I have absolutely no problem with that because they're the sources of knowledge. That said, because I'm in the expert group for Java SE, I have inside knowledge of that. I do talk to people like Brian about what's going on.

For smaller conferences, there's no real rivalry. In fact, a large part of the time I'm actually doing Oracle a favor by talking about the state of Java and where it's going. I get on very well with the other developer advocates I meet at different conferences. There's no antagonism: most people are very happy. We're all part of the wider Java community and we just get on with each other.

**Geertjan Wielenga**: Let's back up now: could you talk about where this all began for you?

**Simon Ritter**: I got into the presentation game way back in 1992, when I worked for AT&T. My boss came to me and said, "We're organizing this conference and I want you to do a presentation for half an hour."

I replied, "No, I don't want to do that because I don't do public speaking. I have no interest in public speaking at all. It's something that scares me and I don't want to be doing any of it."

He said, "You're going to do it. I'm going to send you on a public speaking course and then you're going to do this half-hour presentation." So, he sent me on the presentation course and it was interesting. The course taught the usual basics of presenting.

I did this half-hour presentation and, I'll admit, it was pretty bad as a first presentation. In fact, afterward, the people who were organizing the conference did a survey. They asked all the people who were at the presentations which was the most useful of the day. They had about six or seven different presentations and I scored zero!

I had this survey on my wall in my office for quite a long time because I wanted to code; I didn't want to do presentations, so I had no interest in doing anything further.

Then my boss came to me again and said, "We need you to run this training course." I thought that a training course would not be quite the same as a presentation and would be easier. Eventually, though, I did a few more presentations and found that I started to actually enjoy them.

I joined Sun Microsystems in 1996 and I was sent on a couple of trips to do presentations. I ended up doing a presentation on Java, which is how I actually got into the whole Java scene. Somebody saw me and they said, "Oh, you did a presentation on Java. You could do another presentation on Java, couldn't you?"

It snowballed from there and the job that I had at Sun Microsystems (being a software engineer) morphed into working with the Market Development Engineering (MDE) organization, so I ended up then joining the evangelism team. It was a gradual migration to this role.

## Comparing advocacy to evangelism

**Geertjan Wielenga**: How do you feel about using the "developer advocate" title versus the "tech evangelist" title?

**Simon Ritter**: "Tech evangelist" seems to have fallen from favor as a title in the last few years. People don't call themselves "evangelists" now: they're all called "developer advocates." That's fine; it's the same job, just a different name.

The way I'd describe it is that the idea of developer advocacy is a little bit more toned down. It's more about talking about the tech and explaining the tech, rather than trying to convert people into using the tech, which is what the evangelism thing tends to indicate.

> *"Advocacy is not so much about conversion."*
>
> —*Simon Ritter*

Evangelism has this idea of a belief system and trying to convert people to your beliefs, whereas advocacy is more about promoting what's good about your tech to people who, to a large extent, have already bought into the idea. It's about helping them to then understand that tech and use it in a better way. Advocacy is not so much about conversion.

**Geertjan Wielenga**: You seem to have been doing this for a long time. What's kept you enthusiastic about it for all these years?

**Simon Ritter**: That's actually quite an easy question to answer because the thing that I've always loved about being a developer advocate is that things keep changing. You're not continually talking about the same thing. There's always new tech to look at. I think that's what's really kept me interested in this role for the 20-odd years that I've been doing it.

**Geertjan Wielenga**: Would you say that there are specific attributes that someone ideally should have for this type of role?

**Simon Ritter**: Yes, I think you've got to be passionate. That's really the key attribute. If you're passionate about what you're talking about, the audience will share some of that passion.

I also think that you need a certain level of technical competence. If you're going to stand up in front of an audience and explain something to them, you have to at least give the impression that you know what you're talking about. Having some technical background is often very useful, especially when it comes to answering questions.

The other day Bruno Borges retweeted a `#speakerfail` post. It was asking about situations that people had found themselves in where things had gone really badly wrong with presentations. Bruno actually said that he did a presentation once where he didn't know the subject and every question that he had afterward he couldn't answer.

**Geertjan Wielenga**: What do you do in that situation? How do you respond without being completely embarrassed and never being invited back?

**Simon Ritter**: Well, I think that most people understand that you can't know the answer to every single question. You could be an expert, but unless you're James Gosling talking about Java, or Brian Goetz, you're not going to know the answer to everything.

If you're taking questions afterward and you can answer some of those questions, that shows credibility. If you can't answer some of them, people won't care. You can ask the person for their email address and tell them that you'll find out what the answer is.

You just don't want to be in a situation where you don't know the answer to any question that gets asked. That's when people do tend to get a little bit upset!

As a presenter, you pick up new subjects and you start presenting on them. You might be talking about something and have a slide up and think, "Ah, that's how it works! That's what it means!" You may actually explain it to yourself as you're presenting.

## Navigating technical failures

**Geertjan Wielenga**: The bane of a developer advocate's life is when you somehow can't connect your laptop to the projector. What do you do in those unexpected situations?

**Simon Ritter**: I've been faced with a few issues in the past. Going back to the `#speakerfail` Twitter story, Stuart Marks said that he arrived for one presentation that he was going to do and nobody turned up for it.

> *"Nobody turned up to my presentation."*
>
> *—Simon Ritter*

I actually had that happen early on in my career: nobody turned up to my presentation. I also had one day where one person turned up to my presentation, which was kind of nice because we then just had a chat about the subject. I think, in that case, the most important thing is not to let it worry you. If it happens repeatedly, then that probably indicates that speaking is not for you.

But if it happens once and you've only just started out, then I wouldn't let it put you off too much.

In terms of equipment failure, I remember one session where I turned up, I plugged my laptop in, we were all ready to go, and then *boom*! We had a power cut! An important skill to learn is to be able to present without the slides. If you think about it, a slide should really only be an aide-memoire for you.

There was another presentation I remember doing where somebody came up to me and said, "Oh, Peter's just called in. He's sick. He can't come and do the presentation, and we've got a room full of people downstairs who are all expecting a presentation on this. Can you do it?"

I agreed to give it a go. I knew the subject, but I had no idea what was in the slide deck. So, I just turned up and every slide was a new experience for both me and the audience! I think it probably wasn't my best presentation, but it wasn't too bad. I was able to at least give some value to the presentation.

There are two pieces of advice that I give to people when it comes to presentations. Firstly, do not read the slides because there's nothing worse than somebody who just stands up and does that. The audience can read the slides just as well as you can and you're not adding any value. Secondly, I really don't like scripted presentations because you can tell when somebody's reading from a script. Even if they're good, you can still tell. You should stand up and start explaining something using the slides as motivation or a way of indicating certain points. That comes across better.

**Geertjan Wielenga**: What do you think about the "no slides, just code" type of presentation?

**Simon Ritter**: I think that's a really good idea if you can do it. Personally, that's not for me. I occasionally will do some live coding as part of my presentations, but it's not really where I excel in terms of my presentation style. You need to practice it beforehand to make sure that you know what you're doing. My problem is that I'm useless at typing and my typing gets worse when I'm in front of an audience. So, it's difficult for me to actually do that.

**Geertjan Wielenga**: What would you say are some of the low points or things to be aware of in this profession?

**Simon Ritter**: You need to be a little bit careful because you can end up doing a presentation a lot and sometimes that can be too much.

I've been doing the "55 New Features in JDK 9" talk since the middle of last year and I think I've done that one to death now. It's easy to do that because obviously, with lots of conferences around the world, you can go and do a presentation to an audience that has no idea what you've been talking about. I think you need to continually update your slides and make sure that there's something a little bit different to keep it fresh because, otherwise, you can become stale as a presenter.

> *"You've got to have a fairly thick skin, because there will be times when people won't like what you say."*
>
> *—Simon Ritter*

A low point is that, obviously, you're putting yourself out there in front of the public and there are consequences to that. You've got to have a fairly thick skin, because there will be times when people won't like what you say.

No matter how well prepared you are, you'll always have points where people disagree with you. If you're new to the presenting game, I think that could be more of an issue because people will stand up and say, "No, you're wrong!"

That can be harder to deal with as a young person versus if you're middle-aged like me. If somebody stands up and tells me that I'm wrong, I just say, "Yeah, whatever."

**Geertjan Wielenga**: What would you as a 20-year-old think of the you of today?

**Simon Ritter**: I do sometimes think about this. Being middle-aged, you start looking backward as well as forward. I would probably look at myself and think, "Wow! That's not what I expected!"

When I was 20, if I had seen myself now, I would have asked, "You really travel all over the world and talk to thousands of people, and you just do that all the time? That's what I ended up doing?"

**Geertjan Wielenga**: Would you have expected to be a programmer at that point?

**Simon Ritter**: When I left university and started working in the IT business, I really wanted to be a hardcore programmer working on low-level stuff. Marketing and sales weren't for me.

**Geertjan Wielenga**: What advice would you give to students or young people about developer advocacy?

## Simon's advice for young people

**Simon Ritter**: You have to find a tech to start with. You need to identify a tech that you are interested in and that you can be passionate about. Then, you need to start making sure that you know as much as possible about that tech and building up experience in it.

One of the things that I always say to people, especially when I talk to students, is that a great way of building up experience in something, without necessarily having to get a job (because again, you have the chicken or the egg problem), is open source.

Contribute to open-source projects and get involved. It's a fantastic way of showing a prospective employer, or a prospective conference, that you know what you're talking about. If there's a subject you're interested in and you want to present on it, get involved in some open-source project. Contributing to that project, and becoming known in that project, will help when people look at your background after you apply to a conference.

Then, start trying to think of a different angle that would appeal to developers. You want to be able to say, "Here's the tech and here's what you need to know."

**Geertjan Wielenga**: We've talked mainly about public speaking, so far, but what are some of the other things that you do in your role?

**Simon Ritter**: Since I left Oracle and joined Azul, I've been doing more writing of blog entries and articles.

I write white papers for our marketing department. I also write tech briefs for internal use by our salespeople. I do more writing than I did either at Oracle or at Sun Microsystems before that. That is definitely a shift that I've noticed.

Other things that you do as a developer advocate are related to that. Stack Overflow is another activity and if you're answering questions on Stack Overflow about a particular tech, or a particular area, that can also help, not just in terms of your resume, but also in terms of getting speaking slots. The idea of being a developer advocate covers a number of different areas.

**Geertjan Wielenga**: What kind of career path does one have going forward?

**Simon Ritter**: It's funny because I remember distinctly having this conversation with a number of my colleagues. We were debating what you can do after developer advocacy.

One of the things that actually came up, which we thought would be quite a logical move, was being something like a CTO. You've got that ability to identify tech and communicate tech, which fits into the CTO role. That was one area that we saw as a possible future career move.

**Geertjan Wielenga**: What role does social media play for you? Which social media channels do you use yourself?

**Simon Ritter**: The primary social media site that I use for work is Twitter. That seems to be a very useful tool for me. I use it to highlight activities that I'm involved in and announce when I've created a new blog post.

It's a really easy way of pushing that out to a reasonably large audience because I've got just over 10,000 followers now. But then, of course, stuff gets retweeted.

When it comes to websites, DZone is one of the ones that I use quite commonly and that seems to pick up on the blog posts that I do. I write a couple of articles for JAXenter on a semiregular basis. I don't use Facebook for work. It doesn't seem to fit for me. I know a lot of people post stuff on LinkedIn, but I don't use that either. Maybe I should, but I don't.

> *"When people get things wrong, I'm quite happy to jump in and set them straight!"*
>
> —*Simon Ritter*

In terms of finding information, I tend to use Reddit. I do occasionally post links on there, but mostly I post comments on what other people have posted. When people get things wrong, I'm quite happy to jump in and set them straight!

**Geertjan Wielenga**: I guess an obvious downside to Twitter is that you don't come across anything completely different because you're following the people who you're familiar with. Do you agree?

**Simon Ritter**: I'm not sure I'd necessarily agree with that. I try not to follow too many people because of the sheer volume of input you get. I tend to try and curate the people I follow, so that I get a broad spectrum of information. I don't just follow people in the Java space: I follow people all over the IT world.

I think I get a reasonably good input from quite a range of things.

## Being authentic while working for a company

**Geertjan Wielenga**: When you're at conferences, if you're coming from a particular company, there's the automatic, and probably justified, suspicion that you're there for a reason. How do you balance that authenticity aspect with working for an organization?

**Simon Ritter**: If I go back through my career history, all the roles that I've had were very much about promoting Java. Most of the time, I didn't need to concern myself with having to push a product. We were focused purely on the tech, rather than a product. That's helped in terms of having credibility because people know that I'm not necessarily going to turn up and talk about a given product.

I suppose there's a very thin line; anyone outside of the tech world wouldn't necessarily see the difference between a tech and a product. But then, if you're promoting something that's essentially free, you can hardly be accused of promoting a product. If somebody doesn't have to pay for it, then do they care?

I think it's an easy balance, for me personally, to focus mainly on the tech. People have seen me present before, so they know that I'm not going to just turn up and do a product pitch: I will talk about the tech.

**Geertjan Wielenga**: Do you see any ethical dilemmas in terms of promoting Java?

**Simon Ritter**: One of the things that I need to be careful of is balancing how I present what Azul is doing as a company with Oracle because, clearly, we're in direct competition with Oracle.

Oracle is the custodian of Java. We have a very good working relationship with Oracle in terms of access to the Technology Compatibility Kit (TCK) and access to the source code. We work quite closely with Oracle's engineers on a number of things. There's not so much an ethical dilemma, but I do need to think about how I present my company in relation to Oracle.

With the changes that are happening at the moment, in terms of the new release cadence for the Java Development Kit (JDK), the Oracle binaries will not be available freely for deployment as of JDK 11. JDK 8 support ends in January next year, so people are going to have to think quite hard about how they're going to continue using Java. Are they going to pay for support? There are a number of things around that at the moment, which means that when positioning Azul as an alternative, I do need to be a little bit careful about not being negative about Oracle.

**Geertjan Wielenga**: What were you talking about originally about Java and what kinds of things are you talking about now?

**Simon Ritter**: If I go right back to the beginning of my presentations, which was before Java, I did presentations on Unix. When I joined Sun Microsystems, I was talking about Solaris.

I started talking about Java back in 1996 or early 1997. Most people hadn't even heard about Java or they didn't know what it was. Over time, I've talked about most aspects of Java at some point.

When I joined the evangelism team, I think it was JDK 1.4.2 that had just come out. We were promoting JDK 1.4.2 and then obviously we had the launch of JDK 5, which was a big thing because that had a whole bunch of new features in it, which changed things a lot.

I've gone through every iteration of Java SE since then: JavaFX, both as a scripting language and as the reworked libraries; embedded Java; Sun Small Programmable Object Technology devices (SPOTs); Java on mobile; and all the Lightweight User Interface Toolkit (LWUIT) side of things. I decided that I just wanted to be able to talk about all of the different subjects. I covered Java Platform, Micro Edition (Java ME), Java SE, and Java Platform, Enterprise Edition (Java EE).

Now that I work for Azul, the scope is a bit smaller because we don't cover Enterprise Java, so I don't talk about Enterprise Java at all now. I focus on more of the core platform. That's why I cover topics such as "55 New Features in Java SE 9." I talk about the more commercial side of things: Zing, what we do with garbage collection, and what we do with just-in-time (JIT) compilation, but at a technical level. It's not a sales pitch.

> *"What you don't want is somebody to stand up and give you a sales pitch."*
>
> —*Simon Ritter*

If you go to a conference, what you don't want is somebody to stand up and give you a sales pitch or just a marketing slide.

If you want to be successful as a presenter, one of the key things is keeping the technical content of your presentation good, but you need to avoid going too deep because you can lose your audience. It's quite a challenge to get that level right.

One of the other things that we do at Azul is embedded Java, so there are some interesting areas that I can explore with that. One of the presentations I've done a few times includes building myself a Raspberry Pi cluster, then I use that to do some machine learning in Java, and get it to play Minecraft. It was the idea of taking a more abstract view of Java and looking at how it could be used, rather than just presenting the set of features.

Coming back to what has kept me going in terms of interest in the role, I've been able to do some really weird and wild demos over the years. I would still like to carry on doing some of that, if I can.

**Geertjan Wielenga**: What kind of demos do you enjoy the most?

## Simon's demo ideas

**Simon Ritter**: Building weird stuff, especially with wood, is always interesting to me to put into a presentation. It's a good idea to come up with some original ideas about how you can apply the tech, and the weirder they are the better!

Many people, in their day job, have to do specific things: writing systems that deal with accounts, writing systems that deal with a web page, and things like that.

That stuff is not terribly exciting. If you can show them something that they could do with that tech, and suddenly it's completely out of the realm of what they normally do, it can be very good in terms of promoting a tech, and just helping people to see tech in a different light.

**Geertjan Wielenga**: You're actually quite well known for doing presentations with objects and soldering stuff together. Can you mention a couple of them to illustrate this?

**Simon Ritter**: I think the first one that I came up with was way back when I started with the evangelism team and Lego Mindstorms had just come out.

Somebody had created a very small Java implementation that would run on Lego Mindstorms. When I say small, I mean very small because Mindstorms only had 32 kilobytes of RAM, which meant that it wasn't a full Java implementation. It didn't have garbage collection or anything like that. You had to be very careful about how you programmed it.

> *"I built a blackjack-playing Lego robot and I used a whole range of different techs."*
>
> *—Simon Ritter*

I thought, "Right, I want to build something that can use that." I built a blackjack-playing Lego robot and I used a whole range of different techs. It was great because I got to play with Lego at work. I built this robot that would actually deal cards and then I used FreeTTS, text to speech, so that I could get the laptop to talk.

When it recognized a card, it would deal the card out and say, "You just got the jack of hearts." That was how I got into these demos.

Then Sun SPOTs came along with Sun Labs and that opened up a whole interesting area of things that we could do. We built some gloves that had Sun SPOTs on. There was one demo that I did at JavaOne where I had the projector and the screen, which had infrared LEDs on it. I used a Wii remote control to recognize where the screen was and then project a playing card onto the screen. If you flipped it over, the image would change, so you got the back of the playing card instead of the front.

**Geertjan Wielenga**: To what extent do you care whether people actually do anything with these ideas and to what extent is it just fun?

**Simon Ritter**: I'll have to put my hands up and say that most of that was just about having fun, although it was nice to be able to provide interest and stimulation for ideas that were a bit different. I think people like that.

**Geertjan Wielenga**: What are some developments that you see happening in Java? What areas do you think Java should focus on next?

**Simon Ritter**: The area that most people find that they would like to change is making the Java language easier to use.

I think the JVM itself is very solid. We've got a very good set of core libraries, which provide a very rich set of functionalities. What people tend to criticize Java for is that the language is overly verbose.

If you look at a project like Amber, that's all about trying to simplify the syntax of the language. You need to be careful because it's good to have a simpler syntax when you're writing code, but you need to make sure that the code is still readable. More people are going to read the code than are going to write it, especially if it's used in any reasonable level of deployment.

The other project to think about is Project Loom. It's interesting in terms of addressing the needs of massively multi-threaded code, which means you can share fibers across a single operating system thread. Value types and Project Valhalla is another area that people will like very much.

**Geertjan Wielenga**: To change topics, what was the Siberian adventure that you went on recently? How did you end up there and what did it consist of?

## Travel adventures

**Simon Ritter**: The Java User Group in Russia organizes a number of conferences and so the members approached me about one they were doing in Moscow. The dates didn't work for my availability, but I asked to be invited to any future conferences. They came back straightaway with one in Siberia in March. I had a fantastic time. I was there for the weekend. They took us on a tour and snowmobiling in the wilds of Siberia. One of the best parts of my job is the fact that I get to travel all over the place and meet people from all these different places.

**Geertjan Wielenga**: With the travel that you do, what's your experience of burnout?

**Simon Ritter**: What can become an issue, to some extent, is if you get too involved in this job. The travel can become quite wearing. You can get to a point where you're just traveling too much and you have to dial it back down again.

There are so many conferences now. I reckon that you could literally spend your entire year, if you had the travel budget and the motivation, traveling around the world and going from conference to conference.

**Geertjan Wielenga**: Thank you, Simon Ritter.

## 12

> *Once you start down the path of enjoying something and sharing it, you're already well on the way to becoming a developer advocate.*

# Mark Heckler

# Introducing Mark Heckler

Mark Heckler is a Java Champion, published author, conference speaker, and Spring developer and advocate for Pivotal. He develops innovative, production-ready software at velocity for the cloud and Internet of Things (IoT) applications. Mark has worked with key players in the manufacturing, retail, medical, scientific, telecom, and financial industries and various public sector organizations to develop and deliver critical capabilities on time and on budget. Mark is an open-source software (OSS) contributor and the author/curator of a developer-focused blog (`https://www.thehecklers.com`). Find Mark on Twitter: @mkheck.

---

**Geertjan Wielenga**: When did you realize that you were a developer advocate? Did you set out to do this job?

## Becoming a developer advocate

**Mark Heckler**: This is one of those career fields that it seems you can slide into almost by accident, but I guess it's not really an accident. It does feel a bit more serendipitous than following a carefully plotted path.

There's an old stereotype that those of us who really like to live in the code may not necessarily have the most refined interpersonal skills. It's important to remember, though, that tech is a wide field and categorizations are not overly useful beyond a certain point. There are many of us who love to code and we enjoy the challenge, the thrill, and the intellectual stimulation that coding gives us very viscerally. Then there are people who also really enjoy talking with others and sharing what they do. They really want to be out there mingling and growing from their experiences.

I got into this role by doing a lot of coding and starting to share what I was doing with others. At the micro-level, you have your colleagues. You can say, "Hey, take a look at this." You could tell them that you found an article that was interesting or you found a technique that might also be useful for them. You might then be asked to give a little lunchtime training session or to mentor some junior developers. There are so many ways to start sharing that it almost seems that it just happens.

At some point, you might give a presentation to a local user group or to another group within your company. After that, you might consider attending a conference, but think, "I really don't have much to say; I don't have much to add. What can I bring that anybody would be that interested in?"

Further down the line, you're talking with someone and they say, "You really should present that. That sounds like it would be really useful." Somebody else can see value in your idea.

> *"You may end up learning more than you shared."*
>
> —*Mark Heckler*

You think, "Probably nobody will show up. I probably won't even get accepted, but sure, I'll throw a talk idea out there." Then you do get accepted. It might be such a stressful event and so different to anything you've ever done before that you might just decide it's not for you. On the other hand, you may find that you got some good feedback and had some positive discussions with people afterwards. You may end up learning more than you shared. To me, that's a huge positive.

**Geertjan Wielenga**: 20 years ago, there were computers and there were programmers, but this whole developer advocacy role wasn't there. Something must have happened in the meantime. What do you think that was?

**Mark Heckler**: I think there has been a rise of companies that have more options, more libraries, more framework components, more packaged software, more pieces that you can use in your bespoke or custom software, and so on.

There is now a more heavy-handed marketing push. A little bit of marketing and some kind of presales stuff is good. All of us working in coding and engineering roles can accept that, until it gets to be a deafening roar.

Sometimes, you make contact about a product that you're interested in using and ask for more information. The person on the other end of the line says, "I'm in sales, so I don't know about that." At that point, it becomes a very frustrating relationship. Developer advocates bridge that gap. Typically, most of us are either actively coding or have actively coded.

We know how to apply the tools that we talk about. We can bring the here-are-the-benefits-to-you side of it. We can also bring the here's-how-to-implement-it side of it. That, to me, is invaluable.

When I was just doing development work and not doing advocacy at all, I highly prized the opportunity to talk to somebody who could actually address why I might or might not want to use a product, how best to leverage it, and licensing constraints. I think developer advocacy came into being because the marketing suddenly became much bigger, which necessitated this new role.

**Geertjan Wielenga**: In your case, there was a point where you were an engineer. How did that transition actually happen to becoming a developer advocate?

## From engineering to advocacy

**Mark Heckler**: Initially, I was doing full-time engineering work and then presenting on the side. I was occasionally taking a few days here and there to travel to present at events and conferences. I think many people realized that I had this public-facing level of activities that I was doing. I was out there enough that they felt I was either doing this full-time or maybe should be.

> *"I was offered a full-time gig doing, essentially, what I was already doing in my spare time."*
>
> —*Mark Heckler*

A good friend of mine reached out and said, "I know you're doing this anyway, so how would you like to make this your official role?" That sounded pretty great, so I interviewed and I was offered a full-time gig doing, essentially, what I was already doing in my spare time.

**Geertjan Wielenga**: Did you study software engineering or something completely different?

**Mark Heckler**: Actually, I studied mathematics, computer science, and, interestingly enough, some business. I even got an MBA.

I know that sometimes surprises people, but the value that we produce in software isn't inherently in the software: it's in what it allows us to do as a company for our customers/users/stakeholders. That provides meaning and utility. I felt that an MBA would be something that would help me to understand and get my head around that better.

There are many different types of coursework in any study program, but I tended to gravitate towards the economics and finance topics. Those areas are not entirely dissimilar from engineering: you have numerical discipline in terms of the calculation of formulas and assessing various different variables that go into making a particular outcome. I found it really fascinating.

**Geertjan Wielenga**: Isn't that economics background something that you have been using in a presentation that you've been giving lately?

**Mark Heckler**: Yes, it is! I toyed with the idea of doing that for several years. I finally got around to doing it. The title is something like "This Stuff Is Cool, but How Do I Get My Company to Do It?" The idea is that we, in our industry, tend to go to a conference and hear something, or read something in a trade journal, and think, "This is exactly what we need to do in our company!"

The problem is that it's very hard for us to quantify that and justify a new approach. When we go to leadership, we will get questions coming back to us about the value and the cost. These are very logical questions, but we don't have great responses. We might just say, "We should do this because this is the future! This is the way development is going to go!"

My talk is about learning how to assess things financially. I discuss applying financial formulas and assigning values. It's about taking qualitative measures and turning them into quantitative measures, which is very uncomfortable, very imprecise, and far more clinical than the real world allows. Yet, we have to start somewhere.

**Geertjan Wielenga**: Can you give one concrete example of how you can apply this approach?

**Mark Heckler**: If you were able to go from a release cycle of once per year to once per month, what would that mean for your particular organization? Once per month means 12 releases per year. Could you roll out more functionality faster? Well, obviously you could. You're going to release at least a portion of that functionality in one month's time versus 12 months' time.

The next chunk will be in two months' time versus 12 months' time. A very proven fact is that this increases fidelity.

In many cases, you're working with somebody who in 12 months' time may not even be your subject matter expert. The requirements might shift or the person might leave the company.

If you fulfill some of that functionality within four weeks, the chances of requirements drift are much lower. If you do somehow miss the mark, you've missed it on this much functionality versus that much functionality. So, it's much easier to correct. Those are very understandable concepts.

> *"I always tell people to never try to make a bad idea look good."*
>
> —*Mark Heckler*

When someone asks you how to quantify an idea, that's when you start getting into some numbers. For example, if we're 80% closer on our requirements, if we don't have $X$ amount of rework, how many person months does that equate to? How much do we pay each person on average? When you apply actual numbers to all of those measures, you begin to see this rather convincing picture emerge. Although, it's only convincing if it's a good idea. I always tell people to never try to make a bad idea look good.

All of the predictions are based on assumptions, so these assumptions need to be based on facts. Better assumptions going in means more accurate results coming out, which gives everybody a much more accurate basis upon which to discuss changes.

These conversations help to bridge that divide. The financial types hold the purse strings and so often in this field, we see them as the enemy. But, let's face it, if they didn't make sure everything ran right in our organization, the organization wouldn't still be there. The more we all work together, the better off we all will be.

**Geertjan Wielenga**: On the subject of organizations, what kind of organization pays you to go around the world to talk about the economics of software development?

**Mark Heckler**: A very forward-thinking organization! I think it makes sense for an organization to put people out there to say, "Here are tools you may find useful."

**Geertjan Wielenga**: Could you be speaking on this topic and working for any company out there?

**Mark Heckler**: Yes, this is something that applies universally. At any time, you have to compete for resources. Even externally to our field, any organization has only $X$ amount of money that it can spend on software upgrades and further reach for existing systems. Those are all competing concerns. I think that topic has pretty broad applicability.

**Geertjan Wielenga**: What are some of the other topics that you talk about in your role?

## Mark's talk topics

**Mark Heckler**: I talk about how to solve problems better. Most of that revolves around using Spring or different components that may be considered within the framework, like Spring Data, Spring Boot, or Spring Cloud.

**Geertjan Wielenga**: What kind of reaction do you get to the economics talk and also to your Spring talks?

**Mark Heckler**: The economics talk is a little bit of an outlier. You have people who are looking for something very specific, like a better way to communicate with their management, finance teams, or business units. I get a really good response from them. For the Spring-based talks, there are many problems that are out there that, regardless of their industry, people are trying to solve: better communication, less latency, and more scalability.

The Spring talks fit really well with those topics, so I get good feedback.

**Geertjan Wielenga**: Are there other activities that are part of your role as a developer advocate?

**Mark Heckler**: Every organization does things a little bit differently, but one of the aspects that really attracted me to Pivotal was that you're not just asked to be in front of people at events or at conferences: you also have the opportunity to give workshops with customers and organizations that are actively and wholeheartedly using your software stack.

This is where you really get the trial by fire in terms of your tooling. Just because something isn't in 90% of use cases, it doesn't mean that it's not still very valid. Maybe you didn't foresee something happening, but it makes a lot of sense when you meet with customers. That's when you have your assumptions checked. You think, "Wow, that's actually brilliant. Let's try to work this out and make this a little easier for more people."

> *"If you don't have that variety, you're leaving a huge amount of knowledge and feedback on the table."*
>
> —*Mark Heckler*

Not all companies allow you to speak to people in that way, which is a shame. Some developer advocates just want to write articles and publish them, or they only want to speak in front of small or large groups. But if you don't have that variety, you're leaving a huge amount of knowledge and feedback on the table, and it's being wasted.

**Geertjan Wielenga**: Do you also do blogging and social media in your role?

**Mark Heckler**: I don't do as much blogging as I would like. I need to do more of that because I do enjoy writing. But I tweet all the time and far more often than maybe I should. I live on Twitter. Using Twitter is easier. You can dash something off when you're running to catch an airplane, which is pretty useful. It's harder to blog when you're running to a terminal. But I think each different tool has its place.

## Diversity in tasks

**Geertjan Wielenga**: Would you say that it's the diversity of activities that really appeals to people going into developer advocacy?

**Mark Heckler**: Yes, and it's interesting that you bring that up. To give a really offbeat example, I ordered a keyboard not that long ago and crowdfunded it. It's a great developer keyboard and the construction is superb.

The problem is that the wrist pads that go on it do not detach easily. I literally have to screw them on or off. It's an always-on or always-off design, which means that traveling and portability is pretty much out the window. The keyboard is also unique in terms of its key configuration layout. You have a special key to do this and a special key to do that, which you don't see on any other keyboard.

My first thought at the time was that if you're a developer who sits for eight hours a day in one chair, in one location, this keyboard would be pretty awesome. Even though it's an oddball configuration, you could fully leverage that to really do some neat stuff.

But if you're somebody who tends to do many different things in a day, hopping from machine to machine, and location to location, that is a disaster. It's a great keyboard for certain use cases and a horrible keyboard for others. That's really what our job is: a nice role for some people who really like the constant interruption, but one that certainly involves a lot of change. You're in a field that's constantly changing.

**Geertjan Wielenga**: The flip side of that is burnout. Do you have any tips or insights into how to avoid getting burnout from all the different tasks, activities, and deadlines?

**Mark Heckler**: What's the old saying? Physician, heal thyself. I think much of it comes down to knowing what you need and what will help you to maintain your little island of sanity in the midst of the chaos.

Everybody has a different answer for what they need. For me, I have always eaten, slept, and breathed tech. I've always loved to code. There were a few years when I toned it down.

I took more time away in the evenings and on weekends. I still do that; there are times when I will step away and just have an unplugged day. The truth is that I enjoy this, so, to me, anytime I unplug has the potential to be as stressful or more stressful than when I'm plugged in.

I do think it's important to have different interests and different things that excite you, but if you do thrive on just staying always in the code, then spend time on that. A love of tech could even involve keeping up with the latest cellphones. There's a new range of iPhones coming out. That's pretty exciting to some folks.

It may not interest others at all. But if that's something that excites you, even if it's not strictly in the developer advocate arena, that's valid.

You can also do something fun to recharge. It might be reading fiction or going out on long hikes in the wilderness. Whatever helps you to step away and come back fresh is great.

I think that stress happens regardless of your role or your field. If you're an accountant or a marketing person, for example, you're always going to have those political whirlwinds around you in your company. You're just trying to block that out, so you can get your job done and make a positive contribution.

> *"This is a very creative discipline. It's still a discipline, but you're creating something that wasn't there moments ago."*
>
> —*Mark Heckler*

I love to point out to people who aren't in our field, or who are just starting out in our field, that this is a very creative discipline. It's still a discipline, but you're creating something that wasn't there moments ago. This is something that many people find incredibly rewarding.

**Geertjan Wielenga**: Now that we've talked about all these different highs, what would you see as being some of the lows of this position? What are some things to be aware of before entering this field?

# Negative aspects of advocacy

**Mark Heckler**: I think you hit the big one with burnout. That's not necessarily burnout in terms of just having to get away because you can't take this anymore: it could also be in terms of the pace.

There are 27 things you could be doing at any one point in time. It could be seen as both a positive and a negative that there are 27 things you need to be doing. I always tell people in our field that the good news is you'll never be bored. The bad news is you'll never catch up. I think if you let that loom over you, then it can really bother you.

Plenty of folks love the "Inbox Zero" idea. I'm not a huge devotee because I feel that then you're just obsessed with a number that may or may not be good or bad, depending on the context. Right now, the inbox that I have open is at 2,943 unread emails. Frankly, some of those emails are ones that have rolled in when I've been traveling. I probably glanced at them and decided that they're not important.

If having unread emails is the kind of thing that gets to you, then this role is not for you. You can never catch up on every possible thing. You can never clean off your task list entirely.

If that unsettles you, it will just add to your stress levels and your hatred of all things. If you can embrace developer advocacy as a role that's constantly challenging you, giving you new things to look at, consider, do, and learn, you may never catch up, but you'll never be bored either.

**Geertjan Wielenga**: Would you say that there is a place in this profession for people who are more introverted?

**Mark Heckler**: Yes, sometimes you do need to wall off and be alone with your thoughts. Then there will be other times when it makes far more sense to work with others to try to achieve a goal. No single key unlocks every door.

**Geertjan Wielenga**: One of the downsides of working in developer advocacy is that you're constantly chasing the next shiny thing, but often, your customers are perfectly happy using whatever the tech was three versions ago. How do you get that balance between constantly telling people to get the latest thing and accepting that they could be perfectly happy where they are now?

**Mark Heckler**: In any field, you have people who are really good at their job and people who are just okay at their job. One of the marks of a good developer advocate is not constantly pushing things that people don't need.

Let's imagine we have a very stable piece of software that may have been created 10 years ago, but it's constantly being updated. It's not being updated because we want to try to push out the old: it's being updated because developers are saying, "Hey, we really need this capability. Why doesn't it do this?"

When you actually build that capability in, that's the point where a developer advocate can come in and say, "Look, you were talking about how you really needed this kind of routing or this kind of rate limiting. It's in there now. When you get a chance to update, try it. Let us know what you think."

This is one of the things that open source really helps with. Many times, your customers or your users will submit a pull request to say, "We want this in there. We think that this should be done this way. Accept our code." So, they're actually driving some of the changes.

There's value in showing the new stuff because it solves problems that haven't already been solved. You've added some capability that has been requested by one customer or maybe by several. So, if you do your job right, you're not constantly making your users feel bad for where they are with your tooling. You're just showing them that there are capabilities that they can more fully leverage.

**Geertjan Wielenga**: What do you do when the direction of the company you work for conflicts with your own vision or your own sense of what's right?

**Mark Heckler**: I will have to say that I haven't run into this. I guess everybody's barometer is a little bit different. For me, if I felt that I was working for an organization that didn't have its customers' best interests at heart, I would leave.

**Geertjan Wielenga**: How strongly would you have to disagree with your company before quitting? That would be an extreme step.

## Quitting your job

**Mark Heckler**: There is a guy who is the vice president at a company in my home area. One thing that he wrote was published on Medium a few months ago.

It was a bit of career advice he got early on in his career: "If you see something wrong in your organization and you can't change your organization, then move to a different organization."

I do think that you're right and quitting your job is a drastic step. But if you see something wrong, you have a responsibility to yourself, if nothing else. Even if that issue is something very small and you think that it probably only bothers you, you have to raise that issue.

> *"Sometimes, companies do get things wrong and you have the chance to fix them."*
>
> —*Mark Heckler*

You should say, "This looks a little funny to me. Let's talk about this. Can you explain to me why this is a good thing?" You raise the question and you raise the issue. Sometimes, companies do get things wrong and you have the chance to fix them. Occasionally, the company just has the wrong perception and that gets adjusted. But if the policy is really wrong and it's taking advantage of customers, or somehow abusing public trust, at that point you have to make a decision.

You have to think, "Do I feel comfortable being complicit?" If you don't feel comfortable with the choices that the company is making, you need to move on.

That's a good idea just for your own sanity, as well as because you want to do right by others. In the worst-case scenario, you have to just disassociate yourself.

**Geertjan Wielenga**: This particular question is especially relevant to developer advocates because we tend to be the public face of the company, especially for developers, who are critical people. If you are on stage on a Monday morning after some decision was made over the weekend that everyone knows about, you're the one figure that anyone can actually see from that company. What do you do when the inevitable questions are put to you?

**Mark Heckler**: If you work for a much larger company than I do currently, there are likely far more opportunities for one group within your company to do something that maybe every other group in the company disagrees with.

There will be many times in those situations when you will go out on stage and you don't have an answer for difficult questions. At that point, I always believe honesty is the best policy. Your best answer could be to say, "I found out about this at the same time you did: two days ago. But you can bet I'm going to be looking into this. I want to know how it affects me, how it affects you, and how it affects those of us who are trying to just deploy better software faster."

**Geertjan Wielenga**: How do you deal with the weaker features of the tech that you promote? Do you ignore them and only focus on the strengths? If you're doing a demo and you know that there's a bug at some stage, do you skirt past it carefully?

Do you say that there's something wrong, but it will be fixed in the next release? How do you deal with these kinds of situations?

**Mark Heckler**: I'm not as polished and skilled as some people are. Usually, what I do is swerve right into the bug by accident! That said, I have, all kidding aside, literally discovered regressions in front of a crowded room. It just happens. When it comes to software, as much as you can test and have rigorous procedures in place, you're going to occasionally have something slip through.

Coming back to your strong points and weak points question, there are going to be certain things that a particular component does really well and other things that it either ignores or that are out of its scope. Maybe it's a potential future enhancement. Maybe people aren't even sure if that change really belongs in there. I usually try to point everything out that I'm aware of.

If, as developer advocates, we don't point weaknesses out, I don't think we gain credibility, but, more importantly than that, I don't think we help anybody by hiding them. We can't just think, "I hope they don't notice this until they're in too deep and they can't rewrite." That's crazy. We've all fallen into that situation completely by accident. It's not a comfortable feeling. So, you certainly don't want to have fallen into that because somebody suckered you into it.

**Geertjan Wielenga**: At the same time, you don't want to go out of your way to expose all the bugs that you're aware of. You're not going to do a tour through all the bugs of your product live on stage. How do you strike that balance?

## Honesty about bugs

**Mark Heckler**: I will say that at Pivotal, we have well-developed components that very sharp people have poured years of effort and development into. So, the rough edges aren't usually as much of a problem.

When it comes to new projects, we have Project Riff and Knative. Things like that are being spun up and created early on. In those cases, you pretty much expect there to be a few edges that poke out and surprise you. When you do run into those issues, it makes sense to just say, "If you're using this in this use case, you might want to reconsider until this particular thing gets fleshed out better."

> "I don't think you do anybody any favors by not telling them when there are gaps."
>
> —*Mark Heckler*

These projects are still in early development. Obviously, you want to put your best foot forwards, but ultimately, I don't think you do anybody any favors by not telling them when there are gaps, or particular issues that are being addressed, or issues that may not be being addressed depending on particular priorities.

**Geertjan Wielenga**: It seems to me that many people might think that being a developer advocate means knowing absolutely everything about the tech. They might be worried that if they don't know everything, there's a good chance that somebody in the audience is going to ask a question that exposes that.

The fear of being in a room of 500 people when someone asks an unexpected question can be a blocker for people who are interested in moving into developer advocacy. What's your response to that?

**Mark Heckler:** There's always the possibility that you will get asked a question that you can't answer, but then there's always that possibility in life. That could happen when you're talking to your spouse or your boss. You won't know the answer to every question, but so what? I think all of us, especially developer advocates, but really anybody in our field, get into this line of work because we're curious people. The idea that we can know everything about anything is an absolute fallacy to begin with. We don't know everything and that isn't possible, but we still like the idea of trying.

> *"If somebody asks you a question that you don't know the answer to, that's a positive."*
>
> *—Mark Heckler*

This is something that I've told my kids for years: "Today is the least informed you'll ever be. Tomorrow you'll know more than you did today and the next day you'll know more than you did the day before." That's a good thing. If somebody asks you a question that you don't know the answer to, that's a positive because it gives you a chance to learn something new and to share that.

I look at Spring and it's huge, with a vast number of components, products, and tools. Nobody could know everything about all of that. Luckily, I've got great team members.

I can say, "I don't understand this particular thing. Can you explain it to me?" We are all a team and this is truly a team sport.

**Geertjan Wielenga**: With all that in mind, then, if you're up on stage at the end of your session and someone asks a question that you don't know the answer to, what do you say?

**Mark Heckler**: I just ask them to ping me and follow up with me. I want to get them the right answer. If I know the general concept, I say, "Here's what I would do in this case, but let me get you a more specific example."

Maybe somebody is asking about securing something, but they're using a security mechanism you're not personally familiar with. You could reply, "Let me connect you with somebody who can actually answer your particular question."

**Geertjan Wielenga**: I think that often, the assumption is that if you don't know the whole answer, you don't know anything. Would you agree?

## Handling unexpected questions

**Mark Heckler**: Yes, but everybody who's been in this field for any length of time has had somebody ask a question that initially seemed to have a very easy answer. In that situation, you think that you know the answer from start to finish and you're so proud of yourself. You give the answer, then they reply, "Yeah, but we're using $X$."

You think, "Oh my gosh, I didn't know anyone was using $X$ for that!" Again, assumptions are your enemy.

You should never, even when you think you have the full answer, give your answer right away. There may be unique constraints that invalidate everything you thought you were providing of value. It's a good idea to learn more and get the full scoop before you actually prescribe something that will solve the pain area.

**Geertjan Wielenga**: Let's say that someone reading this discussion thinks that this is an interesting career path to follow. What traits or skills do they need to have?

**Mark Heckler**: You need a love of learning, you need a curiosity about how to make things do things, and you need to know how to code. I say you need to learn to code because that's my background, but, obviously, this is a broad field. So, if there's something that you particularly enjoy in this field, pursue that. Once you start down the path of enjoying something and sharing it, you're already well on the way to becoming a developer advocate. That could be either officially or unofficially in some capacity. In many cases, developer advocacy just happens as natural professional growth in our field. It's all about sharing knowledge.

**Geertjan Wielenga**: Thank you, Mark Heckler.

> *You don't have to be an absolute expert to stand up there and share what you've learned.*

# Jennifer Reif

# Introducing Jennifer Reif

Jennifer Reif is a developer relations engineer at Neo4j, as well as a speaker, blogger, and problem-solver on its behalf. She worked as a developer while studying for a master's degree, before moving into the field of developer advocacy soon after graduation. Jennifer finds ways to organize chaos within large enterprises to help them to make sense of widespread data assets, with the goal of finding an opportunity to leverage the data for maximum business value. As a conference speaker, Jennifer's inventive presentations motivate audiences to stay curious, engaged, and continuously learning. Find Jennifer on Twitter: @JMHReif.

---

**Geertjan Wielenga**: Could you start by explaining what you do?

**Jennifer Reif**: My title is "developer relations engineer" at Neo4j, a graph database company. My role encompasses getting developers familiar with the tech by making sure they know the best ways to use it and how to maximize input/output, as well as the tooling around it. If there are gaps, we will go out and build integrations, tools, or applications to ease the developers' path to accessing the functionality they need with our product.

**Geertjan Wielenga**: How did you find out about developer advocacy and how did you apply for your current role?

## Jennifer's introduction to advocacy

**Jennifer Reif**: Actually, it was when my dad, Mark Heckler, became a developer advocate at Pivotal. That was how I became familiar with what developer advocacy is. He talked about and demonstrated what he did on a daily basis.

I enjoy putting together demos and working on code, but then I also like the organizational aspect, speaking, and sharing information with other developers. So, I thought that type of role would fit really well with the things I like to do, as well as some of my strengths.

I found out that my dad was connected via Twitter with Ryan Boyd, and Neo4j had an opening for what I wanted to do. Ryan and I pinged back and forth on Twitter, then we went to Skype and Google Hangouts as part of an informal interview process. I met Ryan and talked to several members of the team I would be working on. After that, I had an official interview with some of the high-level staff. Then I got hired and I started in late February 2018.

**Geertjan Wielenga**: What observations do you have to share about what it's like to be a developer advocate?

**Jennifer Reif**: First off, you're never bored. There is a variety of things to do. This could be anything from coding to working with the community on projects, going to meetups, and connecting with people.

As a developer advocate, you're often writing tooling around the product, along with working very closely with engineering, as well as sometimes marketing.

You identify where people aren't getting the help or the onboarding that they need. Developers' feedback is used by engineering to help with building our core products.

Then, of course, you could be putting together presentations and demos, sharing the types of things you can do with these tools. You start seeing future trends and hacking those out when you ask, "What would it look like if we were to start going in this direction? How can we enhance and improve the tool this way?"

**Geertjan Wielenga**: What did you do before this? What did you study?

**Jennifer Reif**: My bachelor's degree is actually in music performance, but I took business classes too. I got a business minor with the music major. That was when I started having official programming classes.

When I began taking those classes, I realized, first of all, how much the tech field overlaps with my other interests on the creative and expressive side of things, as well as on the logical and structured side. That overlap, plus the fact that I was really enjoying programming, led me to finish with the business minor and then switch to studying computer management and information systems as a master's degree right after that.

During the master's degree, I got a position with Edward Jones Financial Investments as an enterprise developer. I worked in the financial systems at the company and got some good tasks writing scripts and working with typical enterprise processes, as well as tools.

I experienced working culture and all that great stuff that you learn with your first job out of the gate. That gave me a really good jumping point for my career.

Once I had a lot of skills under my belt—I think it was about two or three years in—I started becoming interested in speaking and presenting, and doing side projects with that. That was when I applied to speak at JavaOne. I'd gone the previous year, back in 2015, as a student, and I really enjoyed that experience. So, I submitted the following year to be a speaker and got accepted.

I submitted to some other small speaking slots when I could get time away from work. Speaking was not part of my role, so I attended all of the conferences on the side. That eventually helped me to get my new developer advocate position.

**Geertjan Wielenga**: What do you think attracts people to this type of role?

## The appeal of developer advocacy

**Jennifer Reif**: Mostly the fact that you can do a little bit of everything. There's a lot of flexibility with it; you're not limited by what has to be built into the product. In a traditional developer role, you need to build certain functionality because certain things have to be incorporated into the product for the next release.

As a developer advocate, you can build tools that, first of all, are very cool, flashy, and fun for demos. Secondly, you can build tools to help developers to integrate with different types of tech. That can be very practical stuff, as well as some hobby stuff. You can find a way to incorporate all of that.

Another positive is being able to share information with people in a variety of formats. So, you can blog, you can speak, or you can do whatever you want to publish GitHub projects. You can use social media to get the word out too, whatever your preferred platform is. You just share that information with other developers and other community people in general. By doing that, you inspire other people to do the same.

**Geertjan Wielenga**: Why do you think so few people know about this role at colleges and universities on computer science-type education programs?

**Jennifer Reif**: I think mostly that's because developer advocacy is relatively new in the grand scheme of traditional job positions. Another point is that it's a blend of not just your typical engineering-type roles, but also roles that require you to have good communication skills, writing skills, presence, and social skills.

> *"There's no degree program out there that has blended both sides of developer advocacy together."*
>
> *—Jennifer Reif*

I almost feel that because of the blend of so many university degree subjects, that makes it tricky for universities to pin course content down. You can't just focus on code, but you can't just focus on the soft skills either. You have to have a mix of skills to be good at this role. There's no degree program out there that has blended both sides of developer advocacy together. You either get the technical skills or you get the soft skills.

**Geertjan Wielenga**: I get the feeling that the demand for this role is going to increase because if it's true that every organization nowadays is an IT organization, then to a large degree, many of those organizations will need a technical person to be the public face for technical people. Do you agree?

**Jennifer Reif**: Yes, and as a developer advocate, you get exposed to many vendor tools and learn how to integrate your particular toolset with all these vendor tools. So, you also get a good handle on how to use your product in the real world. Companies don't run Neo4j, or any other product, in a silo. They have to integrate it and connect it with all these other pieces of the process.

I think this role is becoming more prevalent because we're seeing things that are very highly integrated and every company is pushing out its own IT product in a way, whether it's social media or building its own application. Companies are building their own platforms. To have somebody who's technical but can also speak to people and get the word out is going to be desirable.

**Geertjan Wielenga**: If you're at a party and you're talking to non-technical people, how do you describe what you do?

**Jennifer Reif**: I feel that I'm just now getting a good handle on talking about what I do. The description is getting much more refined as I present it to people more often. Mostly, I just tell people that I work with developers and I show them how to use Neo4j's tools.

**Geertjan Wielenga**: How do you stay up to date with the latest tech developments? Do you use particular social media platforms?

## Consuming information

**Jennifer Reif**: I do a variety of things. I keep up with Twitter; that's how I see the latest releases. People are really good about posting when there are some new updates and releases of tech out there. I read blog posts too.

We also have a community site at Neo4j where people can publish their projects and blogs. If I want to know what people are doing with Neo4j and the tooling around that, I'll visit those types of posts. We also have a weekly newsletter that goes out on key projects.

I go onto DZone and I get some daily emails from a variety of platforms too. I have certain sectors that I've picked. Obviously, I only have time to pick what looks interesting or what I know very little about.

**Geertjan Wielenga**: It does seem like drinking from a fire hose in terms of the new stuff that is constantly coming out. I think an advantage of Twitter is that you're following a large number of people after a while. Would you say that from those people, what comes through is probably worth investigating?

**Jennifer Reif**: Yes, there are certain people who float to your main feed more often because you follow them. Perhaps, hopefully, they follow you as well.

It's usually very concise bits of information because Twitter is a very short-message style. Then there are links to where you can go to find out more. I just keep up with my daily feed and Twitter is very easy to keep track of in that way.

**Geertjan Wielenga**: Do you travel frequently for your job?

**Jennifer Reif**: I work from home—I'm remote out of the St. Louis area in the Midwest—but last year, I traveled quite a bit. That's one thing that's actually unique to this role, at least for my company: you can travel frequently or you can work remotely.

> *"If I have to be the expert and present this material to people, I'm more likely to learn much faster."*
>
> *—Jennifer Reif*

Last year, because I was trying to really dive in hard and get to know the product, the community, the toolsets, and the vendors we work with, I did a lot of speaking engagements. If I have to be the expert and present this material to people, I'm more likely to learn much faster.

I went all over the U.S., as well as some places in Europe last year. This year, I'm looking at presenting to some different conferences, but I'm also hoping to section out some time and really dive into some specific projects.

**Geertjan Wielenga**: Do you have any stories around jet lag, missing your flights, and things like that?

**Jennifer Reif**: I haven't been in a situation yet, knock on wood, where I've missed a presentation because of a flight. However, I've been in several situations where I've had delayed flights when I've needed to be in a particular city that evening for a dinner. I've ended up missing dinners.

I did miss one flight when I was coming back from a conference. There wasn't any major pressure to be somewhere, but I landed in Denver late. The airport is very spread out, so you're running from one end of the terminal to the other end of the terminal to catch your flight. I missed my flight to get home. I just had to rebook that evening. But fortunately, I haven't had anything where I've missed any speaking engagements.

I have had times of stress. Sometimes, I want to practice my presentation but I'm going through the slides on a flight and I can't really give it out loud. Sometimes I stay up extra late to walk through my talk when I get to the hotel.

**Geertjan Wielenga**: Can you describe what an average day is like, or is there no average day for you?

## Jennifer's average day

**Jennifer Reif**: I'm still discovering what average is, but often I get home and start to figure out a particular application or demo that I'm going to be doing for the next presentation.

I spin up a new instance, pump some data into it, start writing queries, and figure out what's interesting, and what I'm trying to get out of this data.

I think, "What would people find interesting about this? Are there some other things that I can do as well? Can I add plugins? Can I run algorithms on this data? Can I pipe in a vendor integration to pipe this information out to a visualization or to another analysis tool of some sort?"

Next, I start putting together a presentation. I usually have a little bit of intro, then I walk through the meat of the technical information, and finally, I give some sort of demo, wrapping up the wow factor there at the end.

The week before I go out of town and present, I start rehearsing and walking through the presentation. The first couple of days that I do that, it's typical for me to go back and tweak slides. Sometimes I change my demo and add a couple of extra commands or fix things that don't look right. Then, I push that demo out to the GitHub repo.

When I do fly out to the location, I present and meet up with people at the conference. I try to attend other sessions as well. Finally, I come back home and do it all over again.

**Geertjan Wielenga**: What are you judged on by your management in your role?

**Jennifer Reif**: We have high-level metrics for the year. I think we're going to start looking at smaller, quarterly results, just so they are a little bit easier to measure. The tricky thing with developer relations is that we're not focused on a sales number or how many people saw this post.

> *"It's difficult to measure what developer advocates do in hard numbers."*
>
> —*Jennifer Reif*

We're really judged on getting developers involved, how we've improved developers' lives, and their experience with the product. It's difficult to measure what developer advocates do in hard numbers, but most of it is just around asking, "How many people are getting access to the tool? How easy is our onboarding process? Are there good training materials out there? Do we have some sandbox instances out there with different datasets that we've created?"

**Geertjan Wielenga**: When you're up on the stage somewhere, you're basically talking about Neo4j, then?

**Jennifer Reif**: Typically, yes. My goal for this year is to go a little bit broader and deeper, and start looking at the internals, how graph databases differ from other types of databases, or how Java interacts with this database in a way that's different from that database. Right now, I'm very specific about the Neo4j tooling, but I'd like to get a broader perspective as well.

**Geertjan Wielenga**: If you're up on the stage, you're essentially, even though it's in as technical and as authentic a way as possible, pitching a product from a company versus someone else who doesn't work for a particular company just talking about various projects that appeal to them.

They're not paid for it, whereas you're paid to present your Neo4j perspective. Do you see any ethical conflict to that?

## Ethical considerations

**Jennifer Reif**: I think it's my role to show what is best practice and show code examples. Other people can get up on stage and present Neo4j as a product, but I'm really showing users what the tool was designed to do. Much of the time, as speakers, we've built these integrations ourselves. Therefore, that often makes us the experts on how the code works. This aspect gives us a leg up when we're speaking.

As far as ethics go, we want people to learn this stuff. We want people to be able to build projects and capabilities with the tools. Our goal is to show people what can be done.

**Geertjan Wielenga**: If there's a bug in the product and you're up on the stage, do you skirt around that bug in your demo? Obviously, you're not going to go and highlight all the bugs in the product. What is the middle ground there? How do you handle that situation?

**Jennifer Reif**: I think that's where you go back to thinking about what the product was designed to do. However, every particular product out there is going to have its ups and downs and its strengths and weaknesses.

In fact, I actually came across something last year where something in our browser didn't show up quite right. It didn't scale when I wanted to maximize and minimize. I just had to say that there was a bug and I needed to talk to engineering about getting that fixed. You just roll with it.

Of course, if somebody asks a question about a weakness in an area, you can say, "There may be other products that do this better or provide more capability here, but we feel that we provide this other aspect and this is really what we wanted to focus on." It's not an us versus them deal. This is an open-source community and open-source product, so it's really about what we feel is important to build and to improve.

**Geertjan Wielenga**: If you're doing a presentation and it gets to question time, and someone asks a question that you simply don't know the answer to, what do you do?

**Jennifer Reif**: I've been there a lot. Being in a new position, I've had that come up quite a bit. There's been a couple of occasions when I've had an expert in the room and then I've just packed up and said, "I have this person who actually is an expert on this topic that you're asking about; maybe he/she can comment on this better." If I do know something about the topic, or at least its basic structure, I will usually say what I know.

> *"I hate not being able to help somebody at a talk."*
>
> *—Jennifer Reif*

I can recommend good resources. Occasionally, I will make a note of the question and reply, "I'm not sure about this, but let me contact one of the experts in our team and see if I can get that answered for you." It really just depends on the question and what kind of level I think I can attack it at. I hate not being able to help somebody at a talk because obviously they've come all that way and they've sat through it. They want to know the answers to their questions too.

If I get asked a question, it could be something I will get asked in the future or some logic I can use when I'm coding or working with something. So, it's a learning experience for me as well.

**Geertjan Wielenga**: If you're a developer working in a company, what might hold you back from doing this kind of work? Is there a feeling that you would need to know everything about a particular topic before being comfortable standing up on a stage and talking about it? What would you say in response to that kind of concern?

**Jennifer Reif**: Nobody's ever going to know everything. I think that whether you're a developer in a small local business or a developer in a massive global enterprise, or a developer in a start-up out of San Francisco, you're not going to know everything.

The best you can do is just try to tackle what you do know, do research, and help as much as you can. When you get confronted with these questions, you do have a good response available of not being sure and needing to read up on something. You shouldn't be afraid that you'll look silly or it will appear that you have a lack of knowledge. More important is whether or not you are actually willing to dive in and learn new information. It can be very daunting, but you have to be willing to just constantly learn.

**Geertjan Wielenga**: I think it would be a logical thing for someone who goes to a conference just as an attendee to notice that what someone on the stage is saying is not the most advanced, complex content, although sometimes it is. Would you say that often it's the kind of information that any generic developer could potentially be sharing?

**Jennifer Reif**: Yes, you don't have to be an absolute expert to stand up there and share what you've learned. That's really all it is: you're just sharing what you've learned. That doesn't mean you know it all. You have to remember that you're not the expert presenting to or lecturing students.

**Geertjan Wielenga**: Do you think you need to be an extrovert to stand up on the stage and speak to a group of people?

## Being an introvert

**Jennifer Reif**: No, I'm actually not an extrovert. I do alright, having gone through school and given presentations in class. I'm comfortable with it, but I still get nervous. I still practice, practice, and practice before I go on stage. Once I finish speaking, then I want some time to myself. That's when I go back home to my remote location and work by myself. I think it's about balance.

**Geertjan Wielenga**: Even though there may be a big crowd of people sitting there, sometimes you don't even see them because of the bright lights. Would you say that speaking can be an ideal role for an introvert in that sense?

**Jennifer Reif**: Yes, it can feel as if you're talking to a blank wall with nobody there. You just have to imagine the people in the audience aren't sitting there.

**Geertjan Wielenga**: The only problem is that you have these people sitting there looking at you very critically sometimes, which can be daunting. How does the preparation work that you do, especially being new to it all, help with nerves?

**Jennifer Reif**: I do go through and shape the talk. I think this is something that I carried over from my musical background. As a musician, you practice really hard and you spend several hours a day refining your performance until it's easy and comfortable. I take that same approach with presentations. I prepare weeks in advance, as much as I can. I walk through my talk in my office at home to get a feel for whether I have enough content or too much content and I need to trim it down.

When I get up on the morning of the talk, I'm typically still getting a feel for whether I should rehearse again or walk in cold. I've found that just getting up early and running through a few things, even if I'm not going through the whole presentation, helps me to get into the groove. I bring that information out of back storage memory when I'm on stage.

I worried at first that practicing the morning of a talk would take the fire and the energy out of it if I had to do it again that same day, but I've found that if you practice up until the very last second, it just resolidifies all that information.

**Geertjan Wielenga**: How often do you do the same presentation again? It sounds like you've done a number of different presentations.

**Jennifer Reif**: Yes, last year included a lot of new talks. I think I might have had one or possibly two repeats, but there was very little repeated information. I'm just getting a feel for new content. There was one session that I presented very early on in the year, then I came back to it and did it again last summer. I was able to refresh that information.

But even in that case, the week before, I went through that presentation and made sure everything was still smooth. I checked there hadn't been any updates to break anything in the code or demos.

**Geertjan Wielenga**: Have you ever been in the situation where a technical glitch of some kind happened?

## Managing technical failures

**Jennifer Reif**: Yes, especially as I'm still relatively new to the presentation and demo activities. A venue that I had one time came with an A/V guy, who had a downstage monitor as well. I was working with my laptop monitor, the screen behind me, and then the downstage monitor.

I was trying to get that to flow, going from presentation mode to demo mode. I had to use a separate display to have my presentation notes up. Then I had to switch and mirror the display to throw my demo up there without having to look at one screen and type. That made me a little nervous, but it was fine.

I had another presentation where there was some trouble getting the visual up. It was just me waiting and trying to figure out how to keep people occupied, while trying to monitor what was going on. I gave an introduction and asked a couple of questions about the audience's background, to just get the room engaged while everything was being worked on in the background.

Another time, I did a half-day training session for our big conference in New York City. Our internet was having issues, which was a major problem. What we ended up doing was getting people to download the software, so they could actually do some hands-on exercises later on in the training session.

> *"Even though you've practiced and rehearsed, you have to be flexible and willing to switch things up if needed."*
>
> —*Jennifer Reif*

I had a copresenter with that one and I had her start by presenting the intro material, the theory, and how it all worked together. While that was happening, me and two other people worked through the room and helped to make sure that everyone's environments were ready to go. In the end, that worked really well. I think it's about always being ready to be flexible. Even though you've practiced and rehearsed, you have to be flexible and willing to switch things up if needed.

**Geertjan Wielenga**: What would you say are the downsides, if there are any, to working in developer advocacy?

**Jennifer Reif**: It depends on the person, I think. If you're not a person who enjoys constantly being on the go, there can be a lot of travel involved. There can also be a constant flow of tasks: anything from publishing a blog post or updating a repo to booking your travel for two months down the line. That is one of those boring admin tasks. There's very little standing still and not doing much. You just have to segment your time and decide what you feel is the highest priority or most urgent.

**Geertjan Wielenga**: Where do you see your role developing in the next 10 years? Do you see yourself doing this for a really long time?

**Jennifer Reif**: Yes, that's my hope. I'm enjoying and thriving in this role, so I would like that to continue. My goal is to become an expert in this area of tech.

I want to start building more integrations and become more involved with working with the product. I hope to understand more about the internals and the guts of how our product is put together. The aim is to become as technical as I possibly can.

**Geertjan Wielenga**: What advice does your father give to you about your current role and future career? Do you see his path as something you want to emulate?

**Jennifer Reif**: From the beginning, he's always told me that a good developer advocate can add a lot of value to a company, as well as to the developer community (whether that is a company's community or broader than that).

A person can be a good developer or a good speaker, but it's not easy to tackle both successfully. Trying to blend and accomplish both facets is what makes the job hard, but it's also extremely rewarding when you succeed. The best things in life are never easy, so if you take on the challenge, you should give it your all.

> *"Staying afloat in this industry requires quite a bit of learning."*
>
> —*Jennifer Reif*

Staying afloat in this industry requires quite a bit of learning. My dad always says to never stop learning and experimenting because it's the best way to succeed at anything. It's easy to feel overwhelmed and like you won't possibly be able to catch up in tech, but each time you learn something new, it only encourages you to tackle the next goal.

On whether his path is something I want to emulate, at a high level, absolutely it is. On a detailed level, each of us faces different obstacles and opportunities that provide unique paths for every individual. In some ways, I've already followed certain steps that my dad took. We both worked as enterprise developers, started speaking at conferences, then ended up as developer advocates for start-ups. Even if we both were faced with all of the same choices, though, we would probably make different decisions. My goal isn't to match each of his steps but to apply to my career what inspires me the most from his career, as well as to avoid any pitfalls that he warns me about!

Another angle is emulating those high-level achievements. My dad has been an important and positive influence and a great source of my current knowledge in tech and other areas. Being an expert in the field, always striving to learn, experimenting, and asking questions are all goals he's accomplished and I want to reach.

He has built engagement and respect extremely quickly at a global level, which has only been gained from his high self-motivation and skill. My dad's contagious excitement about tech and the engagement he pulls from an audience, as well as the buzz he inspires in the developer community, definitely encourages me to do the same. He achieves whatever he chooses (typically with flying colors) and inspires others to be and do their best, and that's something worth accomplishing, not just for me as his daughter, but for any developer.

**Geertjan Wielenga**: What are you most passionate about at the moment in relation to your product and what you're learning at your company?

**Jennifer Reif**: I love the fact that Neo4j has found a way to combine our product and our business with having such a great ecosystem around it. We have a really active, involved developer community that contributes to our toolsets and our main projects. But then, I also feel that my team especially has developed a ton of really nice integrations to go with all these different toolsets and vendors. We have some good partners, we have a great developer community, and we've built some really cool tools.

As I said earlier, you're not using a graph database in a silo: you're using it with a variety of other tools to maximize the value you can get out of it. That's what I've found to be intriguing about my company and our ecosystem as a whole. That makes it really fun and exciting to contribute because you have a variety of people, not just from Neo4j, but all over the world, who are contributing and showing you how you can do other cool things with the product.

**Geertjan Wielenga**: If somebody in their 20s is interested in developer advocacy, what is your advice to them on how to get started?

## Jennifer's tips for young people

**Jennifer Reif**: I think you need a combination of skills, going back to how developer relations touches many different aspects. You need to know the particular tech that interests you in depth. You need to be able to write applications and understand the internals.

Then, you need to be able to commit to projects and open-source work, where you're providing feedback or you're sharing. Basically, you need to have a technical presence to get a job in this field, whether that's GitHub, writing side projects and then publishing them, being active on Twitter, or however you get that word out there that you're a contributing resource to code.

A good idea is to connect with people. If you have an opportunity to go to a conference or to connect with other technical resources in some way, shape, or form, then take it. Places like local meetups are where you really start making connections and hearing about these types of job openings. At a meetup, you could be asked to speak on a topic. If you are interested in standing up to speak, take that opportunity.

> *"You need to be a code contributor and then get a resume built of places you've spoken at, people you've connected with, or projects you've worked on."*
>
> —*Jennifer Reif*

If you want to get your name out there, you can get a recording of you giving a talk and post that to YouTube. Many times, when you're submitting proposals for conferences, the organizers will ask you for any recorded materials or slide decks that they can have as references. If there's anything you can provide to back up your profile, that helps. You need to be a code contributor and then get a resume built of places you've spoken at, people you've connected with, or projects you've worked on.

**Geertjan Wielenga**: Do you have anything else you want to add about being a developer advocate?

**Jennifer Reif**: Just that this is a fun, exciting, and constantly encouraging field to be in. There's no limit on the amount you can do or what you can do. There's a lot of flexibility with this type of position. There are all the extra benefits of getting to travel, working from home, and the flexible schedule that's on offer. In whatever way you want to define it, this is a dream job.

**Geertjan Wielenga**: Thank you, Jennifer Reif.

## 14

> *If I can inspire just one other person, I think my purpose in this industry will be fulfilled.*

# Venkat Subramaniam

# Introducing Venkat Subramaniam

Dr. Venkat Subramaniam is the founder of Agile Developer, Inc., an award-winning author, the creator of `agilelearner.com`, and an instructional professor at the University of Houston. He has trained and mentored thousands of software developers across the U.S., Canada, Europe, and Asia, and is also an invited speaker at international conferences. Venkat is routinely named as a source of inspiration by many of the world's most successful development advocates. Find Venkat on Twitter: `@venkat_s`.

---

**Geertjan Wielenga**: Would you agree that developer advocacy is something that isn't commonly spoken about at universities and colleges and in educational settings?

## Developer advocacy and students

**Venkat Subramaniam**: I would say that even outside of education, developer advocacy isn't well known. I spent years after college as a working professional, and even though it's fair to say that I started working before the time of the internet and browsers, developer advocacy wasn't talked about. Maybe today it's much more prevalent in the industry.

I think we need a lot more integration of what's happening in the industry with the academic world. Students are not generally aware of job roles in the industry once they graduate. They don't know that it's possible to inspire and influence developers.

**Geertjan Wielenga**: You've been mentioned by several of the other interviewees as being someone who inspires them, but what was your own path to where you are now?

**Venkat Subramaniam**: It was a thoroughly interesting journey. A few decades ago, I was on a student visa and finishing up my Ph.D. at the University of Houston. The visa meant that I could do practical training, where you could take up a job while you were studying. That gave me one year prior to finishing my Ph.D. and one year after to work.

I actually had a really strong interest in teaching. When I went to the immigration office at the university, they looked surprised and said, "You need permission to work outside, but you don't need permission to work inside the university. You could work in the industry and teach here in the evenings."

I had a passion for teaching because when I was in the Ph.D. program, I taught a course on C++ for a few years, and I wanted to continue doing that. I followed the suggestion from the university. Once I graduated and started working in the industry, I continued to teach at the University of Houston, this time as a lecturer rather than a teaching assistant.

> *"You can't just decide tomorrow that you want to be a public speaker and then expect results the next day."*
>
> *—Venkat Subramaniam*

Along the way, I got really excited about continuing to speak, learn, and influence. I had an opportunity to speak at a Java User Group and a .NET User Group. After that, I made it a point to speak at them both at least once a year.

I did that for about five years and the reason I mention that is that this is one of the things that aspiring speakers tend to forget: it's a journey. You have to invest in it. You can't just decide tomorrow that you want to be a public speaker and then expect results the next day. It took me years of speaking at user groups.

**Geertjan Wielenga**: What was your big break?

**Venkat Subramaniam**: Hard work met with good luck and I happened to be speaking at the Java User Group in Houston. Due to a complete scheduling error, the organizers had put the wrong date on the calendar. They said, "Oh, we made a mistake, but we're still going to give you the chance to speak."

I went to speak on a different day and that's when a gentleman named Jay Zimmerman had come to promote a new conference that he was starting. In the conference, he had people like Dave Thomas, author of *The Pragmatic Programmer*; Bruce Tate, author of *Bitter Java* and *Bitter EJB*; James Duncan Davidson, the person who pretty much wrote Tomcat and Ant; and Jason Hunter, the gentleman behind the servlet API. Those were the speakers.

After my talk, I was getting my things together and Mr. Zimmerman came over and said, "Hey, good talk. Would you like to come and speak at our conference?" Honestly, I really thought he was kidding because the names I mentioned could not be compared to somebody who had never spoken at a conference, never written a book, and who wasn't known outside of my community. However, I got home that night and I saw an email from him saying that he just wanted me to take the same talk that I had given that day and try it out at his conference.

I went to speak at the conference and for my first talk, there were 11 people in the room. That was a very humbling experience. At the end of the conference, I went to Mr. Zimmerman and he had in his hand a rolled-up piece of paper with all the evaluations on it from the conference. He said, "These are the worst evaluations I've ever seen!"

I thought, "Okay, well there goes my opportunity to speak!" I thanked him anyway and went back to my car to look at the evaluations. On a scale of one to five, with five being the best, almost all 11 people scored me a five. That's when I knew that he had pulled my leg!

The next day, Mr. Zimmerman emailed me and asked, "Would you like to come and speak in Chicago?" In my first year, I spoke in three cities; in the second year, I spoke in 10 cities; and now, it's history. I'm the longest-speaking member at the conference, almost 20 years into it. That's the way the journey started.

**Geertjan Wielenga:** You travel constantly and you're constantly at conferences, drawing in big crowds. You're always talking about cutting-edge developments and how to grapple with those developments in a sensible way. What continues to excite you about speaking?

**Venkat's motivation**

**Venkat Subramaniam:** I'm pretty loyal to user groups and on average, I speak at 15 user groups every single year, even today. I feel that this is part of me giving back to the community and my loyalty to the user groups is because that's where I started.

I am here because so many people inspired me when I was young, and after that as well. If I can inspire just one other person, I think my purpose in this industry will be fulfilled. I think that it's important for students to know that as a child, I had learning disabilities. I was a failure in school. A lot of people, when I say this, laugh and think I'm kidding. Students should know that your education and your ability to do well in school is something that you can turn around.

It took me a while to realize that I really hated studying, but I loved learning. This was a remarkable realization on my part because studying is boring. You have to sit there and read stuff you don't care about because the teacher wants you to read it. Once I got to a certain point in my education, there were things that truly started to intrigue me and it was no longer studying: it was learning.

I remember being in college and the people who knew me in school looked at me and said, "No, this can't be true! You were the dumbest guy in the class and now you're one of the top students. How can this possibly happen?" The answer to that is that this stuff is fun.

Mathematics blew my mind and maybe I was just becoming more mature, but I truly got drawn into physics and science too. Once I started getting curious about topics, I realized that I was absolutely drawn into learning. Learning, to me, is like peeling an onion because you peel a layer and you think you've got it, and then you come back after a few days and you realize there are more layers to peel. Just like when we peel onions and we begin to cry, it can be really frustrating working in the field of programming.

One thing that excites me is when things don't work. When something doesn't work, it's awesome because that's when the learning really happens. I'm more than 50 years old, but if you asked me how old I feel, I feel as young as I was on the first day at school because there's no age to being a learner. As a man or a woman, you have an age, but as a learner, you have no age because you continue to learn every single day.

Another thing that excites me about speaking is that, as Richard Feynman said, if you can't teach something to a first-year student, you haven't really understood it. That is so true because you can't teach what you don't understand. When I started teaching, I really began to hit the limitations of what I knew.

> *"I actually don't think there are complex concepts; I only believe that there are concepts that are not explained well."*
>
> —*Venkat Subramaniam*

When I started learning things, I felt very stupid. Sometimes, complex expressions made me feel stupid. I actually don't think there are complex concepts; I only believe that there are concepts that are not explained well. One of my goals is to take ideas and make them approachable. To me, that is the key. These are the real things that inspire me: the thirst to learn, the thirst to peel those layers of that metaphorical onion, and the thirst to be able to help somebody else to take the journey as well.

**Geertjan Wielenga**: What keeps you interested in teaching at a university?

**Venkat Subramaniam**: I'm still a faculty member at the University of Houston and for that I'm very thankful. About 11 years ago, I left Houston and I moved to Colorado. Six months later, I got an email from the university.

I had resigned when I moved away from Houston, so for six months I was not teaching. The email said, "We had a faculty meeting yesterday and we rescinded your resignation. We want you to come back and teach again."

I replied, "I'm not moving back to Houston."

The university said, "We don't care where in the world you are; all we want you to do is to continue to teach at the university." So, for the past 11 years, I've been teaching remotely. Part of the reason I do that is, as we mentioned earlier, there is a sense of how disconnected students are. I want to do something about that.

> *"I can't change the world, but I can change the small part of the world that I'm exposed to."*
>
> —*Venkat Subramaniam*

I know I can't change the world, but I can change the small part of the world that I'm exposed to. That is part of the reason why I continue to work in the industry and teach at the university also. When I work with my clients, I work on real projects.

I learn about the intricacies of developing software and the challenges that every developer faces. Part of that understanding helps me to go back and teach. I teach at the university, but I also make it a mission to go and teach in corporations.

One experience that I will never forget happened when I was working for an engineering company during the day and teaching in the evening. I was teaching C++ to my students. I was programming in the language during the day for commercial software and then teaching the same stuff at the university.

I would take things from work (without, of course, revealing any work-related proprietary things) and I would teach stuff that my students could actually use. Rather than teaching the theory of the language, I was teaching how to practically use C++ to develop commercial software. What I learned early on is the value of applying the ideas we learn from the industry into the classroom because you're teaching something that is relevant.

One day, we had a crisis call from one of our teams in California. The engineers were making a copy of the model we had created to make some enhancements, but something had gone terribly wrong. We had data corruption and it was a disaster.

This was mission critical. We spent time debugging at work until it got to 4:30 p.m. I had a class starting at 5:30 p.m. I apologized to my team, saying, "Sorry, you've got to continue on this. I've got to go and teach a class at the university, but when I finish my class, I'll continue working on it." Right in the middle of my class, I remember pausing and thinking, "Oh, my goodness! I know the reason we're having the problem at work!"

**Geertjan Wielenga**: What do you think solved that for you?

**Venkat Subramaniam**: I solved it by detaching from the problem. As soon as I finished my class, I ran over to the phone, called my supervisor, and said, "I figured this out while teaching. Here's the reason why it's failing." He looked at the code and he agreed with me. The next thing was to call the developers. We had literally thousands of classes in our system. An immediate call went to all the developers to take 100 classes each. We plowed through the night fixing it.

## Solving a problem

That experience made me realize that this works so much in tandem: I do pair programming with my colleagues in the industry continuously, at every opportunity I get, because the only way I can be effective in teaching is by learning from the industry. I continue to teach because the only way to be really effective in my work is to take the time to continuously learn.

What's the point in learning something if you can't apply it? Much of the time, in a work environment, we're firing through all these problems and struggling to solve immediate concerns. Teaching gives you an opportunity to step back a little bit and say, "While this works, let's also look at these other things that are useful." You never know when those other things will actually turn into something you can apply to that very project.

Whenever I hear somebody say that universities are detached from reality, I always end the discussion by saying, "Thanks for identifying the problem. What are you going to do about it?" I encourage them to go and teach at a university.

I remember when I worked in the industry from 7:00 a.m. to 4:30 p.m. and then I would go to the university. At 7:00 p.m., I would finish my class, but then students would come to me with their questions. I'm not even kidding, there were times when I was at the university at 10:00 p.m., still talking to the students because they wanted to talk. They wanted to talk about tech, life in general, being in the industry, and problems they had to get through.

I was getting peanuts as my salary and if I totaled the amount of time that I was spending at the university, I was literally making less than the minimum wage. Yet my work was so rewarding because to me, the value of teaching is not in the money I take home: the value is in the impact I have on society. One of the things that we tend to forget is that if one person is able to get a really good education and a job because of that, it's not just a personal gain for that person. You're making an economic difference for not just a family, but potentially a generation of people.

> *"Education truly is that one thing that can make a big difference in the world."*
>
> —*Venkat Subramaniam*

I got a fairly good education through very hard work, but because of the investment I put in, my family is doing really well today. I have children who are able to afford a good education. I can definitely say that I'm capable of pulling my own family out of poverty.

If we can help at least a few other people to do that for themselves, then I think that's a really good way to end economic disparity because education truly is that one thing that can make a big difference in the world.

I'm not saying this to boast, but when I go to speak at conferences and user groups, I can't tell you how many times people come up to me and say, "Your talk really changed the way I look at programming."

I'm here today because other people inspired me and it's only logical for me to turn around and give back. You can't be a person in this industry and just program, and then call it done. You also can't teach, whether it's in the industry or at a university, and call it done. I think it's a combination of the two that is absolutely critical.

**Geertjan Wielenga**: This meaningful aspect of what we do as developer advocates can be very difficult to see for people outside of the area in which we work. We're passing on knowledge, rather than just programming. We're inspiring people, we're influencing people, and we're contributing. Would you say that this aspect is hidden from the outside world?

**Venkat Subramaniam**: Yes, and this is something that we should continue to really bring out because the next generation of developers can be so much better if they can learn from our mistakes. I would argue that it is the professional responsibility of every one of us to contribute to the industry's growth in the future.

**Geertjan Wielenga**: With developer advocacy, there isn't a narrow focus: we can branch out and do a whole range of other activities aside from programming, supported by social media and other developments from the past few years. Could you have imagined 30 years ago that this variety of loose, flexible outflows from a central role would exist?

## The importance of user groups

**Venkat Subramaniam**: No, but I remember being part of user groups, even back then. User groups were really the way to bring a community of developers together. The word "symposium" originated from geeks getting together and socializing. There is evidence of Einstein and Planck holding symposiums. People have been doing this for centuries.

I remember as a young programmer going to user groups. When I see my students, I say, "I know you're focused on your studies right now. Your assignment that's due next week seems so much more important, but in the long run, your career is going to be better because of the time you spend at user groups."

Of course, we now have Twitter and Facebook, and other social media channels, but I think that face-to-face interaction is still incredibly valuable. I can't tell you how refreshing it is to go to a user group meeting to hang out with fellow developers.

I say this with utmost humbleness, but today, because I travel so much around the world, it is really hard for me to maintain good friendships with people. I'm not home over the weekends and I'm not home at all for long periods of time. If somebody calls me to get together, I have to tell them that I'm not home. You kind of lose friends over time because of that.

The people who I call friends today are the people who I have met at user groups over the years. In my own local community, those are the people I reach out to.

I remember going back to Houston to give a talk earlier this year. Right in the front seat was a gentleman. He interrupted me in my talk to ask me a question. I paused and I said, "You're as annoying today as you were 25 years ago, and I love you for that!"

> *"This is one of the most important things: be part of the community."*
>
> —*Venkat Subramaniam*

These are the moments I will never forget because 25 years ago, that man was the same as he is today: argumentative, interested, curious, and keen on going further into a topic. It was so refreshing to see him in the front seat. This is one of the most important things: be part of the community.

Contributing to open source is good, but the word "contributing" is a very flexible word. You don't have to be the person writing code all the time. Honestly, I don't write code for open source, but I'm hoping that I still have a contribution to make. I critique the tools I'm using, I speak about open-source products, I inspire other people, I point out bugs in the code, and so on. You can be part of a community in any way you want to be, but the key is to be part of that community. Your activities will be determined based on your passions. Who am I to tell you, or anyone, how you should do things? That's for you to figure out.

Networking is extremely important for developer advocates. Many times, I have walked into a company and somebody has come to me and said, "I saw you at that user group three years ago. When they mentioned your name and they wanted to bring you over, I was all in support of that." When you are applying for a job or trying to seek help in the industry, one of the things people forget is that it's not who you know that matters: it's who knows you.

Being part of the community, going to the user groups, and participating is a way to really get your name out in the community. I'm not suggesting this as a way of manipulating, but I'm saying that this is a way of being effective. We are here to further ourselves in our career, while helping other people. By networking, I think we have a lot to gain.

I can tell you that of all the developers that are out there, only a small percentage actually go to user groups regularly. Whether you're a student or colleague in the industry, going to user groups is something we all need to do.

**Geertjan Wielenga**: I'm also involved in a similar role to you at a university and when students come back from internships, the main problem tends to be that they have run into a problem, but they didn't have enough maturity, courage, or insight to ask somebody to help them. Often, they haven't developed the soft skills that are also needed in the programming field. Do you think that user groups could be leveraged to help students in this way?

**Venkat Subramaniam**: Yes, I do. As an example, I had a student at the university who was supposed to work on something alongside me.

I had set up a version control so we could work together remotely.

I gave her the URL for the version control, told her to access it, and asked her to check her initial work into it. I would then review it and give feedback. A week went by and I was getting a little nervous and frustrated because I hadn't heard from the student. I offered her help but didn't hear anything. Things didn't move. Finally, I suggested that we walk through the task on Skype. I asked to see what she had done so far. There was a pause and then she said, "I don't know how to use the version control."

I replied, "In five minutes, I can show you how to use it. We didn't need two weeks to figure this out." Within a matter of a day, she was able to produce so much work.

I sat back and I thought, "What have we done as an industry? The environment we have created has placed people in a position where they are embarrassed and humiliated to ask for help." If I'm sitting in a corner and I don't know how to do things, but I'm not going to come and ask you for help, it's not entirely that I don't want to ask for help: it's probably because somebody before you called me stupid for asking for help.

When I'm teaching my classes, they are probably the worst classes a student can take at the university. They have very little theory, so my students learn by doing. I do code reviews from 4:00 a.m. to 7:00 a.m. local time every single day when the semester is on. Not many students want to take my course because it is the most difficult course they could ever imagine.

I always suggest the next set of things the students need to do to move forward. Initially, my comments to them are to delete everything and start over.

The students are often in denial, asking, "Are you kidding me? I've written code for three years and you're telling me I have to delete everything and start over?"

> *"As people who are experienced, we should look out because we're the loudmouths. There are so many people who don't have a voice."*
>
> —*Venkat Subramaniam*

When students can learn by doing, they have the courage to take feedback. Students have to break that ice and they have to seek help more proactively. As people who are experienced, we should look out because we're the loudmouths. There are so many people who don't have a voice. How can we remove all these social barriers we have worked so hard to create over the past few decades, and how can we really help another person to open up and ask for help? Today's ignorance is tomorrow's excellence.

## The fear of not knowing enough

**Geertjan Wielenga**: Let's shift this slightly to public speaking, where the situation is similar: people tend to think they need to know everything about a particular topic before they can go and speak about it. What is your advice on that?

**Venkat Subramaniam**: I think that there is another flaw: people think that they need to tell everything as well as know everything. That is the quality of a really poor talk, in my opinion.

One night I saw an email come through saying, "Dammit! I'm still here in the middle of the night, working on the example you gave because this is so intriguing. I've gone on to dig so much deeper and I've gone so much further into this topic. I'm just writing to let you know that you inspired me to learn." Sometimes, you just need to light that fire in someone's mind. You don't need to know everything and you don't need to convey everything.

When I go to conferences and speak, someone in the audience often is the person who wrote this particular language, library, API, or tool that is the topic of my talk. I could ask myself a question: "What qualification do I have to talk about this when the very person who wrote it is right here in the room?"

The answer to that question is: that person can never take away from me my story, my learning, and my experience. I'm never trying to pretend that I know everything. But I'm also genuinely going to say what my learning was. I may not be correct about my understanding of a language, a library, or a tool, but I can never be wrong about my learning because that's my journey and my experience.

For beginners, again user groups are a great place. You're not required to deliver with the intimidation of a conference. User groups are like a family. Even today, I tease out some ideas in user groups before I give a talk to a conference. When my talk is over, there are people who are genuinely interested in staying around for even an hour to argue about and discuss concepts. There's immense learning that I can get from this. Whether it turns into a book, a blog post, or a talk, it's been valuable to get that feedback. Any opportunity to speak in smaller groups is an opportunity for you to get better.

**Geertjan Wielenga**: Do you have any tips for new speakers who lack the confidence to make that jump to conferences?

**Venkat Subramaniam**: Conference organizers are often in a predicament because people pay money and invest time to come to conferences, so it's very critical for them to have talks that actually deliver results. At the same time, many conferences ask a few new speakers to come and give short talks. They can give lightning talks and they can grow from there. A number of conferences are also organizing workshops for new speakers to become better speakers.

There's one more thing I would recommend: you can do a joint talk. It doesn't have to be too formal. When I do keynotes at conferences, I sometimes ask a random person to come and join me. This person comes up on stage and as I'm talking, I direct questions to them and ask for their opinion. It's stage fear for them as much as it's stage fear for me. Afterward, they say, "That was awesome to be up on the stage with you, but I was a nervous wreck."

> *"There is nothing special about us that means we can be on the stage; anyone can be up there."*
>
> —*Venkat Subramaniam*

I reply, "You know what? I'm a nervous wreck too; it's just that I've done it so many times." There's nothing special about us that means we can be on the stage; anyone can be up there. I still have that fear; I stand up and my throat dries up.

I was giving a keynote at Jfokus a few years ago and this lady came up to put the microphone on me. As she was putting the microphone on my shirt, she noticed my heavy breathing, and she said, "Looks like you're nervous! Is this your first talk?" I replied, "No, this is my 10,000th talk! I'm nervous every single time." We never remove the nervousness, but we learn to manage it.

My friends know what a terrible critic I am. I will either email or direct message them to say, "I saw you do this and I don't like it. I don't agree with it." Part of the reason I do this is because they're my friends and I want my friends to be doing well, but I also expect them to do the same thing for me. When authors of a language email me, which does happen because I've earned some of their friendship and acquaintance over the years, I'm so happy that they're able to correct me and I'm able to improve.

The rule that I follow is very simple: you should praise people publicly and critique them privately. When I attend any talk, I quietly take notes. I only give feedback when speakers ask for it. One of the things I've learned in my life is to never give unsolicited advice to another speaker. Not everybody comes to you and asks for help. You can mentor a particular speaker if the speaker has the potential to turn into a reputable speaker. I think we can collectively, as an industry, do so many things that we're not doing right now.

**Geertjan Wielenga**: How do you pick the topics for your talks?

# Venkat's conference topics

**Venkat Subramaniam**: That's a really hard question to answer because I diversify in so many areas. I program in about 15 different languages, but what I normally do is let my brain wander until I find something that piques my interest.

I play with ideas, sometimes for six months or even a year. I may decide to give a talk about something relatively new, but usually I've worked on something similar to it before and I can see the application in that area.

I tend to pick topics based on whether I have a story to tell. This is really the underlying theme. As an example, I was playing with Kotlin for quite a while. I knew that other people were also giving talks on Kotlin, so I thought, "You know what? I don't think I have any interest in giving a talk on Kotlin."

Then, I started struggling to understand a particular concept with Kotlin. I was able to write code to use it and I had read the documentation, but there was this dissatisfaction in my mind. I didn't really connect with it. Suddenly, I realized that the concept was similar to this other language. I switched over and played with it in that other language. Then, I came back and wrote the code in Kotlin in a way that actually worked. I was ready to give a talk on Kotlin after that because I had a story to tell. I always say that the books I write and the talks I give often come from what is curious to me.

*"Having a story to tell comes from critical thinking."*

*—Venkat Subramaniam*

One other thing that I tell students is that having a story to tell comes from critical thinking. Developers and students can have this mode of absorbing APIs and syntax for years, but it's important that they have critical thinking skills. I have had people come up to me and say, "I know all the stuff you were talking about, so I was wondering if I should even come to your talk. I sat there and found that you had some different perspectives in there. I had never thought of it that way, and now it has given me a renewed interest in thinking about it." To me, that is the key: be curious about a topic, but also, spend some time on it using critical thinking.

I've been doing this for a good 20 years now and I often wonder if I'm going to run out of topics. I actually wipe out most of my talks at the end of the year. December is the beautiful month when I retire my talks that I've given in the year. In January and February, I create new talks. It turns out that I don't run out of topics because through the year, as I'm working on things, I develop new understandings, which is that onion layer I talked about.

**Geertjan Wielenga**: In your case, as a developer advocate, you don't work for a specific company. You pick topics purely based on your own interests. Could you see yourself working for a particular vendor of some kind in the future?

**Venkat Subramaniam**: I wouldn't be able to do what I'm doing now without the support of my wife. She has taken this risk with me because one day I came home and said, "I'm quitting. I'm not going to work for a company anymore."

This was a conscious decision that I made nearly 20 years ago. I quit my job when my son turned one. I had a lucrative job that I was doing extremely well at. It was a job that anybody would die to keep. The decision came from nearly four years of unhappiness. I was working for this large engineering corporation and sometimes I would look at myself and my happiness index. I was making money working on cool tech and working with very smart developers, and yet, I was pretty unhappy. I would go to the university and teach in the evening with almost negligible income, but as I said earlier, sharing knowledge was absolutely more rewarding.

Due to the amount of travel involved with developer advocacy, over the years my wife occasionally asked me why I didn't want to have a normal job like everybody else, but she knows that I'm not wired that way now.

I thought, "What if I can do what I truly enjoy doing, rather than going to work and doing what I'm told to do?" In a way, I would say there's a rebel in each one of us. My rebel was a little louder, I think. The reality is that there are times in life when we have to do what other people tell us to. Even today, there are times when clients want me to do things that I may not get excited about. Thankfully, I reduce those situations. I reject a lot of work that comes my way these days, and I only settle on things that I am interested in doing.

To answer your question, part of the reason that I do what I do is that I want to be able to devote my time to creating value. For me, value is not in making a rich company even richer. Large companies are necessary because if you look at the work that some of them are doing, no individual could ever achieve that. I want to emphasize that I'm not naive about this topic.

The beauty of this world is that each one of us has to decide what excites us. I have friends working in large companies. I admire them and I learn a great deal from them, but I can't do what they do. Not everybody could do what I do either.

In the past, people have come up to me and said, "You don't have a position. You don't have a title. You could have been XYZ in your life." In fact, I've had interviews over the years for roles that would have meant working very high up in companies.

To give an example, I was interviewed to be a top person working directly under the president of a company. I was told, "You're the right person for this, but there are some things you have to understand. We're going to give you the weekend to decide. When you walk into this company, we're going to rely on you heavily; we will need you to be on call."

I asked, "What about my teaching?" This was before I got into speaking at conferences.

The interviewer replied, "You have to cancel that commitment because we need you here. We can't have you focusing on anything else."

That was the hardest weekend for me because I was sitting at home biting my nails, thinking, "Do I want to throw away one of the things that I enjoy the most for career development?"

On the Monday, I wrote to this president saying, "I want to thank you for one important thing: you made me realize what truly matters to me, so much so that I'm not going to come and work for you. Actually, I've decided not to work for anyone."

> "Within two years, I had quit my job. That was a pivotal moment in my career."
>
> —*Venkat Subramaniam*

I started saving money like crazy at that point and within two years, I had quit my job. That was a pivotal moment in my career. Today, I get paid by corporations when they call me to come and teach their employees. I get paid when companies call me and ask me to help them with their projects and test-driven development. If companies don't call me, I won't have any income, but at the same time, I have a job at the university that pays me a minimum wage salary based on me being a part-time employee.

There are other ways to make money, but this is the balance that I really wanted to strike. I want to make enough money so that I won't retire in poverty, but at the same time, I want to spend time on the value proposition that I mentioned earlier.

I have to say that I'm very thankful for this opportunity to travel and teach. I'm thankful for everyone in this world who has supported me on this journey in so many different ways. I deeply respect other people for what they do, but I'm also happy that I'm able to be independent. I can critique, express my ideas, and explore things that I feel curious about.

**Geertjan Wielenga**: How would you describe yourself to a non-technical person?

**Venkat Subramaniam**: I would say that I'm a student of computer science and I learn every single day how to apply tech. I help other developers to learn those things too. Part of what I do is turn what is enormously complex into something that's very approachable, and in the process, I make that tech relevant and useful for developers to apply to the businesses they are part of.

**Geertjan Wielenga**: Thank you, Venkat Subramaniam.

## 15

> I came to the point of thinking, 'That guy isn't saying anything that I couldn't say. Why am I not up there?'

# Ivar Grimstad

# Introducing Ivar Grimstad

Ivar Grimstad is a software architect working as a principal consultant for the Cybercom Group in Sweden. A Java Champion and Java User Group leader, Ivar is deeply involved in giving back to the Java community, having joined the Java Community Process (JCP) as a member of the executive committee. He is also an Oracle Groundbreaker Ambassador and a frequent and well-reviewed speaker at international developer conferences. Since this interview, Ivar has become a Jakarta Enterprise Edition (EE) developer advocate at the Eclipse Foundation. Find Ivar on Twitter: @ivar_grimstad.

---

**Geertjan Wielenga**: Do you think that developer advocacy is still quite an unknown area?

**Ivar Grimstad**: It's only recently that I've started noticing that companies are now searching for and hiring developer advocates. Previously, you just became a developer advocate in some way.

My position at Cybercom is not formally described as "developer advocate" because we don't have that in our company. I just started doing talks because the company wanted to be more publicly known and I wanted to attend conferences. Kind of a win-win situation!

**Geertjan Wielenga**: As you don't have an official position in this sphere, is it correct that there's not a tech from your company that you're actually promoting?

**Ivar Grimstad**: Yes, Cybercom is a consulting company, so there aren't products to promote. I just find topics that I think are interesting and I speak about them.

**Ivar's ideal job**

In a perfect world, I would have some kind of freelance role and companies creating products would just fund me somehow. I could go out and talk freely about anything and everything. But I don't know if that role exists right now; it would be called "freelance developer advocate" or something like that.

**Geertjan Wielenga**: I know that Cybercom exists because of you. Although you say you're not promoting anything from your company, all your sessions do begin with you saying who you are and where you're from. Would you say that the promotion part ends after you've mentioned Cybercom's name?

**Ivar Grimstad**: On the contrary, I would say that's just the beginning. Since we're a consulting company, and we don't have any products, the tech we're using is what our customers need to create their products.

Standing up and promoting our clients' products in some context could be okay. I can do showcases of what we're doing for clients, but then we have to have approval from the clients that I can use their stuff on stage and so on. It's easier to just promote open-source tech. Most of the work that we do involves using open-source tech anyway.

> *"By being out there and talking about tech, we actually contribute a little bit back as a company."*
>
> —*Ivar Grimstad*

I'm trying to convince my company that giving talks about the tech we use is also one way of giving back to the community. We're consuming a lot of open-source tech and we're using it in our client engagements. But, as with most consulting companies, we are not very good at contributing back. By being out there and talking about tech, we actually contribute a little bit back as a company. It also helps with recruiting. When I go to conferences, people say, "Oh, this guy works for Cybercom. That must be a good company; I'll apply there."

My work helps with creating business too. Tomorrow, actually, I'm going to meet a client. That meeting is solely based on a talk I did at a conference last year. The client said, "We saw you there and we want you."

Another client said, "We've seen you at this conference. Do you want to come and speak at our company's internal conference?" The company paid for me to go there and speak.

The business that my role generates is not always something that you can connect with my talks directly. For example, if my company sends me to Oracle Code, I don't think there will be a direct return on investment just as a result of me being there. But if I go and build the brand by getting my name and the company name out there, it may generate business in a year or two.

**Geertjan Wielenga**: I think it comes across as really authentic when you're not representing a company producing a product. Do you feel that you can speak more freely?

**Ivar Grimstad**: Yes, and it has also given me the luxury of being able to write in my abstracts that my talks are totally vendor-neutral. Even though I sometimes show IBM, Oracle, or Red Hat products, I mix them and I can discuss them freely. I think that's one benefit of being seen as independent, which I am.

I've joined the Oracle Groundbreaker Ambassadors. Consequently, the talks I submit to Oracle events have an element of Oracle and Oracle Cloud products because that's what Oracle pays for. However, that doesn't mean that my talks don't have any other topics in them. I do have talks that have been accepted on the Oracle Code tour with MicroProfile in them. I just add a flavor of Oracle Cloud into that kind of talk.

**Geertjan Wielenga**: How did you end up doing developer advocacy in the first place?

**Ivar Grimstad**: I've attended many different conferences in my working life and I always really enjoyed going to them. After some years of regularly attending conferences, I came to the point of thinking, "That guy isn't saying anything that I couldn't say. Why am I not up there?"

I just wanted to try speaking, so I started submitting abstracts. I already gave talks at meetups locally, but I began feeling comfortable enough to approach conferences. I continued submitting abstracts until I got accepted.

As it turned out, while I was becoming interested in speaking, my company was struggling to raise its profile. Nobody, even in Sweden, knew what we did. So, my company was super happy for any publicity it could get. I could provide it with that by just going out and talking about tech. It didn't have to be related to anything we did; I just had to be there with the company name on the slides. That was good enough in the eyes of my company. After a while, about 50% of my time became dedicated to activities such as speaking at conferences and contributing to open-source projects.

**Geertjan Wielenga**: When did you feel that you were becoming successful on the conference scene?

## Finding success

**Ivar Grimstad**: I think the real breakthrough was getting accepted for JavaOne in 2013. Suddenly, other conferences were reaching out to me just because they wanted JavaOne speakers. Getting that conference under my belt was important. Then the ball started rolling and my hands became free; I could more or less just submit wherever I wanted.

**Geertjan Wielenga**: What are the topics you mostly talk about?

**Ivar Grimstad**: Nowadays, I usually talk about MicroProfile or Jakarta EE. I have done some talks on serverless as well. Sometimes my topics are related to the Java Specification Requests (JSRs) active on the JCP.

**Geertjan Wielenga**: How did you get started in the tech industry? What's your background?

**Ivar Grimstad**: I came out of university after studying systems engineering at the Norwegian University of Science and Technology. I'm a decent programmer, but my strengths are in systems engineering. I started working as a consultant and got exposed to a lot of tech when working with clients. It has been Java all the way, though, since the very beginning.

**Geertjan Wielenga**: You said that you started by speaking at meetups. What attracted you to speaking in that way? Not everyone who is a programmer, or who is involved in IT, wants to stand up in front of a group of people and talk.

**Ivar Grimstad**: I think, personally, being up there at the front of the room gives you a little kick; it's adrenaline. I have to learn this stuff to be able to present it, so it keeps me learning.

At the same time, I like giving back and I like being involved in the community when having these exchanges of knowledge. You can't do this job by yourself, so you're relying on other people. You need to have discussions with good people. The best way of starting a discussion is just to throw something out there in a talk, then discuss it with people afterward. My talks are prepared well and pretty decent, but the discussions afterwards are what I'm after.

> *"You also get to meet all these amazing speakers whom you usually just hear about."*
>
> *—Ivar Grimstad*

Another thing that motivates me is that I like to travel and see new countries. You also get to meet all these amazing speakers whom you usually just hear about or you've read their books and maybe only seen a video of them. Now you have the chance to sit down and actually have dinner with them!

**Geertjan Wielenga**: If somebody wanted to do what you're doing, what would the process be to get to that point?

**Ivar Grimstad**: My experience is to start small, but don't be afraid of going up there. Start by speaking internally in your company and after doing that for a while, look up some local meetups. Meetups and user groups are always looking for speakers. Anyone who just wants to speak about something is always welcome. It's so low key; you don't have to be super glossy and prepared. You just go up there and say something. You'll get the discussion going that way.

Don't be afraid of just signing up for a talk either. Many companies have put some kind of infrastructure in place for this. In my company, we have what we call "Cozy Fridays." Every Friday morning, we have somebody speaking about something. In that kind of session could be where you practice a small part of your talk. As an example, that's where I did my serverless talk for the first time. Next, I gave it at a meetup, then at a conference. Now, I'm giving the talk at Oracle Code.

**Geertjan Wielenga**: If you're at a party and there are no technical people around, how do you describe what you do?

**Ivar Grimstad**: I would say that, at a party, I'm probably more of a silent person. That contradicts what I do, I know.

I thrive on the stage and I like being there, but I don't get involved as much in social situations; I'm pretty introverted.

Being at these conferences is always kind of stressful. You want to pull back and go to your room to just relax a little bit. I'm not this super social guy, but I manage and I do this job. I'm definitely not the type who takes over the party, though!

**Geertjan Wielenga**: There are many people in software and the whole IT industry, in fact, who are introverted. They might think that they need to have a different kind of personality to be a speaker. Are you saying the opposite is actually the case?

**Ivar Grimstad**: I've talked to many speakers and most of them are actually like me in this way. When I talk about introversion, it's not that introverts don't like to talk to people, but it pulls the energy from them. I feel that is reversed when I'm on stage. Of course, I was really nervous for the first couple of years as a speaker, but you get used it. I get more energy when I'm on a stage, but then afterwards I find that I feel drained.

**Geertjan Wielenga**: Having a stage, a lectern, and a microphone in some ways creates a very confined and safe space because you know that everyone is safely away from you and sitting on chairs. Does that make you feel more in control?

**Ivar Grimstad**: Yes, you are in control: you control the topic and the pace. Even though I'm pretty sure I'm never the smartest guy in the room or the guy who knows most about a topic, just by being up there on the stage, I'm the smartest guy for that moment in time. Of course, I can still get tricky questions at the end of the talk.

**Geertjan Wielenga**: What do you do with a tricky question that you can't answer?

## Difficult questions

**Ivar Grimstad**: You've got to be honest. If I can't answer a question, I have to say that I need to look it up and come back to them. Being polite is always important, but you shouldn't start making up answers. If you don't know it, you don't know it. The hardest thing is when you end up having a discussion with somebody in the audience, but you just have to cut it short because nobody else in the room wants to hear that.

**Geertjan Wielenga**: What does your typical day look like?

**Ivar Grimstad**: I would say that there are no typical days in my work life. They are all unique in some way or other. One day, I may be coding the entire day. Another day, I could be busy with customer meetings. Then there is the developer advocacy work, which is divided between blogging, writing demos, preparing talks, traveling to conferences, speaking, and contributing to open-source projects.

**Geertjan Wielenga**: Can this multitude of tasks lead to you experiencing burnout?

**Ivar Grimstad**: The risk is always there, but at the same time, I think that our industry is kind of special in that regard. Even if I'm programming and coding all day on some work assignments, it can actually be relaxing to go home and just write a presentation, do a demo, or work on some pet project.

Even though I'm still coding and thinking, I'm doing it in another context, which allows me to unwind.

**Geertjan Wielenga**: What about when you travel too much or have too many early mornings on the road? Do those situations affect you?

**Ivar Grimstad**: I think I've managed to not get into those situations too often. That is mainly because I like to travel and I don't get stressed by delays. Sometimes, I've had three weeks in a row of just being home for half an hour, changing my bags, and then going away again. That's not fun, but there is an end to it. I try to limit that and have periods without travel in between.

You need to relax when you can and do fun stuff at a conference as well. When I was in South Africa last July, my workshop was canceled on the Wednesday. I had a day off, so I just went to Table Mountain and hiked down from there. I had a day outside in the sun.

**Geertjan Wielenga**: Are you traveling regularly right now?

**Ivar Grimstad**: It goes in periods. You get a period of heavy travel in the spring and then also in October/November.

**Geertjan Wielenga**: Do you have any tips for avoiding jet lag? What do you do to remain fit, focused, and ready to present on any stage in the world?

**Ivar Grimstad**: I have to get enough sleep. I also try to always arrive the day before the conference, just so I don't have issues with being late. I usually try to stay in the city until the day after the conference too.

If you have a talk at lunchtime, then you have to check-in at the hotel in the morning and have your baggage taken somewhere. That can be stressful, but I try to be as relaxed as possible when I travel. When I select flights, I try to do it carefully, so I don't have long layovers. If I go to San Francisco, I will pay more to go directly from Copenhagen, rather than stopping in New York, for example.

Regarding time zone travel and jet lag, I always try to get into the local time zone as fast as possible. I turn my watch to Pacific time the minute I get on the plane. Then I normally try to sleep on the plane. When I get to my destination, I stay awake until at least 8:00 p.m. I don't take naps in the afternoon.

I try to take advantage of waking up early and just go for a run or something. If I wake up at 5:00 a.m., I don't see that as a big deal; I just get out of bed, have some light snacks, and go for a run. I'll be back for breakfast and ready to get the day going. Eventually, I get into a new rhythm.

The last couple of years, I've been avoiding staying for extra time after a conference. I used to stay longer and spend a weekend in a new city, but nowadays, I value getting home more. I try to spend all my weekends at home.

**Geertjan Wielenga**: What about the technical issues one runs into? If you get to your faraway conference and then your laptop has an issue, how do you handle that?

**Ivar Grimstad**: The technical issues I largely avoid by using a MacBook. I'm a Linux guy, but I see the limitations there and when I go traveling, I bring a MacBook. I never have problems with the displays or anything like that.

**Geertjan Wielenga**: Let's say there is some signage problem at the venue and only three people manage to find your session room that you've traveled across the world to get to. How do you approach that situation?

**Ivar Grimstad**: I have had sessions where I had four or five people in the room. That's not fun, but you just have to accept it. I would do the talk anyway, but it would get more personal. I could have more of a dialog with them individually maybe.

As a speaker, you can submit as good an abstract as possible to describe the session and try to get people there, but the conference organizers have to know their audience. If they accept your talk and nobody comes, you can't take the blame entirely. You've done your best with writing an abstract and the organizers accepted you.

> *"It's not fun when you get star speakers right next door to your session, so nobody attends yours, but you can't take it personally."*
>
> —*Ivar Grimstad*

In some conferences, there is a scheduling conflict. It's not fun when you get star speakers right next door to your session, so nobody attends yours, but you can't take it personally. You just have to accept the situation and write a better abstract next time or try to promote it more.

**Geertjan Wielenga**: Do you have any advice on being accepted at more conferences or writing a good abstract?

**Ivar Grimstad**: You can always talk to the organizers and just ask them what would work well. However, I think most people are like me in that I generally only realize I need to submit a paper when the last call goes out. You just have to throw something in before the window closes. You should, at least, submit a week before the deadline, so you have time to actually tailor your abstract to the conference. But usually, the dates hit you unexpectedly and you have to just throw in what you have.

## Managing controversy

**Geertjan Wielenga**: Let's say you're talking about a tech that is very controversial at a particular point and there's been lots of information in the news. You're up on the stage and on the one hand, you have the good fortune that you're not representing a particular company. On the other hand, you're trying to describe a solution that attendees can use. If you get a question on this kind of topic, how do you handle it?

**Ivar Grimstad**: You just have to try to answer it the best way you can, from the background you have. I try to avoid the provocative talks, but I touched on them a little bit a couple of years ago, when doing talks where I compared Java Platform, Enterprise Edition (Java EE) and Spring. Then there was always a risk of upsetting people.

You just have to be respectful about both sides and try not to bark back or be opinionated yourself when answering.

You can, for example, say, "This is my opinion, but it doesn't have to be your opinion."

**Geertjan Wielenga**: Would you say that Spring is useful for one particular kind of domain and Java EE, or Jakarta EE, for another?

**Ivar Grimstad**: Yes and no. They solve more or less the same problem. Nowadays, it's just a matter of taste, I think, and what your developers are more comfortable with.

**Geertjan Wielenga**: What do you think about the situation with Jakarta EE now being in Eclipse?

**Ivar Grimstad**: I think it has good momentum. There have been some delays, but we will get Eclipse GlassFish out of the door. One thing I think we have not been successful with is communicating what's actually being done. I have five meetings every week in different committees and we're discussing the same things, but there's actually a lot of progress and we're informing each other.

**Geertjan Wielenga**: Let's take a few steps back. You've been involved in the JCP process, which made you known in the Eclipse Foundation. How did you get started with that?

**Ivar Grimstad**: I think it was at a JavaOne back in the day. I noticed some participants had these ribbons on their badges saying they were experts. I thought, "What's this? How do I get there?" I had been an individual member of the JCP for a long time and I started browsing for JSRs that were looking for experts.

**Geertjan Wielenga**: Are there many individual members?

**Ivar Grimstad**: I'm not sure how many individual members there are. There are not that many, but there are some. My breakthrough came when the new Model-View-Controller (MVC) specifications were being announced. I'd created many MVC frameworks myself, so I thought, "I'll join that actual group." I signed up directly and was accepted to that one. Now I'm actually the specification lead for it.

I joined the security specification because security is as important as ever and I wanted to be part of that. It also looks good on my resume. I was asked if I could join the Java Message Service (JMS) specification as well, so I did.

**Geertjan Wielenga**: How did you get into the Jakarta EE Eclipse Foundation discussions? Was it from the MVC point of view?

**Ivar Grimstad**: No, not really. I think it had more to do with me being on the JCP Executive Committee, as well as being independent from the vendors involved.

I've done all these MicroProfile talks, even though I'm not formally in any MicroProfile project, but it was an easy topic for me. I remember at the last JavaOne, we had this MicroProfile breakfast, where all the members of MicroProfile were there, and I was invited as well. At that breakfast, David Blevins said, "I think Ivar here is the one person who is doing the most talks promoting MicroProfile out of all of us in the room." All these vendors were there, so that was kind of surprising. I've been accepted at a lot of conferences with the MicroProfile theme, but I think that's the way it is: people like hearing from speakers who are not too biased toward a particular product.

When Eclipse Enterprise for Java (EE4J) projects were formed to get Java EE over to the Eclipse Foundation, we wanted the project management committee (PMC) to be equally weighted between the vendors. Oracle was there, IBM was there, and Red Hat was there. There was a dilemma: who was going to lead this PMC? If Oracle did it, then Oracle would move the stuff from itself to a cluster and continue to run it; that would be the community reaction. Then if IBM took the lead, IBM would be the big bad guy in the eyes of the community, and the same went for Red Hat. I thought, "We need a neutral party in there." I've been the PMC lead for a year.

When the Jakarta EE working group started up, I was there as a PMC representative. Since then, I've been a committer at the Eclipse Foundation. I ran for the elections to the working group, so I got elected in there as well.

**Geertjan Wielenga**: You're really an example of what you can do as an individual in the community, but if you could change one thing about your professional life, what would it be?

**Ivar Grimstad**: I think being a consultant or having a consultancy background is very good for being exposed to many different types of tech and that provides a solid foundation for doing developer advocate activities.

> *"In an ideal world, I would be doing more of the developer advocacy work and less of the consulting."*
>
> —*Ivar Grimstad*

However, in an ideal world, I would be doing more of the developer advocacy work and less of the consulting. Right now, I have both elements in my role, but given the choice, I would have the developer advocacy side be more formalized than it is now. But it is useful to have consultancy behind me. It provides hard facts that I can use in my developer advocacy.

**Geertjan Wielenga**: How do you stay up to date with the latest tech developments? Are there particular sites you follow?

**Ivar Grimstad**: It's getting more diluted, I think, but I remember when `TheServerSide.com` was the one place I always went to for updates. Now I get my information from Twitter more than anything and I just click on links from there. I don't have any sites I regularly go to for tech stuff, actually. I've seen that Medium is getting very popular, but I haven't figured out what that is yet or how it works.

## Making use of Twitter

**Geertjan Wielenga**: It makes sense in our tech space that if you follow a certain number of people on Twitter, you only focus on 20 or 30 people out of that group, and you get all the information that you need from those people. Do you find that getting information from a few knowledgeable people, by following their posts, is more valuable than reading some anonymous article by somebody who you have no connection with at all?

**Ivar Grimstad**: In some ways, but at the same time, you have to be a little bit careful that you don't fall into this bubble that means you only ever listen to people who are like you.

Getting influenced by ideas from all around you is always good and that's where the conference side becomes important.

I go and listen to other talks at conferences still. I never go to a conference with a particular narrow focus in mind; I just look at the schedule and think, "Okay, what's cool here?" I might select a talk on web tracks, mobile tracks, agile, project management, or backend, for example. I listen to the speaker on those topics and if they mention a book, or they recommend some other speakers to follow or blogs to read, I just look those things or people up and read up on the information. I used to learn from tech books and I've bought many books over the years, but I don't do that so much anymore.

**Geertjan Wielenga**: What are you most passionate about at the moment? What's a new tech or something that's on the horizon that you think is really interesting right now?

**Ivar Grimstad**: I'm most passionate about the future of Jakarta EE right now. I'm interested in how we can get all the good stuff from MicroProfile to become more cloud-native, in order to actually become a real competitor to other tech out there. That's what I put my energy into these days.

At the same time, I can see that there are so many things happening very fast in the cloud space. There is this mix of functions and microservices, and a focus on getting all this architecture up. I think that Jakarta EE has all the foundation there to be successful, but we need to show something within the next couple of years to really be competitive.

**Geertjan Wielenga**: On the personal career level, you have a role now where you can be a semi-official developer advocate, but where do you see your professional path developing in the next five, 10, or 20 years? Do you see yourself doing this job forever or do you foresee moving to some other role at some point? What does the future look like for you?

**Ivar Grimstad**: It's a hard question, especially in this industry. Developer advocates could be obsolete in five years, so we never know what the future holds for us. Maybe in 20 years speaking at conferences won't be allowed anymore because we may not be encouraged to travel by our companies or we won't need to travel because everything will be virtual.

I can see myself taking on a more official developer advocate role in years to come, as long as it doesn't get too strenuous. If the travel starts wearing on me, or I stop enjoying what I'm doing, then I probably will look somewhere else for a new career path. But right now, developer advocacy is where I get my energy from.

**Geertjan Wielenga**: Thank you, Ivar Grimstad.

## 16

> *Having a voice that people are willing to listen to is an opportunity for the greater good of humanity.*

# Regine Gilbert

# Introducing Regine Gilbert

Regine Gilbert is a user experience designer based in New York City. She is a professor at NYU Tandon School of Engineering, where she teaches user experience design to students in the Integrated Digital Media program. Regine has taught at General Assembly in New York City and is an alum of its part-time UX program. She has more than 10 years of experience in the tech arena with much focus on inclusion and accessibility. Regine has a strong belief in making the world a more accessible place and is passionate about advocating for good user experience that starts and ends with the user. Find Regine on Twitter: @reg_inee.

---

**Geertjan Wielenga**: You're a designer, but you interact a lot with developers and you promote your vision of user interface (UI) design. Do you see yourself as an advocate?

**Regine Gilbert**: I feel that, as a user experience (UX) designer, I advocate for the user, ultimately, but that means not making things hard for the developer either.

**Geertjan Wielenga**: Do you see a very strong difference between designers and developers?

**Regine Gilbert**: I think there is a difference. At the end of the day, we all want to get our jobs done, but our perspectives are a little bit different. From a designer's perspective, we want something that will look good. From a developer's perspective, they want to get things done, but they also want to make things good for users, so we come together on that. There is much more collaboration than you might initially think.

**Geertjan Wielenga**: Would you describe yourself as an accessibility advocate, then?

**Regine Gilbert**: Yes, I would say that. I do my best to be aware and mindful of not only what I design but what I teach. As an educator, it's so important to get your students thinking about this.

I have had students in the past who were injured or had accidents that caused temporary and sometimes permanent disabilities. It changed their perspective on things when they experienced the challenges. Once you know something, you can't undo that. Moving forward, I hope that my students continue to learn about accessibility and continue to speak about it. I've worked with companies who don't really care about it. All I can do is plant seeds and hope that they grow at some point.

**Geertjan Wielenga**: How did you get into the work that you're doing?

## Regine's career path

**Regine Gilbert**: I was working as a product manager in supply chains in the fashion world. I was a designer before that, but a different type of designer: a fashion designer. I really missed designing when I was a product manager. This was around 2013/14 and I paid attention to what was going on in the news. It was reported that everything was going digital. I decided that I wanted to go more toward the digital world too.

I started learning on my own. I decided to take a formal class in UX design at General Assembly and that led me on a path that I never expected to be on today.

I'm now writing a book on inclusive design and designing with accessibility in mind. Over the years, I have become an accessibility advocate, as you say. I not only create guidelines for the workplace but I also teach and incorporate accessibility into my classroom.

I was a certified project manager and a scrum master when I was doing project management. Getting an understanding of what people were programming has been very helpful in my career. I've taken classes on HTML, CSS, and JavaScript, but I don't sit there and code. I can look at code and say, "Okay, we can fix these things," and I'm not the person who sits there all day doing that.

**Geertjan Wielenga**: How did your particular interest in accessibility come about?

**Regine Gilbert**: I became very passionate about accessibility when I realized that it's not being taught in the curriculum. I remember when I took my first UX course and there was one slide on accessibility in a 12-week course. When I started teaching, I built in the accessibility topic early. I actually mention it in the first class.

We often exclude people with disabilities from the very beginning when we're making a product. I ask my students to complete an empathy exercise so that they start thinking about accessibility. Sometimes I bring people with disabilities into my classroom, so my students can do a design sprint, come up with an idea, and then pitch it to the person who they're building it for. They then get real feedback.

**Geertjan Wielenga**: You speak at conferences on these topics as well. What are some places you've spoken at recently?

**Regine Gilbert**: Most recently I spoke here in New York at General Assembly. I was on a panel talking about accessibility and design in digital products. I've also spoken in previous years in Boston at HOW Design, which is a very big design conference. I do little talks within the New York community about accessibility as well.

**Geertjan Wielenga**: Could you talk more about the book that you're writing?

**Regine Gilbert**: Yes, the book is geared toward designers, project managers, and people who have a general interest in accessibility. It addresses web content accessibility guidelines and incorporating accessibility into design systems, as well as covering past and future innovations to do with accessibility.

When I'm talking to my students, I ask, "Do you text? Well, texting was initially created for people who are deaf." Many people don't know that. Curb cuts were initially made for people with wheelchairs, but we all benefit from them. There are many innovations from the past that we use today.

**Geertjan Wielenga**: Typically, when we think about accessibility in terms of software, we automatically think about sight-related disabilities. Are there other disabilities that are related to accessibility and software?

**Regine Gilbert**: Yes, when thinking about accessibility there are four categories: visual, hearing, cognitive, and motor.

For example, one of the first things that I do is see whether I can keyboard through a site. If I can keyboard through it, am I able to see where I'm going? Not everyone can use a mouse.

If there's a video on a website, is there closed captioning available for that? Is there a transcript available? Can I turn on my screen reader? Will it read the page? What's the hierarchy of the page? Those are things that I've learned. I'm continuing to learn more from friends who have visual and hearing impairments.

Twitter is great for learning about what's going on and what people are talking about too. #a11y is a numeronym for accessibility. Some people say, "Ally."

## Different avenues in the IT industry

**Geertjan Wielenga:** This is very interesting from the point of view of this book. I'm trying to make the argument, among other things, that being involved in the IT industry isn't necessarily a dry day job of programming and being very code-oriented; there is also a range of other types of work that you can do. Do you agree that your work is an example of this?

**Regine Gilbert:** Yes, it's very interesting to think about. I teach UX design at the New York University Tandon School of Engineering. The undergraduates work with a real-life client each semester.

> *"There are many areas in which accessibility is just not being addressed."*
>
> —*Regine Gilbert*

This semester, their real-life client was an accessibility consulting firm called Equal Entry. Each student was given a different topic area, ranging from creating accessibility awareness in Vietnam to making more accessible maps and creating accessibility awareness around virtual reality (VR). There are many areas in which accessibility is just not being addressed. Because VR and augmented reality (AR) are still so new, we have an opportunity to get accessibility awareness out there.

For the web, a lot of people are now talking about accessibility, especially because in the U.S. there have been many lawsuits around accessibility. People aren't talking about it in relation to these mixed realities just yet.

What I like to remind people of in my talks, especially in the U.S., is that we're an aging population. In this country, by the year 2035, which is 16 years away, we'll have more old people than young people. If we're not creating products for our older selves, what are we doing?

We're constantly on our devices, which means that low vision and blindness are probably going to rise. Are we creating these products to work with future sight problems? How can people who already have those disabilities use them now?

With my students, I ask, "Who do you think about the most?" They sit for a second and then realize that they think about themselves more than anyone else.

We think about ourselves the most, so when we're designing for someone else, we have to take ourselves out of that equation.

You should think about everyone who could use your product. You're not your user, basically. I have to keep reminding my students of this because even when they start to come up with solutions, they sometimes stop thinking about the user.

As designers and developers, I think we fall into that trap. When we're making this really cool thing, we stop thinking about who we're making it for. We get caught up in the fun that we're having making it.

**Geertjan Wielenga**: Would another way to approach it be to think about yourself with low vision, a hearing problem, or a limb missing?

**Regine Gilbert**: Yes. Microsoft has a really great inclusive design toolkit that I like to show people. It splits disabled people into being permanently disabled, temporarily disabled, or situationally disabled. For example, if someone is born with one arm, that's permanent. If someone has a broken arm, that's temporary. If someone is holding a baby, that's situational.

Thinking about disability from all contexts is important. You're creating this cool product, but what if somebody has a baby and they're trying to use it? I really like that perspective because it makes things more relatable. When you can relate, you can connect. When you can connect, you can understand. When you can understand, you can build better products.

**Geertjan Wielenga**: You mentioned VR and AR; where would accessibility fit there?

**Regine Gilbert**: One big thing that I learned at the CSUN Assistive Technology Conference is that Microsoft is investing heavily in artificial intelligence (AI) and accessibility. Ultimately, you have to get disabled people working in these areas alongside able-bodied people in order to create the best products.

> *"Co-designing will be the future when it comes to AR, VR, and AI."*
>
> —*Regine Gilbert*

From what I've seen, co-designing will be the future when it comes to AR, VR, and AI. There's no way to come up with better ideas than to incorporate the people who will be using the products into the development process. That's my hope for the future as well. There are already some companies, like Magic Leap, creating accessibility teams and thinking about it from the start.

**Geertjan Wielenga**: I was working with a group of developers some years ago. They were creating software to be used by farmers and one of the team members was actually a farmer. Is that similar?

**Regine Gilbert**: Yes, it helps immensely. The British Broadcasting Corporation (BBC) has done a good job of incorporating accessibility into a lot of its workflows, in part because it does hire people with disabilities and do thorough testing.

**Geertjan Wielenga**: What are some new developments happening in accessibility in general?

## Accessibility awareness

**Regine Gilbert**: Firstly, people are becoming more aware of it. Secondly, there are organizations, like Teach Access here in the U.S., that are promoting incorporating accessibility into the classroom.

I'm biased because I just got a grant from Teach Access to incorporate accessibility into my curriculum. I've been doing that on my own, of course, but it's great to have the extra help.

I think accessibility is an education issue because I've taught computer science students and engineering students who had no knowledge of the Web Content Accessibility Guidelines. I asked, "You want to work in the web and mobile, but you don't know that there are these Web Content Accessibility Guidelines?"

Even designers have no idea that they exist. It's important to increase awareness. Obviously, there are exceptions to every rule, but these international standards have been put in place for the good of everyone. Everyone should be able to access the web.

**Geertjan Wielenga**: I work at Oracle as a product manager for a JavaScript toolkit. We're always talking about these topics and trying to integrate these guidelines. Can you incorporate accessibility outside of this type of large enterprise?

**Regine Gilbert**: 100%, yes. Look at small businesses; they have no idea that they need to adhere to these guidelines; they don't even know about them. It's just not something that's discussed.

Unfortunately, because of certain lawsuits that have occurred, which I referred to earlier, there are now federal guidelines around accessibility. The web is so new that lawmakers are trying to catch up. They've applied an old law to new tech, so this blanket rule has been implemented. Businesses that are just not aware may end up getting sued. That's been a catalyst for a lot of businesses to learn more.

> *"We're not helping people to feel good about using our products."*
>
> —*Regine Gilbert*

I think the bigger motivation should be not excluding anyone from being able to use your product. There's a wonderful book called *Mismatch: How Inclusion Shapes Design*, by Kat Holmes. She talks about inclusion but also exclusion. We all know what it's like to feel left out. In essence, that's what we're doing when we don't make things accessible. We're not helping people to feel good about using our products.

**Geertjan Wielenga**: Aside from being an educator at a university, you work inside companies as well. What kind of advice do you give?

**Regine Gilbert**: I have my own consulting business, so I work with companies big and small. I typically help them with overall UX and then provide some guidance around accessibility. I create guidelines around what's needed for their site and what the responsibilities are for each of the different teams.

For web copy, this could be having an understanding of what needs to go in the alt text and how you need to write certain things to send users in the right direction. For visual design, this could be making sure that you're creating the right color balance. For developers, it could be making sure that they have an understanding of where to test things and how to test them. For UX, you need to have an understanding of what's needed from an accessibility perspective.

**Geertjan Wielenga**: What's an example of something that needs to be provided?

**Regine Gilbert**: When creating a wireframe, most of the time there are details needed in terms of the interaction design. For example, when you're creating a password, you can choose to see your password or not see your password. What is that like if you're using a screen reader? For privacy concerns, would you want it to read the password? Those are the details that are often left out.

**Geertjan Wielenga**: Can you give any more examples that you might not think of immediately but are quite obvious when you think about them?

**Regine Gilbert**: One of the things that many accessibility consulting firms do is add a "skip to content" button at the very top of the screen. For example, there are plenty of power keyboard users and also people using screen readers. If they don't want to see or listen to all this content, then at the very top, when they first start to tab through, a button will appear that will allow them to skip all this other stuff and move to the content that they need.

**Geertjan Wielenga**: In applications, does this mean that the introductory text before the content needs to be as concise and specific as possible?

**Regine Gilbert**: Yes. Ultimately, as designers and developers, we want the user to get to the next thing so that they can accomplish their goal. If we're preventing that in any way, that's when we need to look at wireframes to make sure that all those interactions are clear.

**Geertjan Wielenga**: What's something new that you've recently learned?

**Regine Gilbert**: I mentioned the CSUN Assistive Technologies Conference earlier. It's been running for 34 years in California. It's been around for longer than the internet has been around, which is very cool.

Marcie Sutton is a developer and she did a presentation on CSS flexbox. She was talking about the web in the past and the present. The *Space Jam* website still exists. Do you remember the movie? The website is from 1996, but it's actually more accessible than what we have today! The movie *Captain Marvel* came out recently and it had a 90s look and feel to it, so the website did too. However, the backend was not as accessible as the old *Space Jam* website. We have to think about what's gone on in the last 20 years from a development and design standpoint. We have, in some ways, a less accessible world.

There's heavy use of JavaScript today, which isn't bad, but it's not that great for accessibility at times. We have moved away from semantic HTML.

Many people don't get to learn HTML and everything that you can do in it.

To answer your question, what's new is what's old in some ways. What can we do to make things better for the future? First things first, we can look at the past.

**Geertjan Wielenga**: 10 or 20 years ago, what we had available was less complex. Is that what made things more accessible?

> *"The simplest things still work."*
>
> —*Regine Gilbert*

**Regine Gilbert**: Yes, keeping it simple is the way to do things. Nobody likes a convoluted webpage where you can't figure out where to go. The simplest things still work. When you look at Craigslist, that's not changed; people can still use it. There are simple things that don't need to be made complex.

**Geertjan Wielenga**: Where do you see your role and your interests developing over the next few years?

## Regine's future projects

**Regine Gilbert**: I definitely will be more focused on AI and mixed-reality worlds. I'm currently creating a UX course for mixed realities. The course will obviously have accessibility in it from the beginning, but I'm also going to be thinking about creating designs for an environment when 90% of the environment is uncontrollable.

What does it mean from a design perspective when you're not dealing with a static webpage or mobile app?

You have to think, are the people using this able to see? With AR, instead of having the visual, could there be something that people feel? There are other ways to think about it. We tend to think about things just from our sense of sight and hearing, but other senses could be utilized in these fields that we're not utilizing right now.

There's one VR that was created by some university students. I got to see it last year. It's designed for people who don't have mobility of their hands. Usually, with VR, you have to hold something in order to do the thing. With this VR application, you have the headset and instead of using your hands, you use your head to control where you go next. That's not only something that could be good for people who don't have mobility of their hands; it could be used by anybody.

We need to think about how our bodies physically work when we're dealing with some of these things. There are still people who get sick with VR. What's happening in our brains? I'll be doing more research around that in the next year and beyond.

I've had people in the past tell me that I should shame people or companies into doing better and I've always said, "That's not my job; I won't do that. I will work to create a level of awareness and to educate people."

**Geertjan Wielenga**: People involved in any field of advocacy tend to be so full of zeal that bringing a message across in an effective manner, and in the right tone, can be a challenge. Have you experienced that?

**Regine Gilbert**: I've been in companies where I've had strong opinions about accessibility and that just didn't work in my favor. That's how I learned about planting seeds. I'll say something and if people don't want to do it, I'll wait for a few weeks and then say it again. I will continue to say it. Eventually, if you repeat something enough, people will start to listen.

**Geertjan Wielenga**: Browbeating isn't effective, is it?

**Regine Gilbert**: It's not. We've all been in meetings where somebody was so insistent about their idea that they became completely closed off to hearing anyone else's idea. One thing I like to do is question things. If I'm trying to plant these seeds, I'll question the way that things are being done.

**Geertjan Wielenga**: Is there a danger of being seen as the accessibility person who only talks about accessibility?

**Regine Gilbert**: I don't worry about that. I hope that everybody will become an accessibility advocate. It's every person's responsibility, not just one person's job. People come to me and say, "Well, you're the expert."

I reply, "I'm not the expert. You're the expert because you're the developer, so you need to do this." I'm trying to get other people to realize what their responsibility is.

**Geertjan Wielenga**: Are you trying to make yourself obsolete, then?

**Regine Gilbert**: Basically, yes. One person can make a difference; we see it all the time.

Having a voice that people are willing to listen to is an opportunity for the greater good of humanity. Why would you want a group of people to feel left out? When you think about more than just yourself, it connects you to other people.

**Geertjan Wielenga**: Thank you, Regine Gilbert.

## 17

> *You need to be an insider
> if you're going to have
> credibility in front of people.*

# Tim

# Berglund

# Introducing Tim Berglund

Tim Berglund is a teacher, author, and tech leader with Confluent, where he serves as the senior director of developer experience. He is also the co-presenter of a bevy of O'Reilly training videos on topics ranging from Git to distributed systems. Tim can be seen speaking at conferences across the U.S. and around the world. Find Tim on Twitter: @tlberglund.

---

**Geertjan Wielenga**: Could you start off by explaining what you do?

**Tim Berglund**: I work for Confluent and I run a team there that we call the "developer experience (DevX) team." It's really a developer relations team, but we call it "DevX" because we think it sounds cool. I have a background as a full-stack Java developer, trainer, and speaker.

**Geertjan Wielenga**: A basic discussion between people who do this particular profession is whether they describe themselves as "tech evangelists" or "developer advocates." How do you see yourself and what is the difference between those two descriptions?

## Debating job titles

**Tim Berglund**: This is a perennial discussion: we always talk about it. 10 years ago, I was involved in a meetup for software architects.

The first 50% of the meetup was about what it means to be an architect and then the other 50% was something useful.

In our line of work, we all do the same thing. I don't think there is a difference, especially if you stack up all the people who do this type of work and arrange them by title. When they talk about titles, some people say, "They're so different because a developer advocate is working for the developer and an evangelist is just trying to make something look good." That's not true.

This discussion does bring out some interesting aspects of our work. There are some ethical issues, such as who are we really fighting for? That said, I'm almost completely uninterested in the distinction. I usually say I'm a "tech evangelist" and at my company, we use the word "evangelist."

There have been people who have said, "I don't like the religious overtones of that. I don't want to be called an evangelist." Of course, I completely respect that and I'm not going to make somebody uncomfortable, but the work that we do is the same either way.

**Geertjan Wielenga**: How does the term "spin doctor" feel to you?

**Tim Berglund**: There are conferences that won't accept anyone whose title is "evangelist" or "developer advocate." I'll be straight: they make me mad.

I think the accusation of us being spin doctors is ridiculous only because some of my best professional friends are people who do this work. I know them and they do it authentically.

They're not interested in misleading people because that's wrong and they don't want to do a wrong thing.

The product marketers I've known are not developers or developer advocates; they're marketers. They're obsessed with facts and the logic of the claims they're making. These marketing people are a little too hung up on the lawyering of their statements.

We think, as tech people, that marketing people just lie and distort. You're going to find that there are unethical people everywhere, but my experience with actual marketing people is that even their spin doctoring is really careful and thought through.

Computer programmers will always call you out. There's this culture of software development where you can just raise your hand and say, "You're dumb and I don't agree with you!" Somehow that's okay! We even have a little bit of rudeness in this industry sometimes; people call each other out online.

> *"The controversy around our work is a lot smaller than we think."*
>
> —*Tim Berglund*

I just don't know how you'd get away with being a spin doctor when talking about code. This could be pure self-defense because it's what I do and I don't like being accused of spin doctoring. I just think the idea is nonsense because I don't see much of it happening. Actually, I think the controversy around our work is a lot smaller than we think.

As a developer advocate, your money is on the table, as it were, relationally. Your reputation is integrated with the community and you can't just lie to people. Also, you speak to people all the time, so you're good at it and you're a professional communicator. I don't see that as a negative.

**How Tim got started**

**Geertjan Wielenga:** How did you become a developer advocate in the first place?

**Tim Berglund:** I started my career as a firmware developer and I loved that. Then I moved into Java and the web, right as the first dot-com bubble was collapsing. That was my impeccable timing: getting involved in the web while the web was crashing!

A while later, I found that I like being in front of people and I like teaching. I'm good at teaching and it's a really energizing and rewarding thing for me to do. This was a time in my career when I was an independent consultant. I had some freedom to explore teaching, as long as I could get somebody to pay me for it.

During that time, my practice shifted from custom software development to training and conference speaking. That's how I got into speaking. I'll always remember the first meetup I spoke at. It just felt like I was on fire, in a good way, and I knew I needed to do more of it.

**Geertjan Wielenga:** The speaking aspect gripped you immediately, then?

**Tim Berglund:** Yes, it wasn't the first time I'd spoken in front of a group, but I felt that this was the right time to take speaking forward.

I wasn't a professional developer advocate or a tech evangelist, but I wanted these activities to be part of my brand and my personal identity. I wanted to take tech that was important to us as a community and help people to get started. I wanted to take something, learn it, and teach it. I was sucked in by that.

I started speaking at meetups and I thought, "I need to do something bigger and speak at conferences." I wanted to make this happen, so I pursued it. I got some breaks and began speaking. I was a guy just doing speaking at conferences because I wanted to, then later, I got a job where that was my role. I figured out how to build teams and align this work with what a company's priorities are.

**Geertjan Wielenga**: Which organizations have you worked for in this role and what did you advocate/evangelize?

**Tim Berglund**: The first regular army job I had in this space was at GitHub. My title was actually "trainer." GitHub was a flat organization back then and there was only a small group of trainers. This was 2012, so Git was still super scary to people and it was strategic for GitHub to drive adoption by helping people to be comfortable with using the core tech.

We did training and conference work, but the evangelism function was informal. As trainers, we were good in front of people, it was a role we loved, and we had friends in the community we were part of. We wanted to be out there talking about our work. We absolutely did evangelize the platform and the tech.

> *"We started to figure out how to evangelize a commercial product."*
>
> —*Tim Berglund*

From there, I went to DataStax and that job was also, by title, a training role. I ran a curriculum team and we built online training. We evangelized open-source Apache Cassandra and Spark, and the integration. We started to figure out how to evangelize a commercial product and play with that boundary a little bit.

During my tenure at DataStax, we put together some plans to formalize this process. We said, "Here's how we train our customers, here's how we evangelize the tech, and here's how we make documentation work together with that." We tried to make this a coherent vision that we could articulate.

At Confluent, there are people who function as evangelists throughout the company. I don't manage a big team of them, but I coordinate that overarching program.

**Geertjan Wielenga**: Is developer advocacy recognized sufficiently within your organization?

**Tim Berglund**: Yes, there's absolutely no question about it. I'm fortunate to have a CEO who functioned, historically, as the public face of the underlying open-source project. He really understands the value of this work and the company culturally understands the community of developer advocacy, so that's a big win.

**Geertjan Wielenga**: Clearly, you're very enthusiastic about all of this. What keeps you interested?

**Tim Berglund**: This is like breathing to me. I need to be able to speak.

**Geertjan Wielenga**: If someone doesn't enjoy speaking, is there a place for them?

## If you don't want to be a conference speaker

**Tim Berglund**: Yes, certainly on my team there is. I've got a member of my team who doesn't like speaking and doesn't like being in front of people. She's an amazingly high performer.

My view of the evangelist role is that at meetups and conferences, this is a performance role, but you also have to deliver content that's useful. On my team, we have a content person. What she does, for example, is take different parts of the open-source stack that we've built, and even parts of the enterprise product, and say, "These things are supposed to work together. Product marketing says this works this way. Let me try and build something that does that."

This is amazingly valuable work because we can find out that the product doesn't work, so we need to fix that. We can also find out that the product works well and create content around that.

**Geertjan Wielenga**: Is the variation of tasks part of what you find enjoyable about this role?

**Tim Berglund**: Yes, although what lit my fire initially was the performance aspect of the work; that remains critical to me.

Documentation is a function that reports to me. It's a rich developer advocate function that needs to be there. That's part of the way that we communicate with developers.

> *"The variety of my work is important to me."*
>
> *—Tim Berglund*

Leading a team is a big part of my role. I could just be a guy on the road performing and I'd love that, but it's also motivating to me to have a group of people and give them a vision. I give them a context in which they can thrive and grow, and I find the next thing that they're going to do. The variety of my work is important to me.

**Geertjan Wielenga**: What kind of advice do you give to your team?

**Tim Berglund**: My team is more than just developer advocates. I've got a tech writing team that's growing. Then I've got a community team that's much more operational. I have a video producer who reports to me right now. Then I have one and a half developer advocates. Most of the people who do developer advocacy are distributed, as I mentioned. They're off in other teams being solution engineers or things like that.

When it comes time to give advice, I give feedback on new decks, along with helping to shape a narrative structure and providing those nuts and bolts of how to do the basic job well.

I also talk about how to deal with the various problems that can occur on stage when presenting, including dealing with hecklers. That's rare, but it happens.

A lot of conversations involve a member of the team asking, "Should I speak here? This conference reached out to me, but is it a good one for us?" We then try to assess community impact and commercial impact, and make a strategic decision for the company.

**Geertjan Wielenga**: How often do you refresh your own talks?

**Tim Berglund**: There are some things, like an introduction to Kafka, that are going to change slowly. Where the raw content doesn't change too quickly, a talk can live for a long time. Although, I don't actually want to be giving the same deck for more than two years. You get tired of it and you realize that you have to change it.

# Requirements for being a developer advocate

**Geertjan Wielenga**: What are some minimum requirements for this role? Are there any personality traits needed?

**Tim Berglund**: As my boss has put it, my team is a rare zoo of unusual, unique animals: we're all different.

For the developer advocate role, I think you need to have an engineering background. This is a role where you are communicating with, relating to, making friendships with, and helping computer programmers. Let's not lose sight of that.

These are people who write code for a living; it's hard and scary. They never know how things work and everything's new all the time, and it's your job to help those people. I don't think it's realistic to say that you're going to be good in this role if you're not also one of them.

**Geertjan Wielenga**: You said that you need an engineering background, but imagine you're somebody interested in switching from a different career. Would that even be possible?

**Tim Berglund**: I'll put developer advocacy to the side and just think of developer as a role. We already see people coming into professional software development without a computer science degree. That's wonderful.

I'm not particularly bent out of shape about what path people take to get into tech. I certainly don't think you need to come through a university. You can do that, but it doesn't matter if you don't. However, I'm a little opinionated. I think that to be a developer advocate, you have to have spent time as a developer.

I wrote my first program when I was 10 and never looked back. Other people take different paths, but I think you need to spend time as a developer because you just need to understand that life.

There are very technical product marketing people who are very smart and are able to talk about the tech. You've got to be careful with that role, though, because you're never going to get it quite right if you're trying to use a marketing voice to talk to developers.

I think of this anthropologically because it's not just the practice of coding: there's a set of shared traditions, values, vocabulary, and myths that we have. To give an example, I'm from Denver and I think this is evident when I'm in Europe because I'm as American as one can be. When I speak, I don't try to hide that. There are all these things about me that I now recognize as being American things.

> *"There is this shared software development culture globally."*
>
> *—Tim Berglund*

As developers, there is a sense that we have more in common than we do not. There is this shared software development culture globally and you need to be an insider if you're going to have credibility in front of people. That's why I think you need to spend time as a developer. You've got to have spent time writing code.

Just in terms of the standard evangelist/advocate public role, you should have a certain level of comfort in front of people. It is really a performance role, as I said, and that's a core skill.

If you look at professionals like Venkat Subramaniam, you may think that you can't live code and tell jokes for 60 minutes, to a whole room full of people, as he does. And no, you can't. Maybe you never will be able to, but you need to want to do that. You need to love the interaction at that level. You don't need to be an extrovert and you don't need to be a people person.

Not all performers are extroverts, but you're going to be on stage and that needs to be at least a little bit exciting to you.

## Tim's tips for progressing to advocacy

**Geertjan Wielenga**: Based on your experience, what would be the best way to progress from being a developer to being an advocate?

**Tim Berglund**: If this profession sounds like a good idea to you, then it probably is. That's one of the nice things about developer advocacy. There's a large community of developers who think, "I guess I might be able to give a talk, but doing that work full-time sounds terrible." If anybody does want to do this full-time, then they should pursue it. They are probably qualified.

The way you start is to make up a talk on something. If the work that you do is with very bread-and-butter tech, you may think, "It's a good tech, but it's not super cutting edge. The world already has a Josh Long talking about Spring. I'm not going to be him overnight. How am I going to make something interesting about my day job?"

My advice is that if the code that you write in your day job isn't very cool, then find something you think is cool and learn about it. Make a talk about it. It's not dishonest to do that; you're not a fake. You'll have actually done the work to learn about the tech and know enough about it to be able to then talk about it for 45 or 60 minutes at a meetup.

I'll say it again: find a tech you're interested in, build a talk, and then find a meetup in your area that deals with that tech. Maybe it will take four or six months to get on a schedule, but you probably can do that.

In terms of the mechanics of how to build a good presentation and how to speak well, there are great books on that. Dive in! After you do a meetup, do another one. When you've done four or five of those, submit at a conference. Submit a talk at five conferences and you'll get in.

**Geertjan Wielenga**: Do you need to know absolutely everything about a tech before you can promote it?

**Tim Berglund**: No, you don't. You will find, as you talk about the tech, that you learn as people ask you questions that you don't know the answers to. I learned as a professional trainer that you need to make peace with the fact that you're not going to be able to answer every question. No matter what, somebody's going to be able to think of something you don't know.

**Geertjan Wielenga**: What do you do in that situation?

**Tim Berglund**: You darn well better say you don't know! I've just switched tech stacks in the last year. I didn't know anything about Kafka a year ago. Sometimes, you are in situations that are embarrassing. There are things that you should have known, just as basic knowledge of the tech, but get over it! Take the hit. Often, you will receive good, thoughtful questions that nobody could have anticipated. You just have to say that you'll look up the answers later.

**Geertjan Wielenga**: What do you do when you're not completely behind the direction that your organization is taking, then you're up on the stage and you get a question about that?

**Tim Berglund**: Firstly, I should say that, happily, I'm not in this position right now, so none of this is personal. There are a couple of dimensions to this. You're the face of the company and even if you're an individual contributor, you're functioning as a leader. You're in front of a group of people who are asking you a question.

Whether or not you have any say in the direction of the company is one thing, but there's an assumption that you do. I think you should get to the point where you at least have a shared understanding with the company about its direction and your shared commitment. You can say that you have a consensus and even if you don't agree, this decision has been made by a team and you're going to carry that ball.

> *"If you think there are actually ethical principles on the table, you have to quit your job!"*
>
> —*Tim Berglund*

If you get up in front of people and you say, "My company is doing this but it's dumb and I wanted to do this instead," that's weak leadership. If it's something that you feel strongly about, or if you think there are actually ethical principles on the table, you have to quit your job!

It would be better to say to yourself that you're on board and representing this decision, but you've still got your own opinions. In a private conversation, it's fine to give a private opinion, especially if it's a big community thing or relates to open source versus commercial, but in public, you have to represent the consensus position you hold with your employer.

If the organization is employing developer advocates, there's the assumption that the product has some surface that developers can touch, such as a development tool or an API. In my company, it's infrastructure. Only programmers use Kafka, which means there's a community. The leadership team should be relying on the developer advocate team to understand what the community thinks.

## Being open about bugs

**Geertjan Wielenga**: How honest are you when you know that there are bugs in the tech that you're promoting?

**Tim Berglund**: I will 100% cop to the bugs. I think that's a different matter altogether because it's a fact that software has bugs.

**Geertjan Wielenga**: Would you cop to any and all bugs? How far do you go?

**Tim Berglund**: You have to take that case by case. I'm not going to go out of my way to say, "Well, here are all the bugs!"

Nobody wants to know that. They're just thinking, "How can I succeed with this?"

**Geertjan Wielenga**: As a developer advocate, you can certainly grow attached to a tech and to the community around it. A downside might be that you could end up being too attached to it. Have you experienced this?

**Tim Berglund**: No, I love tech, and I can't imagine a life of mine that didn't have tech in it, but I've always been able to decouple myself from it emotionally.

When something is going wrong in a community, or a company is making a wrong business decision about how to handle open source, I'm far enough removed that I don't feel like the real me is threatened.

That doesn't mean that things don't happen at work that get to me. I've got my buttons, but the tech is always kind of wrong; you've just got to love it for what it is. For my many weaknesses, getting too attached to any particular piece of tech is not one of them.

> *"If the tech goes wrong, it's not you that is broken."*
>
> —*Tim Berglund*

I worked for a company a few years ago that viewed itself as not just a cool company but a completely different idea. It wasn't just a good start-up: it was a shining city on a hill. I saw this attitude and I thought, "Guys, your god is going to bleed at some point and it's going to be a bad day for you!" That day came and it broke a lot of people. You've got to have other things in your life. You also have to realize that there's a boundary around you. If the tech goes wrong, it's not you that is broken.

**Geertjan Wielenga**: What does a typical day look like? Is there a typical day?

## An average day for a developer advocate

**Tim Berglund**: My answer will be colored by the fact that I'm a leader of a developer relations team, so an individual contributor would have a slightly different answer.

On the road, I can be speaking at a conference during the day or traveling to a conference in the evening. There are meetings with people too. Those people might work with completely different tech or they might be people in my tech community who I'm catching up with. Maybe we're only going to see each other twice this year, so I have a lot of relationship maintenance to do in a short time.

At the same time, I still need to be on certain calls. I also need to attend to emails and Slack. Being on the road doesn't mean that office life stops. Since I'm the leader of a team, those management responsibilities don't go away.

At home, it will again be email, Slack, or phone calls that dominate my day. Every once in a while, I'll have some time to create a new presentation. I'll spend time writing and editing content. One of our responsibilities is the company blog. We also make video tutorials. A couple of times a month, I'll have a day in the studio recording some video content. But a typical day looks like it does for any manager.

**Geertjan Wielenga**: Do you prefer to work from home, then?

**Tim Berglund**: Yes, that's very important to me. I'm traveling at something approaching 50% of the time, so when I'm not traveling, just from a lifestyle and family perspective, I really want to be at home.

There's no reason for me to go to the office. In this role, since we tend to be road warrior people, there's a strong preference toward home office work when we're home.

**Geertjan Wielenga**: Then the follow-up question would be: what percentage of the week do you get up before lunchtime?

**Tim Berglund**: I happen to be an early riser. A normal day is 5:00 a.m. for me and a late day is 6:00 a.m. or 6:30 a.m. That's just me: I get up early. A few times in the winter, there'll be a day when I don't have to go anywhere and it'll be pajama pants all day. That's a major victory!

**Geertjan Wielenga**: How do you deal with things like jet lag, missed flights, and all the typical problems of the traveler?

**Tim Berglund**: In the U.S., there's melatonin available over the counter. It might be complete nonsense, but I take a couple of those tablets before bed. Just anecdotally, I feel better for it.

Generally, jet lag is tough. When I come to Europe, for my first two or three nights I'm going to wake up at 3:00 a.m. At lunchtime, I'm going to be super tired. If I have a session, I'll feel pretty rough.

**Geertjan Wielenga**: Do you tend to try to arrive a couple of days beforehand to deal with that?

**Tim Berglund**: Not generally. I don't plan business meetings or talks on the first day now. I did it because of a delayed flight once and it was the worst experience.

I was supposed to leave on a Sunday but flew out on a Monday instead because of a delay. I landed in London at 6:00 a.m. and had to teach at 9:00 a.m. There was this guy coughing and there was a baby crying on the flight, so I couldn't sleep at all. It was terrible.

**Geertjan Wielenga**: Imagine you've traveled across the world and, for some reason, your projector connection to your laptop doesn't work or only two people turn up to listen to you. How do you deal with that?

**Tim Berglund**: A little over a year ago, I had a projector on a Mac that flat out didn't work. That talk was actually in California. In that case, happily, the deck was a simple one and I exported it from Keynote to PowerPoint and threw it on somebody's Windows machine. That worked.

> *"Just do your job and don't worry about the number of people at your talk."*
>
> —*Tim Berglund*

In terms of the second problem, give those two people a great talk! Just don't worry about that. Yes, I want there to be 2,000 people attending too; everybody wants that. But just do your job and don't worry about the number of people at your talk.

## Taking a break

**Geertjan Wielenga**: Have you encountered burnout? How do you know that you're on the verge of it and what are some ways to deal with it?

**Tim Berglund**: I don't know how to define it. My pace hasn't really changed over the years, so if I have flirted with burnout, it hasn't taken me down. Everybody needs to recognize that there are walls, though. That can be in terms of physical health or even emotional health. Anybody can be preoccupied with thinking, "I'm not sure if this is right for me," but burnout is different.

What you need to look out for is thinking, "I actually can't do this now. My body is preventing me and my mind is preventing me. I'm unable to do the work." That's burnout. That hasn't happened to me, which is something I'm very thankful for.

You need to take time to rest. I have for the past eight or nine years tried to build in a no-travel December. I make small exceptions to that. There's a conference in South Florida that I usually speak at in December. My wife and sometimes my adult children come. My wife and I used to live in Florida, so we get to see friends and there's warm weather, so it doesn't feel like travel to us. Otherwise, I think, "I'm on the road a lot. Let me take a month to reset and be at home for a while."

**Geertjan Wielenga**: One thing that's quite special about you is that you've been doing *DevRel Radio*. What's the background to that?

**Tim Berglund**: We actually recorded a few episodes early last year and then for various reasons, relating to each of the three co-hosts, we put it on hold for a while. We've picked it back up now. Viktor Gamov, Baruch Sadogursky, and I said, "Hey, we should do a podcast." We're all friends. Viktor and Baruch are already famous Russian podcasters.

I'm pretty good at being a radio host. We realized that this profession needs some community around it. We're all community builders: serving various communities, doing our thing, helping people, and mentoring new people. The podcasts are just the wisdom of people who have built things and have been doing this for a long time.

**Geertjan Wielenga**: Where can you find the podcasts and are there going to be any new episodes?

**Tim Berglund**: You can find them on iTunes, but `devrelrad.io` is the easiest way to find them. We're going to be producing approximately two episodes each month. That's ambitious. It's okay if we don't hit that target; we won't feel bad about ourselves.

**Geertjan Wielenga**: How do you stay up to date with the latest tech trends?

**Tim Berglund**: I work with smart people and I talk to them. This is a little embarrassing, but I read Hacker News every morning. I don't read the comments, though, just as a life choice.

My Twitter feed is mostly professional, so I see things there. I'm part of a few communities with old-style mailing lists too. Those aren't really sources, but I rely on those people.

**Geertjan Wielenga**: How do you explain what you do to a non-technical person?

**Tim Berglund**: I tell people that I mostly just write emails, talk on Zoom calls, and occasionally fly to places. Functionally, my role is easy to describe. The shortest shortcut I can come up with is that my job is the intersection of marketing and engineering. I have a team of technical people who are trying to explain a piece of tech to a community of users of that tech. We're doing that in a way that is fun and winsome.

My work is explicitly outreach. Saying that usually lets people at a cocktail party know that if they're not careful, I'm going to talk for a lot longer and they need to change the subject fast!

**Geertjan Wielenga**: Why do so many people not know about the profession that we're in?

## The progression of developer relations

**Tim Berglund**: I think it's just very new. I traced the origins of the controversial word "evangelist" to 1984 and Guy Kawasaki. That was a slightly different kind of work he was doing: he was trying to convince what we used to call independent software vendors to go and write programs for the Macintosh. He was evangelizing the platform.

> *"Developer relations, as a discipline, is really just emerging."*
>
> —*Tim Berglund*

Developer relations, as a discipline, is really just emerging. It's a consequence of open source maturing and businesses forming around open-source projects. There are all these activities happening. In the last five or 10 years, more people have realized that there's a discipline here.

The word that comes to mind is "inchoate." Developer advocacy is not completely formed. As a result, not everybody appreciates that it's a thing. Everybody's been to a conference. Everybody knows that there are meetups. Everybody likes sample applications. But as a coherent whole, the role is not fully known yet.

**Geertjan Wielenga**: You mentioned Guy Kawasaki. Are there other people in the industry who inspire you or who you've learned something from?

**Tim Berglund**: Yes, there are a number of them. I've always been a fan of Scott Davis. I always thought, "Wow this guy's just everywhere. He's such a great presenter. He's got this cadence of a Baptist preacher!" I really admired that fun stage presence.

Ken Sipe, Stu Halloway, and Neal Ford are also people I admire. I learned a lot from Neal about presentation structure and narrative.

He's done some pioneering thinking and it's had a huge impact on me. Matthew McCullough and I worked together in the early 2010s too. These are all people who shaped me.

**Geertjan Wielenga**: We've talked about many positive things thus far. What would you say are some lows that you have experienced in your years of doing this?

**Tim Berglund**: It's a trope that we're on the road all the time, even though there are ways to structure the role so that there's not as much traveling. If you have a young family, you have to ask, "Is this going to work?" I got into this when my kids were not so little anymore. My youngest was around 10, so that wasn't such a stretch. You've got to be willing to travel, though.

I'm always thinking, "Where does this go? What's the career arc in this industry?" It's a middle-aged, sole-breadwinner kind of anxiety. To speak frankly about age and tech, somewhere around my mid-30s, I was looking around a bullpen full of developers and I thought, "Does your mom know you're here?!"

These were grown men and women, not children. It just struck me that many developers are really young, although, in the evangelist/developer advocate community, this is less the case. It doesn't mean that you can't be young and do this role well, but these roles seem to be a magnet for more senior-level people.

In the U.S., the assumption is that past 35 or so, you're not really going to write code anymore. You're going to get into management or a product role or something else. I don't know if that's true. I'd like to validate that. You have the celebrities who are not, in any sense, young anymore, but they're still doing this. Short of that, what happens for everybody else?

> *"What's our career arc? What should it be?"*
>
> —*Tim Berglund*

What's our career arc? What should it be? How do we feel about it? How should we prepare young people? I do think it's possible to do developer advocacy over the long term and ride with it into retirement. I think that can be done, but I don't know where my story will go yet.

**Geertjan Wielenga**: What are some roles that would flow naturally from this if you did want to change paths?

## Career options for developer advocates

**Tim Berglund**: You could be in the leadership team of organizations that do this. If you're working as a developer advocate now, you're on the road, you're teaching, and you're doing talks. You're getting results and people are benefiting and your reputation is increasing. You could go from there to leading the same type of people.

The issue is that not everybody wants to do that. They might be gifted at all the work I just described and not gifted at leading. We should let people do what they're good at, but if they're motivated to lead, they can apply their own experiences to help other people to come into the role.

Marketing could be an option. I've mentioned that I tell people that developer advocacy is where engineering meets marketing. That's scary language among developers, but I don't think it should be.

**Geertjan Wielenga**: Right now, you're working within a company, but initially you were giving talks for your own enjoyment. How would you compare that experience?

**Tim Berglund**: I think, just with my particular set of capabilities, I'm able to create more value within a company structure than completely independently. The part that I miss is the greater creative freedom that I had when I was on my own. I could just write talks about cool things.

**Geertjan Wielenga**: Could you take some cool things and combine them with the work that you do now?

**Tim Berglund**: Probably, but the problem is with the workload that having a full-time job presents. My role doesn't leave much time for creative exploration. It hasn't worked out to be practical to do that. I haven't figured out how to combine anything new with our go-to market and responsibly give a talk in the community. It's theoretically possible, but I'm skeptical.

**Geertjan Wielenga**: Do you see yourself working forever in a company setting, then?

**Tim Berglund**: Definitely in the short term I will keep working for "the man." I'm pretty happy with it. There may come a time when I don't need an income. I don't know what I'll be like, or be interested in, or be doing at that point.

If there is some kind of retirement phase in my life, then I could just go and creatively explore fun things and still have a platform to be able to talk about them. That would be a pretty great retirement!

I could go back to advocating independently and certainly put food on the table, but it doesn't seem like the right move for me right now. There are good things going on with some of the companies that I've been involved with.

**Geertjan Wielenga**: Would you say that some people in our domain, who don't work for companies, really need the conference scene because that's where they see people in the industry?

**Tim Berglund**: Yes, I've got all kinds of those peers. That's really a good reminder that you should make time for your colleagues who are independent when you're at conferences. They need you.

**Geertjan Wielenga**: What would the 20-year-old you think of the current you?

**Tim Berglund**: There's just no way I would have been able to predict this career path. When I was 20, I wanted to write code, do digital logic design, or do signal processing, or a mix of those things.

As I mentioned, I actually had a job writing firmware while I was a college student. I was coding professionally and that's all I wanted to do. I wanted to build embedded systems and write firmware. I just couldn't imagine a cooler thing.

There wasn't a culture of developer advocacy like there is now. The only conferences I knew of were the Computer Dealers' Exhibition (COMDEX) and the big networking or consumer electronics conferences. I just wouldn't have had any concept of developer advocacy as a role.

For advice, I probably would tell the younger me to start a little earlier. Not that I feel I missed any kind of boat, but this job is so great that I wish I had got into it sooner. "Start now" is the best advice I could give primordial Tim.

**Geertjan Wielenga**: Thank you, Tim Berglund.

## 18

> Everything I do is for the community and for the good of the community.

# Ray Tsang

# Introducing Ray Tsang

Ray Tsang is a developer advocate and Java Champion. Ray has worked in tech and consulting companies, helping customers to develop and design information systems and enterprise architecture and adopt new platforms. Ray has also contributed to open-source projects and is the creator of the JDeferred library. Despite having had a lot of fear of public speaking, Ray has forged a successful career delivering both presentations and new tech to developers. Find Ray on Twitter: @saturnism.

---

**Geertjan Wielenga**: When did you realize you were a developer advocate and how did you get to that point?

## Ray's path to developer advocacy

**Ray Tsang**: I've been in the industry for a very long time, through all the Java days, starting with Enterprise JavaBeans (EJB) 2.0. I worked in consulting for large companies for a while as well.

In every role, what I ended up doing was introducing new tech and techniques, and bringing that to the team of developers to make their lives easier. This meant that we could streamline some of the boilerplates and the whole development process.

Then I joined a company called Red Hat and there I was a solution architect. I helped people and taught them about the tech that we had.

That's how I got to meet quite a variety of people and that made me think, "Oh, this is an interesting thing to do." Developer advocate, to me, is not a position: I think it's a mindset. Anybody can be a developer advocate and it doesn't have to be a specific job.

I remember at Red Hat, I'd seen many of the engineers working on the open-source projects, such as Hibernate, Infinispan, and JGroups, and speaking and writing about their tech. They talked about the things that they had done and how people could better use the tech to solve their problems. That really inspired me to think, "Well, I want to be able to do that one day."

At Red Hat, there was an opportunity to speak at one of its conferences in my role as a solution architect. I was selected to speak for one of the sessions on the things I was personally working on as well. That was the first time I ever spoke at a conference, but afterwards, I felt that was the job I would really enjoy doing.

Speaking was never something I liked doing; I'm actually terrified of public speaking. I never really liked speaking in front of anybody. During my high-school time/university time, I always avoided speaking in front of the room. I absolutely did not enjoy it.

The first time I had to present professionally was at a consulting company where we were presenting a project. I just remember that I had to memorize the scripts. I rehearsed for two weeks and on the day of that presentation, with only 20 people in the room, I wasn't able to stand up. My legs didn't have any strength. I had to push myself up. My hands were clenched into fists. It was a terrifying experience speaking at all in front of people.

**Geertjan Wielenga**: That's very interesting that you're terrified of public speaking. Have you become more comfortable with it?

**Ray Tsang**: Over time, public speaking has become something that I can handle. That's not to say that I enjoy every moment of it because it's still terrifying, but I have overcome some of the fear; that's the change.

**Geertjan Wielenga**: What's the terrifying part?

**Ray Tsang**: I used to be terrified of making mistakes and not knowing what I needed to say. English is not my first language. I do lose words from time to time. I can't speak fluently in some cases. My train of thought doesn't come out the right way, for example. I can't gather my thoughts quickly enough to just speak the next sentence.

> *"Was I really qualified to be speaking on the topic?"*
>
> *—Ray Tsang*

I was also afraid that all of the things I was presenting were wrong or fundamentally flawed. Was I really qualified to be speaking on the topic?

**Geertjan Wielenga**: Did you study IT? What was your educational background?

**Ray Tsang**: I actually studied computer science and I had the opportunity to use computers really early on. I had always known that I wanted to be in that industry, doing something with computers and programming as an engineer.

Then, somewhere along the way, during university, I really wanted to be a consultant.

There are campus interviews, where companies come to the university campus and they interview you. On one occasion, I got through to the last round. The partner of the company asked, "Why do you want to be a consultant?"

I replied, "It would be really nice to write some code on the beach somewhere and travel the world." I didn't get that job, for obvious reasons.

Ultimately, the people at Red Hat inspired me to want to bring tech to developers in a way that solves their problems. That is when I started to do this.

**Geertjan Wielenga**: Today you're a full-time developer advocate, then?

**Ray Tsang**: Yes, I'm a developer advocate full-time. I'm very lucky to be in an organization that's actually part of engineering. Much of what I do is engineering-heavy and engineering-focused.

I definitely try to focus on the developer stories and developer issues. The other part of that is advocating for the developers. I want to make the developer experience as good as possible. It's not just teaching people new things and trying to make that consumable in terms of information, but also seeing everything as a two-way street.

## The appeal of advocacy

**Geertjan Wielenga**: When you compare this role to pure programming, which is what you were doing before, what is the attractive aspect?

Why are you no longer purely programming and instead you're a developer advocate?

**Ray Tsang**: I enjoy the pure engineering, but I also enjoy the relationship part of it and working with people. I'm fortunate to have the opportunity to be able to travel and to meet great people.

I learn so much by talking to people. That helps me to expand my view and my knowledge base because there are always these new ideas that pop up when I get to talk to a diverse group of people.

I don't feel that I would get those opportunities if I didn't get to know the community. Of course, there are ways to get that balance in pure engineering too, I'm sure. Some of the most inspiring engineers not only create great tech, but also engage with the community. However, in addition to being able to work on projects, I have the people aspect in my work.

**Geertjan Wielenga**: Travel can be problematic sometimes. Do you have any horror stories to share?

**Ray Tsang**: First of all, knock on wood, my luggage has never been lost. I try to never check in my luggage.

Mainly travel is just something I choose to do. If I ever want to not travel, I believe I can totally do that, and I'll probably advocate in another form, through blogs or videos, or using other ways to get the information out. But to get information out there, and also for being connected to the community, I do feel that meeting people in person is one of the best ways.

> *"I don't think travel is required. Advocacy takes on many different forms."*
>
> —Ray Tsang

I love to connect with people in person, but I also know that some people like to just live code and show the video stream. So, I don't think travel is required. Advocacy takes on many different forms.

When I do travel, it's about just coordinating all the flights, figuring out what time I'm arriving, and thinking about how much time I can spend at the conference. One thing I don't like to do is just go in and out of the conference for my session because then I don't get to network with other people. I try to make sure that wherever I go, I can stay for the entire duration of the conference, or even sometimes a little bit longer, and connect with the local community and customers/users while I'm there. I try to speak at other local Java User Groups or other developer groups that are out there.

People may experience struggles with their extensive travel schedules, but at the same time, I feel we're all responsible for our wellbeing. I'm responsible for my own schedule, so I try to manage it however I see fit. If I do feel overwhelmed, I will definitely cut it down.

**Geertjan Wielenga**: Have you ever not made a speaking engagement in time?

**Ray Tsang**: No, between organizers and the speakers, there is a certain amount of trust. They know I'm going to show up with, hopefully, good material that meets audience expectations.

So far, I haven't had many issues. Sometimes I don't get the email or I lose the email of acceptance, then I forget about it until I remember that I accepted and was supposed to be somewhere. There was only one time when I double-scheduled by accident and that was because I didn't see the acceptance email.

**Geertjan Wielenga**: How do you deal with jet lag?

## Managing jet lag

**Ray Tsang**: For the eastbound flights, if I can't sleep, I usually just stay up all night on the airplane. Then I stay up all day once I land and just sleep on my evening off. If I try to stay up as long as I can, that second day and third day will be great. On the fourth and fifth days, the jet lag is going to hit me again and it's just a matter of drinking coffee and tea to stay up.

On the way back, I think it's also a little easier. Basically, when I come back, it's usually evening and I just sleep through the night. But I personally haven't had much trouble with jet lag. I don't take any melatonin or any other things to stay awake or go to sleep.

One tip is to eat on time. Eating on time is something I do follow rigorously. Even at work, I always try to eat on time. I don't like lunch meetings for that matter. Eating on time sets my schedule during the day and keeps me away from working too much as well. When I move to another time zone, that really helps me to reset my internal clock.

**Geertjan Wielenga**: There's always this discussion about tech evangelism versus developer advocacy. What's the difference to your mind?

**Ray Tsang**: Are they supposed to be different? I don't know the difference between them! I think the title doesn't define who we are: it's what we do that defines who we are.

Engineers can be great advocates for what they do and for the things that they've learned. Whether some people like to do that or not is a separate discussion.

> *"There are other people who have the same fear of public speaking.'*
>
> *—Ray Tsang*

I know there are other people who have the same fear of public speaking but the people I've seen on stage who give some of the best talks are, in fact, engineers who talk about the things that they work on. They get to learn from the audience and hear what other people think about what they're doing, so they can actively improve it. You also get great talks/content from users, where they provide insight into really hard problems, show how they solved those problems using certain tech, and discuss improvements that can be made to a project.

As for advocate versus evangelist, I truly don't know the difference between the two.

**Geertjan Wielenga**: I'm still a bit fascinated about how on the one hand you're terrified of speaking and on the other hand, you're speaking all the time. How does that work?

## How Ray prepares for a talk

**Ray Tsang**: As I said, I'm not as terrified these days, but I do have fear every time before I get on stage to speak. Speaking is just one way that I do my job and one way for me to connect with the audience, but there are many other ways to do it. I chose to do a lot more public speaking because I wanted to face my fear. I wanted to know if I could actually do it.

Constant rehearsals help. It's about just repeating what I want to say and drafting the story to make it, hopefully, a fun presentation that is also informative/useful.

I start from the beginning when rehearsing. I make sure the slides will guide me in terms of the story I want to speak about. But if I ever make a mistake somewhere during rehearsal, I will go back to the top and restart the whole thing again.

I do this until I feel comfortable with the whole talk from end to end. I also record myself, so that I can potentially hear any part of a sentence that I'm going too fast on. I usually go too fast anyway. Are there any pronunciations I need to correct? Does it sound right? I have to prepare myself to feel confident when I'm presenting.

**Geertjan Wielenga**: Do you do this every time you go to a conference and you have a presentation?

**Ray Tsang**: Yes, every time when they ask me to bring a new talk, I do this process. The first dozen times I do the same talk, I will still prepare in the same way.

You probably won't see me in the conference area before my talk. That's because I'm always in the room practicing the presentation. Even if I've given the same presentation more than once, I always have to go back and rehearse the same thing, especially when it comes to live demos.

**Geertjan Wielenga**: In general, what are the themes that you've talked about over the years? Is there a commonality across all your presentations?

**Ray Tsang**: I come from the Java backend world, with a heavy enterprise focus. I had the opportunity to go through the EJBs, the service-oriented architecture, and all that, so I'm heavily rooted in backend Java.

The things I do today are still focused on backend Java, particularly with the cloud because that is what people have been talking about for a number of years. Although, I think that this is happening at a faster pace now.

Beyond the cloud, what I focus on is architecture. Many of things that I do surround the Java microservices architecture. This includes orchestration with Kubernetes, the microservices communication itself with gRPC Remote Procedure Call (gRPC), and the monitoring and tracing aspects of microservices.

Recently, when I went back to see the different talks I'd done over the past couple of years, I realized that they actually link up into a whole series based around the Java microservices architecture from the bottom up. This is building the microservice, the communication that we need to use, the orchestration, resiliency, tracing, and monitoring. They all tie up end to end.

**Geertjan Wielenga**: What's on the horizon? Where do you see the themes of future conferences going?

**Ray Tsang**: I don't actually chase the hot topics, but if there's a certain new tech that really works, and is really useful, then I would love people to know about it.

It's not so much about what the latest and greatest new theme is, but more what is actually useful and relevant for developers today to solve today's problems. Potentially, there are some people who want to talk about future problems as well, but I like to be more practical.

I don't know what else is going to be relevant in the future. I was lucky enough to be interested in the right thing while it was popular, but that doesn't necessarily mean that I'm going to jump onto the next big thing.

**Geertjan Wielenga**: How do you stay up to date with the latest developments? Do you use social media alerts or any online sites?

**Where to go for information**

**Ray Tsang**: Mostly, I just follow Twitter. Sometimes I do check Hacker News and some mailing lists as well. As a Java Champion, I get to see the mailing lists there. I also read other Java-oriented mailing lists to see what new things are being considered or worked on, and those are very useful.

I personally find some of the developer surveys to be really awesome, at least for understanding the landscape.

Of course, every one of them will be slightly different, but in the greater scheme of things, it just helps with understanding a little bit of the current trends.

There are other things that are getting popular, like serverless and machine learning, but I think that at the end of the day, there are always these practical problems that we all have to solve.

> *"We have to go beyond just always chasing the latest thing."*
>
> *—Ray Tsang*

I spoke to Bruno Borges and he has this idea of going back to the basics, which are things that have been forgotten that we all have to do as best practices. We have to go beyond just always chasing the latest thing. We have to have deep roots in engineering to make things great.

**Geertjan Wielenga**: In the conference scene, you're known, along with people like Josh Long and Matt Raible, as being a very dynamic and entertaining speaker. Is this just how you present or has this developed to where it is today?

**Ray Tsang**: I remember going to conferences where I saw only slides and I just realized that everyone likes different ways of consuming information. For me, personally, the slides thing usually doesn't work.

When I'm trying to present a new concept or topic to my audience of mostly developers, I find that showing code is one of the best ways.

With live coding, some people may find that boilerplates don't really demonstrate the points. That's why when I live code, I want to make sure every line of code counts, so that it does demonstrate some issues or points, and I have explanations around why this is done a certain way.

**Geertjan Wielenga**: What do you do when someone asks a question and you don't know the answer? Has that happened? How do you solve that?

**Ray Tsang**: Who hasn't had those kinds of questions at sessions or conferences? I just say, "I don't know the answer." It's impossible for me to know everything and sometimes the questions are very involved, which is actually great.

> *"There are definitely times when I don't know an answer."*
>
> —*Ray Tsang*

I think that what's important is for me to understand where the question is coming from and what problem it solves, and follow up after that. There are definitely times when I don't know an answer and the worst thing that I can do is to pretend I know.

**Geertjan Wielenga**: How do you follow up? What does that mean in your case?

**Ray Tsang**: That could be exchanging messages on Twitter or just making sure that the answer is in a written form somehow for that person. I love questions. I think I've learned so much through questions and the insight from them.

**Geertjan Wielenga**: What about the situation where you get to the conference and your laptop doesn't connect to the projector or there is some technical problem? Has this happened?

## Battling technical issues

**Ray Tsang**: Yes, there have been a few times when the adapter was faulty, but I didn't figure that out until, say, 20 minutes in. One time, the screen was projected and it just went off, then after about five minutes it came back on. We had no idea why that was happening. There was nothing I could do. I couldn't really just stop, so I tried to talk through the concepts and do as much as I could.

As you know, I do a lot of live demos. If I can't do live demos, I have to talk through the concepts in more detail and that becomes a very difficult thing to do.

There was another time when I had to do the entire presentation from the back because the connection in the front didn't work, so there was no way for me to project my screen. I actually had to, after about 10 minutes of introduction, run to the back of the room, and sit right next to the A/V people.

If there's a complete outage of Internet, then what can you do? Life goes on. That's beyond my control. Again, knock on wood, that hasn't happened yet. I do require the Internet for all of my sessions because I do many of the demos on the Internet in the cloud. Without the Internet, it's going to be very difficult for me.

**Geertjan Wielenga**: We've talked mainly about the speaking activities that you do as a developer advocate, but there's more to being a developer advocate than that. What are the other activities that you're involved in?

**Ray Tsang**: I mentioned advocating for developers and that could be the needs of the developers in terms of bugs that need to be fixed, or experiences that could be better, or the products that could work better for certain developer communities. When I'm not speaking, I'm trying to make all of these things accessible and easy to use.

The feedback for a product is not just from the conferences, though: it also comes from users within other companies. I go and speak with other developers within other companies and try to understand how they're using our tech, what troubles they're running into, and what kind of features they'd like to see.

As a developer advocate, I think it's important to have a central network or to be empowered to have a channel of communication. Ultimately, it's up to the products team to make the decisions on what needs to be done and then what can be done.

**Geertjan Wielenga**: Do you have a basic schedule?

**Ray Tsang**: I don't have a regular schedule. It's determined mostly by the conference schedule when I'm traveling. If I've got a session, of course my schedule will be rehearsal and practice. After the session, I get to relax a little bit and can chat with colleagues and friends in the community.

If I'm not at a conference, then it's meetings and catching up with the many colleagues I need to talk to. My schedule is a little bit fluid and dynamic. I don't really have a set schedule. I know some people may have study time or experiment time in their working day. I'd actually like to add more structure myself.

**Geertjan Wielenga**: What do you find most interesting and what do you find most boring to work on?

**Ray Tsang**: I think I'm in the fortunate position where there is a lot of trust from the team. Everything that I choose to do is something that I want to do. Whether I decide to go to conferences or do something like produce videos, it's all completely up to me.

> *"As advocates, being truthful about what is good and what is not good is what we need to do."*
>
> —*Ray Tsang*

I'm passionate about the Java developer community specifically, so everything I do is for the community and for the good of the community. To some extent, I can tell them what not to use and what is a bad practice. I can also tell them what I feel is really great. As advocates, being truthful about what is good and what is not good is what we need to do. I can choose my own path in terms of what I think is really awesome right now and if there are bad practices, I will call them out.

## Honesty when doing a demo

**Geertjan Wielenga**: If you're doing a session and you're doing a demo, do you avoid the areas that you know don't quite work the way they should, or do you talk about that very openly?

**Ray Tsang**: I think it's important to talk about things that don't work well. I always add in a caveat if something's not production-ready, for example, because we've got to make that clear.

459

I think it's very important to call all things out: saying what works and doesn't work. I try to do that as much as I can. I may say, "Don't use that for now." Say, for example, that we're talking about databases. If you have object-relational mapping, you have these complicated graphs of objects relating to each other. Is it right to always use those things? It depends on the use case. So rather than saying yes or no, when I get the time, I want to make sure I understand what the use case is and figure out if it's something that can work.

**Geertjan Wielenga**: If you're a developer advocate coming from a company, then there sometimes is the suspicion that you're only pretending to be authentic because actually, you're being paid by that company. What would you say to that?

**Ray Tsang**: I actually think that most of the great developer advocates don't necessarily talk about the tech from their company per se.

I do a lot of work around open source and I like to show things that could be done in many different environments. I remember the days when I had my own 286 computer. I could read a book and write a few programs, and that just worked without anything else. That is the power that every developer has and that's what I feel that I want to bring to the table as a developer advocate.

If you are, in fact, working in a large corporation, then of course there are other pressures and things that can be worrying. You need to think about building a network in a large team, getting to know who to talk to, and how to potentially have an influence on the direction of a certain product to make it better for the developers. These internal things can be stressful for anybody in a company.

Without passion, I think it's very easy to just give up, but I feel that most of the advocates I know are really passionate about what they are talking about and what they want to achieve. We keep on going at it to make sure that it's good for our users.

**Geertjan Wielenga**: What would you say are the core personality traits or characteristics that are ideal for being a developer advocate?

**Ray Tsang**: I think everyone has the capability to do this when they are passionate about their tech or passionate about the community. It's all about information sharing. People from all over the world have different kinds of personalities. I wouldn't say that there's a single trait that you need. Developer advocates do what we do to make tech better. That's our story, I suppose.

**Geertjan Wielenga**: Thank you, Ray Tsang.

## 19

> *I can't imagine a company out there that won't eventually have a developer program.*

# Tori Wieldt

# Introducing Tori Wieldt

Tori Wieldt is a developer advocate for the New Relic Digital Intelligence Platform. She writes blog posts, speaks at New Relic User Groups and conferences, and works to empower and educate the New Relic developer community. She has had experience as a system administrator, technical writer, and marketing leader. Tori's style and inclusive approach make her writing and presentations both educational and engaging. Find Tori on Twitter: @ToriWieldt.

---

**Geertjan Wielenga**: What are you doing right now with developer advocacy?

**Tori Wieldt**: I'm about 40% a developer advocate. Where the slider is for me depends on how much pure marketing I'm doing.

## Tori's day-to-day work

At the minute, what I'm tasked with doing for my organization, New Relic, is the messaging around DevOps for marketing. That's creating messaging docs and presentations, and training the salespeople on how to talk about DevOps to people who are interested in our software. The rest of the time, I do things that are more classically considered evangelism, which means going to conferences, giving presentations, talking to developers, gathering up information to take back to my company, and so on.

**Geertjan Wielenga**: How are you not a developer advocate, then? That entire breadth of activities is what many people would see as advocacy.

**Tori Wieldt**: The difference, for me, is that I'm not a coder, so I don't know if that breaks the mold or not. I don't build sample apps; I have people to do it for me. I do feel that I bring value to my company, though.

Developers are allergic to marketing, so you have to have a measure of respect for the person you're talking to. Developers at my organization say, "I just created this new feature."

I get to say, "So what? The feature by itself has no meaning: you have to provide context. Why would anybody care about this?" Developers (our customers) are really good at sniffing out fluff, so you don't want to waste their time.

It helps to understand what developers deal with on a daily basis. Then you can say, "Here's a thing that'll help to make your work life better or maybe even your home life better if it can get you home sooner."

**Geertjan Wielenga**: What is your job description, then, at New Relic?

**Tori Wieldt**: They want to call me a "solutions manager." My role has been through some evolutions during my time with my company. When I came on board, the title was "developer advocate" and then I was a "community manager." It does feel like a slider, depending on what the focus is and how much I adjust what I'm doing.

**Geertjan Wielenga**: How did you get to where you are now? What's your story?

**Tori Wieldt**: I have to be honest here and say that I do have a lot of experience, but you have to be careful in this industry when talking about how old you are. I've felt that in my current environment.

I have a degree in cinematography and I was planning to be a director of feature films. When I graduated, there were no jobs in that field, so I got a job as a media specialist for a school district. In that role, I helped to deliver films to schools.

When the schools got 100 Apple IIe computers delivered, I was told, "They aren't books, which must mean they're in the 'media' category. You need to figure out how to use them."

I installed the first computers for the school district, then I started looking at and recommending software for teachers. That got me into the world of computing. I loved it and thought it was fascinating.

Next, I got a job at a phone company as a sysadmin. That included running some really old microcomputers that were the size of large rooms. I had to pull up sections of floor and pull cables. In that role, I learned Unix, which was really invaluable at the time. I came out to California for a Unix conference, which made me want to move to California. I've been in tech ever since.

I worked at Sun Microsystems as a tech writer, then I started managing the team that took care of the website and most of that was a delivery mechanism for software.

It took the whole team to make that happen. When Sun Microsystems got acquired by Oracle, I moved from developer tools—NetBeans, which I adored—to being a community manager for the Java community.

Mostly, I was actually trying to explain to Oracle how things worked in the Java community. I felt that was a good way to be an advocate for developers. Oracle was very used to a hierarchical way of running user groups. It was all about who was in charge of the user groups and what the rules were. The Java community has a very different mindset to that, so I was responsible for bridging those two worlds.

I had a really good manager at Oracle who explained, "Much of your job will be saying no to marketing people." The marketing team wanted to fill all our social media channels with things that weren't relevant to our audience. They were just trying to broadcast everywhere. What we needed to be doing was building trust with our users. The reality is that every time you send an advert—especially an advert for a webinar that has nothing to do with that audience—you chip away at that trust.

> *"Acknowledging that we needed to push back against marketing meant that we were empowered to do the right thing."*
>
> —*Tori Wieldt*

Acknowledging that we needed to push back against marketing meant that we were empowered to do the right thing. My newsletter contained topics of interest to Java developers and even topics that were outside the sphere of the company.

I would point to a good article because it was a good article, not because it pushed a particular product. That's important.

I left Oracle and came to New Relic, and it's been a great ride. New Relic is a company that's growing really well and you get the opportunity to build out a process as you're using it. You're creating the work and deciding how to do the work at the same time.

Right now, the world is getting eaten by software. New Relic is very much at the heart of helping companies to make that transition, including moving to the cloud, moving to doing DevOps, and understanding that your user experience is literally determining whether you're going to stay in business or not. It's a really interesting space.

**Geertjan Wielenga**: Do you feel that the demand for the kind of function that you describe is just going to increase?

## Knowing your audience

**Tori Wieldt**: Yes, absolutely. The old notion used to be that the developer audience is very different from other audiences. You can't say that literally everybody's becoming a developer now, but consumers are much more sophisticated. You have to treat them with respect and understand where they're coming from. Why is your widget of value to them? You have to prove its usefulness within minutes.

This whole notion of a three-year sales cycle, with hundreds of people involved in terms of purchasing software, is out the window. I feel good about that because it enables choice for consumers.

Although, I do feel for legacy companies that have the monolith. In order to stay in business, they're really going to have to flip the table.

Who would look at a features and benefits table right now? That's classic marketing but it's not specific enough. I don't think that kind of marketing is useful anymore. Maybe it never was useful, but the feedback loop was so long that you could never prove or disprove it.

The phrase in tech writing was "easy reading comes from hard writing." Easy consumption of an app comes from really hard work on the backend. Our expectations for how an app should work on our phone are based on the last best experience that we had.

> *"The reality is that if you're not doing it, your competition is."*
>
> —*Tori Wieldt*

I was doing a presentation yesterday. A guy wanted to know about site reliability engineering (SRE) and how you can start getting your teams out of their silos. He asked, "How do you get support from management for this?" The answer was a little bit brutal because the reality is that if you're not doing it, your competition is. It's very easy for consumers to jump from one app to another.

When I was at Sun Microsystems, the first product I worked on as a tech writer was Sun WorkShop TeamWare. I begged for customer feedback and finally, I was able to go to the support room and eavesdrop on phone calls from customers.

80% of the calls were about installation. That totally blew my mind because there I was, working really hard on a manual that helped people to walk through features that often, they weren't even getting to. That would just not happen today. You pivot your entire organization to make sure that installation is easy and as frictionless as possible.

**Geertjan Wielenga**: Do you work from home or at the office?

**Tori Wieldt**: I'm primarily based in the office. Our headquarters are in San Francisco. Most of our engineering work is based in Portland, so I go up there on a regular basis too.

Otherwise, I'm on the road, training salespeople or speaking at conferences. I have the best of both worlds because I'm not a complete road warrior, but it is important to get out and hear what people are talking about.

**Geertjan Wielenga**: What percentage of the time are you on the road?

**Tori Wieldt**: I travel about 25% of the time. That feels like a good amount to me. If you don't see what's happening on the ground, you can be blinded by the online clickbait discussions. I think you need to be grounded in the reality of what developers have to deal with. It's about meeting likeminded people as much as it is about the content. The network is your career.

I also meet with customers to talk to them about our DevOps story, giving them ideas about where to get started and ways we can help them. I really like the variety.

**Geertjan Wielenga**: What kind of personality, temperament, or characteristics fit very well with this kind of role?

## The right personality

**Tori Wieldt**: You've got to like people, variety, and learning new stuff. I remember at Sun Microsystems, whenever somebody would use an acronym I'd never heard in a meeting, I'd decide that before the end of the day, I would figure out what that was.

Being able to read between the lines is really important. I'm a vendor but when I look at other vendors' information, I have to be able to determine how much of that is vaporware versus what's really out there. You've got to have a sense of curiosity.

> *"You must be able to deal with uncertainty."*
>
> *—Tori Wieldt*

Crucially, you must be able to deal with uncertainty. It's a rollercoaster being in this role. I keep seeing the word "uncertainty" in more and more job ads, which, at first, made me a little bit nervous. Then I thought about it one morning when I came into a conference and the booth was in the wrong place, so the demos weren't working. I had to go in there and do some firefighting. I thought, "This is actually great because if everything always worked as expected, I could be replaced by a bot."

I recommend this job for women. I think tech is a great place for women. I know it's challenging, there's sexism, and we certainly have to play the game at a higher level of difficulty than our male counterparts do, but I really think it's a fantastic area to be in. One of the things I'm particularly proud of is being able to get other women into tech.

**Geertjan Wielenga**: What's so good about working in tech, would you say?

**Tori Wieldt**: You get to meet smart people who are doing really interesting stuff and the money is good. Tech is not a typical "ghetto" for women; it's not like nursing. In the U.S., careers that are more typically done by women have salaries artificially deflated. The salaries in tech are better.

**Geertjan Wielenga**: What should you do if you don't feel confident about your tech knowledge?

# Having the confidence to get started

**Tori Wieldt**: Read the comments on an article, take a look at Twitter, or try out the software yourself. Even if you aren't really technical, everybody should be able to download and try software. More and more companies allow you to do that.

People tend to undercut their abilities. If you're starting a user group or you want to get people together online, just try a tech and write down the experience you've had. That is the great start of a presentation. You can say that you tried XYZ tech and what you learned. Explain what was easy, what was really frustrating, and the resources that got you going. That's really valuable information. If you're interested enough and willing to share your thoughts with other people, then do so.

**Geertjan Wielenga**: Do you need to know absolutely everything about the tech from your organization to be able to share knowledge with the salespeople and the community?

**Tori Wieldt**: Absolutely not and actually, that would be impossible. Tech is a Swiss Army knife: there are so many things you can do with it. I don't even think our CEO, who wrote the software to begin with, knows everything that our software does now.

The old tech writer mantra applies here: "Know your audience." I try to predict where customers will be coming into the software and what their questions will be. If I do a call with a customer and we've already done the basic introduction, then they want to go a little bit deeper, I make sure that there's a more technical person on the call who can do that. That seems to work really well.

**Geertjan Wielenga**: What do you do when you're running a session and someone asks a question that you don't know the answer to? Do you just wing it?

**Tori Wieldt**: I say that I don't know the answer and I'll get back to them. In my session yesterday, a couple of people asked questions. I said, "I don't know, but this is how we do it at my company. Do other people have answers?" That started a really great discussion about people who are at different levels on the path of this DevOps stuff. After the session, there were four or five people out in the hallway having a conversation about that. I always used to tell my tech writers that a manual is the start of a discussion.

**Geertjan Wielenga**: What do you do to stay current?

**Tori Wieldt**: I spend time on Twitter and I talk to the other people in my organization. I spend as much time as I can with the engineers too. They do unconferences regularly and I go to those.

**Geertjan Wielenga**: Are there any websites that you read?

**Tori Wieldt**: I go to Slashdot, but otherwise, I have enough of a network on Twitter that I can see what's going on. We get a weekly report that shows the new users for our software. I go to Twitter and start following them so I can understand what's important to them. We're all guilty of thinking our customers are sitting around waiting for us to deliver something to them. It's nice to have the reminder that we are a small percentage of a much broader world that they're looking at.

**Geertjan Wielenga**: What is the tone that you use when you talk to customers?

**Tori Wieldt**: I hope it's a helpful tone. I want to get across that our software can help them to accomplish XYZ. We're highly aware that it's the user experience that's key, so you have to really pay attention to that. We don't have all the answers, so my tone is respectful, reflecting that this is hard work. If it was easy or if a company could sell you DevOps in a box, we'd all be able to go home!

> *"The software can come and go, but we have to change people and processes."*
>
> —*Tori Wieldt*

This is hard work because we're changing people. The software can come and go, but we have to change people and processes. We're saying that our software is a lever that will help our customers, but they have to do the hard work too. We aren't fixing bugs for them: we're pointing bugs out to help them to get their job done.

476

# When to talk about competitors

**Geertjan Wielenga**: In the area of ethical dilemmas, what if you're doing a presentation and you get a question, and you know that your competitor does the job better than your product does. How honest are you?

**Tori Wieldt**: It depends on the context. If I'm in front of a room of people, I'm not going to give any praise to my competitors. If I'm at happy hour having a beer, standing next to somebody, then that conversation will go a little bit differently. "Does it better" is also highly dependent on a user's situation.

**Geertjan Wielenga**: What if you know that there's a bug in the tech and you're doing a demo? Do you avoid that particular bug area without saying anything?

**Tori Wieldt**: I will skirt imperfections, although I would never lie knowingly. I've always been heartened by how intelligent and reasonable developers as customers are. You can just be upfront and say, "This is not the direction the company is going in." People can handle it. I have yet to have the reaction that I think we all fear so much.

Often people reply, "Okay, I just wanted to know." They're going to figure out how to do their job with the tools that are best for them, so I think honesty is the best policy.

In the presentation yesterday, I had a question: "It would be really great if your software did blah, blah, blah. Will that ever happen?"

I knew a lot about what he was asking about, but all I could say was "stay tuned." I gave a nice smile as I said that!

**Geertjan Wielenga**: What happens if the company you work for takes a direction that is completely against everything you stand for or you just disagree with it? If you're on the stage in a big room and everyone really wants to know about the controversial topic of the moment, how do you handle that?

**Tori Wieldt**: In my many years doing this job, I've learned to "trust" the experts. If it's a PR issue, I let the PR people handle it. That said, I was at a community user conference and did an unconference session titled "Working at the Dark Star." It focused on how to be a community manager in a large company and that really resonated. Many people attended and were really honest about their challenges in those areas.

**Geertjan Wielenga**: What did you discuss in the session?

## Disagreeing with your company

**Tori Wieldt**: How challenging it is to work for a big company that wants to be able to dictate things. In one of my roles, there was a bit of a culture shock after having gone from one company that was very lenient and open to a company that was not that way at all.

The company wanted to run every blog post through a legal organization. I was fighting hard and saying, "That's crazy! We need to be able to have comments on blogs. The whole point is engaging with people, which means they can say good and bad things about the company."

> *"You have got to learn not to freak out if one person says something about you that you don't like."*
>
> —Tori Wieldt

Modern companies have Twitterfall at their conferences. You have got to learn not to freak out if one person says something about you that you don't like. The arena has changed and it's a mindset shift. You have to let go of that control or the illusion that you ever had it. If there are conversations happening somewhere, I would rather they be out in the open where I can engage with them.

**Geertjan Wielenga**: You mentioned that you travel regularly in your role, so how do you avoid jet lag or do you not encounter it? Do you have any travel horror stories?

**Tori Wieldt**: I try and give myself a day to rest. I don't know how people step off a plane and go right to a meeting. I have just learned to accept that I'm going to be running at 75% when I'm traveling. I'm not going to be at 100% and that's okay. I'm a little afraid to say this out loud, in case the gods are listening, but I have yet to have a really horrible travel experience.

**Geertjan Wielenga**: What about the technical glitches that you can encounter when you arrive at these faraway destinations? What do you do in those situations?

**Tori Wieldt**: You try to take it in your stride and just remember that you're a human among humans: glitches happen to everyone.

I was at one conference and in every room, there was a big red button. If there was anything wrong with my A/V, I could go to my room early and press the button. Just knowing that was there was so cool.

I've been lucky when using adapters. Usually people carry stuff that they can help you with. Sometimes the software is down. We're a Software-as-a-Service (SaaS) company and sometimes the response time on the service is not as snappy as we'd like it to be. You get pretty good at talking about stuff while the page reloads.

**Geertjan Wielenga**: What about burnout? Have you been on the verge of that and how do you avoid it?

**Tori Wieldt**: You need to have an outlet. I love being on some of the Slack channels with the other community managers. We just talk about travel stories and recommend good airports, or suggest avoiding a particular airport at all costs.

One of the difficulties about this job is that people are naturally going to be jealous of you getting to fly to all these places. They don't realize that you're inside a hotel conference room. You have no idea what the weather is like because you don't go outside. Sometimes you get to explore the city and sometimes you don't; that's just how it rolls.

**Geertjan Wielenga**: What would the you in your 20s think about what you're doing with your life today, professionally speaking?

**Tori Wieldt**: I think I'd be really thrilled with it. I have had jobs that didn't exist when I was going to college, so even the best of schools wouldn't have been able to train me for them.

I loved being a tech writer and riding that wave. I also love doing developer stuff right now. I think if I met my younger self, we'd high five each other.

**Geertjan Wielenga**: It's hard not to go back to what you were saying earlier about age. What's the concern about age in this business?

**Tori Wieldt**: I don't want to start generational wars, but the assumption is that somebody who is older is not an up-to-date person and so isn't as valuable to the organization.

I don't feel like experience is valued much anymore. Maybe that's San Francisco-specific in Silicon Valley. All these companies are set up and run by young upstarts. Millennials just don't think we know anything as old folks. I don't necessarily want to bring up that I worked at that phone company and I had a pager!

> *"You don't want to lead with your age. I just think it's the reality of tech."*
>
> —*Tori Wieldt*

You don't want to lead with your age. I just think it's the reality of tech. Luckily, I look younger than I am and probably act younger than I am too.

**Geertjan Wielenga**: What is the professional trajectory for the kind of work that you're doing? Where can you go with your career?

**Tori Wieldt**: I think the world is your oyster. If you want to do an engineering role, you could go in that direction. If you want to go into marketing, you can do that.

When people start talking about API-first or API-everywhere, I think that just emphasizes how important it is to have developers who like your products and want to help to build your ecosystem.

I can't imagine a company out there that won't eventually have a developer program. If you think setting up a forum and walking away counts as a developer program, you're going to be sorely disappointed. It's all about human-to-human connections and you need people to make that happen.

**Geertjan Wielenga**: Thank you, Tori Wieldt.

## 20

> *Once I got a taste for being able to help others in this way, I wanted to do more.*

# Andres Almiray

# Introducing Andres Almiray

Andres Almiray is a developer with a passion for Java and Groovy. A Java Champion with more than 20 years of experience in software design and development, he is an enthusiastic speaker and one of the founding members of the Hackergarten community events. In his own words, Andres is a "true believer" in open source, and he supports this by working on projects including the Griffon framework, of which he is a founding member. He served a two-year term on the Java Community Process (JCP) Executive Committee. Since this interview, Andres has become a product manager at Oracle. Find Andres on Twitter: @aalmiray.

---

**Geertjan Wielenga**: Are you an official developer advocate?

**Andres Almiray**: Yes. For years I didn't officially have that title. I followed the same path as someone in a developer advocate role while remaining in an engineering role. Currently, I'm a principal developer advocate at Gradle. It's a start-up with a well-known open-source product (Gradle) and it also has a commercial product (Gradle Enterprise).

What I did in the past was talk to people about the tech and the experiences that we had in-house. The point was to showcase both good and bad experiences, and how we solved problems as a company. Nowadays, I do more of the same, but I focus on specific products and offerings that my company has.

**Geertjan Wielenga**: Do you focus on developers when you talk about these products?

## Talking to developers

**Andres Almiray**: Yes, I do. I prefer to do that because being a developer myself, I can understand how developers think and how we react to certain news.

The marketing department of any company knows how to deal with and reach out to the decision-maker—the chief technology officer (CTO) or chief executive officer (CEO). They know how to speak to them in such a way that they can share the benefits of the particular solution they want to offer. But it's different when you need to do that with developers. If you come up with your standard marketing jargon for a developer, either the developer won't understand you or will simply say, "That's not for me and I just don't want to deal with this particular thing." You have to understand the person on the other side, and that's why I want to talk to developers.

**Geertjan Wielenga**: You travel the world to visit conferences and you speak everywhere, so how does that fit into your job?

**Andres Almiray**: Previously, I had to strike a balance on how much time I could spend outside of my billed time with customers. My previous employer and I agreed upon a certain percentage of time that it made sense for the company to spend in the Java community.

Now, as a developer advocate for Gradle, things are somewhat similar: one of my responsibilities is to reach out to users and potential customers. This means I can use all means at my disposal: articles, blog posts, videos, and, of course, face-to-face meetings, which usually happen at conferences and Java User Groups (JUGs) worldwide.

**Geertjan Wielenga**: Does your company pay you to go to conferences and speak around the world?

**Andres Almiray**: Yes, where it makes sense for the company to do so. For local and regional events, that's not much of a problem. For events that are far away, such as Oracle Code One, my company does cover some of the costs.

It would be great if the conferences would pay or if I could find another way to expense these things. After all, the company can only spend so much. There has to be a balance between what you actually do in your day job and going to these events.

**Geertjan Wielenga**: Can you say whatever you like at conferences?

**Andres Almiray**: I can, kind of, speak what's on my mind. When it makes sense to push out what we're doing within the company, I say, "This is what we're doing. If you want to know more, then come back to us." That could be translated, hopefully, into a sales pitch and a lead.

**Geertjan Wielenga**: When you go to a conference and you see other speakers who are officially involved in developer advocacy, do you believe that what they're saying is really just marketing, or do you think that they're being completely honest and authentic in what they're selling on stage?

**Andres Almiray**: Most of the people who I see in this area are definitely authentic. They wouldn't be in a developer advocacy role if they didn't believe in it.

I have hardly met anybody who is doing this particular job just because they want to travel. Even though you might think from the outside that it's exciting to go to many different countries, one city to the next, it's actually tiring. You can get sick of doing that every single week. So, lots of travel is not something that many people want to do for work. What developer advocates actually want to do is share knowledge and have an experience face to face. The transfer of knowledge happens quicker that way.

**Geertjan Wielenga**: How did you get into this industry? What is your background academically?

**Andres Almiray**: I majored in computer science 20 years ago. The reason I got into computer science was because, at the time, I just wanted to create my own video game. I really had no idea what I wanted to do with my life, except that I wanted to create a video game! When I finished my studies, I wanted to do different things. One thing led to another and a few years later, I gave my first presentation in my home city.

It was a year later that I traveled to the U.S. I decided to participate in a community-led event in Silicon Valley. That was my first international event and it was a turning point for me. I saw that there were very well known people in the industry attending.

> *"I thought, 'This is a great opportunity. Even if I fail and even if I do a terrible job on stage, I will still have given myself the opportunity to try it.'"*
>
> —*Andres Almiray*

One of the people who presented there was Douglas Crockford, who is very well known in the JavaScript world. Next to him, there were completely unknown people, like myself. We were sharing the stage at the same time. I thought, "This is a great opportunity. Even if I fail and even if I do a terrible job on stage, I will still have given myself the opportunity to try it."

The result of this particular experience was very positive for me. The reaction from the attendees was pretty encouraging. I decided to continue. That was 12 years ago and I've been talking to people and going to conference events for 12 years now.

After that U.S. conference, I looked for other options close to the area I was living in. I was already very much into the Groovy community, so when I noticed that there were a few conferences popping up on that particular topic, I joined immediately. I jumped into the first opportunities that I had to participate in such conferences, even when that meant going to the other coast of the U.S. or a different country.

**Geertjan Wielenga**: What are some of the topics that you talk about? Is there something that they all have in common?

## Andres' conference topics

**Andres Almiray**: What they mostly have in common is that they're based on the experiences that I have had in trying to solve a particular problem. I have definitely talked about many different types of tech. When I started doing this, I talked a lot about the Groovy programming language.

I was quite new to the language. I had fallen in love with it based on the capabilities that you get by using it.

As time passed by, I jumped into alternative Java virtual machine (JVM) languages. I did a little bit of Swing and I've done meta programming also. Now I'm doing benchmarks, Java Microbenchmark Harness (JMH), and testing. So, there are many different things that I've covered these past 12 years.

**Geertjan Wielenga**: Don't you also do a session about the best Java libraries?

**Andres Almiray**: Yes, that's a session that I created a few years ago. It's been very popular and well received. That particular talk is a collection of libraries that are framed within a particular use case. I try to make it as broad as possible so that many other people who encounter this particular problem can find an alternative way to solve the use case.

The great thing about this session is that there are no silver bullets. There are places where you can switch one particular library for another to get a similar effect, depending on whether you're more oriented to, let's say, the Spring way of doing things or if you want to do things closer to Java Platform, Enterprise Edition (Java EE). You can mix and match. It's not like there's one single path to solve the problem. I want to showcase two messages to developers: "Look at this set of libraries and pick which one you want, but also, you can find a path to be able to select the next library that will help you."

**Geertjan Wielenga**: What do you think makes a good topic for a conference when you're submitting abstracts? What works well?

**Andres Almiray**: In my experience, what has worked well is finding a particular use case where I had trouble in the past and I was trying to find a particular solution. It could be something that took me a while to figure out, but when I found the solution, I realized it wasn't so difficult.

You have to know all these steps before you can give a talk. Perhaps you need to be aware of this other condition or this other library, then you can make the jump and the connection. I want to make developers aware that connections exist.

I tend to stay away from the hype topics because for those topics, you will always find somebody else willing to talk about them. If it's the new reactive programming framework or the new JavaScript framework that came out last week, those topics are definitely not for me.

**Geertjan Wielenga**: You address topics that relate to day-to-day work and solving problems in day-to-day activities, then?

**Andres Almiray**: Yes, unless that particular hype has some legs and you can actually see that this thing is going to really make your life easier, and it's not going to disappear within a couple of years.

I want to feel that I'm talking about something quite stable that can go the distance. Otherwise, it just doesn't make sense. For example, if we want to pick on a tech that was very hyped and lots of people got very excited about, before suddenly it just died, then we can talk about Flash and Flex. Right now, nobody's talking about Flash and Flex, even though there are still some people maintaining legacy applications written with that tech.

**Geertjan Wielenga**: Something isn't just hype if it was useful for a particular period. If a tech has been replaced by other things, does that mean that it wasn't useful at the time?

**Andres Almiray**: True, I can give you that point. There is tech that can solve a particular problem very well, but once you start to get off the beaten path and outside of the box—I'm not saying that this was the case for Flash and Flex—there's just nothing that can help you. You're out in the wild and it's difficult to know how you can find your way or if there even is a way to reach your goal. This is true for pretty much every tech. What we need to do is find out what the limits are if we haven't found them; every single tech has a limit.

**Geertjan Wielenga**: In many ways, you had a comfortable job as a consultant. Why would you go and extend that in the way that you have by being part of this global community of people where you're sharing this knowledge? What are the motivations for you to go beyond your standard profession?

**Andres Almiray**: It has to do with having a little bit of extra passion. In my particular case, I was just a regular consumer of open source for a long time. One day, it dawned on me that there was a bug in a particular library and the developers didn't have enough time to fix it because it was quite a small one. The bug was annoying to me, so I thought about fixing it myself. Instead of just keeping the fix for myself, or for the company I was working for, I decided to publish it back to the open source. That's how I got the ball rolling.

Once I got a taste for being able to help others in this way, I wanted to do more. Then I figured out that I needed to create something that did not exist, so I created a project to solve a particular issue and decided to open source it as well. That kept going and going.

> *"If you believe that your solution can be useful to others, then going down the path of open source is pretty much the only way to go."*
>
> —*Andres Almiray*

If you're someone who has a bit of extra passion for solving a particular problem, and if you believe that your solution can be useful to others, then going down the path of open source is pretty much the only way to go. Once you're in this environment, then you figure out that sharing knowledge and sharing your experiences is the next logical step. Whether you become a conference speaker or meetup attendee, building your activities is very likely to happen once you go into open source. You don't have to go to face-to-face events if you don't want to—you can also do it online. You can blog, you can tweet, and you can share content in many different ways.

## Developer advocacy's recent growth

**Geertjan Wielenga**: It seems to me that very few people know about this profession. Do you agree with me?

**Andres Almiray**: I definitely agree with you. I think that we have seen, in the past few years, more and more tech people jump into the option of traveling around the world, which involves letting potential customers and developers know what's happening in their particular neck of the woods and what they're doing in a particular niche.

I believe that this change is because companies have figured out that if you don't reach out to developers directly, then it's much harder to sell particular solutions. It doesn't matter how easily you can convince the decision-maker, or the people at the top of the chain, if once they push down a particular solution the developers won't accept it. You have to find a way to convince both the people at the top and the developers. You have to find a way to do it properly too.

**Geertjan Wielenga**: What kind of person do you think fits this role? What kind of qualities do you need to have? Do you need to be really extroverted, for example?

**Andres Almiray**: In my case, I can say that I'm still very introverted. Many of us developers are introverts. We function very well within certain boundaries and with our friends and colleagues. However, when presented with an environment that's completely different, or when they encounter a culture that's very different to theirs, some people freeze. That's fine.

There are some other people who just go with the flow, even though they might be scared. I have to confess that every time I go on stage, I'm still very nervous. I don't know how the audience will react. I don't know if the cultural references will make them feel good or if there will be some negative reactions.

You always have to play with your emotions and you have to be very aware of what's happening in front of you in developer advocacy.

If you happen to be an extrovert, I guess it is easier to strike up a conversation with people. You can do it very quickly. If you're an introvert, then you feel safe talking about the tech and the things that you know. If I can move a conversation into that arena, then I definitely feel much more comfortable. Perhaps once I open up a little bit more or if the other person opens up a bit more, we may begin talking about different things later.

There are so many different topics that can arise once two people who are participating in a conversation have reached a level of understanding. This is one of the things that I like about unconferences, where pretty much every attendee is also a speaker. That makes it very easy for all of us, regardless of whether we are extroverts, to reach the same level of understanding quickly.

**Geertjan Wielenga**: What is something that would have been useful for you to know right at the start of doing all of this? What would you say to somebody getting started in this area?

**Andres Almiray**: I would tell them that failure is always an option and that's okay; don't be afraid to fail. What you can do after you fail for some reason is just learn the lesson from it and move on. I was very much afraid about how audiences would react to me. I was afraid about my command of the English language, at the time.

I was afraid of embarrassing myself or being seen as a clown on stage. I was worried that I would look like I didn't know what I was talking about. All those things could happen at some point, I suppose, but if they happen, then just figure out a way to recover.

> *"Be more prepared, but definitely believe in yourself."*
>
> —Andres Almiray

Plan ahead. We can always solve many things if we just stop, reflect on what we're doing, make a plan, and come up with contingencies in case that something happens. Be more prepared, but definitely believe in yourself.

**Geertjan Wielenga**: Do you need to know everything about a particular topic in order to present a session about it?

**Andres Almiray**: Not necessarily. I actually have encountered this situation with previous colleagues. Once they saw that I was going to places and sharing knowledge, they said, "Oh, I want to do the same thing. I want to go to this other country. I want to go to this particular event. But I don't feel that I know the topic very well, so I don't think I will do that."

Then, after the event happened and they saw the list of the speakers, the videos, or the content that was presented at the conference, they said, "I know all those things and actually, I know a few more than that. So, I was definitely ready to do this." I tell them to take the opportunity next time it comes up.

It's okay to not be a full-time expert. If you eventually get asked a question that you don't know the answer to, it's okay to let people know that you don't know the answer at that moment in time. If you follow up with them in some way, maybe by email, or some other contact mechanism, then you can probably give them the answer that they expected.

## Experts in your audience

**Geertjan Wielenga**: What do you do when you're in a situation when you know your audience is more knowledgeable than you? Maybe you have some experts sitting in the audience and you're a bit concerned about that. How do you react?

**Andres Almiray**: What I would do first is try to understand the audience and discover at what particular level they are with the tech. If you figure out that they know more than you do, you will have to find a way to finish what you started.

If you have a few more points that you can make related to your talk, then make them, but if you definitely feel that there is no way that you can climb this particular slope, and that the audience is at the top of the mountain, I don't know how you would try to solve that.

Personally, I haven't found myself in this particular situation yet. Some people in an audience will figure out that I'm not very well known for a particular topic. They may decide that they have two choices: they can jump in and help me, so that the audience gets a much better picture of the topic, or they can just stay quiet and see what happens.

Once the talk is finished, they will often come up and talk to me about how the session could have been improved.

**Geertjan Wielenga**: Have you done that? Have you gone up to a speaker and given them tips and things like that?

**Andres Almiray**: Yes, I've done it a couple of times, especially when I've seen somebody looking a bit nervous on stage. You can often see the potential for the person on stage to be a really great speaker and convey the message in a much more natural way. But there are a few things that may be stopping that person from doing so.

You might notice that the person is in a particular comfort zone: repeating the same phrases or going back to the same place. You can see that they want to get out of their shell, but they don't feel very safe about that. What you can do on the spot, perhaps, is ask a question and try to move the discussion into a different place.

After a session, you can give suggestions, but not in a way that makes the other person feel like you are much higher up and that person will have a difficult time reaching your particular level. Make the other person feel welcome with your message; that's the best thing that you can do.

**Geertjan Wielenga**: What do you do when you're at a conference and you're about to speak and you discover that there is some technical problem? Have you got stories about that situation?

**Andres Almiray**: Yes, I had my laptop reboot on stage when I was talking.

Luckily, that particular time, the computer rebooted very fast, so I didn't lose much time.

When I started doing talks, I got nervous when something didn't work correctly with the projector or the computer. I would freak out and try to solve it. But you have to recognize, again, that failure is always an option. Sometimes the physical things will break down and there's no way that you can come back from that in every situation.

You have some options: be prepared by having your slides, your presentation, or whatever you want to showcase in an alternative format. You can put your presentation on a USB stick and ask for a second laptop so that you can connect quickly. You might even decide to carry a second laptop to every conference.

If it's a projector issue, one thing that I've seen is someone using a screen sharing application. I think they were using the local network. They set up three or four computers to share the screen. Then people would line up next to the different screens so that they could still see the content. That was very cool.

> *"The most important thing is to keep engaging the audience and not go silent."*
>
> —*Andres Almiray*

When something breaks down and you can't recover, the most important thing is to keep engaging the audience and not go silent. Let them know what's going on. If it's something that's recoverable, such as when my computer rebooted, you can say, "Oh, my computer rebooted, but by the way, I was talking about this, this, and that."

In my case, the reboot took 30 seconds, so the audience didn't have to wait for me to enter my credentials and so on. I was lucky that time. Continuing to talk to your audience is my advice.

If the hardware gets busted and the network no longer works, and there's no way for you to continue with your demo, then just let the audience know that these things can happen. You can continue to show your content in another way. If not, then ask the audience if it's okay to continue just talking without any sort of backing material. It depends on the topic, of course. There will be topics where this is fine and there will also be topics where you definitely need to show something on your computer. There's nothing you can do in those situations.

**Geertjan Wielenga**: How do you stay up to date with the latest tech? What social media channels do you use?

**Andres Almiray**: There are several channels that I use. From time to time, when I go to a conference and I see a new topic appearing, I will attend that particular session. Maybe in the hallway track I will encounter a particular speaker, or somebody else, who I know is a good person to ask about that relevant topic. Maybe there's a chance to hack something together with that particular person, whether it's within the confines of the conference or maybe somewhere outside of that.

I also read certain articles and blogs. You have the option to go with the fire hose, which is Twitter. Depending on who you follow, someone will eventually say, "Hey, look at this particular project. It solved my problem with X and Y." If I'm suffering from X as well, I'm definitely going to look at that.

I use Twitter a lot. That's how I get the news about certain releases, libraries, or projects that would be much more difficult for me to find otherwise.

**Geertjan Wielenga**: What about travel? We talked about this briefly earlier. There's a lot of flying, jet lag, and running around to get to conferences. What are your tips in that area?

## Travel advice

**Andres Almiray**: When you're doing a very long trip, especially going west, it makes sense to fly at least one day before the event. Flying west is easier. When you're flying east, I recommend flying two days before, if not three. In my experience, flying east is way harder on the body.

Many people who I see at conferences as speakers go to an event and then they either go back immediately after the event finishes or even during the event itself. They just do one talk and then leave. Those people go very quickly about their business. They don't have time to relax a little bit, interact with people, or even visit the city.

It's nice to have one extra day perhaps to just discover what's around in that particular area. Given that if you do this you will be taking some extra time off from your company, if you have some kind of opportunity for remote working, then taking those extra days will be very helpful. If you have much stricter limits on the time that you can spend away from the office, then I recommend not traveling either so often or so far away. If you have to go to the other side of the world for a particular event, then make that event the exception; perhaps have one of these events each year.

**Geertjan Wielenga**: What about burnout? Is that a danger in this area?

**Andres Almiray**: Definitely, yes. At some point, you will get tired of flying or traveling too much. Last year, I did an event that was a tour around here in Switzerland, Germany, and Italy.

We did that for two weeks and we planned it in such a way that we had an event every single night during the week, and we used the weekend to relax and recharge our batteries. We traveled by train, which made it a little bit easier. On the train, we didn't have more than four hours for each trip. On the train, you can do some work and you can relax. It's not as stressful as flying. If we had flown to all those 10 different cities, I think that would have been harder.

What made me a bit worn out last year was that there were definitely too many events. So, again, you have to strike a balance on how many events you go to, in terms of which ones you consider more important regarding different dimensions. Once you figure that out, then pick and choose your battles.

**Geertjan Wielenga**: Is it true that you're quite special in the sense that while other people need to go back home again to be with a partner, you bring your partner with you?

**Andres Almiray**: Yes, we tend to travel together. That's part of the deal. I'm able to travel as much as I do not just because of my employer, but also because of my spouse. When the trip is short, maybe one or two nights away, then I just do it alone. But when it's a longer trip, or if it's an exotic destination, or it's a place that my spouse would like to visit, then we certainly plan for a trip together if we can make it happen.

**Geertjan Wielenga**: Does she also join you in your sessions?

**Andres Almiray**: Yes, we have participated in a handful of sessions together. I think the first session we did together was back in 2009 at JavaOne. I think that was her first ever event too and it was a big one.

**Geertjan Wielenga**: What are the benefits of traveling to conferences together?

**Andres Almiray**: We can practice the sessions together. We have found a rhythm where she will pose as someone asking questions or be a skeptic about one particular topic. I'll be the one answering the questions or showing how things could be done. From time to time, she will say something or showcase the content in such a way that I think we switch roles. It's funny to see how we do this dance together, depending on the topic that we've chosen.

**Geertjan Wielenga**: Thank you, Andres Almiray.

## 21

> *Developers are the new kingmakers.*

# Arun Gupta

# Introducing Arun Gupta

Arun Gupta is a principal technologist at Amazon Web Services (AWS). He is responsible for the Cloud Native Computing Foundation (CNCF) strategy within AWS, and actively participates at CNCF Board and technical meetings. Arun has built and led developer communities, has spoken in 45+ countries on a myriad of topics, and also founded the Devoxx4Kids chapter in the U.S. He is the author of several books, a globe trotter, a Docker Captain, a Java Champion, and a Java User Group (JUG) leader. Find Arun on Twitter: @arungupta.

---

**Geertjan Wielenga**: Could you start by explaining what you do?

**Arun Gupta**: I help service teams at Amazon to engage with open-source communities, help to define our open-source messaging and positioning, and share that outside of AWS.

I've been working in developer relations for over 13 years now at a wide variety of companies. I started at Sun Microsystems, then Oracle, then Red Hat, and then Couchbase. I've been an individual contributor, bootstrapped developer relations programs, built teams from the ground up, and taken existing teams and made them highly performant and efficient.

**Geertjan Wielenga**: Would you describe yourself as a "tech evangelist" or a "developer advocate" or a "developer relations person"? What's your title of choice?

**Arun Gupta**: I think a rose by any other name would smell as sweet. I've seen people freaking out over the term "evangelist." They think that evangelism is a one-way street and advocacy is a two-way street. I've worked as a "technologist," "developer advocate," "tech evangelist," "developer evangelist," and "developer relations person." I've had all sorts of titles, but my tools and techniques have stayed consistent across the roles.

I think the fundamental requirement for whatever you call this role (I generally refer to this work as developer relations) is believing in your product, making other people believe in your product, and keeping your eyes and ears open. Be willing to listen to feedback, whether it's positive, negative, or constructive. Bring that feedback into your team and fix the product. You want to be able to feel the pain of the end users before they do. You should be able to understand where the product fails. Don't hide that from your users; be willing to acknowledge it, because that helps to build credibility.

**Geertjan Wielenga**: In some sense, are you a spin doctor?

## The spin doctor comparison

**Arun Gupta**: No, I don't think that I'm a spin doctor. I have a true belief in my product that comes with the understanding that there are limitations to it. As a practitioner of the product, I'm aware of them and I'm not shy about sharing my experiences. All software has limitations anyway, but the key part is that we're listening to customers' feedback and constantly improving it.

I've always believed in the value of education and selling happens because of that. Selling has never been the main focus of whatever I've done.

**Geertjan Wielenga**: What do you like about this type of work?

**Arun Gupta**: I created a role for myself in this area back in my Sun Microsystems days. In the early days of my career, I focused on writing code, getting a piece out, and fixing a bug. That was exciting to me. But the more I started talking to customers, the more I realized that the most exciting part is telling customers how to be effective users of your product. My role evolved from an engineering role to a developer relations role.

Back in 2005, at Sun Microsystems, we were working on Java and .NET interoperability to provide a seamless experience to our customers. We were at the Microsoft campus in Seattle creating and running interoperability tests for the Web Services Description Language (WSDL) and Simple Object Access Protocol (SOAP). We were testing on the wire interoperability, fixing the implementation, and trying it out. I wrote a blog post on `java.net` that said, "This is what we're doing and this is why it's relevant to our customers. We want to give you out-of-the-box interoperability." That blog post got picked up by the media. At that time, blogging and social media weren't so common. The fact that my blog got picked up piqued my interest and more importantly, it piqued my management's interest. The thinking was that "customers care about what we're doing and they want to be informed."

As I started doing more testing and fixing of products, I began to talk more about that as well. Management was happy as that blogging was helping with customers' perception of our product. Eventually, conference organizers started reaching out to ask, "How about you talk about that at our event?" I realized that I enjoy that part far more than actually building a product. Solving problems for customers is exciting.

I can summarize that as going out and saying, "I'm excited about my product and I want you to be as excited about it." Developer relations allows you to have a holistic view of the product, learn the superpowers, gaps, and workarounds, influence product roadmaps, and help customers to be effective users of the product.

Traveling around the world across six continents (still waiting for an invite from Antarctica!), meeting people from different countries and cultures, eating local food, running in different terrains, and yet using the same "developer speak" is very fulfilling.

**Geertjan Wielenga**: Are there any downsides to this role?

**Arun Gupta**: Yes. Passion is very important. If you're not passionate, people will think, "It seems like this person isn't convinced. Why should I be convinced?" That requirement is a downside of this job because it affects your work-life balance.

You might be on the road for 365 days of the year, literally hopping from city to city and visiting all of these exotic countries and meeting exciting developers. I've had a bit of that lifestyle for some time and it has a physical, emotional, and mental toll. You need to strike a balance on that.

Pay close attention to avoiding burnout. What kind of food are you eating? What kind of air are you breathing? Are you working out regularly? All of these things add up very quickly.

It may sound exciting to go to Italy, then Turkey, then Brazil, then India, and then back to Canada in a month, but that's not good for you. If you're just starting your career, you can do that for a while, but what if you want to go on a date but that date lives in your home city? If you have a family, your kids have activities like soccer games and swimming classes. You're not participating if you're always on the road. If you have a wife or a domestic partner, you're not spending time with them. You may be missing anniversaries and birthdays too.

> *"Work is a means to support my life and my family, not the other way around."*
>
> *—Arun Gupta*

There have been several times when I've committed to a conference but then realized that my son had a recital or performance on the same day. I've had to decline, saying, "I understand that I committed to your conference, but this recital came up at the last minute and that's much more valuable to me. I'm going to make it up to you some other time, but I have to cancel." My philosophy is that work is a means to support my life and my family, not the other way around.

**Geertjan Wielenga**: Is there a typical day for you?

**Arun Gupta**: It's more like a typical month. In a typical month, there are a few events that I do, sometimes in person and sometimes via a webinar.

Those in-person events are typically planned a few months ahead of time because you have to make sure that your talk is aligned with the conference agenda. The online events are a lot easier as they can typically be delivered from your desktop and they scale much better because they're recorded. These days, conference talks are recorded as well, but that's still time away from your family.

I spend time keeping track of the conferences where I need to submit a talk. Certain conferences have a policy of only accepting brand new talks, so that means constantly thinking about content. I do a lot of conference-driven development, essentially, whether that's writing, speaking, or discussing internally.

At a conference, no offense to any speakers, but I typically don't attend talks. However, I thoroughly enjoy hallway tracks. This is where the freeform and most engaging conversations happen. It is where you learn the most and can typically open up a laptop and hack together, and that could be much more worthwhile than attending a talk. There are, of course, numerous customer conversations as well, which involve helping them to understand our products or listening to their feedback.

A good part of my time is spent providing feedback from these customer communications to the product teams inside the company. This helps with defining the roadmap, removing paper cuts, and learning what matters to customers. I also participate deeply in architectural discussions about the product design. For anything that has ever been built at Amazon, there is a narrative for it that explains what we are trying to build, how it will help customers, what the user experience will be, pricing, and many other details. I participate regularly in these narrative reviews.

As a CNCF Governing Board member, I also spend time coordinating and tracking activities around that: participating in different Slack channels, engaging on Twitter, and reviewing blog posts, and the list goes on.

A big part of each month is also taken up with writing code. I continue to build new samples and play with code. Right now, I'm working on machine learning using Kubernetes. I'm playing with different machine learning frameworks and asking, "What do customers want? What's available in the market? How do you run them in Kubernetes? If I talked to a developer, would they understand the concept of machine learning? How can I simplify it for them?"

**Geertjan Wielenga**: What are the qualities that you need to be successful in this role?

## Requirements for success

**Arun Gupta**: It's a unicorn role in a sense. I mentioned passion earlier and that is indeed a fundamental requirement; otherwise, you can't get your audience excited about the product. You also need to be a good developer; you need to know how to code and preferably a wide variety of languages.

You need to be a really good tester because often you're involved in bleeding-edge products. You should be able to debug the configurations and figure out what's working, what's not working, how it's working, why it's working, what command-line options you need to try, where in the menu you should click, and so on.

You should be a really good technical writer too. This means not only reviewing the documentation but understanding what's happening and being able to talk about it or write articles about it on Medium, your personal blog, or your company's blog. In this Twitter-centric world, you should be able to provide the value of your product in less than 280 characters.

You need to be a good storyteller. When you're at a conference, you should empathize with the developer and tell them a story that they can believe in; that's what makes a talk entertaining. That's the difference between an average developer advocate and a good developer advocate.

You also need to be a very good product manager because from the engineering perspective, you act as a bridge between the external and the internal, so you bring that feedback in. Don't think that you are in any way less powerful than the actual product manager; you bring customer feedback right back to the product. Think of yourself as the chief technology officer (CTO) of your entire product. You're the person who defines exactly how that product is going to be built, tested, exposed to the users and customers, pitched, sold, and adopted.

**Geertjan Wielenga**: What do you admire and respect about other developer advocates?

**Arun Gupta**: A trait that I admire in other developer advocates is having the ability to pick up some tech in a matter of days and become the biggest champion of it. That's pretty admirable. It could be a language, a product, a feature of a product, and so on. That's a very unique capability. I also admire people who use analogies from their daily lives, because that's when the product or the feature sticks in your mind.

515

> *"Failure is inevitable and we need to embrace it."*
>
> —*Arun Gupta*

I admire developer advocates who do code-intensive sessions because if you do a code-intensive session, there are so many things that could go wrong. You can't expect a demo or talk to be absolutely flawless. Failure is inevitable and we need to embrace it. I admire developer advocates who can gracefully recover from a failure. This is a basic tenet as well.

**Geertjan Wielenga**: When a demo goes wrong and the speaker on the stage is confused, the people watching can feel uncomfortable. How should you handle that as a speaker?

**Arun Gupta**: To start with, it shouldn't be your first time playing with the product. You should have broken the product before and failed with it before. You should know that there are places where it breaks and you should be honest about them. Audiences learn a lot from the failures. If the demo gods are not favorable, then demos can and will fail.

In such cases, I've seen some speakers lose their train of thought and spend several to many minutes debugging on the stage, without sharing anything with the audience. This is where it gets uncomfortable. My demos have failed and, in such cases, I try to talk through the different steps to reproduce the error so that the audience understands, and often helps with, debugging the problem. If the issue does not get resolved, then acknowledge this as a configuration issue, make a note, file a GitHub issue, and move on.

Always have a plan B and C in case things don't work. Have a screen capture or pre-recorded video that can be played.

**Geertjan Wielenga**: It seems to me that not many people know about developer relations. How has this profession developed?

**Arun Gupta**: This profession has definitely grown and picked up in the last few years. When I created this role for myself many years ago, it was definitely very niche and we had to explain the purpose to everybody: where it fits in the organization, whether it is marketing or engineering or sales, what we do, and so on.

Moving from a pure engineering role, where you're chunking out code, creating new features, and fixing bugs, to developer relations, where you're talking about the product as opposed to building the product, took some convincing. I would say that that change is not uncommon these days: I've seen people move from engineering to developer relations and vice versa.

In the last few years, many companies have started to focus on building dedicated developer relations teams because they've realized that developers are the new kingmakers. I've had discussions with early-stage start-ups with 10 to 15 employees and even they're considering having a developer relations person on the team.

The ultimate end users, who are the architects and developers, need to believe in a product and they don't want to be sold to: they want to be educated. Developers have an allergy to marketers, but developer relations people tend to be much more hands-on.

That's where this developer relations function has more credibility and respect. The profession is a lot better understood, but there are definitely things that can be done to improve it.

**Geertjan Wielenga**: The people who aren't sat in suits and ties can actually have the deciding vote in a sale. Would you agree?

**Arun Gupta**: Yes. I used to run the GlassFish evangelism efforts back in my Sun Microsystems days. I once walked into an account meeting that was supposed to be an hour-long discussion. It went on for almost two and a half hours. These guys were firing deeply technical questions one after the other. When we finally got out of the room, the salesperson who had been sitting silently next to me the whole time said, "That was one of the best conversations we've had with this customer."

In the meeting, we'd discussed GlassFish clustering, GlassFish high-availability, the sticky session, scaling an application, and so on. As a developer relations person, I had played with the product very deeply and the client loved that authenticity. These architects are the ones who have to deal with a product on a day-to-day basis, so they have a deciding vote. This is one target audience for developer relations.

**Geertjan Wielenga**: What advice do you give to companies that are considering hiring developer relations people?

## Allocating resources

**Arun Gupta**: Last year, I was talking to a 10-person start-up. The team said, "Arun, we're so busy building the product. We have maybe the equivalent of half a person doing sales. How many of our 10 people should be dedicated to developer relations?"

The start-up world is very tricky. My advice was that things change very rapidly. The entire company could pivot based on one deal or a couple of deals. Start-ups need to be strategic and focused on who their target audience is. For example, if you're building a product around microservices and security, look at where you can participate in online media, deliver webinars with existing parties that have brand credibility, attach to hashtags, and speak at meetups and conferences that address that target audience. Don't try to spread yourself too thinly. For the company in question, we concluded that half a person on developer relations would be relevant.

In a much bigger team, of course, you can write more blogs, tweet more, build more hands-on demos, deliver webinars, and present at more conferences. With a start-up company, your funding is going to be an issue. Can that person travel to a conference from San Francisco to Singapore or China? Does that market even matter to you? See where you want to target geography-wise, language-wise, product-wise, and audience-wise. Maybe pick one conference in a quarter and make sure you have your pipe and funnel very clearly identified.

At Amazon, for example, our focus is heavily on education: we want to educate customers and help them to make the right choice. In the start-up world, if you have half a person working on developer relations out of a total of 10 people, that's a lot of resources. So ferocious focus, clarity of role, and metrics are critical. They're also important in a bigger company but more so in a start-up because of constrained resources.

**Geertjan Wielenga**: Is part of the problem the measurability of developer relations work?

**Arun Gupta**: Yes, that is indeed where it becomes tricky. From a marketing perspective, you can very easily set targets about page views, adverts, and lead generation. There are very clear metrics and goals. However, it's very difficult to say, "This product sale happened because of developer relations."

The question is, do you measure number of blog/YouTube views, Twitter followers, impressions on tweets, audience numbers reached in conference talks, new demos created, having "helped" in sales deals, field enablement, or something else? Unfortunately, none of this is typically tied to revenue and so there is always passionate debate about what the right metrics are.

In developer relations, we are generally seen as enablers of sales. I'll share an anonymous example. My employer was trying to secure a bank in Europe as a customer. This bank found out using my tweets that I was going to be in its country and invited me to give a talk. I explained the concept of microservices and related tech for about three hours, and didn't mention a single product name. There were six salespeople from my company standing at the back and at the end, they said, "Arun, we're glad you didn't mention a single product. That was the best sales pitch that we have ever seen. Now that the company understands the tech, you have started a conversation for us. Now we can talk about our products."

My public persona led to the company reaching out. That's the relationship that you have to build. Salespeople often add developer relations people to their calls and say, "Here's our developer relations person. They're going to tell you about the product and then we'll talk about the selling part later." These are good stories but not a good measurable metric.

**Geertjan Wielenga**: We've been talking about developer relations at start-ups, but more than anyone that I know, you've seen the large organizations from the inside. You've worked at Sun Microsystems, Oracle, Red Hat, Couchbase, and Amazon. What are the advantages and disadvantages of that kind of enterprise-based journey?

## Arun's experiences at large companies

**Arun Gupta**: I think one of the biggest advantages of being at a bigger company is that your scope, impact, and outreach is significant, and typically global. Pick any of these companies; they've always had a huge product portfolio and an extremely impressive number of customers have been excited about their tech and products.

Of all the companies that I've worked at, Amazon has the most comprehensive portfolio. The services that we offer include compute, database, containers, artificial intelligence/ machine learning, and security. Then you have a range of services within each type, such as relational, document, key/ value, cache, time series, and ledger databases. The global availability across 22 geographical regions and 69 availability zones is just mind-blowing. This truly allows us to help customers to innovate and build applications without worrying about the undifferentiated heavy lifting.

At Couchbase, a much smaller company, the advantage was that we had one product, so that allowed me to have ferocious focus. There I could put the pedal to the metal and apply my developer relations experience to build, grow, and nurture the community.

I immediately started thinking, "How are we going to make the tech relevant at developer watercoolers? How are we going to make it scalable? What are the metrics? What's going to be our meetups and conferences strategy for sponsoring and speaking?"

> *"We're at the bleeding edge of tech and our customers want to hear about it."*
>
> —*Arun Gupta*

I asked, "How am I going to be more strategic? Where are my developers going to live? How am I going to attach Couchbase to the latest set of topics or tech?" With AWS, that's typically not the case. We're at the bleeding edge of tech and our customers want to hear about it. There are a different set of challenges.

**Geertjan Wielenga**: If you're presenting product A from company A and then a few years later, you're presenting product B from company B, which competes with company A, does that have any impact in terms of authenticity?

**Arun Gupta**: Not really. I'll give a specific example: I moved from Oracle to Red Hat. At Oracle, I was doing GlassFish. I moved to Red Hat and started doing JBoss. GlassFish and JBoss are competing products. The common theme that tied the two was Java Platform, Enterprise Edition (Java EE). Some people thought, "Yesterday you were preaching GlassFish and now you're preaching JBoss. Why should I trust you?" That's the way it came across. I faced that response multiple times as a matter of fact.

It helps if you explain your rationale for moving. I said, "GlassFish is still a good product, but here is the need it serves. JBoss is also a good product and here is the need it serves."

I've always avoided bashing a competitor's product. That might be done in a closed setting, but in a public setting, I want to understand what your problem is and I will tell you how my product solves that problem. If it solves it, good. Don't ask, "Why shouldn't I use your competitor's product?" That doesn't get us anywhere.

**Geertjan Wielenga**: If the company that you represent makes a decision that you don't agree with, how do you handle that?

**Arun Gupta**: It happens all the time. At Amazon, we have leadership principles and they are the driving force for each employee on a day-to-day basis. One of the principles is "disagree and commit." This means saying, "I don't agree with how this should be done, but because the rest of the team believes that this is the way it should be done, I will disagree and commit. I'm going to go and talk about it in the way that you tell me to talk about it, but if I get feedback, then I have the right to come back and provide that feedback." Always be flexible in that sense.

**Geertjan Wielenga**: What do you do when the direction that the company you work for is going in really conflicts with your vision?

**Arun Gupta**: I think there is a tipping point, but you've got to think about it carefully.

My philosophy is to change what you cannot accept and accept what you cannot change. If a direction fundamentally conflicts with who I am, I possibly will move on. It could be a diagonal move, a horizontal move, or a completely orthogonal move.

The tech industry is booming like crazy, but I want to give it my best shot in my current company. In a company like Amazon, there is such a wide variety of roles. If the current role isn't working out, I could look for a different team or even have a career change. That's the exciting part about Amazon: it provides many opportunities.

**Geertjan Wielenga**: Is this what you expected to be doing with your life?

**Arun Gupta**: I had no clue what I would be doing. I'm a runner. I like to run long distances and I run by feel. I don't look at my heart rate; I run as far as I want to run. I approach life in the same way: I take it as it comes.

I'm not at all disappointed by where I've ended up. I'm very happy working at Amazon. One of the most exciting parts of my job is the huge range of customers that we have across the world. Anywhere that I go, there are customers talking about what they like and don't like about Amazon. I can bring that information back into the company and make a change. When customers thank me for listening and making it easy for them, that's really satisfying.

**Geertjan Wielenga**: Do you see yourself being in this role for the rest of your life?

**Arun Gupta**: I'm really enjoying this role. I've also done consulting work for start-ups and other companies and I've helped them to build their developer relations programs. That's something that I really enjoy too. I've realized that developer relations comes very naturally to me. I'm a social person; I like talking and explaining things. I've always had compliments that I break things down into simple terms very well.

No matter what kind of role I pick up and what it evolves into, I think developer relations is always going to be in the background, even if I'm building a product. How are we going to promote it? How are we going to talk to customers? Developer relations is very much part of my personality, but only time will tell whether it stays as my official title or not.

**Geertjan Wielenga**: What's the best way for someone to get into this sphere today?

**Tips for getting started**

**Arun Gupta**: One of the most important things to do is build your online profile. I don't necessarily mean your Facebook profile: that's for your family and friends, but I really want to see that you have a good GitHub profile. That tells me what languages you're proficient in, so I can look at your coding style, what areas you're comfortable with, how long you've been contributing, and much more.

The second thing that I want to see is writing and speaking skills. There are tons of blogging platforms available, such as WordPress, Medium, and GitHub pages. Pick a platform and start writing about what you care about.

You may think that nobody else cares about it but I bet you'll be surprised. In this YouTube-centric world, start creating a video series explaining topics that matter to you. If you want to take it up a notch, start a podcast, have discussions around tech, and bring communities together.

> *"Most tech communities are very inclusive."*
>
> —*Arun Gupta*

The third thing that you can do, and you don't need to be employed anywhere, is to find a local meetup. There are meetups happening every day of the week in most of the major cities and most of the smaller cities as well. So, pick a city. Speak at a local meetup and get over that stage fright. Most tech communities are very inclusive. They will love you participating and sharing.

It's a great time to be in developer relations, particularly for people who are starting their career. Instead of getting into a silo of engineering, testing, or product management, start with developer relations. It will give you a holistic perspective of what a product is about and experience of communicating with customers.

Of course, if you don't have a family or partner then you can spend your time traveling around the world and building your credibility. It's exciting when people come up to you as if you're a celebrity and say, "Hey, I've seen you on a YouTube video. Can I take a picture?" When that happens, you feel proud.

**Geertjan Wielenga**: Thank you, Arun Gupta.

## 22

> *My market is global. I spend time with people on six continents, every year.*

# Josh Long

# Introducing Josh Long

Josh Long is the first Spring developer advocate, a role he's held since 2010. Josh is a Java Champion and the author or lead author of more than five books and numerous training videos. He blogs routinely at `http://spring.io/blog` and `http://joshlong.com`, maintains a regular podcast, and is prolific on YouTube. Considered by his peers and audiences to be one of the most engaging speakers in developer advocacy, Josh pays property tax in San Francisco but spends most of his time talking to audiences all around the world. Find Josh on Twitter: `@starbuxman`.

---

**Geertjan Wielenga**: How did you end up being a developer advocate at Pivotal in the first place?

## Josh's introduction to developer advocacy

**Josh Long**: I was contributing to a project called Spring Integration in 2008/9 and the lead of the project was a gentleman named Mark Fisher. He now works on a function-as-a-service offering for Pivotal called Project Riff. I contributed several modules to Spring Integration.

Right after the acquisition of Spring by VMware, Pivotal had a bit of money to expand the team. Mark said that there was this new role open on the Spring team called a "developer advocate." I had never heard of that term, but I'd seen James Ward, at that time an Adobe evangelist, speak, and James, of course, is a living legend. So, I knew what an evangelist was and Mark likened one role to the other.

At the time, I was already out there in public debates, and on forums and panels at conferences. I'd written books and articles, so I was already in the community on my own time and dime. I had a full-time job as an engineer, but I was talking about Spring when I could. I loved it. This stuff was open source and it was super easy to use.

Mark offered me the advocacy role, but I said, "That doesn't sound like it's for me! I couldn't do that! Thanks, but no thanks." I walked away from my Skype session and about 20 paces away from the desk, I thought, "What am I saying?" I ran back and said that I would absolutely take the role. Mark was offering me a chance to join the family. I joined and I've never looked back.

**Geertjan Wielenga**: What is your role as a developer advocate?

**Josh Long**: I champion the developers to the engineering team and I champion the engineering team, and their work, to the developers in the community.

If I give a talk and the audience is less keen on that talk, then I know that the topic is not something people care about and Pivotal can turn that into feedback. If I give a talk and it's packed to the gills, then I know there is an appetite and we should hone in on that topic.

I try to be a conduit for feedback from the community and a big part of that is being on the ground, being able to talk to people, and being there by the water cooler so that someone can come and talk.

People maybe wouldn't be so eager to reach out in the community if all they could see was an inaccessible series of Twitter handles and public chatrooms. Developer advocacy is about being that feedback channel for people in the community who are using our stuff.

I think we forget that very few people have the itch to go onto GitHub and file an issue or try to debug code. Not many people even get to the point where they have a problem with the code.

Anecdotally, I have found that there are a lot of people at conferences who love what they're working on, but they aren't in a place where they feel they could contribute back or even comment with authority. They may not have the motivation to overcome that initial wall.

If somebody is standing there, they feel that they can talk to them. They then don't need to post a question on a public forum and expose their name or get into a long debate. I think it's very natural for people to want to be able to connect face to face. Being an active participant in the community is a huge part of that.

At Pivotal, the engineering group does good work. I meet the engineers behind Spring and I talk to them. I try to understand what they're doing and how that empowers our users.

**Geertjan Wielenga**: It seems to me that at colleges and universities, people generally don't know about developer advocacy at all. They assume that the world of software is about development and testing, and maybe architecture. This whole role is completely unknown. Do you agree with that?

## Making an impact

**Josh Long**: Yes, I agree. It depresses me to think that for all the people I've met, all the hands I've shaken, and all the eyes that I've made contact with over the years, that is a super-tiny percentage of the aggregate population that may ever use our software.

It depresses me to think that I haven't made a big difference and that people are completely unaware of what people like myself do but, at some point, you have to accept that you're not the majority. Even if you change many people's minds, you're still not going to connect in a meaningful way with as many people individually as the tech itself does.

Many people are just self-starters and learn tech from their friends. There are people who learn from developer advocates like us, and they take whatever they can learn from the source. Those cutting-edge people, at the edge of the pack, then teach their friends and bring the information into their organizations. It becomes part of organizational standards.

It's very interesting that people don't know about developer advocacy because many of them end up, in effect, doing that job for their organizations. Nowadays, I think there are a lot more of us out there. People are talking about big data, Android, Jakarta Enterprise Edition (EE), security, microservices, and so on. It all converges.

> *"One problem is the improper categorization of developer advocacy."*
>
> —*Josh Long*

It's hard to miss that there are people out there who are successful in this role. Having said that, I find that even with organizations that have accepted that they need a developer advocate, they don't quite understand that it's not a function, necessarily, of marketing. One problem is the improper categorization of developer advocacy. If you tell a hardcore developer that they're going to be doing marketing, they will probably flinch and say, "I think you've got me all wrong: that's not what I do."

That was my response when Mark asked, "Hey, would you be interested in this role?" I felt that the idea didn't sound like me because I'm an engineer, whatever that means. Of course, I realized how stupid that was two minutes later.

To be successful in engineering and developer advocacy, it's important that you have soft skills. You need to be able to articulate ideas, communicate with a team, and empathize. Those skills are as important, if not more important, than promoting or pushing your career in an organization. The best engineers are also evangelists or advocates.

**Geertjan Wielenga**: Let's go back to the distinction between marketing and developer advocacy. What, to you, is the difference between them?

**Josh Long**: It is blurry, but I do see a difference. I think of marketing as a function that is going to help to promote something. For example, what I do is talk about open source. My goal is to take back what the community tells me and turn that into direction, or insight, for our engineering group, whereas I think marketing is more of a unidirectional channel.

Marketing is trying to inform an ecosystem and a market. I don't think people in my organization do this, but to some people, marketing is also about deception or at least misdirection.

You see these car commercials and they're trying to suggest that a car will get you a better rapport with your peers at work and better success with your love life. The suggestion that one has anything to do with the other is just silly.

I'm not out there trying to mislead people in my role. I limit myself to the topics about which I can speak authoritatively. I do that by demonstrating ideas. If you come to see my performances in talks, I spend a lot of time just writing software live on stage.

> *"There's no rabbit up my sleeve."*
>
> —*Josh Long*

I start from absolute zero and I build something, so it's very hard to say, "Oh, you've got a rabbit up your sleeve." There's no rabbit up my sleeve. I believe that developer advocacy is as technical as anyone wants it to be, but also, it's informative, fun, and entertaining.

**Geertjan Wielenga**: Is there an overlap with being a spin doctor?

## Criticizing competitors

**Josh Long**: I'd say that's more a marketing function. All of us are given to being snarky, especially these days. It's so easy to be critical about competitors, or take pot shots, but if you do that, you're not the best advocate.

I'm not trying to diminish other techs: I'm only trying to let things I care about sell themselves. There's a difference between force-feeding somebody conclusions versus giving them the facts that they can use to, hopefully, arrive at conclusions. I sometimes poke fun at a tech, but I then proceed to use that exact tech on stage. So, I'm poking fun at myself, ultimately.

You can point people in a certain direction, but I know what it's like to have gone to a talk and felt like I just had the wool pulled over my eyes. I feel that way with slideware talks. You walk out at the finish line at the same place, but you don't quite know how you got there, so you feel like something was missing.

I think that developer advocacy, when done right, never leaves you wondering how you got to the conclusion, whereas marketing might, for convenience, skip a step or two. It might leave you just a little confused and clutching for a conclusion.

**Geertjan Wielenga**: Have you always been 100 percent behind the tech that you've promoted? Can you still be a developer advocate if you're not?

**Josh Long**: Sure, just look at Spring. Spring is massive and there are so many corners, or ecosystems, that it's impossible for me to say I've tried every single piece of code in all the modules everywhere, and I would do everything exactly the same way as I see it. That's not going to happen and it would be disingenuous to suggest otherwise.

I have good friends who are working in Java and doing advocacy for Java. Java is massive, so there's no way that they can say they approve of and have worked on everything that's possible with Java.

**Geertjan Wielenga**: For those topics that you do talk about in your presentations, and that you blog about, do you need to be 100 percent behind them?

**Josh Long**: Nobody tells me what to say, so if I say it, it's something I have tried, liked, and thought it would be interesting to talk about. Nobody has ever given me a script. Nobody tries to conditionally approve what I say.

You've only got so many chances to turn an audience to your tech, so I don't scattershot; I don't hit every single possible new thing. If I'm talking about a topic, I have found that thing to be useful and it's worth sharing.

That said, sometimes I'll find a feature to be limited in some way or I'll wish that maybe it did more, but I almost never need to get on stage and say that. By the time I've started playing with something, and I've got to a place where I'm at an impasse, or something didn't quite work as I hoped, it's dead simple for me to just go on the Gitter channels, which are open to the public, and ask questions, get feedback, or set up pull requests on GitHub.

By the time I get on stage, I've already invested enough time in an area that any kinks have been worked out, and if I can't work them out because they're insurmountable, then I don't talk about it (and I often try to fix them). I don't want to give my audience something that is not going to help them.

Spring has this massive ecosystem and for everything you can imagine, there's a tech or module for that. I can't hit every conference out there. I have to know my audience, so if I'm going to Oracle Code One or Devoxx, I'll talk about something related to building web apps or backend systems.

I'll talk about Spring, but I have to cluster the topics that are relevant to the conference that I'm speaking at.

I only talk about things that are less than desirable about Spring when I want to have fun or make a joke. For example, these days, I like talking about Spencer Gibb, a cofounder of Spring Cloud. One of the things that I joke about is that he's too damn responsive!

I made a video on how to use this tech from Spring Cloud called Spring Cloud Gateway. I rehearsed it, recorded it, post-produced it, and then put it out there. The video was well received and Spencer, after watching the video, asked if I had any feedback on the tech. I told him that it would be nice to have this and that happen. That same day, he went and instigated those changes and had it working perfectly. My video was made irrelevant in less than 24 hours! Spencer is so receptive, helpful, welcoming, and indulgent! That cad!

Sometimes, I'll talk about that kind of topic as a joke, but I don't spend much time talking about tech that didn't make the cut. I talk about the cutting-edge stuff instead.

## When you disagree with your company

**Geertjan Wielenga**: What happens when the company you work for does something that you disagree with, then you're on stage representing that company? Has that happened to you?

**Josh Long**: No, but it could have happened. I tried to love the Open Services Gateway initiative (OSGi) support that Spring had put forward before I joined Pivotal. I wrote about it to get a feel for it, coded it, and got feedback.

I never fell in love with it, though. By the time I joined the company, it was in the rearview mirror, so I didn't have to talk about it.

> *"Nobody forces you to talk about anything in a good organization."*
>
> —*Josh Long*

In fact, nobody would have forced me to talk about the OSGi support. Nobody forces you to talk about anything in a good organization like Pivotal. I can't speak for every organization, but at Pivotal, there is nobody who drives my direction, except the community. The community drives what I'm doing next. I don't have anybody who asks, "Would you please tell people about this or that?" Instead, I get people in the engineering organization saying, "Give this a shot." If I like the feature, I'll take it with me on my next talk and I'll stand by it.

If you're in an organization where you can't find something that you like, then that's the wrong job for you. I wouldn't want to be a developer advocate and champion things that in my heart of hearts I just didn't like.

With Spring, there might have been one small corner in the stack of the OSGi stuff that I wouldn't have been super enthusiastic about, but I would have just focused on all the other wonderful things that Spring supports and provides.

**Geertjan Wielenga**: If you're a new developer advocate standing in front of a big crowd and someone knows more about the tech that you're promoting than you do, how do you respond to that?

**Josh Long**: First of all, there is nothing wrong with saying that you don't know, especially if somebody throws a question from out of left field.

If it's a question on the topic that I'm talking about, then, of course, I hope to have an answer for that. If the question is on a tertiary subject, or secondary subject, in the satellite topology of the talk, then that's fine. I just try to point the person in the right direction of where they should look.

I also try to not get into a situation where I'm nervous that I would be made to look silly by any random question. I don't go on stage and talk about things that I'm not somewhat qualified to talk about.

**Geertjan Wielenga**: Something else that tends to happen in very opinionated communities, especially where developer advocates are active, is that there can be conflicts between people and it can, potentially, get personal. Have you encountered that and what advice would you give around that?

## Conflict between developer advocates

**Josh Long**: To the people who find conflict, or want conflict, I would say that developer advocacy is a very small community, so don't piss in the pool. There is only a tiny pool of people doing this worldwide, in any given ecosystem. I can't imagine trying to join my particular ecosystem, with all these wonderful people, just to start picking them off and starting conflicts.

You do find that in open source you've got these very opinionated people who are motivated to focus on this stuff.

They are out there working on these projects, so I don't begrudge them for being opinionated at all. It helps to harness their passion without letting it yield conflict.

> *"If you pick a fight with someone, you're going to ruin the best part of this ecosystem—the community."*
>
> —*Josh Long*

I love our community. I would say that in the Java ecosystem, and the cloud ecosystem, there are not many people I wouldn't break bread with. There aren't many people I would argue with. If you pick a fight with someone, you're going to ruin the best part of this ecosystem—the community.

**Geertjan Wielenga**: Do you have a typical day as a developer advocate?

**Josh Long**: The nice thing about this job is that there is no such thing as a common day; every day seems to be different. You're learning about something different, you're talking to different people, or you're in a different city or country. At any given time, I'm writing, reading, speaking, and listening about code. Then, of course, I have to spend time on the dreaded expense reports, which are the bane of all of our existences!

**Geertjan Wielenga**: That is one of the downsides of lots of travel. What specifically about expense reports is annoying and what are some other things that you dislike about doing what you do?

**Josh Long**: Expense reports are the only part of the job that feels like work. It's slow, tedious, repetitive work, so I have a hard time staying awake.

Obviously, if you're international, you're going to be moving around and conferences never start on a Tuesday and finish on a Thursday. They always, for some reason, start on a Monday and finish on a Friday. That means you're flying on the weekend.

You've got all sorts of stuff happening at any given moment and basically, you don't have much free time in this role. It's not like you can just sit there and stare at the sky. So, when you're told that you've got one day at home but in order for you to get on a flight, and make the next round of travel, you need to submit the expense reports, it's just so depressing.

I look back on a particularly busy year, a few years ago, and I can remember sitting there on December 24th doing expense reports. My goodness, they can stack up if you travel enough!

**Geertjan Wielenga**: Can you sketch out what amount of travel you actually do?

**Josh Long**: Let's start by saying that travel is not the job; you can do this job sitting in your underwear at home. You can write blogs that reach as many people, if not more, as you can reach talking to audiences. However, I like the boots-on-the-ground factor: being there and being able to meet people. Travel is part of that, but I don't think it's the job.

I travel because it's a way to connect. I find that being on the road, and having the time on the plane to myself, gives me an opportunity to write and do the other functions of the job. I actually find that traveling helps me in that respect.

Right now, I don't want to sit at my desk ignoring this opportunity. We have this amazing window that is just a brief flash in the pan. There are developers out there building applications that need to scale.

At Pivotal, we happen to have tech that not only helps with things that aren't easy to do but also supports things that people just don't do but should. Spring expands the use cases and makes things easy, which resonates well with the developers. I've been in a place where there was less of an appetite for what I was talking about, so if there is demand, I want to make sure that I don't ignore it.

Flying 25,000 miles per year with United Airlines puts you in the silver category, then there's 50,000 miles, which is gold, then 75,000, which is platinum, and then 100,000. Above that, there are no more tiers. There's an invitation-only tier called Global Services that you get if you exceed a certain dollar spend and miles flown. I've been Global Services for three years running. Last year, I flew more than 500,000 miles.

I'm very lucky because open source is the great equalizer. As long as you have an internet connection, which, I grant you, excludes some of the human population, you can participate. For that reason, my market is global. I spend time with people on six continents, every year.

## Josh's busy travel schedule

**Geertjan Wielenga**: Do you have any tips about handling flights and all the other problems of traveling the world?

**Josh Long**: On my team at Pivotal, we have a person, Tasha, who manages air traffic control.

She's an events coordinator and she manages my appearances. While I'm free to manage them myself, I've realized that if I just lean on her, I get infinitely better results. She's got the bird's-eye view.

It's hard to reach out to conferences and ask them to move your appearance so that you can make another conference nearby on that day. When it comes to your schedule, there's only one of you and so many places to be. With a big conference like Oracle Code One, that's a whole-week affair, but there could be five other events I want to be at in that same week. Somebody like Tasha can help to coordinate these appearances so I can be in different cities every day.

A couple of weeks ago, I was in Sydney on a Sunday and I was in Dubai by Monday night. By Thursday morning, I was in Bangalore, India, and then Boston by Sunday. For that kind of planning, you need somebody who's thinking about this stuff. It's hard enough for me to get on the plane, get there, and be prepared, and do all the other stuff that I talked about. To have someone else managing that schedule is invaluable.

I don't miss many flights because of that support and I don't have many horror stories anymore.

Every now and then, I'll get snowed in or something will get canceled. That's life; you can't win 'em all.

Several years ago, I was stuck in L.A. traffic, so I missed a flight to Russia. I was due to attend a wonderful conference in Novosibirsk, but I couldn't get to the airport in time. They closed the gate before I could board and that just killed me. Nothing kills me more than knowing that had I got there 10 minutes earlier, I would have made it. That was very disappointing.

**Geertjan Wielenga**: Do you have a morning ritual?

**Josh Long**: Morning for me is checking my calendar and then sometimes checking my TripIt to see which city I'm in. Sometimes I know where I am right away if I got in the night before and I've had enough sleep that my brain is booted up by the time I wake up.

I will try and get to Twitter, Slack, and then email, in that order. Email is my direct channel for people at conferences. I put my email in every single one of my presentations and I tell people about it. I encourage people to reach out to me, so I'm very happy if people email me. Ditto for my Twitter. I do check for those messages.

> *"If I have time, I'll listen to the cascade of noise from the organization itself."*
>
> —Josh Long

I also have a Pivotal email and if I have time, I'll listen to the cascade of noise from the organization itself. I don't spend much time being engaged with the machinery of my organization. I don't know who most of the people in my company are. I know the engineering teams behind Spring and some of the satellite techs, like Reactor and Cloud Foundry. I also know who our CEO is and basic stuff like that, but I don't spend much time in the organization itself.

I don't meet people in Pivotal because I don't spend much time in my office. I'm usually on the road talking to our customers and our community, so as a result, I find it to be very helpful to compartmentalize that noise.

I would love to engage with what's happening in my organization, but I find that I can do more, and bring more value, by focusing on today's talk, for example.

In 2014, when Spring Boot was starting to become a little more popular, people began asking me for help internally, but I didn't know who to reach out to. The problem was that I didn't know who the directors were of these different offices all around the world, which my colleagues wanted to know to help them to ramp up Spring Boot. Nowadays, things are different. We're internally visible and people, on the whole, know to reach out to us.

These days, everybody at Pivotal knows that Spring is a good thing and they know where to look for the new content. We do have an internal Slack, as well, and people ask questions there, but nobody needs to be convinced. Nobody needs to be told that they should be interested in this stuff anymore; they just naturally are.

**Geertjan Wielenga**: What's something new that you've recently learned?

**Josh Long**: There's always something to learn. Working with Java 12 was fun.

**Geertjan Wielenga**: What were you doing with Java 12?

**Josh Long**: It was about trying to make everything work, seeing what blew up, and moving things to modules. I love Java because it's always fun to get down to the basics with the Java virtual machine (JVM).

Recently, I've also been researching a number of different monitoring systems, such as Dynatrace and Datadog, because we have this relatively new project called Micrometer. I've just been going through and learning about dimensional metric tools.

I enjoy not focusing on the same topic over and over. No day should be the same for a developer advocate, unless you're doing something wrong.

**Geertjan Wielenga**: Do you feel that you end up being a jack of all trades, master of none?

## Spreading yourself thinly

**Josh Long**: Sometimes I feel, after a while, that I'm okay at 10 different things, whereas some people are really great at more. You start getting used to feeling mediocre, at least I do. But still, I'd rather be focusing on many topics than be bored.

**Geertjan Wielenga**: Where do you see your role developing in the next 10 years or so?

**Josh Long**: I love what I'm doing and our advocacy team is growing. I spend as much time as I can with people on the team to try and help them to do this job effectively. I'm privileged to have been doing this job for a good deal longer than anybody else on my team, so I try to help them.

As regards our larger company story, we're getting better and better. Every day there is a really amazing opportunity for these services.

We have more and more opportunities for synergies, and the synergies between all these different techs are really interesting to me.

I like Spring, I like microservices, I like cloud computing, and I like building distributed systems, but there's a cultural discussion behind that. You have to be more agile and have test-driven delivery, test-driven development, and cloud computing. There needs to be a circular arc: one concept leading to another, which leads eventually back to itself. In my role, I hope to address a larger spectrum of things.

**Geertjan Wielenga**: Would you say that there's a generic career path for developer advocates, or is a developer advocate doomed to be that for their entire life?

**Josh Long**: I think that engineers have a path to go into advocacy and vice versa. If you tried advocacy and it wasn't for you, there's a different ladder you could climb.

Some people just decide they want a change of pace or they switch career track. You aren't stuck in one role by any stretch of the imagination. I think the skills that make me a good developer advocate would lend themselves to me being a good part of an engineering team in an engineering organization. I would be better off for having gained this advocacy experience, not worse off.

**Geertjan Wielenga**: Is burnout a particular risk of doing developer advocacy for a long time?

**Josh Long**: If it's creative work, then many people will feel particularly invested in it.

There is this desire to contribute and keep contributing well past dinner time. That may seem positive, but the impact on your body is negative and at some point, it will manifest as a negative feeling that you have in your heart and mind.

> *"Anybody who loves what they do runs the risk of that feeling souring."*
>
> —*Josh Long*

That's a risk for anybody who is creative and invested in what they are doing. Programmers feel it too. Anybody who loves what they do runs the risk of that feeling souring because it becomes too much.

In our industry, it's very important to stop and smell the roses. Not every day involves going to the office. You can do much of what we do from home and you can be with your family. People have this misconception that this isn't possible in our role. In reality, some days you'll be out of the country, but some days you'll be home all day. What free time is taken away from you on some days is given back to you on others. Just make sure that you take advantage of the opportunity to be with your loved ones or to do whatever replenishes you.

Right now, it's 70 degrees here in San Francisco. There's a whole gaggle of people swimming in the pool in my condo building. I'm looking at that view and just thinking, "I need to go for a swim."

**Geertjan Wielenga**: Thank you, Josh Long.

## 23

> *Developers will listen to us because of the passion and authenticity, and because we are one of them.*

# Trisha Gee

# Introducing Trisha Gee

Trisha Gee is a Java Champion and a developer advocate for JetBrains. She has expertise in Java high-performance systems, dabbles in open-source development, and is passionate about enabling developer productivity. As the leader of the Sevilla Java User Group, Trisha is a strong promoter of healthy development communities that share ideas, learn from mistakes, and build on successes. Find Trisha on Twitter: @trisha_gee.

**Geertjan Wielenga**: I don't think that many people know that this profession exists outside of the people who are actually doing it. Would you agree with that?

## Raising the profile of developer advocacy

**Trisha Gee**: Yes, a lot of people don't know much about developer advocacy, so from a visibility point of view, I think we need to change that. I do get approached by people who are developers and are really interested in what's involved in this job and finding out whether they could actually do a job like this. I also think it's important to expose the profession to graduates and newbies to tech, and tell them that yes, this job exists.

One of the things I really love about developer advocacy comes from the fact that when I was a child, I wanted to be a teacher. That was because my parents are teachers, but also, I liked the idea of teaching people stuff; it's a cool thing to do.

If I had known that I could be a programmer and a teacher at the same time, I think I would have aimed for this career much sooner because this is my sweet spot: being able to do something that's creative and logical like programming, but also focusing on the documentation, the teaching, and the speaking. It's just a weird blend of skills and often people don't realize that you can make the most of that blend.

When I was at school, I knew I was interested in computers, mathematics, and physics, but the idea of being seated 9 to 5 behind a computer absolutely horrified me. I'm not really a massive people person, but I am a physically active person and I do like to talk to people. I thought, "I don't want to sit there not talking to anyone all day while I struggle with a computer. That sounds like my idea of hell!"

**Geertjan Wielenga**: Was there a point where you just realized that you were an advocate, or did you intentionally end up where you are now?

**Trisha Gee**: I intentionally steered my career toward this, but there was definitely a fuzzy period in the middle when I didn't know what I was steering myself toward. I was a traditional developer in the sense that I did computer science at university. I graduated in 2001 and it was a new, exciting field; the web stuff was taking off. We learned Java at university, so I became a bog-standard Java web developer.

> *"There is a niche for technical people who can also write."*
>
> —*Trisha Gee*

In those early years of my career, I read a lot. I read many blogs and books, and I discovered that there are these technical people who are also good at writing—people like Joel Spolsky. There is a niche for technical people who can also write, even if it is just them writing the documentation or writing their experiences using something. Much of what you do as a developer is googling how to do stuff. I decided I was going to scratch my writing itch because one of the other things I wanted to be when I was younger was a journalist.

Quite early on, I started with the blogging side of stuff, but in 2006 or 2007, when I was around seven or eight years into my career, I went to a QCon London conference and I saw loads of ThoughtWorks people presenting. It just blew my mind. I thought, "This conference thing is amazing!"

Sharing ideas, telling people about cool stuff that you've worked on, and being able to talk about process stuff at conferences is so creative and inspirational. I didn't think that I was good enough to do it myself, but I did like the idea. I carried on with the blogging for a few more years after that.

**Geertjan Wielenga**: Were you working for yourself while you were blogging?

**Trisha Gee**: No, I was working for different companies. I moved from one standard Java developer job to another. I worked for Ford Motor Company and for a credit card company.

At the time of going to my first conference, I was a consultant working for a small consultancy that specializes in farming out Java developers to the financial markets.

I was doing the blogging in my own time. When I was working for this consultancy, there was a guy called Simon Brown there who was speaking at conferences. I thought, "This guy Simon is more experienced than me, but he's not that much more amazing than me. I could actually do this."

Then a few years on from that, I actually did end up working for ThoughtWorks. I met Martin Fowler and I was complaining about the lack of women speakers at these conferences. He was the one who said, "Well, you should be speaking at conferences."

I replied, "I'm not ready for that."

**Geertjan Wielenga**: Do you think that there is this perception that conference speakers are geniuses who know absolutely everything about their topic?

## Trisha's advice for aspiring speakers

**Trisha Gee**: Yes, but the thing that you learn when you're doing this job is that, actually, an hour is not that long in terms of the amount of time you have to present an idea or a set of ideas.

You don't have to have very deep knowledge to fill an hour with something interesting and useful. I don't mean that in a bad way, and I'm not trying to criticize or put down speakers. What I'm saying is that it's much easier for pretty much any developer to do this role than they realize, even if it's just a talk on their own experience of learning tech. I say this to beginners and people who want to get into speaking all the time.

Out of my initial blogs, the most successful was about getting aspect-oriented programming (AOP) caching working with Spring. It's a very specific piece of functionality, but there was no good documentation. I was writing the blog without very good knowledge of the Spring Framework or even about annotations or caching. But it turned out to be very successful because there are many developers in that same position of not really knowing anything and starting from zero.

There are actually not that many developers who need to know the expert-level, deep stuff. Way more developers need to know the introductory stuff. Sometimes, there is no documentation on how to get different techs working together. If you are an experienced person, you could probably throw stuff together after a bit of trying, but often there's no one central place for that.

> *"I was quite worried about writing my blog posts in case they were wrong."*
>
> —*Trisha Gee*

It's very easy for us in this industry to have opinions and just chuck them out there by blogging. I remember in the early days, I was quite worried about writing my blog posts in case they were wrong. So, even if it was an opinion piece, I would worry. I quite often write opinion pieces about being a woman in tech and my experience of being a woman developer. I used to spend a long time doing research, and finding facts and studies to back up what I was saying, because I felt like someone was going to say, "Quote your sources! You're wrong!"

If I did my research, I thought I would be able to come back to that person and say, "I'm not wrong because this, this, and this." But actually, that never happened! All of that research that I did was pointless because people just chuck their opinions out on the internet all the time, back them up with nothing, and then get into a massive argument with someone else who's done exactly the same thing! I think in many ways that's a good thing about the industry. I'd like to encourage more people, particularly women and people from underrepresented groups, to overcome all the things that are stopping them from blogging.

I'm doing my "Career Advice for Programmers" talk this week and next week, so on Twitter, I asked, "What advice would you want as a programmer?"

I had a lot of beginners saying, "I don't know how to get started. I don't know what I should be learning and I don't know how to learn it. I'm intimidated by all of this stuff." If you just put content out there aimed at beginners, there's way more of a market for that than for the deep-level expertise that we think is needed.

**Geertjan Wielenga**: Would you say that open source is a good entry point for beginners?

**Trisha Gee**: Absolutely! When I worked for MongoDB, we hired people from the community all the time. Even if you're not hired by someone to come into that organization, you have a portfolio to show other employers.

# Being involved with open source

Submitting a CV to a job opening is probably not how most developer advocates are hired. That's how I got hired for all of my developer positions, but for developer advocacy, it's easier to interview someone for that role by not even interviewing them. Often, you can see their conference talks and their blog posts. If you've got a developer who's not officially a developer advocate yet, but they do have some user group talks, a couple of blog posts, and so on, it's much easier for an organization to come up to that person and say, "You've got the right sort of profile; come and work for us."

**Geertjan Wielenga**: There's always the obligatory topic around the title of "tech evangelist" or "developer advocate." How do you see yourself, and does it make a difference?

**Trisha Gee**: In terms of title, I use "developer advocate." But it's easier for me to do that because my product is aimed at developers, and I also want to pitch myself as a developer. I'm a developer talking to developers.

Also, I don't really like the word "evangelist" because it has certain overtones of being slightly overzealous and a bit religious. An important part of the advocate role is that it's supposed to be a two-way thing. "Evangelist" just says that you're going to stand up and tell people why your product is amazing. An advocate is meant to stand between the company and the user. We're going to tell developers what's new in our product, why it's useful for them, and how to use it.

We also really need to hear back from the developers about what they want and what the pain points are. Apart from the fact that we don't really talk about the role enough anyway, I think we don't focus enough on the bidirectional nature of it.

**Geertjan Wielenga**: There's another distinction between developer advocates who work for companies, who are paid by those companies, and the segment of developer advocates who don't represent a particular company or product. What differences are there?

**Trisha Gee**: When I'm doing advocacy around the Java space, but not being paid to do it by a company, I am much freer in a way because I can express my opinions and I'm not representing my organization's opinions.

Then, of course, if you're truly independent, a lot of the goal of that is to drum up business for yourself. That's actually a good thing and not a criticism. If you're an independent person, you want to be seen as being an expert because that's how you get business.

> *"People like us have been hired for being passionate about those products in the first place."*
>
> —*Trisha Gee*

I guess some of the suspicion around advocates or evangelists is people thinking, "Are you trying to sell something to me? What is your end goal?" For independents, they have one particular type of goal. For people like me who work for companies, we get paid to talk about how amazing our products are, but one of the interesting things about the developer advocate role is that, often, people like us have been hired for being passionate about those products in the first place.

An important point for people who are interested in doing this sort of role is that while some of the skills are transferable between companies regardless, like the ability to write, the passion for the thing that you're talking about is really important, and the passion can be fairly broad. I'm interested in Java, but not in a really techie "this is how you create new languages" kind of way. I'm interested in Java in terms of asking, "As a developer, what in the language is going to make my life easier?"

I could work for Oracle and talk about that. I could work for, obviously, JetBrains and talk about that because our main product is aimed at Java developers. I could work for any company in the Java space. I've just chosen to work at JetBrains because its interests align nicely with mine.

In my last role (I don't want to say this in a negative way about the company I was working for because the company is fine and is successful), my interests as a developer advocate did not align well with the interests of the company. What the company wanted to do for engineering and for product marketing did not align with my views. I moved on from there because as a Java developer advocate, it didn't work well being employed by a NoSQL database company.

## Advocacy and spin doctoring

**Geertjan Wielenga**: Would you see yourself as a spin doctor in any way?

**Trisha Gee**: Interestingly, we've had a similar conversation about this inside JetBrains recently with all the advocates.

We've got about 12 advocates for the different products and the different languages, and we actually don't work that closely together because we're all in our own independent communities, with our own independent languages.

A core element that pulls us together is that we really want to be honest about things. That's not to say that we're not going to try and present things in a positive way, but there's no way I'm going to say my product supports Java 12 when it doesn't support Java 12.

> *"I need to be honest about the weaker points of the product."*
>
> —*Trisha Gee*

I need to be honest about the weaker points of the product. We won't be able to improve functionality if we're out there lying. Trying to put a spin on things is ultimately not going to work well for this role. People won't trust you, people won't listen to you, and you're not going to benefit the company or the community by not being honest in both directions.

Developers are really averse to being sold to or marketed at, and they're smart enough to smell that a mile away. Even though developer advocates are effectively doing a presales-type job, developers will listen to us because of the passion and authenticity, and because we are one of them. We're not some sort of salesperson trying to sell them something.

**Geertjan Wielenga**: What does your day consist of, typically?

**Trisha Gee**: When I'm not traveling, I have fairly structured days. Part of this is due to my kids, but it's also partly due to having a spouse who I should spend time with.

Even before the kids were born, I was fairly structured about work. I'll say I work 9:00 a.m. to 6:00 p.m., but it's not really those exact hours. I usually start work around 11:00 a.m. I used to be a morning person, but I don't think I'm very productive in the mornings now. I generally catch up on emails and all the admin rubbish. That might be when I do my expenses. I know that the morning is the time when you're supposed to use all your energy and willpower to get the creative stuff done, but I just don't seem to be able to get stuck in in the mornings.

I usually break for lunch at 2:00 p.m. Then I come back and start work again at 3:00 p.m., until I stop at 6:00 p.m. In the evenings, you can't really contact me. I don't get a chance to look at my phone because I'm trying to tire the kids out for a couple of hours.

**Geertjan Wielenga**: Some of the highs of this role have been pointed out, but what are some of the lows of this particular profession?

**Remote working**

**Trisha Gee**: They're going to be different from person to person, not just because of the individuals and the companies, but also because of the different types of situations. For me, one of the great things about my role is that I work remotely. I'm the only person in JetBrains who lives in Seville, but Hadi, my boss, is a couple of hours away in Malaga.

I work in my office at home, so that's great. It gives me flexibility, should I want it, but it's also potentially quite lonely.

In my case, working from home requires willpower and self-motivation, which is fine because I'm good at that stuff. But if you're the sort of person who just can't quite force yourself to sit down and do the work, I think certainly working from home might be quite challenging.

> *"Sometimes, the role can force you to do something that's routine instead of creative."*
>
> —*Trisha Gee*

Another challenge is that developer advocacy covers loads of different types of things. I do conferences and blogging, but I also do screencasts, Twitter tips, and animated GIFs. I write a monthly newsletter and I have to create material around releases, which means that at a given time of the year, I have to be working on release content and on the functionality that's in the releases. Those tasks are good because they counter the lack of willpower thing: you've got external deadlines that have to be hit and very specific things you have to do. But you can sometimes think, "Oh, wouldn't it be great to just sit down and blog about this thing that I've got in my brain?" I have to sit down and do the newsletter instead. Sometimes, the role can force you to do something that's routine instead of creative.

I've been ignoring my emails for three weeks because I just really needed to get some content done. I've literally spent the last two and a half days just replying to emails, and because of the way that advocacy works, many of those emails are time-sensitive.

There might be conference invitations, abstracts that need to be written, and titles that need to be sent.

Often, at the end of one day, you've done many small things and if you're a tick-box sort of person, your to-do list looks amazing because you've ticked everything off. The problem is that you haven't got to anything that you wanted to do, like a screencast on the future of Java or something a bit fluffier.

One of the main problems is prioritization. This is something that we struggle with as a team at JetBrains because it's difficult to measure your impact on the bottom line. You don't really know if doing this Twitter tip is going to sell more licenses, for example. Somewhere down the line, maybe someone will see it and say, "That's a good idea."

When you're doing development, you've usually got a product owner or someone who can say, "We need to work on this feature because X-many users have requested it and they really need it." When you're a developer advocate, it's difficult to weigh that up. For a start, you've got lots of different types of content. For a blog post on, say, new features in Java 11, how do you weigh that up against a webinar on code best practices? They're two different topics and two different audiences. I don't know how to prioritize those two different things because I kind of want to do both. So, prioritization is really difficult for a developer advocate.

There are so many things to do and sometimes that can be a bit overwhelming because I like to be able to prioritize things according to some sort of point system. But I'm coming to the conclusion that given that I have a certain amount of experience in this now, I'm just going to have to go with my gut.

I can just decide that I think this is the right thing to work on because it feels like the right time to do that.

**Geertjan Wielenga**: Do you have experience with burnout?

## Burnout in the industry

**Trisha Gee**: For me, it's the difference between being externally motivated versus being internally motivated. If you're sitting at a job and your boss is telling you that you need to get all this stuff done for the release, which is next week, and you just don't have enough hours to do it in, and that happens again and again, then you end up burning out.

I think it's also possible to get burnout when you're driving your own goals. I definitely see this in some of the developer advocates around me because there is variety in what we do, but there are just so many things to do. People like us are very passionate and very driven, so we just want to be doing the next thing all the time.

> *"I've seen people faint on stage because they were working too hard."*
>
> —*Trisha Gee*

I think probably one of the reasons why more of us don't experience burnout is because, generally, advocates are a bit more senior and maybe we're better at spotting if something is not productive behavior. I don't know what the statistics are, but I've seen people faint on stage because they were working too hard.

What stops me from burning out right now is that I have two small children at home and I have to put the work down for them. I think if I didn't have the kids, I would work harder and longer, but the kids force me to work smarter. I have to work within the hours I've got available, then I have to put the work down. I have to be off at the weekends and take my vacations too.

**Geertjan Wielenga:** Would you be more productive if you were working much more, though?

**Trisha Gee**: Before having kids, I was using my free time to make up for the fact that perhaps I hadn't done the right things during my working hours. I was working harder but not more productively.

Then, when you don't have the time for that anymore, you decide that you're just not going to do that thing and it's not that important. I might decide that I'm not going to give the same talk five times; I'll give it three times, but at three big conferences. You just have to be much more brutal in your prioritization.

I've been on maternity leave twice at JetBrains, which people noticed, but I don't think they noticed as much as you would think when taking four months off work. My problem is trying to figure out what things to do in that "less" time that I have. What are the productive things to work on? You could churn out 12 blog posts or you could do three really good ones.

When I was pair programming, I was probably at my most productive because out of the eight hours a day you were there, you'd get six hours of solid work done.

But when I was working in a traditional office, just sitting at my computer, I probably spent a third of the time emailing friends, checking Facebook, and looking at cat photos. I don't want to say that in an "I'm a lazy developer" way, but it's just what you do in an office environment. You reach a point in the project that you're working on where you feel blocked, but because you have to sit at your desk, you don't go for a walk, so you just look at something else on your computer instead.

I've spoken to loads of people who work from home. When they get stuck, many of them just stop and have a shower. In the shower, that's where they have their most creative ideas. Being sat at a computer is not the most productive place for a developer, an advocate, or pretty much anyone because the problem is not the typing: it's the thinking and it's the creativity. You can wake up at 3:00 a.m. with an idea; you don't have to sit at your desk to have that happen.

**Geertjan Wielenga**: How important is the travel aspect of the role for you?

**Trisha Gee**: When you're a developer advocate, you meet other developer advocates at conferences. We're a bigger community than we think we are. So, my colleagues are other developer advocates who work for other companies.

We don't work in the same office and we don't even necessarily do the same sort of job. We work in competing companies sometimes, but we hang out and we chat, and we have much more in common with each other than with other people. That's one good part of the traveling.

Also, the travel is an appealing part of the job if you don't normally have the chance to travel. Many people think, "Oh, developer advocates are really cool because they get to go to these exotic places." That's not necessarily true, but it can be.

I've started trying to cut down on the travel because I'm not sure it's the most productive use of my time right now. I've had kids and they're only little. I'll start doing traveling when they're at school and they won't miss me as much.

The travel is actually a really important part for me because that's where I meet our users and where I get my energy levels back up. I'm not really an extrovert or an introvert. I am an introvert in that I like having plenty of time alone to recharge myself, but I also need time with people to give me that boost and that spark.

When developer advocates get together at conferences, we don't talk about what's new in Java; we ask, "So, how many miles did you rack up this year? Hasn't Hilton got so much better in the last year?" The conversations will be something travel-related.

**Geertjan Wielenga**: How do you deal with the jet lag? How do you cope with missing a flight? Do you have horror stories to tell?

**Trisha Gee**: I don't miss a lot of flights because I'm very paranoid. I like to get to the airport early. In Seville, we do have an international airport, but it's not a major one.

## Travel difficulties

One time, I was going to OSCON, which is quite tricky to get to because it's in Portland, Oregon. It's right on the other side of the U.S. Even from London, that was quite a challenging flight.

From Seville, it was easier for me to get the train to Malaga, which is two hours away, then get on a flight from Malaga to New York, and then fly from New York to Portland.

That wasn't the worst set of circumstances, but the trains between Seville and Malaga are really weird. They're not once an hour: there's a weird clustering of trains at certain points of the day. I caught the earliest possible train to Malaga and I got there, but I was five minutes late for getting through security at the airport. I had this brilliant business-class flight lined up that I was really excited about, but I wasn't allowed on the plane. I had no luggage and the flight wasn't for 45 minutes, but they said no.

I had to get on the train and go another two hours back home to Seville, but I couldn't rebook because Malaga has one flight a day to New York. Malaga is not London. In London, you just book the next flight. If I got the next flight from Malaga, I was going to be two days late for the conference!

I used to suffer from jet lag. I had a way of dealing with it because I worked in New York for a bit, so I was traveling back and forth between London. I had techniques for drinking the right amount of alcohol on the plane to get me to go to sleep, which, incidentally, is slightly more than one glass of red wine but definitely less than two glasses of red wine!

> *"I just don't have jet lag anymore because I'm permanently sleep-deprived."*
>
> —*Trisha Gee*

One of my children is 10 months old and one of them is just under three. In the last three years, I've not been sleeping and now I've realized I just don't have jet lag anymore because I'm permanently sleep-deprived. I don't notice it. I feel tired all the time, so it makes no difference.

Last time I traveled, I went to San Jose, which was a 23-hour journey, and I said, "I'm never going to do that again!" That was a terrible journey, but I still felt normal amounts of tired the next day. I was pregnant at the time, so I was just tired anyway. I'm just always tired; that's the secret!

**Geertjan Wielenga**: How much time do you spend on social media and what are some sites that you make use of?

## Using social media

**Trisha Gee**: I publish frequently to Twitter. I don't really read Twitter. I don't know if that makes me a bad person! I just don't have time. If I've woken up at 3:00 a.m. because the baby wants to feed, then I'll read Twitter. Reading Twitter at that time is a mistake because you don't sleep properly if you do that. I'm responsive on Twitter if people ask me questions. Support requests come through Twitter quite often.

I use Facebook and I have a bunch of developer advocate friends on there, but Facebook is very much a case of keeping in touch with family, more than anything work-related.

The good thing about doing a monthly newsletter is I quite often have to seek out news, and figure out what's going on and what's interesting. I use InfoQ for that and DZone. DZone updated its emailing recently, probably due to the General Data Protection Regulation (GDPR), so I don't get those emails anymore.

Medium gives me notifications on my phone and I don't know how it decides what I should be interested in, but sometimes it's interesting and sometimes it's not. There's just so much news out there that I don't try to read everything.

I'm signed up to a bunch of mailing lists, like the Java Development Kit (JDK) and OpenJDK mailing lists, but mostly, I wait for something to have enough momentum that I hear about it through friends and colleagues, then I'll go and find out about it. There's just too much noise and so much to stay up to date with.

**Geertjan Wielenga**: What sort of tech have you been advocating recently? What sessions do you do at conferences?

**Trisha Gee**: I generally focus on keeping developers up to date on Java for my sessions, usually with live coding. It's nice because it means I have to stay up to date with Java, especially now, with the new six-monthly release cadence.

I can show new features that are in IntelliJ and I still get to write real Java code. I've been doing a Java versus Kotlin kind of talk, which is mostly because I was on maternity leave until last March, so I had to steal someone else's talk and make it my own! A lot of the JetBrains people obviously do stuff around Kotlin, so I got to play a little bit with it, but I still haven't really used Kotlin very much. I want to do more of that.

I'm going to update that talk in time for JavaOne to include some Groovy, which I'm still a big fan of, even though it's dynamic and sometimes a bit weird in terms of not behaving the way you would expect it to. I'm also going to update it for Scala because I actually had to write some Scala code last month for the first time in my whole life!

I give a talk called "Is Boilerplate Code Really So Bad?" The point is that as an old-school Java programmer, I just don't see why people keep calling it "boilerplate" because this is my language; this is what I'm used to. Many people, certainly from the new Java virtual machine (JVM) language world, quite often talk about minimizing boilerplate in languages like Kotlin. So, I was interested to see some of the new features in Kotlin, particularly as some are already in the Java language, such as the variable declaration. Also, `switch` expressions are coming into Java.

> *"You can't objectively say that one language is more readable."*
>
> —*Trisha Gee*

It was interesting looking at Scala because Scala goes, in my opinion as a Java developer, a little bit too far in terms of stripping out boilerplate, and things just happen magically. The feature that I was demoing in IntelliJ was putting the boilerplate back in, so that you could understand what the code was magically doing under the covers. It's nice to compare and contrast, and it makes you realize that readability and understandability are totally a personal thing to do with your own experience, the team that you work with, and the code base that you're familiar with. You can't objectively say that one language is more readable because it's all about familiarity.

## Trisha's areas of interest

**Geertjan Wielenga**: What would you say you are really passionate about at the moment in terms of tech?

**Trisha Gee**: I actually don't think I'm extremely passionate about tech. I'm really excited to see how fast Java is moving at the moment with the six-monthly release cadence. I think that's really cool because in many ways, it's going to make everything less exciting around the releases and it will be less exciting to see new features. It's just going to become normal, and I like that.

What I'm really passionate about is around the people side of being a developer. I write stuff about code reviews for our other product that I do advocacy for, which is Upsource, our code review tool. I don't really talk that much about Upsource as a tool. I talk more about how to talk to other developers about improving their code. I talk about what good code is or isn't. Essentially, it depends on the other developers, on the domain, and on the experience of the people around you. We shouldn't get really religious about saying things are good or bad. I'm passionate about conversations that we should have within our teams about code. It should be about trying to make the product better and not about nitpicking this formatting or this semicolon.

The other area I'm really interested in is around the "Career Advice for Programmers" talk that I mentioned earlier. That is why this interview is interesting: the career path for developers/programmers/technical people is not very clear.

Traditionally, you might start as a programmer and be promoted to being a team lead, then a manager. Maybe, if you're in a senior technical position, you might be a chief technology officer (CTO) or something like that. The issue is that, over time, good programmers don't necessarily want to do that. Someone who's got 20 years' experience as a Java programmer would be wasted if you stuck them in middle management.

> *"Our industry is new; we still don't really know who we are or what we do."*
>
> —*Trisha Gee*

There is information out there about careers advice for programmers, but I think this is an area that is still very new. Our industry is new; we still don't really know who we are or what we do. So, it's difficult for developers to know how to become programmers, how to grow themselves technically, and what sorts of roles are available to them that aren't just programming, like being a developer advocate, or DevOps, or a full-stack developer. These sorts of roles are still evolving in our industry, so that's something I'm really interested in.

To go back to the diversity topic, which we've touched on a little bit, there is a distinct lack of visible diversity in our industry in that, generally speaking, most of the developers you meet are white and male. Obviously, there's a big contingent in South Asia, but typically, we're talking about white men. We have a very low proportion of people of color and of women.

People don't really know how safe the industry may or may not be for the LGBT community also.

I think if we understand a bit better what our job is, what the role encompasses, what it's like to work within a team as a developer, what the career path is, and how fulfilling it is or is not as a human being, as opposed to just a coder, that can help us to address some of these diversity problems.

**Geertjan Wielenga**: Nowadays, working in tech is a much more sociable path because there's social media, WhatsApp, Slack, and pair programming. Do you think that a greater range of possibilities is opening up for people from all backgrounds?

**Trisha Gee**: Yes, I completely agree with that. I'm really passionate about highlighting to people outside of the industry, and not just to kids who might be considering it as a career path, that this idea of the lone-wolf programmer that gets shown all the time on TV is not true.

In fact, it's becoming more and more desirable to not work with people like that and to not hire people like that. Programming or being a developer, as opposed to being a programmer, means talking to users. It means pairing and it means communicating. The difficult bit of our job is not writing the code: it's understanding what is required, turning that into something vaguely useful for the machine, and having conversations with people to figure out what that looks like.

> *"This job is a highly social, very communicative role, but we don't necessarily present that even to ourselves."*
>
> —*Trisha Gee*

This job is a highly social, very communicative role, but we don't necessarily present that even to ourselves. We certainly don't present that to the outside world. I still think people outside of tech think of programming the way that you and I thought about it when we were at university: being seated in front of a computer for nine hours a day, and it's just not true. People who want to work that way are not going to integrate well into the current developer role because it's so social and so dependent on good communication.

I have a friend who's a tech writer and I realized that her role and my role are very similar. We have to have tech backgrounds and we have to have an interest in the tech. We went to university and both studied Java, but she went off to do the tech writing much earlier in her career than I became a developer advocate. Really, these roles are much more about communication.

People don't know about these sorts of roles, but they're becoming more and more important. I'm seeing more adverts for tech writers, developer advocates, and tech evangelists. How I got into advocacy was I was working at LMAX and we open sourced the disruptor. That's fine because you can check anything on GitHub, but what you need is people to go and say, "This is what it is. This is why it's cool. This is the way you can use it."

My boss, Martin Thompson, was doing that, and my other boss, Dave Farley, was doing advocacy around the continuous delivery stuff that we were doing inside LMAX. I wanted to help. They helped me to get into that scene.

Martin has this deep technical knowledge and I didn't have that, but the good thing was that I didn't need it because Martin was doing that role. What I had to do was take his deep technical knowledge and just make it accessible enough for developers like me. I got into developer advocacy because we, as a company, open sourced our product, and we open sourced that product partly for recruitment and partly for marketing purposes.

**Geertjan Wielenga**: What kind of career path do you see yourself as having as a developer advocate? Do you see yourself being in this role forever, or do you see it developing somewhere else?

## The career path for advocates

**Trisha Gee**: It's actually ridiculous that you've asked me the obvious question, considering that I'm working on a talk about career advice for programmers, and I've not actually thought about that for myself!

I've been at JetBrains for nearly four years. This is the longest I've ever worked for a company, for a start. I expect to be here for a while because my interests align with the company, as I mentioned.

Beyond this specific role for this specific company, I definitely think developer advocacy, in one flavor or another, is going to be my job for the next five or 10 years. Developers can't really see beyond about five years anyway.

With the variety, you can tweak whichever levers you want. If I don't want to travel so much and I don't want to do so many conference talks, then maybe I'll focus on doing some more tutorials. If I decide that I'm really fed up with struggling to use Camtasia, then I will do something else.

One of the challenges of being a developer advocate is that you have to use different types of tech. I'm not using IntelliJ IDEA to write code all the time. I have to use screen-capturing tech and GIF-rendering tech, and stuff that I'm not an expert in. If I decide I don't want to do any more of that and I want to do more writing, then I can do more writing. So, I can see myself doing this for a long period of time.

> *"I can definitely see myself in this kind of weird hybrid role of being technical and being a teacher."*
>
> —*Trisha Gee*

Something I would like to do more of is in-person training, and I would like to, at some point, write a book. Although, I've been saying that for 10 years now! I want to do the career advice stuff as a book. I was just going to write it as one blog post at a time, but then I'm ridiculous when I write blog posts.

I write a blog post about code reviewing something, for example, and it ends up being 3,000 words. I'd like any job that would let me reach these goals. I can definitely see myself in this kind of weird hybrid role of being technical and being a teacher.

Most of the time, if you're putting stuff on a website, you have no idea if anyone's using any of your code. One of the best things about being a developer advocate is when people come up to you after a talk and say, "That was really great." You get instant gratification from that.

**Geertjan Wielenga**: Thank you, Trisha Gee.

## 24

> *What I'm doing now addresses the problem that I faced as a young person: gaining real and practical coding skills.*

# Bilal Kathrada

# Introducing Bilal Kathrada

Bilal Kathrada is the CEO and founder of IT Varsity, an education business focused on transforming South African computer science graduates into fully employable junior developers. As well as speaking at conferences and advising businesses about strategic digital transformation, Bilal writes a weekly tech opinion column for *The Cape Argus*, a South African newspaper. Passionate about transforming the tech landscape of the future, he has also launched CompuKids, an educational program designed to provide a 21st century computer science curriculum in primary and secondary schools. Find Bilal on Twitter: @BilalKathrada.

---

**Geertjan Wielenga**: Can you briefly talk about your background?

**Bilal Kathrada**: I'm a software engineer by profession, I'm a certified Java programmer, and I've done some Java development in the past. Now I run an online institute that trains people to become developers.

**Geertjan Wielenga**: In many ways, I think that you're a developer advocate. You work with developers, you give them skills, and you update them on the latest tech developments. You fit into a long history of people around the world doing this work in the tech space. Would you agree?

## Encouraging young people

**Bilal Kathrada**: Absolutely. Besides running my institute, I also travel to schools around South Africa to talk to children about careers in development. In South Africa, the level of computer science education in schools is pathetic. I try to get young people clued up to give them advantages in the future.

I run developer workshops for young people and speak to universities and businesses to encourage people to get into tech careers. I also write for four major national newspapers about tech and run a weekly podcast called *TechWatch*, where we speak about getting into tech and developer careers.

**Geertjan Wielenga**: Could you say more about the South African context behind your work?

**Bilal Kathrada**: The South African context is a very problematic one. Since apartheid fell away, the expectations that people had have not been fulfilled. There's a lot of corruption, an economic crisis, and massive youth unemployment. I think the latest reports said that we have 45% youth unemployment. That's the first issue.

What further compounds the problem in South Africa is that we're likely the most developed nation in Africa and potentially we could be the tech gateway to the whole of Africa. Unfortunately, we've fallen way behind on this simply because we haven't prepared our youth for entrepreneurship and innovation in the space of tech and development. We've taken a back seat compared to other countries like Kenya.

Roles are being outsourced to international workers because there aren't many South Africans who are skilled enough to do development work. That's compounding the problems we already have. The South African context is pretty much defined by this.

> *"South African youth are getting the lowest possible quality of education that you can imagine, especially when it comes to tech."*
>
> —*Bilal Kathrada*

The reason that this is all happening is that our universities haven't kept pace with what's going on in the world. South African youth are getting the lowest possible quality of education that you can imagine, especially when it comes to tech. Thousands of graduates are emerging every year from our universities and the one word to describe them is "unemployable." They're unemployable because they just don't have the skills that they need. They have some theory, which is usually outdated, but no skills to go into development work.

**Geertjan Wielenga**: What specific skills do they need?

**Bilal Kathrada**: They need three levels of skills. Level one is knowing the very basic theory around development. Most universities offer a very theoretical qualification as far as IT goes, but they stop at this layer.

The second layer is marketable skills. There's a vast difference between learning to code in Java and learning to create an application in Java, for example.

Java coding will consist of the fundamentals of the language, which is great, but over and above that you need additional knowledge, such as knowing how databases operate and how your application will connect to the database.

If you go to a typical South African university, there are HTML courses with a little bit of JavaScript thrown in and some Java here and there, but it's a very basic level of education.

The third layer that's needed is soft skills, such as entrepreneurship, personal branding, digital marketing, and all of the skills that help you to accelerate yourself from where you are to where you want to be in life.

**Geertjan Wielenga**: There's a pressing need for new developers throughout South Africa. Is that correct?

**Bilal Kathrada**: There are plenty of jobs, yes. You've got your fair share of companies that have adopted the Java ecosystem and others that have adopted .NET or Python. You're not confined to any one specific tech. The role I'm trying to play in South Africa is helping people to fulfill all three layers of the pyramid. That's why I left my development job.

I felt the same pain as young people do now when I left university and went to get my first job. I approached a couple of non-profit organizations that needed systems to be developed and I did that at no cost. That got me an interview and then I had to prove myself to get the job. I discovered that there was a lot that I didn't know. Seeing this skills gap, I decided to design a curriculum to teach people these skills. I now have students from countries including Nigeria, Haiti, and Kenya.

**Geertjan Wielenga**: What are the subjects that you teach?

**Bilal Kathrada**: The focus is on full-stack development, so we started using Java, HTML, CSS, MySQL, and full-stack applications, then we introduced PHP because there's a lot of demand for it in South Africa. Recently, we've noticed that there is demand for .NET too; there seems to be an upswing in terms of companies looking for .NET developers.

Students are free to choose what stream they want to get into and we advise them accordingly. We've noticed that there are many learners who are enthusiastic about getting into IT, but they're not quite hardcore developer material. Rather than turn them away or demotivate them, we offer them the option of going into web design. Our bright sparks continue with mobile and full-stack development. We place a very strong emphasis on good coding practices, such as code documentation, testing, and writing clean code.

**Geertjan Wielenga**: Do you see a place for open source in your curriculum? These projects are on GitHub and even if you're not very technical, you can get involved in all kinds of other ways: finding issues and bugs, trying out the software, and writing documentation.

**Bilal Kathrada**: Yes, we constantly encourage our learners to get involved. Open-source projects are an excellent way of expanding your knowledge of development.

**Geertjan Wielenga**: What does your average day look like?

**Bilal Kathrada**: The first few hours of my day are focused on content creation and this will take the form of tutorial videos, online advice, podcasts, or any other free content that we put out. Some days I might plan new courses or improve our existing offerings.

The next portion of my day is spent catching up with students around the country. The last part of the day I usually reserve for meetings. That could mean networking with business people, companies, or corporates. I spend my evenings researching. If my article is due the next day or in a few days, I'll do research for that.

## The risk of burnout

**Geertjan Wielenga**: What I've noticed with people in the advocacy field is that they're very passionate. The flip side of that is burnout and exhaustion. Have you encountered that and do you have any insights about it?

**Bilal Kathrada**: Yes, I've experienced that. About eight months ago, I got sick very frequently and my doctor was concerned. It wasn't one related illness but many different ones. He warned me and said that it was all related to stress.

> *"I remove myself from tech and when I come back to it, I have better ideas."*
>
> —*Bilal Kathrada*

Since then, I've disciplined myself to do exercise and eat well. I also take time out. Every three months, we make it a point as a family to disappear for three or four days into the wilderness. That could be going camping or into the mountains. I remove myself from tech and when I come back to it, I have better ideas.

The engine needs time to cool off. My family plays an important role in avoiding burnout. Our wives know us better than we know ourselves! My wife acts as an early warning system that I'm getting stressed.

**Geertjan Wielenga**: How do you keep up to date with tech?

**Bilal Kathrada**: I read a lot. I subscribe to Feedly, read websites and blogs, and follow people on Twitter to find out what's going on in particular areas. I also network with companies. I was talking to a company the other day that said that Amazon Web Services (AWS) is a big thing. That surprised me because I thought that Microsoft Azure would be bigger. The feedback I received was that AWS seems to be doing better than Azure in South Africa. Those are the insights that you can get from speaking to people in the industry.

**Geertjan Wielenga**: As a young person, did you envisage this path for yourself?

**Bilal Kathrada**: No, but what I'm doing now addresses the problem that I faced as a young person: gaining real and practical coding skills. I started coding when I was a child in the '80s. Coding wasn't even a popular thing. I started with BASIC on my Commodore computer.

When I needed to choose a career, everybody was passionate about their own direction in tech. It was confusing. I was worried about making a move in one direction and then finding out that those skills were no longer in demand several years later. It was a scary decision.

Fortunately, I networked with people who recommended Java to me, but within Java itself, there are so many fields. In those days, I was writing Java applets or Java full-stack applications. I needed mentors and I needed to know where to go to learn about tech. I now offer mentorship for free to anybody who needs it and I light a clear path to learning.

As much as I'm passionate about Java and the Java ecosystem, I'm not a radical; I'm not religious about it. People often get into extended debates, but we need to keep an open mind. I help to get people into the development space in a way that is fun and accessible.

**Geertjan Wielenga**: Thank you, Bilal Kathrada.

## 25

> *In developer relations, we fight to prove the return on investment (ROI) every day.*

# Baruch Sadogursky

# Introducing Baruch Sadogursky

Baruch Sadogursky is a developer advocate and the head of developer relations at JFrog. His passion is speaking about tech and he is a regular speaker at the industry's most prestigious events including DockerCon, GopherCon, Devoxx, DevOps Days, OSCON, Qcon, and JavaOne. A JavaOne Rockstar, the co-author of *Liquid Software*, and a Cloud Native Computing Foundation (CNCF) Ambassador, Baruch is a vocal champion for the interests of the developer community. Find Baruch on Twitter: `@jbaruch`.

---

**Geertjan Wielenga**: You're very knowledgeable about what's been going on in the developer relations world over the past few years in terms of conferences and podcasts. Could you just sketch out the landscape as you see it?

**Baruch Sadogursky**: Developer relations is on fire. Every day, there are new books, podcasts, and conferences. People are doing more and more in this area. In terms of the landscape, there are a couple of very good conferences. There is the whole franchise of DevRelCon, which runs in three different locations: London, San Francisco, and Tokyo. It was in China for a couple of years too, but I'm not sure whether that's continuing.

Those are, for me, extremely important conferences if you're in this space because all the practitioners get together and talk about the stuff that matters. There are so many topics covered if you count all of the three different conferences. The good news is that all of the talks are online, so you can go and watch all this content for free.

**Geertjan Wielenga**: What kind of topics are addressed at these conferences?

## Developer relations conferences

**Baruch Sadogursky**: You'll find general topics like empathy and ethical questions, then you'll also find very practical topics, such as how to create a successful presentation or what the best style for technical writing is. There are talks about the stuff that we all care about, which includes key performance indicators (KPIs), measurements, justification, budgeting, and so on.

**Geertjan Wielenga**: Are you saying that there is this whole community supporting people who are doing developer relations?

**Baruch Sadogursky**: Yes. There is another conference, run by Evans Data, called Developer Relations Conference. I've never been, so I can't really testify, but from the content and the organization, it looks like more of an old-school evangelism thing. Also, it costs $1,000, which makes it not really accessible for most of the community.

**Geertjan Wielenga**: How did these developer relations conferences come about in the first place? They seem to have boomed in the last five years.

**Baruch Sadogursky**: Developer relations, as a discipline, has become more established. In the past, there was some planning and theory behind it, but it was more niche.

The Evans Data conference has been running for 15 years, so it's not new. However, in the last five years or so developer relations has become more mainstream for our industry. All kinds of companies are looking for approval from developers or looking to hire a group of developers. Realizing that developer relations is important, companies have started to invest in it and plan for it. An entire industry has subsequently been built up around developer relations. All these podcasts and books have been created due to the realization that almost every software company now needs developer relations.

On my way to the office today, I was listening to a webinar from a bunch of developer relations specialists at companies that do developer relations purely for HR. There was a company that sells home improvement equipment and it has a developer relations department that actually helps it to build a better brand and to recruit better developers. Everybody now wants to do developer relations.

**Geertjan Wielenga**: How did you end up in this domain yourself?

**Baruch Sadogursky**: I've worked with the two cofounders of JFrog, Yoav Landman and Fred Simon, since 2004. Before JFrog, we worked together doing Java consultancy at a company named AlphaCSP. We did a lot of Java 2 Platform, Enterprise Edition (J2EE) back then and also Spring. We drifted toward the automation of continuous integration and started to use Maven and stuff around it. At some point, we realized that Maven had great potential, but it was missing this key element of having an in-house repository.

Yoav and Fred wrote an open-source tool named Artifactory for our customers at AlphaCSP. They realized very early on that there was huge potential. Very large and important companies had started to use the tool from day one. Yoav and Fred eventually left AlphaCSP to start JFrog.

I stayed with AlphaCSP and also worked at a couple of other places. Eventually, Yoav and Fred called me and said, "Okay, it's time to come home. And by the way, we've invented a new job for you that we're going to call 'The Secretary of State' or 'The Minister of External Affairs.' You need to represent JFrog to the community and help us to spread the word. You need to get feedback from those people." That's how I got into this line of work.

That was seven years ago and, back then, we didn't really know how to do developer relations. We made many mistakes. We did evangelism instead of doing developer advocacy, for example, which meant one-sided communication and just trying to increase our audience size, instead of creating a dialogue and ongoing engagement. There wasn't much information out there about developer advocacy at the time or, at least, I wasn't good enough to find it.

**Geertjan Wielenga**: What do you like most about this role that you're in at JFrog?

**Baruch Sadogursky**: For me, it's the perfect job because it allows me to both be technical and network with other developers. I get to help and see the impact of that. When I was a developer, it was satisfying when I was able to create new things, but the feedback loop was very long, if it existed at all.

As a developer, you write something and maybe you see your code running in production, but that's it.

> *"In developer relations, you actually have a full feedback cycle."*
>
> —*Baruch Sadogursky*

The question is, how does your work improve the lives of other people? In developer relations, you actually have a full feedback cycle, which is extremely important for me. If JFrog manages to help developers, we hear it from them. If we don't do something right, we get feedback on what we can do better. We can take that feedback, implement changes, and have another try at helping the developers. Developer relations is the pipeline through which feedback travels. That's very satisfying because we can see how our organization is making an impact and how developer relations is making an impact.

In this role, we represent something that other people create. If we do developer relations to increase the adoption of a product by developers, to be able to hire better developers or to get better feedback, those outcomes allow us to support other functions in our organization.

**Geertjan Wielenga**: What kind of personality fits this role best?

**Personal qualities needed**

**Baruch Sadogursky**: I'm constantly recruiting because the right kind of people for these roles are hard to find. Most of the functions in developer relations are technical.

There are obviously some roles that are not technical, such as a community engagement manager or a community builder, but developer advocates, engineers, and technical writers all have to be technical.

The other side of this role is that you need to be an outspoken and community-loving person. I used to say that people in developer relations need to be extroverts until I was corrected; I was told that many people who do these roles are not actually 100% extroverted. They don't necessarily get energy from other people, but they still know how to engage. I'm more cautious now when I talk about requirements in developer relations, although I think that it is easier for extroverts, who naturally get their energy from engaging with other people.

**Geertjan Wielenga**: Why is the combination of technical knowledge and people skills so difficult to find?

**Baruch Sadogursky**: The majority of technical people are not necessarily very engaged with their tech community, either because they don't like doing that or because they're not very good at it. I don't want to get into generalizations and make statements about mutual exclusivity, but that's been my experience when trying to recruit.

Both when hiring internally and externally, I've found that whenever we have good technical people, they are either not interested in or not capable of being community beasts at the same time. I don't know why; I'm definitely not a psychologist. My observation is simply that it's very rare to find people who are both very technical and outspoken in their community.

**Geertjan Wielenga**: Do you have a typical day in your role?

**Baruch Sadogursky**: Developer relations is very diverse. We try to do tons of stuff around community engagement, including staying in touch with different communities and finding out what those communities are, where they are, and what is of interest to them. That's one end of the spectrum: pure social engagement. The other end of the spectrum is writing code, contributing to projects, doing code samples, and so on.

Other tasks include writing presentations, giving those presentations, taking part in webinars and conferences, and writing blog posts. On top of that, you have to make sure that all of this work is trackable and measured. That involves writing event reports and managing the influencer or networking database.

In an ideal world, all these tasks would be done by a team of diverse people, but in the real world (this ties back to our struggle with recruitment and also the fact that we're a pure cost center for the organization), we don't always have the luxury of five people at our disposal who each have a narrow domain to focus on. Everybody does everything, so a typical day is quite chaotic.

**Geertjan Wielenga**: Is developer relations really a cost center, then?

**Baruch Sadogursky**: Oh, absolutely. We cost JFrog money and we need to justify this money in terms of providing a ROI. This ROI is not 100% clear or trackable, of course.

Imagine that you're speaking at a conference and people hear about your project. Some of them will like it and try it. Although it's clear that you're making an impact, how much impact?

Was it worth sending you to this conference? Does it even work having you on the payroll? It's not clear. In developer relations, we fight to prove the ROI every day, so, yes, we are a cost center for the organization. We hope that we're a justified cost center, but we do cost money.

**Geertjan Wielenga**: As a consequence of all these diverse activities, I can imagine that each person must take on a lot of work. Can the result be that you work far harder than you really should?

**Baruch Sadogursky**: I think that's true for most of us in developer relations. The people I know in these roles are some of the most hardworking people in their organizations. We care about so many things from so many different domains that it naturally creates work. If you spend an entire day writing a marvelous piece of code because it's important and you enjoy it, that then leaves you working into the evening to get everything else done.

**Geertjan Wielenga**: I recently heard an interesting idea: "If you're a very hardworking person and you work 30% less, nobody will notice the difference, and you will still be productive." What do you think about that?

**Baruch Sadogursky**: Yes and no. I understand where that's coming from, but if you just start doing 30% less, I bet people will notice. Things that have to be done won't be done. It's better to ask, "Can I optimize and be 30% more efficient?"

It isn't effective for developers to work very long hours. If you do one thing all day, you're in this zone for $X$ number of hours.

Piling on more hours will actually diminish productivity to zero very quickly. However, in developer relations, we don't have the same excuse because we do so many different things.

If you've been writing code for five hours and you feel that your code is only getting worse, do something else; get in touch with the organizers of your next meetup. It requires almost zero mental effort on your part to do that, but it's still something that needs to be done. When you're done with that, write a blog post or an event trip report for your last trip. Choose a completely different activity that you definitely can do effectively even when you're tired from writing code. When everything else fails, fill out that expense report you've been postponing for weeks.

It's very important to work efficiently, but I don't think we can cut our work down and expect that no one will notice. Maybe I'm just lying to myself about how important I am, but I would like to believe that the stuff that I do is important enough that I can't just throw it into the garbage.

## Caring too much

**Geertjan Wielenga**: Sometimes people care too much about the tech that they represent, which means that they work too hard. Do you not agree that, in some cases, we should take a step back?

**Baruch Sadogursky**: I completely agree that we carry too much on our shoulders, but I think that's part of the job. We're in developer relations *because* we care too much. I don't see how that's a bad thing. I don't want to lose my investment in this work because I need that passion to do my job.

**Geertjan Wielenga**: If the company that you represent starts going in a different direction, how should you respond to that?

**Baruch Sadogursky**: You need to be invested in the vision of your organization. If you're aligned with this vision and if you understand why the pivot was made, then that pivot is natural for you as well.

We had this come up at JFrog when we started being a tool for Java developers. We then became a tool for .NET developers and JavaScript developers. There came a point when we realized that the people who really care about our tools, and the people who we should care about, are actually the tools teams or the DevOps enablers in organizations and not necessarily the research and development teams themselves.

That was a huge pivot for JFrog. We started speaking about data centers, tooling, and DevOps for entire organizations. We basically switched our entire community in terms of our targeting. You now see us less at developer conferences, especially Java conferences. The people who we care about are now different and that wasn't an easy change to make. I felt perfectly comfortable with the change because I understood that it was the right thing to do. Our tool is much more helpful to some people today than it was 10 years ago. We need to talk to those people and help them instead.

> *"We need to understand what our organization's needs are and put them above our personal relationships and tech communities."*
>
> *—Baruch Sadogursky*

I often see developer relations people who care about their tech communities too much. They stick to those communities, even if they move to companies that should target different communities. I'll give you a hypothetical example: say someone was working for a company that does tools for Java development and now they're working for a new company that does tools for JavaScript development. At the next Java conference, you see that they're there with their booth again. It's not because this is what their organization wants: they just feel comfortable in their old community and building relationships in a new community is hard. That's a mistake. We need to understand what our organization's needs are and put them above our personal relationships and tech communities.

**Geertjan Wielenga**: Another difficult situation is when the company that you represent makes a decision that the community doesn't agree with and you're on stage on a Monday morning receiving questions about this decision. How do you handle that?

**Baruch Sadogursky**: That's a very tough spot to be in. That goes back to the question of how much we care about what we do. There may come a point where you have to say, "I can't defend or justify this decision." That's when you should leave the company.

However, there have been times when although I didn't 100% agree with a decision, I still rallied behind it because I understood why it was made. I can live with that. It's like every other leadership situation: you might disagree during the process of making a decision, but once that decision is made, you're either behind it or you watch that the door doesn't hit you on your way out.

This is our world in developer relations. If you're a developer and you disagree with your boss' decision, you will be grumpy for the rest of the day and that's pretty much it. If you're in developer relations and you represent the company, you might find yourself in the position where you need to advocate for and defend a decision that you don't 100% agree with. Your integrity should step in and you should decide where to draw the line.

**Geertjan Wielenga**: Do you need to know everything about a subject to get up and talk about it on stage?

**Baruch Sadogursky**: As I mentioned, a developer relations person can be non-technical, but for developer advocates, the more technical they are the better. How technical you need to be depends on the nature of your product and your company.

You need to be extremely technical if you're advocating one product and you need to dive deep into how this tool works and what the use cases are. On the other hand, JFrog's tools integrate with over 25 different tools and programming languages. There is no way that I can be proficient in all of them. I do my best to keep track of the principles of how they work, but that's all I can do. We have communities that we see as being more valuable or worth the investment of our time, and they are where I dive much deeper, but still, it's impossible to know everything about everything. T-shape is the best I can hope for—broad knowledge with deep specialization.

**Geertjan Wielenga**: What happens if you're giving a talk on the stage and you get a question at the end that you don't know the answer to?

**Baruch Sadogursky**: The right approach is to be very honest about it and just say, "I'll have to come back to you on that because I'm not sure." Alternatively, you could pretend that you know more than you do. Sometimes that works, but I'd say that it's not worth the risk of being caught.

**Geertjan Wielenga**: Might another option be to open up the question to the audience?

**Baruch Sadogursky**: That's a little bit dangerous because you don't really know how to validate the answer. Someone might say something that sounds like the right answer but is wrong. You would have to endorse it or not endorse it, without knowing the answer yourself.

**Geertjan Wielenga**: What are some current developments that you find very interesting in developer relations and also in tech?

## Baruch's hot topics in tech

**Baruch Sadogursky**: As we discussed, more people are starting to understand what developer relations is and how to do it right. I track those developments as part of my professional growth as a developer relations specialist. I try to go to all the DevRelCons, read the books that are available, and participate in podcasts and conversations.

> "We have the ability to evolve software all across the board at a velocity that we've never seen before."
>
> —*Baruch Sadogursky*

One of the most exciting areas in tech is accelerating the continuous delivery of software and migrating from continuous delivery to continuous updates. We have the ability to evolve software all across the board at a velocity that we've never seen before. That's exciting because this proliferation of software at a previously unseen speed is something that is extremely important for the world today. When you try to think for a second of something that exists in the modern world that isn't powered by software, you can't. Our ability to ship software has become critical.

**Geertjan Wielenga**: Do you see software writing itself, delivering itself, and updating itself in the future?

**Baruch Sadogursky**: The writing itself element is the most problematic of them all because the domain is not easily automatable. Business problems are, at least at the moment, too complex for algorithms to solve by themselves.

Building and delivering are easily automatable, but they will be even more automatable in the future. I don't think that needing to write software is going to go away. I definitely think that the other aspects can be minimized to a level that we see in elite teams, where a team of five people can take care of building and delivering software for a huge development organization.

**Geertjan Wielenga**: What advice would you give to anyone interested in entering this field?

**Baruch Sadogursky**: There is a lot of knowledge out there today. Blogs and newsletters are great places to start. There are podcasts like *DevRel Radio* too. The first step is to decide what your function in developer relations could be. This doesn't mean that you will end up doing only that, but it will give you a clear starting point.

**Geertjan Wielenga**: Thank you, Baruch Sadogursky.

## 26

> *I'm filling the role of
> a community manager
> for community managers.*

# Mary
# Thengvall

# Introducing Mary Thengvall

Mary Thengvall is a consultant for companies looking to build a developer relations strategy, and the author of the first book about developer relations: *The Business Value of Developer Relations*. A connector of people both personally and professionally, Mary has been engaged in building and fostering developer communities for more than 10 years. Her membership at Prompt, a nonprofit that encourages people to speak openly about mental illness in tech, attests to the personal approach that Mary takes to developer wellbeing. Find Mary on Twitter: @mary_grace.

---

**Geertjan Wielenga**: Could you explain a little about where you fit into this world of developer advocacy?

## Mary's background

**Mary Thengvall**: I fell into developer relations and I say that a little facetiously. I have a journalism background, but I grew up around tech. My dad used to bring computers home for us to try out, but he wasn't a developer and wasn't involved heavily in code.

I taught myself how to create a website when I was in middle school and the Yahoo! plug and play websites were around, but that was about it. I graduated from college with a journalism degree, but at that time, here in the U.S., many of the newspapers were letting their editorial staff go. I was trying to figure out what was next for me and I ended up taking a public relations job at O'Reilly Media.

I was writing about technical topics and having been a journalist, I like to know what I'm writing about. I did a lot of research into Drupal, Python, and Java as I was writing press releases for the books. I was soon asking, "How do we know that these are the topics that people want us to be writing about? How do we know that these are the most relevant things to be talking about these days?" I asked those questions often enough that the company accepted that they were fair questions. I was given a budget and I had a year to go and investigate them.

I became involved with community management by working with a technical audience, without having any idea what community management actually is. I didn't even realize that there's an industry around it, although I had been the publicist for Jono Bacon's book, *The Art of Community*.

I just listened to people in the industry for six months, traveling to different cities and talking to influencers, authors, and conference speakers. I wanted to know what topics they were interested in, what websites they were browsing, and what blogs they were following. We ended up building up a team of community managers at O'Reilly Media to manage different areas of focus. I focused on DevOps and web performance.

Eventually, I moved over to a company called Chef, an open source infrastructure, and worked for the community team there. When I left Chef, I worked at another company called SparkPost, helping to build up the community team and figure out what developer relations meant to the company.

> *"Companies didn't understand the value of developer relations and building relationships with a technical community."*
>
> —*Mary Thengvall*

Along the way, I noticed the patterns that many of us now see: an increase in burnout being experienced by community managers and people getting frustrated by being pigeonholed into areas that they didn't really fit into. Companies didn't understand the value of developer relations and building relationships with a technical community. I kept having these conversations as I was building my own teams.

Finally, I had a couple of companies pull me aside and ask me to come on board and do consulting. I've always loved solving puzzles and working on strategy, and that's what I'm doing these days for clients, along with providing resources for the community.

**Geertjan Wielenga**: Do you mean providing resources for companies that are doing developer relations?

**Mary Thengvall**: Yes. Up until a few years ago, there were a few books on online community and a handful of articles here and there, but nothing solid. My main goal with my company is to provide resources for developer relations professionals, which could be developer advocates, community managers, or people who are responsible for documentation.

**Geertjan Wielenga**: In a way, then, you are offering developer relations as a service?

**Mary Thengvall**: To a certain extent, yes. I'm filling the role of a community manager for community managers.

**Geertjan Wielenga**: Would a company outsource its developer relations work to you?

**Mary Thengvall**: That has happened. I've come in and helped to build an editorial calendar, provided some content, and explained how to go about the events side of things. Sometimes I'll come in and do that work for a short time to see the company through the gap until someone is hired.

More of what I'm doing these days is strategy, which means coming into a company that is either looking to build a brand-new developer relations team or has a team, but needs some help figuring out if it's heading in the right direction. I do an assessment of what the company needs to reach its goals.

**Geertjan Wielenga**: Do you bring in developer relations people to implement strategies?

**Mary Thengvall**: Sometimes I'll help with recruiting. With the network that I've built, I'm able to make connections with the companies and often find people who are a good fit for the role.

**Geertjan Wielenga**: Something that may put many people off developer advocacy is that, on the one hand, they don't want to program all day, but on the other hand, they don't want to be a spin doctor either, which is what you are, more or less, as a marketing person. Can you relate to that?

**Mary Thengvall**: Yes, developers who tend to succeed in this role are very focused on people. Whether or not they have a technical background, I've seen that there's a common thread of caring deeply about people. They want to solve problems and they want to make sure that people are taken care of.

Developer advocacy is about figuring out and understanding what people's needs are first and then solving the problem in the best way possible. The developers who have succeeded in these developer relations roles might still be passionate about coding, but they balance that with the people side.

Spinning information isn't part of developer relations at all, though. It's about being authentic with your community, even if that means telling them that your product isn't the right one for their needs. It's about building relationships and solving problems for a technical audience so that when, one day, they do have a need for your product, they know exactly where to go because they trust you and know that you have their best interests at heart.

**Geertjan Wielenga**: Do you have to know everything about a topic, or rather a tech, to be a developer advocate?

**Mary Thengvall**: No, and I actually think it's almost better if you don't know everything. Being able to dig into a topic with a community member and figuring it out together is very powerful. It's a good humility statement, but also, it deepens the trust between you and the community.

The worst possible thing that we can do as developer relations professionals is try to make it sound like we do know everything.

That puts us on a pedestal above our community members; it makes it seem like we're better than them. Acting like you know everything is also problematic because when there comes a time that you truly don't know something, and you're trying to make up an answer, you might say the wrong thing, which might lead the person down the wrong path. Giving bad advice makes it very obvious that you either led someone astray due to your ignorance or that you intentionally lied because you wanted to save face.

## Advice for young people

**Geertjan Wielenga**: How can you become a developer advocate as a young person? You came from a different background and fell into developer relations, which can happen, but there are also real job advertisements for developer relations roles. How do you get the skills you need to successfully apply?

**Mary Thengvall**: For college students who are interested in getting into this field, I think this generation has a huge advantage: there are developer relations internships popping up, at least all over the U.S. I noticed a handful of internships last year and there are even more this year, so students have an opportunity to get into a team early on.

As far as classes and things to get involved in, I always tell people to take some writing courses, even if they're just basic. Get involved in the technical writing courses or get a technical writing minor. That relates far more to the documentation side of things, but it'll teach you to write in a technical manner and be aware of all of the common grammar mistakes.

Take public speaking classes too and work on some of those skills while you're in college. It's really easy to take a writing class and a speaking class in addition to completing a computer science degree.

If you really don't like speaking or writing, then maybe developer relations isn't the best thing for you. You might discover that you really like the writing side and feel terrified of public speaking. You could research how to either get better at speaking or find a larger developer relations team where you don't have to be doing everything. You could stay on the documentation and tutorials side, rather than being the person who's on stage all the time.

> *"You'll learn the people skills to be able to navigate all the politics that come along with developer relations."*
>
> —*Mary Thengvall*

The other thing that I tell people to do is try and get involved with some open source projects. If someone needs help with documentation, see if there are easy issues that you can fix. See if the maintainers need guidance on how to make it easier to contribute to their project. Getting an idea about how open source projects work, even if you end up working at a company that's all proprietary software, will give you a huge leg up in getting to know the community and learning to work with other people. You'll learn the people skills to be able to navigate all the politics that come along with developer relations.

This last point is a little more difficult if you're a full-time student, but you can also see what conferences are happening in your area.

I think far too often people think about a conference and assume it will be a $2,000 ticket and a lot of travel to get there. There are actually so many community-run and volunteer-run conferences that are popping up all over the world these days. You might have to miss a day of classes, but the ability to network and get to know people who are in the community is priceless.

**Geertjan Wielenga**: Have you been involved with developer relations conferences?

**Mary Thengvall**: I haven't organized any developer relations conferences, but I've spoken at a couple and have attended some as well. The turnout is pretty good and they're happening all over the world. I spoke at a developer relations summit in Seattle a couple of years ago. I also spoke at DevRelCon London last November.

A few hundred people from the industry attend these conferences, but being able to be in a room with even just a couple of dozen people who do what you do, and understand the challenges that you face, is incredibly encouraging and validating, especially for those of us who don't have a technical background. You sometimes feel that you've been making things up as you go along for years!

I think that there's a generational gap now with regards to imposter syndrome. There are so many of us who have been doing developer relations for a decade or two, and a lot of it has felt like guesswork, but now we're being looked at as people who know what we're talking about!

I've spent most of my career flipping switches and seeing if something works; there's been so much trial and error. My generation is now getting to a point where we can share our experiences and pass much of that learning down, which is fantastic, but then you've got junior-level developer relations people joining who know things that took me six years to figure out.

Anyone joining now is lucky enough to have internships they can join straight out of college or straight out of code school. Now they have the books to read, the mailing lists to join, the Slack teams to join, and all of the places to go to for resources. I would have given anything to have those types of resources when I started out in 2006.

**Geertjan Wielenga**: You're working on a podcast and a book, so let's talk about each of those. What's the podcast about?

**Mary's podcast**

**Mary Thengvall**: The podcast is called *Community Pulse*. I started it almost three and a half years ago with Jason Hand. He was at VictorOps at the time (he's at Microsoft now) and we didn't think there were enough resources out there. We were struggling to find resources ourselves, so the podcast frankly ended up being a nice way for us to share our experiences and learn from other people. PJ Hagerty joined us about eight episodes in, so the three of us run it now and we've released over 30 episodes.

**Geertjan Wielenga**: What sort of topics do you deal with?

**Mary Thengvall**: Everything from social media and how to navigate it to writing content and submitting calls for proposals (CFPs). We're recording an episode next week that's about event organization and creating community-run events. We talk about anything that developer relations people or community managers might run into.

**Geertjan Wielenga**: Your book is on the business value of developer relations. Could you explain more about that?

**Mary Thengvall**: The biggest takeaway is that one of the most valuable things developer relations brings to the table is connections, both within the community and between the community and the company. This could be introducing community members to each other, furthering open source projects, working on content together, or introducing people to sales teams. I started calling them "developer relations qualified leads," which is similar to marketing qualified leads.

Developer relations people are responsible for making sure that introductions are made. We aren't responsible for whether or not those introductions are successful. Far too often, people in this industry are given goals to get a certain number of leads from conferences or to increase signups. Our goals are often based on work output (such as speak at three conferences in Q2) or things that we don't have control over (such as whether a community member that we referred got hired), so it's not fair to set those goals.

> *"I want to be making the best connections possible, but I'm not responsible for the end results."*
>
> —*Mary Thengvall*

In my role, it's my responsibility to make connections, so of course I want to be making the best connections possible, but I'm not responsible for the end results. Making sure the hiring manager is happy with the candidate or making sure that the potential hire handles all of the interviews correctly and actually gets hired is out of my control.

**Geertjan Wielenga**: What are some appropriate goals for a developer relations team, then?

**Mary Thengvall**: I think it depends on the overarching goal of the company. If the overall company goal is that it needs more signups or needs to increase general revenue, then maybe there is a brand awareness problem.

It can help to spread the word about the cool things that the company is doing on a technical basis. Developer relations people can speak at conferences about interesting problems that the company has solved, or spread the word through its own networks when there are new features released or interesting blog posts that go out.

If the developer relations team can show that what it's accomplishing directly impacts the company goals, then there's no question about whether or not that work is valuable.

I think, all too often, work output ends up being the goal rather than the *impact* of the work output, and that's a huge problem. If you're judging us on our work output, then the chief financial officer (CFO) is going to notice how much money we spent traveling to all those conferences or sponsoring those events. The chief technical officer (CTO) is going to notice that we weren't involved in anything technical regarding sample apps. The marketing team might get pissed off because that's not the content they were looking for or we weren't helping with generating leads, but we were helping with technical content, which increases general awareness.

**Geertjan Wielenga**: Many people are attracted to developer advocacy because they want the excitement of travel or being on a stage. Those activities are actually a subset of reaching some larger goal and that goal is not about the work output, as you said. Would you agree that, first and foremost, your values should align with the values of the company when you look for a position?

**Mary Thengvall**: Absolutely, and that's a big thing that people don't take into account. If they aren't passionate about the product, they're going to have a really hard time continuing to write content, continuing to serve that community, and continuing to research those topics.

It's more than just finding a company that's a good fit or finding a company that will work with you to get you to conferences around the world: it's about finding products that you're passionate about, finding topics that you're interested in, and being willing to invest in them.

So much of developer relations is a mixture of building your own brand as well as the company's brand. That's a symbiotic relationship. I'm not talking about the number of followers on Twitter but the number of people you have in your network, the number of people who you know you can go to if you need help making a particular community connection, or the number of people who would be willing to help promote a new open source tool. If you continue to grow that group, then the company benefits as well in terms of its reputation.

## Answering difficult questions

**Geertjan Wielenga**: If you're representing a company, that company might have made a decision on a Friday that impacts many people and there could be bad press about it. If you're standing on the stage of some big international conference on the following Monday, you're going to be asked why your company did that thing. How should you handle that?

**Mary Thengvall**: There's a phrase that I go back to on an almost daily basis: "To the community I represent the company and to the company I represent the community. I have to have both of their best interests in mind at all times." There's a very fine line there!

There are times when I need to stand up for the community within the company and my coworkers really aren't going to be happy with me because I'm pushing for this particular change that has to happen. But I'll continue to advocate for that change because I understand that if it doesn't happen, we're going to have people asking all sorts of difficult questions during my talks.

Likewise, the company needs to make money because if the company can't continue, then the community is nonexistent as well. It's about navigating those conversations and understanding where both parties are coming from.

Sometimes, you have to say that you don't understand why a decision was made, but when you fly home, you're going to be on the phone to figure out what happened and why it happened that way. The company can then build up processes internally to make sure that similar situations don't happen again.

**Geertjan Wielenga**: There's often a discussion about terminology in this industry. The term that you've used is "developer relations professional." Does it matter what title a person has?

**Mary Thengvall**: I think it does. I use "developer relations professional" to refer to anyone who could be on the developer relations team. That could be a developer advocate, technical evangelist, community manager, technical writer, developer relations operations manager, or someone else.

The titles within a team are incredibly important as well. The strategic lead of the team is usually called a "manager." Your technical contributor is a developer advocate and that's the only person on the team who, I would argue, should have been a developer in a past life or have a computer science degree of some sort. They tend to be the one who is doing the technical demos, building out the sample applications, and really digging deep into the code with community members.

> *"You need to be able to have deeper conversations, rather than just giving an elevator pitch."*
>
> —*Mary Thengvall*

The next person is the technical community builder or community manager. I like to use "community builder" instead of "manager" because I'm not so much managing the community as I am working to build it, strengthen it, and give it a good foundation. I put "technical" in front of that mostly because even if you don't have a technical background, I think you need to be tech savvy; you need to be able to have deeper conversations, rather than just giving an elevator pitch. I believe strongly that that person needs to be able to hold good conversations. Once they hit a point where they can't answer the super technical questions, they also should know who to point the person to next.

Developer experience manager I think is an important role as well because you're getting feedback as a team from people who are using your product, working to improve the website, and working to improve the documentation. The training and documentation team usually lives under that developer experience person.

With technical evangelists, I choose to call them "technical ambassadors" and I do that specifically because many companies and people take issue with calling someone an "evangelist."

There are so many people who have a visceral reaction to that word that I think "ambassador" is better. I also like the word "ambassador" because it implies that you're traveling and networking with the intent of taking feedback back to the company, but you're also interacting with your community of people.

The biggest difference I see between developer advocates and technical ambassadors is that the advocates are sharing interesting information about the technical side of the product. The technical ambassadors are showing why this product is important at this time within this industry lens, so they're framing the product against what the current issues are for the broader community. The role also has a sales arm to it of working with some of the vice presidents (VPs) and C-suites to show the importance of the product and why it's beneficial to the larger technical community.

**Geertjan Wielenga**: Another aspect of your engagement in this industry is that you're a member of Prompt, a non-profit organization that encourages people to talk openly about mental illness in tech. This connects to burnout, due to the number of different tasks that developer advocates have at any one time. Do you think that burnout can be a risk?

## Avoiding burnout

**Mary Thengvall**: Yes, I think burnout has a tendency to hit people in developer relations that much harder. I'm a people person and that sometimes means that I never get a chance to switch off.

I'm at conferences frequently and when I'm not at conferences, I'm interacting with people on Twitter, or on Slack, or helping people out. I have such a drive to help people and to provide whatever I can for them that I lose that balance of taking care of myself.

I really do need to make sure that I have that downtime. I think burnout can hit all of us in these roles because we don't want to turn off that side of ourselves. Interacting with people is what gives us energy and meaning. The problem is that we're not paying attention to how much energy we give to our jobs versus the energy that we need to keep going with our day.

Part of what's fascinating to me is that there's a commonly held notion that people in community management or developer relations roles don't last more than 18 months. Some people decide they will give these jobs a try because they sound awesome. Then, for whatever reason, the role either ends up not being exactly what they expected or it doesn't work out.

I've seen people go back to previous careers after 18 months, returning to engineering, product, or marketing. I've seen people drop out of tech entirely too. For some people, it's not a matter of getting away from developer relations: it's just a matter of switching jobs. Often, you get a year and a half or two years into a job and you're exhausted with the politics at work. You're exhausted with constantly having to advocate for what you want to do and what is best for the community. Because it's always a fight, that's draining. Helping the community is such a high that that keeps you going.

The problem is that you can only oscillate between those highs and lows so many times.

**Geertjan Wielenga**: What can happen as a developer advocate is that you become completely disconnected from the company that you're working for; in fact, you disagree with it and you have this whole community of people you're supporting more or less independently. Your company is not that interested in what you're doing, but because you're enthusiastic, you continue doing it. Would you agree that you're not really helping anyone in that case because, in a way, you're acting as a facade for the company?

**Mary Thengvall**: Yes, and then you've got that burden of worrying that the community will eventually find out that you're the facade for the company. What happens when the company does something that you can't explain away?

There's the guilt of feeling that you're not really doing your job because you're not actually representing the company, but you're still trying to help the community in the ways you can. So many of us end up feeling trapped.

> *"You may feel that you desperately want to leave the company, but then you would be leaving your community high and dry."*
>
> —Mary Thengvall

*Mary Thengvall*

The hardest thing is that because we are people pleasers, we often find ourselves stuck between a rock and a hard place between the community and the company. You may feel that you desperately want to leave the company, but then you would be leaving your community high and dry. You have personal relationships built up in that community. Can you leave a company that you really despise and at the same time leave a community that you love deeply? There's no easy answer. Even when people switch jobs, they often try and switch into another company that will keep them connected to the same community.

In the same way as when you meet someone new in dating, when you change jobs there's all of this great energy surrounding it and it fuels you for a while. You see all these great things happening with the community in your new role and that takes some of the burnout away. But in the end, you still find yourself having to advocate for the community in ways that you wouldn't need to if the company actually understood what you were doing. The burnout then hits even harder than it did before. Every company has its dysfunctions; it's just a matter of when you're going to figure out what they are.

I think one of the biggest problems is that so few of us are trained in any sort of business negotiation. How do we even have a business conversation with VPs and C-suites? How can we advocate for our plans? How do we write a business plan?

You've got this collection of really talented people who are great in their field, but they don't have the skills, yet, to build a solid business plan, build a strategy, and then defend that strategy up at the board level. People in developer relations don't always know how to communicate value to people in different departments.

They become really frustrated and discouraged, often leaving the industry simply because they don't have the tools that they need to do the job effectively. As an industry, we're investing in how to do developer relations better, but we haven't yet solved how to have those difficult conversations.

**Geertjan Wielenga**: What would you say has happened over the last few years that has resulted in a minor boom in developer advocacy?

**Mary Thengvall**: I think part of it is the increase in companies whose end users are developers. Some of that is just as a result of Silicon Valley, more tech companies, and more APIs.

I also think a handful of companies have really figured out how to do developer relations and have succeeded in ways that are getting attention. Twilio is the main company that comes to mind. Twilio is huge and enormously successful, and from the beginning the company has said that it is developer-focused. A successful developer relations team has been built up and other companies are noticing that. Developer advocacy has finally started to gain traction.

**Geertjan Wielenga**: Thank you, Mary Thengvall.

## 27

> *If I learn something and think
> I can explain it, I want people
> to know about it.*

# Yakov
# Fain

# Introducing Yakov Fain

Yakov Fain is a Java Champion who works at the IT consultancy Farata Systems. A fiercely independent speaker and the author of a number of technical programming books, he has extensive experience in the tech field, having taught multiple classes and workshops on the web and Java-related tech, presented at international conferences, and published more than 1,000 blog posts. Find Yakov on Twitter: @yfain.

---

**Geertjan Wielenga**: If you're at a party and you're with non-technical people, how do you describe your profession?

**Yakov's job title**

**Yakov Fain**: At one point, somebody described me. They used this word that I wouldn't have come up with myself, but they said, "He's a technologist from New York City." I just share what I know. If you need to hire me for a project, I will call myself a "team lead." That's the closest definition of what I do.

**Geertjan Wielenga**: For people who don't see themselves being programmers their whole lives, would you say that developer advocacy presents another option?

**Yakov Fain**: I actually went through several stages of thinking about different roles in tech. I remember many years ago, I thought of programming as the most important part of the IT process of any project because if I don't write a program, there will be no product.

Eventually, I started to think that if a salesman wasn't ready to sell this idea, I wouldn't even be writing this program. Then there is quality assurance to consider and also managing relationships between people, which is very important. When I started managing people, I realized that I have a lot more responsibilities than before. So, there are many different things around programming that you can do. I don't believe writing code is actually the most important task: the most important task is creating a software product. People are involved in the process and all of them are important.

If you wrote a piece of code, you have questions from that: is it what people expected? Did you even know what they wanted? Maybe not. Would your piece of code work with someone else's piece of code? Maybe not. All these little things usually have some friction associated with them and they need to be ironed out. This is where you end up spending a lot of your time. All these agile methodologies, tickets that you have to close, and meetings that you have to attend eat up time.

Different people find pleasure and comfort by doing different things. Some people would like to do coding all their lives. Some people, at some point, will get bored of doing programming all the time. Programming is a pretty similar activity regardless of what framework you use. You want a convenient screen and a simple user interface. The data should arrive quickly and the system should be stable. What language you use and whether you use curly braces after a statement or not is not that important.

I don't get much positive energy if I just sit and program all day long. After a while, I realized that I wanted some additional activities. Now I have different activities in my work, including writing books and running classes online. This is, in my opinion, much more interesting than just sitting and writing code.

**Geertjan Wielenga**: One significant part of your work is that you speak at conferences. How did that happen?

**Yakov Fain**: In the '90s, I had a second job teaching programming classes. I gave out these little handouts for every class and the students were saying, "We like your handouts. Why don't you write a book?"

I did decide to write a book, but major publishers didn't want to publish it. It was a Java tutorial book. To promote the book, I started writing blogs and speaking at conferences. When you write a book, you have tons of material because you usually research a subject well. Any book can easily give you material for a dozen presentations at any conference. I had my research, so it was not difficult for me to present.

I was working as an independent consultant at that time. Right now, I work for a company, but for a large portion of my professional life, I was working as an independent consultant, and if you are independent, you have to be known. How do you get people to know you? I didn't have a budget for a marketing campaign that would scream, "Yakov is a great guy!" But if you're speaking in front of 100 people, or more, if they like you, maybe someone will invite you to join their project later on.

**Geertjan Wielenga**: Have you seen a correlation between speaking at conferences and getting consultancy requests?

# Getting leads from conferences

**Yakov Fain**: Yes, in some cases, although it may not be immediate: it may happen in a year or even two. Somebody might send me a message saying, "Two years ago you were doing a so-and-so presentation and we spoke for a minute." I may or may not remember that guy, but that presentation and short conversation could turn into a project.

You have to do a lot of talks and not only at conferences. I also organized the Java User Group (JUG) in Princeton, New Jersey. From that JUG, I got some consulting projects.

**Geertjan Wielenga**: Have the topics of your talks changed in the last few years?

**Yakov Fain**: They have changed substantially. For many years, I was doing mainly Java and everything related to Java. It was as if I could only speak one language. I can actually speak English, Russian, and Ukrainian. That has opened up information streams, along with entertainment, movies, articles, news, and audio books; it's great.

> *"It's not that interesting to be a single-language programmer."*
>
> —*Yakov Fain*

The same is true in programming. These days, at least for me, it's not that interesting to be a single-language programmer. I still use Java, mainly on the server side, but for the frontend I've been using different things.

My interests are around the frontend more than the backend now. I've written a couple of books on the development of the frontend of web apps.

I speak at smaller gatherings as well as larger ones. For example, I speak at the Angular Summit twice a year. It's a conference attended by 300 people. I go there and I deliver six, seven, or eight presentations and a workshop during two days. It's hard work, but it's an interesting experience for me.

I just came back from Ukraine. I was participating in the Devoxx Ukraine conference and gave a couple of presentations there. One of them was on modern JavaScript and the other one was about blockchain tech.

**Geertjan Wielenga**: You talk a lot about Angular. What makes it a good topic for a conference speaker?

**Yakov Fain**: Angular has many different facets; there are so many things to talk about. Angular on the frontend is kind of like Spring or Java Platform, Enterprise Edition (Java EE) on the backend. You can talk about the build tools, the programming language TypeScript, state management, inter-component communications, communications with web servers, and more. It's like a goldmine of subjects.

Now I'm interested in learning TypeScript more deeply, so I will prepare a number of talks on TypeScript. I don't sell anything when I talk: I just talk about the technical aspects of a specific language, framework, or tech.

**Geertjan Wielenga**: You aren't promoting anything from your company, then?

**Yakov Fain**: No, although, the fact that I speak, present, and promote myself also works well for my company. If I wasn't running a consultancy, I could work for Google, or for Oracle, being a developer advocate. I know I could do that because I know how to take a complex subject and explain it in simple language; I've done it many times.

I'm not saying that I'm the best programmer, or even a great programmer, but I'm a decent programmer, that's for sure. However, I'm definitely good at explaining things. I can explain Java and Angular to your grandma. You give me the software that your company wants to promote and I will find a way to help people to understand it. I have that skill. One day I may have an official "developer advocate" title.

**Geertjan Wielenga**: Since you don't work for a company, other than the consultancy that you are part of, does that mean that you can talk completely freely about any shortcomings in a piece of tech? Are you honest about bugs?

## Speaking honestly on stage

**Yakov Fain**: Yes, but first of all, I'm not afraid of announcing my opinion on anything. If we're talking about Oracle, and before that Sun Microsystems, I was awarded the title "Java Champion" in 2005. This basically means that you have to promote Java, no matter what.

Despite that, I've never had a problem saying that I don't like something about Java or a particular area in Java. The fact that I was given the title is great, but I don't think twice about speaking up if I don't like something.

Having said that, I've never been an employee of Oracle and I didn't work for Sun Microsystems. If an employer was to ask me to avoid showing negative parts of its software, I would listen. The company would be paying my salary, so I would have to play fair.

In terms of hiding bugs, back in 2009, I cofounded another company that automates the work of insurance agents who sell life insurance to people. When we started the company, we didn't know anything about insurance. One of the partners knew about insurance as a salesman, but he was not a developer; we were the developers.

He said, "In three months, there will be a very important trade show, which all our potential clients will attend. We need to show something on the expo floor." We showed a small demo. Of course, this demo had tons of bugs. It's not technically possible to implement a complex app in three months. We knew how to do the demo, but it was like a minefield. The point was, though, that people started to know who we were and that we had a product.

> *"I don't have any moral problems with the fact that the product wasn't ready."*
>
> —*Yakov Fain*

I don't have any moral problems with the fact that the product wasn't ready. I knew that we could create the product and I knew that we would do it. The cycle is so long between demoing a product and selling it. I knew that we had plenty of time to fix all the bugs and deliver the product. I don't have an issue with not showing bugs because bugs can be fixed. I don't feel like I'm cheating anyone.

**Geertjan Wielenga**: What do you see as being the differences between you and someone who is actually selling a product for a company?

**Yakov Fain**: It's not necessarily about selling for money because there are many developer advocates who speak about open-source tech. Typically, you're offered most of the product for free, but if you want to have extra services, tech support, or an additional piece of software, then it'll cost you.

These companies hire developer advocates, who go around places saying how great the product is. They talk to clients to see what kind of problems they are planning to solve and explain how the product can do that. In that sense, I don't have any product to promote.

I talk about software that is available for everybody. I'm not a member of the Angular team. I have no direct connection with the people who create TypeScript; they didn't hire me to promote their tech at all. I do it all for myself. I can tell people that I have technical expertise, so they should listen to me, watch my presentations, and read my books. That works well for me.

Whether you work for a company or not, one thing that is important is your personality. You have to enjoy speaking in front of people. For me, it's easy and I'm not afraid. Maybe it comes from my teaching all these different software subjects. Unless you enjoy speaking, it won't work for you. People are not stupid. If they don't like the way you present, even if you are technically good, developer advocacy won't work for you.

**Geertjan Wielenga**: Becoming a good or adequate speaker is a process, right? What would you say that process consists of?

# Traits needed to be a good speaker

**Yakov Fain**: Firstly, you have to be an outgoing person in general and secondly, you should be a friendly person. You should not be afraid to speak to one person, or two, or three; that's a minimum requirement.

If you have no problem in that area, then you need to try preparing a talk and delivering it in front of a large group of people. The best place is a local meetup. These meetups are usually looking for speakers. You don't have to be a high-profile person at all. You can pick up an interesting topic from the software industry, spend your time researching it, and then you can say that you know the topic well.

It doesn't matter how many people show up to hear you speak. If you can speak in front of five people, it's progress. Usually, these days, people use video recordings. This wasn't the case 20 years ago, but right now, how many people are physically present at a meetup is not very important because the organizers often post the talks on YouTube and many more people see them.

The same goes for conferences. For example, I was delivering a presentation at Devoxx in the U.S., in California, about two years ago. There were about 50 people in the room.

Then the organizers posted the talk online. That particular talk was "Angular 4 for Java Developers." You can find it easily; it has more than 30,000 views. If somebody needed a person with my skills, they would find me. You need to start speaking regardless of how big or small the audience is. Don't reject opportunities. Don't be rude to people; if somebody is giving you an opportunity to speak in front of five developers, take it.

**Geertjan Wielenga**: Do you have any advice for improving a talk?

**Yakov Fain**: You need to do timing well, meaning that you need to deliver the material within the allocated time slot. Initially, if you're not an experienced speaker, you need to do training around this. Do the talk in front of someone and time it.

Eventually, over the years, I created a formula for myself: two minutes per slide. It may not work for everybody, but if I have a 60 minute talk, I need to have 30 slides. In some cases, I need 10 seconds per slide, but two minutes on average gives me a good estimate for how many slides I should have.

> *"People should get the content that was advertised in the abstract of your talk."*
>
> —*Yakov Fain*

Another point is to avoid getting into a lengthy discussion with one person in the audience. This is a huge mistake and everybody else will suffer because you may not have enough time to deliver the material that you planned and put in the abstract of your presentation. Try to give a short answer to that person. If necessary, say that you will talk about it afterwards. People should get the content that was advertised in the abstract of your talk.

Another mistake is when developer advocates spend five minutes talking about themselves. I don't understand how you can spend more than a minute on that. Enough! You're not there to explain what a great person you are. I feel cheated when I sit in an audience and the speaker is five minutes into the talk and has still not started presenting on the subject of the talk.

You should also always be prepared for all the different disasters that may happen. Internet is a common problem. I know that some speakers like to say, "If the presentation gods will be favorable to me, then I will show you this and this."

I'm thinking, "What are you talking about? What is a presentation god? Didn't you know before the presentation that something might go wrong? Where is your plan B?" If the connection is down, then prepare something locally that doesn't depend on the connection. The other option is to come with your own connection.

You need to spend time preparing the talk and you need to start early. Even if you're an experienced presenter, you can't start preparing only a week before. I start two or three months ahead. I'll put my notes aside, but I'll come back to them frequently to make improvements.

One time, a guy was coming from Washington D.C. on the train to present at a little local meetup in New York City. The train journey was about two hours and he started his presentation by saying he had prepared his slides for us on that journey.

I found that insulting. Was he a prima donna? Was he doing us a huge favor by coming to see us? I think that shows disrespect. If you're going to do a presentation, then spend some time on it. It doesn't matter if you're getting paid for it or not; people pay with their time.

**Geertjan Wielenga**: Do you do live coding? What's your experience with that?

## The problem with live coding

**Yakov Fain**: I know only one person who can do it well: Venkat Subramaniam. Firstly, most of his talks are recorded on video, so, you can watch them later on and see how he did the coding. Secondly, he maintains a site and all of his presentations, with the code, are published there.

Unfortunately, many other speakers, who are not as good as Venkat, just enjoy themselves in front of the people in the room. They say, "Look at this! Look how I can code in front of you!" They show all these different shortcuts, copy-pasting snippets of code, and in 10 minutes, they have created the project. You're thinking, "Slides are boring. Look at what this guy does! In front of an audience, he does all that!"

Now the talk is over and you're at home. After this talk, what's left? What are the resources available to you? In the case of Venkat, you do have them, but in the case of many other people who do live coding, you have nothing. There should be a healthy mix. I prepare slides, I prepare all the code samples, and I run the code samples live when it's appropriate. I give all that to the audience. I'm not one of these guys who will say slides are bad.

**Geertjan Wielenga**: Do you need to be an absolute expert on a topic to be able to talk about it at a conference?

**Yakov Fain**: No, you don't, but you need to research the topic well. I don't want to be rude, but any software developer can research a topic. If you invest hours of your time into researching something deeply, you can speak about it at a conference.

There is no expert in everything. Don't be afraid of saying that you don't know something. You will be standing in front of 100 people. Yes, you researched the subject, but there is a chance that in the audience there will be other people who have also researched that subject. They may have specific questions. Don't be afraid of that. If you don't know the answer, say, "I didn't have a chance to work with that, sorry, but I can look it up for you." Don't try to pretend that you know everything about the topic.

> *"You don't have to be an expert and you don't have to lie about it either."*
>
> —*Yakov Fain*

You can definitely prepare a presentation that is interesting and useful for people. How you present it is a different story, but in terms of material and coverage, you don't have to be an expert and you don't have to lie about it either.

**Geertjan Wielenga**: I think many developers are afraid that if they blog about their code, in a future job application that blog will be found. If that code is found to be wrong, they fear that they will not be taken seriously in their job interview or something along those lines. What would you say to that?

**Yakov Fain**: I understand those fears, but you need to develop a thick skin. If you become a public person by writing blogs, or books, or anything else, you need to be prepared because there will be some mean people. They will say bad and insulting things about you.

I would say there are two major groups of people: those who create content and those who consume content. You've got all these platforms like Facebook and YouTube. Most of the people on Facebook just repost videos made by someone else, but if they don't like something, they will be very vocal about it.

I remember when I wrote my first book, people started nitpicking. Of course, mistakes slip through. My first book was self-published, but even when you work with technical editors, still some mistakes will be missed and you'll see mean comments about them.

> *"I thought, 'Who are you to criticize me? What did you create?'"*
>
> *—Yakov Fain*

People will say, "He is a book author but is using `var` instead of `let` when declaring a variable." As if that's a crime!

Many years ago, it bothered me seeing these comments, but after that, I thought, "Who are you to criticize me? What did you create? What did you contribute to the community?"

Don't try to be a perfectionist. When I started doing developer advocacy, all these people around me knew the subject better than me, but when it came to writing a blog about it, they kept postponing it.

In their opinion their content was not perfect; they were afraid of criticism. The problem is that time goes by and then the subject of that never-published blog is not even relevant anymore.

There is a concept of the minimum viable product. You need to release what you're working on. The same goes for conferences, books, and articles. Push it out. Yes, there will be something wrong with it and people will tell you that. The criticisms can be constructive, though, so you will learn and do better, but don't wait and try to release a perfect thing. I don't remember who said it, but if you release a product that's perfect, you've released it too late.

**Geertjan Wielenga:** What has kept you going in this direction all these years?

## Yakov's motivation

**Yakov Fain:** I like the fact that I can have freedom. I have the freedom of not going to work every day. I have the freedom to work with multiple people. I have the freedom to go and see places. I like travel and going to conferences covers my travel.

As opposed to going to the same cubicle every day and doing the same thing, I work remotely. If I want to be in good shape financially, I take on a project and I work for a client for two or three months. Then again, I can decide not to work for a month or two. Instead, I will teach a class.

**Geertjan Wielenga:** What is enjoyable about teaching others?

**Yakov Fain**: I can't give you a common answer that would work for everybody; it depends on your personality. Whenever I learn something, I have an urge to tell someone else. If I read about something that I don't understand and all of a sudden it clicks, the first thing I want to do is write a blog about it.

I have my personal blog, where I've written more than a thousand blogs. Maybe 80% are technical blogs with different software, mainly Java, of course. I'm not afraid of releasing these blogs. If I learn something and think I can explain it, I want people to know about it.

**Geertjan Wielenga**: You've mentioned that you enjoy the travel element of developer advocacy. Can you give some highlights of your travels when going to conferences?

**Yakov Fain**: One of the important things for me when you go to any conference is the speakers' dinner, because typically a large conference brings together many prominent people from around the world. During these dinners, you have the chance to meet speakers in person and get some new ideas.

I like seeing places. If I go to Ukraine, for example, I like walking around. I'm originally from Ukraine. If I go to Belgium, it's a great country to be in. There are so many good things to explore. In December, I went to a conference in Florida and found interesting things to explore there. If there's a concert in the area, I will go to it.

The only thing is that sometimes it's too much travel. If you go to one hotel, then another hotel, it gets annoying. Other than that, I do enjoy seeing and meeting people, or simply walking around in different cities.

**Geertjan Wielenga**: As an international traveler, do you have any tips around jet lag, avoiding losing your suitcase, and so on?

**Yakov Fain**: In terms of jet lag, I try not to switch time zones, if possible. Of course, if I'm going to Hong Kong or Singapore, this won't be possible. If I go to California from New York City, it's a three-hour difference. I will live by the New York City clock, even though I'm in California. If I go to Europe and let's say it's a six-hour time difference, I will go to bed a couple of hours later than at home.

I've learned that my luggage should be small. Initially, I had an actual suitcase and a bag with my laptop. In some cases, they wouldn't take the bag on the plane in the cabin or I needed to pay extra for it. Eventually, I bought a good backpack. That's all the luggage that I have and my luggage won't get lost.

The backpack was expensive, but I can fit in everything I need for a week of travel. There's a special pocket for a computer and a place for clothing. If you go on Amazon, or other online stores, you can find really useful travel accessories to keep the contents of your backpack neatly arranged. It looks like I don't have anything with me, but I have tons of things in my backpack. So, invest in a good backpack and you'll be safe in terms of travel.

**Geertjan Wielenga**: How do you stay up to date with the latest tech developments?

**Yakov Fain**: There is no silver bullet; you should just sleep less to stay ahead of the curve. You have to understand that our profession is about learning until you're retired.

The amount of information available for consumption is tremendous. Hopefully, over the years, you will find a way to narrow down your online sources and you won't just read everything. But in the software industry, you should have an interest in learning something new all the time.

> *"I spend the first couple of hours every day reading about something and learning."*
>
> —*Yakov Fain*

For me, it's natural. I'm an early bird, so I spend the first couple of hours every day reading about something and learning. Everything is quiet in the house and everybody is asleep. It's the perfect time for learning.

**Geertjan Wielenga**: Which social media platforms do you consult for new insights?

**Yakov Fain**: First of all, YouTube; it's available for everybody. Secondly, I use a site called Pluralsight that publishes video courses on different subjects. I go there if I need to. I do have an account on Twitter, where I have more than 5,000 followers. I use Twitter mainly for announcements. I will post that I'm going to this conference, or I want to announce this training, or that I posted a blog.

**Geertjan Wielenga**: If you could change one thing about your professional life, what would that be?

## The idealjob

**Yakov Fain**: I would like to be able to afford to do only teaching and speaking. As of today, it wouldn't pay my bills and that's why I have to work on other projects. Ideally, I would like to be able to do learning, teaching, speaking, and writing. This does not pay the bills, unfortunately.

The same thing is also true with writing books, unless you author another Harry Potter book, of course. Software books are not something that you write for a living. I remember, maybe 15 years ago, David Flanagan wrote a bunch of good books. One day, I saw his blog where he stated that he couldn't write computer books for a living anymore. The minute the book is out, it goes onto all these pirate sites and people get it for free. People don't want to pay for books. David is a talented writer, but people don't want to pay for good content. What can you do?

**Geertjan Wielenga**: Do you think that books are still important in the tech field? People go to Stack Overflow, or they watch some YouTube clips, or they watch a series on a particular topic, and they think that they have all they need. In many cases, they learn in practice by applying those sources to their projects. Is there a need for books still?

**Yakov Fain**: Yes, there is a need for tech books. A book is a collective set of opinions and skills from a particular author or a group of authors.

You can't replace that with a short video on YouTube. I'm not saying that short clips don't have value; of course, they do, but it's different. Short clips show you a specific technique, but for seeing the big picture, and how multiple pieces of the puzzle work together, you need books.

**Geertjan Wielenga**: Possibly one problem in this particular domain is that there are so many things to do, and so many interesting things to learn, that potentially you're spending your entire day moving from one different thing to another. Have you had any experience with burnout?

**Yakov Fain**: I've never been in that situation. Burnout usually happens when you do things that you don't like. For example, if you put me on a project and my main responsibilities were fixing bugs in someone else's code, closing tickets, reporting every morning how many tickets I'd closed, and reporting why I didn't close a ticket, this could be a reason for burnout.

I've seen all these people who are promoting agile tech. It's all about daily meetings, standups, sending each other emoji symbols, and so on. That environment is something that would burn me out much faster compared to developer advocacy, which is a set of different activities and has no deadlines.

**Geertjan Wielenga**: Listening to you, I wonder why anyone would not want to be in this subject domain. Is it the perfect job?

**Yakov Fain**: For me, yes, but not everybody is willing to share what they know. There are some people who are very introverted and keep information to themselves. I don't blame them; it's their choice, but I'm not that kind of guy.

**Geertjan Wielenga**: Thank you, Yakov Fain.

## 28

> *I stress this often: developer advocates need to build their personal brands.*

# Patrick McFadin

# Introducing Patrick McFadin

Patrick McFadin is the vice president of developer relations at DataStax and is devoted to making users of DataStax and Apache Cassandra as successful as possible and improving their experience as developers. Previously, he served as a chief evangelist for Apache Cassandra and was one of the leading experts in Apache Cassandra and data modeling techniques. Patrick has been fortunate enough to help with building some of the largest deployments in the world and he publicly speaks about the design of highly available distributed systems. Find Patrick on Twitter: @PatrickMcFadin.

---

**Geertjan Wielenga**: Would it be true to say that this whole profession is fairly new?

**Patrick McFadin**: As a job description, it's fairly new. If you go back to the early days of software, Apple employed evangelists in the '80s to help to build its developer ecosystem. That was a formal job, but it was more of an engineering advocacy role at the time.

If you look at the history of software, developer advocacy has been going on for a lot longer than many people realize. There might not have been an established job field, but there was somebody working at Apple, for example, who spent time with developers at conferences. Microsoft had a similar person. In the '80s, there was a small group of people doing advocacy, it just wasn't a really big field.

# The growth of developer advocacy

**Geertjan Wielenga**: Over the last five years, developer relations has even become a service: you can hire a company to come in and set up a program for you. What has led to this progression?

**Patrick McFadin**: I think it's just a maturing of our industry and more companies understanding how much developers make a difference. Developer advocacy has grown so much in recent years because software is eating the world.

The dynamics of how we consume and buy software have changed. Open source, I would say, is to blame for that. Previously, when you bought software it was the most expensive part of your IT budget; now it's not. There's been such an explosion of options. Companies are fighting to get noticed and they're going to employ any strategies they can to make that happen.

> *"Businesses are starting to realize that developer relations is a significant way to get market share."*
>
> —*Patrick McFadin*

With marketing, you used to buy a full-page advert in a magazine to get your message out. You could go to a conference and have a big booth. By doing that, everyone would know your company. Nowadays, there's zero marketing budget for some of these small projects. If you have an open-source project that grows into a company, who's going to get people to use the software? Businesses are starting to realize that developer relations is a significant way to get market share.

Compared to marketing, there's a different voice needed when you're talking to developers. There's this old adage that developers are allergic to marketing. That's not entirely true, but you get great results from developer-to-developer discussions. Companies have to understand that flashy adverts or balloons flying in the sky alone aren't going to get them into a market; the key is knowledge transfer.

**Geertjan Wielenga**: Does being called a "tech evangelist" versus a "developer advocate" make any difference?

**Patrick McFadin**: That's actually only a recent debate. I started the evangelist program at DataStax about five or six years ago. "Evangelist" was the term that made the most sense at the time. We've since decided to use the term "developer advocate."

To my mind, evangelists are more about promotion and doing a lot of conference talks, whereas advocates spend time with the product and the engineering team, while also spending time with users and customers. Developer advocates not only advocate for the company, but they also advocate for the developers themselves. We switched the name for our team because "developer advocate" is a better description of what they do. I would hope that anyone who talks to a developer advocate at DataStax feels that they have a direct connection to our engineering team.

**Geertjan Wielenga**: What kind of personality is needed to be successful in this role?

**Patrick McFadin**: I've hired many advocates in my time and all types of people fit, but I think being a natural learner and explorer is important.

You need to be someone who wants to push the boundaries a little bit and you need to be excited about sharing your learnings.

Developer advocacy is not a desk role; you don't sit in a cubicle and write code all day. If you're not okay with getting out there and talking to people, you'll be really miserable. I've hired developer advocates who just wanted to spend time working with the code. That's straight engineering, so developer advocacy didn't work out for them.

**Geertjan Wielenga**: Isn't it true to say, though, that not every developer advocate needs to be out there doing public speaking at conferences? In some companies, there's also a need for blogging, research, creating samples, and so on.

**Patrick McFadin**: That's a great point. Recently, it seems that there's as much of a need for the online component as the in-person component, but creating connections with people is critical.

**Geertjan Wielenga**: How many people are there in your team of developer advocates?

**Patrick McFadin**: We have six developer advocates right now at DataStax. I'm sure that the team is not going to stop growing. We're always adding developer advocates because the plan is to put them closer to where people are.

I don't want to have a team of developer advocates in San Francisco serving India or Asia. People should be strategically placed so that they don't have to spend their lives on airplanes. Every region in the world has different needs, requirements, norms, and conferences. I also wouldn't want to have a purely online team; I think that would be really plastic.

**Geertjan Wielenga**: Are these developer advocates all doing the same type of work for your company?

**Patrick McFadin**: Mostly, but the key is that everyone is different and everyone has their own way of doing what they do. There's a requirement for speaking publicly and for working online, as we discussed. Those percentages are different for each person.

I stress this often: developer advocates need to build their personal brands. When I'm talking to my team, I always say, "Your personal brand and trust relationships are what we're building here. Don't worry about creating DataStax branding; we have people for that. You need to be the brand with your voice." If I needed someone to be Mr. or Ms. DataStax, I'd be looking for a product marketing person, which is a different role. I need someone who can bring their personality because it's a trust relationship that we're building with developers.

**Geertjan Wielenga**: Should a developer advocate ideally be someone who is seen as being more or less independent of their company through having a personal brand?

## Building a personal brand

**Patrick McFadin**: Yes, not compromising on your personal brand is really critical. You don't have to be exactly following the party line, although that can lead to some conflict. Be true to yourself; if you don't want to talk about something, pick something different. There are plenty of choices.

**Geertjan Wielenga**: What's your personal brand?

**Patrick McFadin**: At this moment in time, my personal brand is just being a large-scale application person. Most of what I do is around data modeling. I'm known for data models and deploying Cassandra, but my brand is around building applications in general.

That has worked out really well because when developers walk up to me, they already know who I am. I don't know them, but they can immediately say, "Hey, I really want to deploy this application and here are some of the parameters. Can you help me to look at this?"

**Geertjan Wielenga**: What are the personal brands of the other people on your team?

**Patrick McFadin**: There are several different directions that people take. For instance, we have one person on our team who's just an amazing networker and they have a brand around DevOps. They're at conferences all the time.

We have another person who's very focused on frontend development and women-in-tech issues. They have a very strong voice and participate in outside groups. We then have some people who are well-respected for their enterprise software chops. They're known for being people you could trust to know about enterprise architectures.

You don't always have to be known for something cutting edge. It could be that you've been doing something for a long time and you know what you're doing. You just have to have a voice.

**Geertjan Wielenga**: This voice doesn't have to be 100% aligned with the company, then?

**Patrick McFadin**: That's a dangerous conversation to get into, but this is what I worry about: if company dogma says, "We need you to talk about X, Y, and Z; if you don't do that then you're wrong," that's not letting people find their path.

An example would be that, at DataStax, we sell tech in and around Apache Cassandra, but if a developer advocate wants to spend some time researching something else, within reason they can go down that path. Sometimes that turns into a product direction over time.

A specific example is that our advocacy team led the charge in Docker and Kubernetes. Before the rest of the company was ready to do that, we were already there. That direction could have been a dead end, but it wasn't.

> *"Embrace the crazy for a little bit and let your team be natural explorers."*
>
> —*Patrick McFadin*

You just have to embrace the crazy for a little bit and let your team be natural explorers. They may find a dead end or they may find something interesting. My only guidance is to make sure that what you're doing is adjacent to the company somehow. I don't want my team to go out and build a self-driving car, for example, because that's not what we're about.

**Geertjan Wielenga**: What can happen is that the company that you're working for takes a direction that conflicts with your own vision and/or with what you know the community is focused on. What would your advice be in that situation?

**Patrick McFadin**: Don't compromise yourself. If you really feel strongly about something, there are plenty of other jobs out there. I would never recommend that anyone just sucks it up and deals with something that they don't support. That's generally good advice for anyone who works for a company. If you don't believe in what the company is doing and you can't find a way around that, then you should leave.

If you just do whatever the company says with no conviction, then you're a mercenary at that point. Advocates should believe in what they do; I think that's so critical. If you don't believe in what you're doing, that's going to just start eroding your credibility. I've had discussions with advocates in my team who started changing their tune. I've asked, "Is this the right place for you right now?"

With every advocate I hire, I say, "You have an expiration date. We just don't know when that is." Developer advocacy is likely not a permanent position for the rest of their life. They will eventually have this moment where they realize they can't do it anymore. Maybe that will happen because they just want to get back to pure engineering. Maybe they will decide that they can't spend that much time on the road anymore. Maybe, as a result of the company naturally going through change, they just won't feel the passion anymore.

I'm not going to try to push someone up a hill. Passionate people, just by nature, can't pull passion out of thin air. I just don't see how that could ever work.

**Geertjan Wielenga**: You could have a really passionate developer advocate who sees things going the wrong way within their company and thinks, "I'm going to go along with it. In principle, I could quit right now because I don't agree with this, but maybe in six months or a year, things will have changed again. I'm going to stick it out for the interim." Is that a good plan?

**Patrick McFadin**: In that case, you could use your voice to advocate for going in another direction. I can't tell you that everything that DataStax has done has been awesome. I have had moments when I've said that we shouldn't go in a certain direction.

> *"You don't need to rage-quit your job."*
>
> *—Patrick McFadin*

When you get enough respect in your company, you're seen as being pure in your ideals. You don't need to rage-quit your job. You can say, "I believe our community of users will be negatively affected by this. I'm now going to advocate for all of them." Often, the company will make some changes because it didn't think about these roadblocks initially. When I see other companies making weird changes, I always wonder whether anyone actually said anything about that.

**Geertjan Wielenga**: What would you say are some of the disadvantages of the life of a developer advocate?

**Patrick McFadin**: There's a high likelihood of burnout. I try to live a healthy, balanced lifestyle and I really pay attention to burnout because I've burned out before. I've been an engineer for a long time; I get it. You don't see the warning signs until it's too late.

**Geertjan Wielenga**: What happens when you reach the burnout stage?

**Patrick McFadin**: You're done; it's an abyss that you can't escape from. Going on a quick vacation won't help because burnout really does ruin you in a lot of ways. The worst kind of burnout means that you need a career change and that's unfortunate.

When you hire a developer advocate, you're usually taking an engineer out of their natural habitat. When you do that, you put the engineer into an environment that they weren't originally planning on being in. That can be a risk.

Sometimes, what leads to burnout is getting too excited; for example, many new people get excited about going to all these conferences. By about the 10th conference, they're pretty sick of living out of a suitcase or just the continuous nature of the travel. I've done two weeks solid on the road bouncing through Europe to go to different events. By the time I got back to San Francisco, I didn't want to see another human, let alone talk to one.

**Geertjan Wielenga**: Developer advocates tend to be very passionate about what they do. We can work 24 hours a day and still have other things that we want to do. The problem is that if you're working from home, no one prompts you to take a break. How do you encourage finding a balance?

**Patrick McFadin**: My advice is always to block out a day on the calendar, put Slack into sleep mode, and take naps. I tell my team not to feel bad if it's only the afternoon and they need to take a nap. I'm not worried about my team using that as an excuse to not work; I'm worried about the opposite.

If I don't step in sometimes, I'm effectively helping my developer advocates to throttle themselves. This is a wonderful job; everybody that I've hired for developer advocacy says, "This is my dream job. I can't believe this exists." Then they are at risk for burnout.

**Geertjan Wielenga**: How did you get into this role yourself? What's your background?

## Patrick's route to developer advocacy

**Patrick McFadin**: This career is not what I was originally planning. I have a degree in computer engineering and distributed computing. I'm classically trained as an engineer. I worked in the dot-com industry in the '90s and had a lot of fun. I made good money, but when the dot-com boom ended in the '00s, I got involved in large-scale infrastructure. I loved it.

I had my own consulting company for a long time until I sold that to another company. I ran an infrastructure team and in 2011, I started using Cassandra quite a bit for problems that I was having. I thought, "This is a really great database that no one knows about."

A friend of mine started a company called Riptano, which eventually changed its name to DataStax. He kept trying to get me to join the team. Finally, I acquiesced. I was about employee number 50. When you're in a small start-up, everybody has about 10 unofficial jobs.

I was mostly working as a consultant. I was traveling around helping people to do large-scale Cassandra projects. It was fun, but along the way, I started doing meetups and webinars. I became known for that.

Eventually, our CEO, Billy Bosworth, called me into his office and said, "I think that there's a good reason for you to just do this work full-time." For him to believe in me and pull me out of my field was a significant thing. I was given a budget to hire people and I was told to go out and do nothing but grow the Cassandra community.

I asked, "Is that a job?" But in fact, I believed in what the CEO was saying; I believed that this would be really good for the company and for Cassandra. At the time, the title I was given was "chief evangelist." Everyone said Steve Jobs was the chief evangelist for Apple, so I said, "Okay, I'll take that job!"

That's what got me into this role. This is a nice part of my career. I've spent 20 years building and doing things. Now, as I'm getting older, I can talk to the younger people who are coming in.

This is my personal journey. I'm almost paying back into the community that I learned from. After all, this is the most important job field in the 21st century.

**Geertjan Wielenga**: Why is this the most important job field?

**Patrick McFadin**: Because software is everything. It's also the biggest immigrant story that there is. I'm obviously a descendant of immigrants to the U.S. My wife is a first-generation American. Immigrants came to this country for a reason. My ancestors came to this country because they were looking for a better life and the same thing is true right now with software. The top three professions for green cards in the U.S. are all software positions.

> *"Software is building the future."*
>
> —*Patrick McFadin*

People are leaving their towns and their villages. They're coming to the U.S. from all over to do one thing: build software. It's exciting because people are making better lives for themselves. Their kids will have better lives because these people have chosen to go in this direction. Software is building the future.

**Geertjan Wielenga**: Where does the developer advocate role fit into this vision of software that you're talking about?

**Patrick McFadin**: Almost everyone in software is probably stressed out. They're behind schedule.

They have a boss somewhere telling them to go faster, make things happen, and not make any mistakes. There's a stress level built into this system right now.

Developer advocates are a friendly face. Support teams are great, but a developer advocate is the helpful face when you go to a conference. I know that look: someone with their laptop open looks at you and asks, "Can you help me?" That is a wonderful moment right there. That person realizes that they're not going to lose their job. Their kids are going to be okay. Just being a helper is such an important part of the tech world.

**Geertjan Wielenga**: What topics do you cover at conferences?

**Patrick McFadin**: The last talk I did was about the importance of the developer experience. That's a really critical part of a product, especially an infrastructure product. It doesn't have to be ridiculously hard to use a product. Developer advocates are at the cutting edge of delivering that message.

**Geertjan Wielenga**: What are some aspects of making a product easy to use?

**Patrick McFadin**: Everything from having great documentation and examples to providing a smooth path. How do you install the product and what's the user experience like? It's also important to have a strong community around a product.

**Geertjan Wielenga**: When you go to a conference as an attendee, rather than as a speaker, do you look first at who the speakers are? Which topics do you find inspiring?

**Patrick McFadin**: Sometimes it's the speakers who draw me to a conference. There's always someone who can make a topic interesting. I also look for names I know, but I think the topic is probably more important to me.

Knative is an example. It's a new Kubernetes project and at a recent conference there were people I'd never heard of talking about it. You should look for keywords that pop up in a conference. This is a good time for me to mention that you should always pay attention to the title of your talk because that's normally all that people read!

**Geertjan Wielenga**: What are some good titles that you would recommend?

**Patrick McFadin**: I wouldn't recommend a particular formula beyond making sure that people know what you're talking about in the title. If you're talking about Kubernetes, put that in the title. If you're talking about Cassandra, put that in the title. If you're at a Cassandra conference, you may get away with less, but you still need to be specific. If you have a title such as "The Glorious Ending to my Unicorn Lifestyle," people won't know what that is. I've seen fun titles, but speakers often end up having too much fun. If you're not a big-name speaker, don't get too fancy.

**Geertjan Wielenga**: What's the atmosphere like at conferences that are specifically for developer advocates?

**Patrick McFadin**: Along with the developer advocates attending, there's also a mix of marketing people. Many people are just there because they're trying to figure out the role itself.

It does seem a little chaotic, but the major theme is people asking, "How do I convince my company that this role is valid?"

## Proving your worth

**Geertjan Wielenga**: This is the standard problem. How do you prove to upper management that you're not a cost center or that the cost center is justified?

**Patrick McFadin**: I've talked about this at conferences before. The pitfall in developer relations is that we get sucked into the same kind of measurement statistics that marketing does. We start to focus on qualified leads and key performance indicators (KPIs). We start trying to calculate how many people we've talked to. That's the wrong approach; we already have a marketing department for that.

Developer relations is about awareness and the developer experience. How do you measure that? It's very difficult convincing a business that you should be measured much more like an engineering team and much less like a marketing team. What's the return on investment (ROI) on a developer building code? Give me the metrics that show the ROI. They don't exist. We hire developers to work toward an overarching goal. We set that goal and we say, "Go and do that thing."

> *"Businesses now understand how success for developer relations is measured."*
>
> —*Patrick McFadin*

I think a change that is happening in developer relations is that businesses now understand how success for developer relations is measured. What I do for my team is set goals such as making inroads into a community. I can go back and report to my executive team, saying, "Here's what we tried to do. We wanted to be a larger voice in Kubernetes. Here's some stuff that we've done and look at the effect: we're being invited to these Kubernetes conferences."

From an awareness standpoint, that's really good. You've got to have people who believe in that approach. You can't have an executive team that replies, "No, we want marketing leads from you." In that case, they should go and hire more marketing people!

**Geertjan Wielenga**: Do have any KPIs with numbers, such as the number of conferences to attend per year?

**Patrick McFadin**: Yes, I want every developer advocate to try to get at least two speaking positions per quarter, but it's not the end of the world if they can't achieve that. It's not like you can magically get your name into a conference. I try not to put many numbers into our goals because when you add a number, that's all that people focus on.

**Geertjan Wielenga**: Are you still traveling a lot or do the developer advocates in your team do that now?

**Patrick McFadin**: I thought I wouldn't be traveling as much, but I end up doing it anyway. Travel is just in my DNA now.

I still really love meeting our developers and I can't stop doing that. I could never be relegated to a desk and be okay with that. I'm not as much of a road warrior as some of our younger advocates, who are out there all the time, but I make it a point to attend at least one event every month.

**Geertjan Wielenga**: If you could change one thing about your professional life, what would it be?

**Patrick McFadin**: I would like more acknowledgment in the tech industry that developer advocacy is a really critical role. DataStax is a full believer in developer advocacy, so I have no problems there. I'm very proud of our work, but I wish developer advocacy was more accepted and formalized in our industry as a whole.

When we start seeing senior executive roles related to developer advocacy, that's when we'll know that developer advocacy has arrived. If there was a chief advocacy officer, developer advocacy would then be on the same level as sales and marketing. That's the dream.

**Geertjan Wielenga**: Is a developer advocate within an organization doomed to be that forever? Is there a route into different positions?

## Career development

**Patrick McFadin**: There aren't many options at the moment. In the industry, we're having discussions about what the path should be for individual contributors. Do we send them down a management path or an executive track?

If you're just starting out in developer advocacy, you can move up into more senior roles where you're managing groups of advocates, doing more substantial projects, and creating programs. Many people end up moving out of developer advocacy into pure engineering. I'think there are many distinguished engineers who it could easily be said are developer advocates.

**Geertjan Wielenga**: How do you stay updated on the latest tech developments?

**Patrick McFadin**: Twitter is always a good channel. I have a pretty healthy diet of online sources, including TechCrunch and Hacker News. Hacker News is the bleeding edge of the bleeding edge. I just see what people are talking about, along with going to conferences and meetups. It's about paying attention and talking to other developers.

**Geertjan Wielenga**: What are you most passionate about at the moment in the tech industry in general?

**Patrick McFadin**: For me, it's the impact of what the cloud is doing to this entire industry. I think people are missing how disruptive it is and what it's doing to open-source projects, along with the changes we're seeing to how developers get their work done and how we do business internationally. The cloud came on fast and we can't measure its impact just yet. I'm very interested in the topic because it reminds me of when we went from proprietary software to open-source software. The cloud will have the same level of impact.

**Geertjan Wielenga**: Thank you, Patrick McFadin.

## 29

> *If you're doing this role for the right reasons, this is your life and what defines you.*

# Reza Rahman

# Introducing Reza Rahman

Reza Rahman is the principal program manager for Java on Azure at Microsoft. He brings more than a decade of experience with tech leadership to his contributions to industry journals, and he authored the popular book *EJB 3 in Action*. A frequent speaker at Java User Groups (JUGs) and conferences worldwide, Reza has been the lead for the Java Platform, Enterprise Edition (Java EE) track at JavaOne, as well as being named a JavaOne Rockstar. Find Reza on Twitter: `@reza_rahman`.

---

**Geertjan Wielenga**: Not much is known about developer advocacy outside of the industry. Would you agree with that?

**Reza Rahman**: Yes, but it shouldn't be that way. It's difficult because developer advocacy is more of a function than a paid profession in many cases.

**Geertjan Wielenga**: What's the difference between a function and a profession?

**Reza Rahman**: Let's take me as an example. I was hired to do evangelism full-time for a relatively brief period. Oracle hired me as a Java EE evangelist and that formal role only lasted for about three or four years, but informally, I've been performing this function for most of my career.

For at least 15 years, I've been doing developer advocacy in one sense or another, but it's always been something that's been a small part of my job, at least in terms of workload. Other than that, I've done this type of work in my spare time.

**Geertjan Wielenga**: How would you describe what developer advocacy entails?

## Defining developer advocacy

**Reza Rahman**: It's very difficult to define. The only other role I can compare it to is an architect. You're always switching roles and doing many different things as a developer advocate. There's not a defining activity about which you can say, "Okay, that's developer advocacy."

Some people will be tempted to say that developer advocacy is public speaking, but that's not true. There are full-time developer advocates at Microsoft who never do public speaking, so that's not a defining characteristic. Developer advocacy is about two-way communication.

An interesting debate that we can get into is the evangelist versus developer advocate question. An evangelist's output function is much higher than their input function, and their job is to deliver a message. They deliver that via blogging, doing social media, speaking, writing books, or even writing code. A developer advocate has an input function. They listen and then deliver impact. You could say that about other roles too, such as a business analyst or salesperson.

The other defining characteristic is communicating and listening without an immediate agenda. There's not a sales quota that you need to meet. There are no concrete requirements to deliver. There is no download number that you must reach. Instead, you're communicating a message and listening to what people react to. You can then fine-tune that message or product.

**Geertjan Wielenga**: How did you end up doing this in the first place?

**Reza Rahman**: I've always done public speaking. It's always been in my portfolio because it's an area of interest for me. I've always enjoyed writing and communication in general as well. The fundamentals of developer advocacy go way back to almost middle school.

I have a passion for communicating ideas. That morphed into something more professional when I entered the professional world as an engineer, but it didn't happen right away. Obviously, you have those initial few years where you're just an entry-level developer and all you're doing is learning, churning out code, and producing software. There was a period of that but then I reached a stage where my passion for communication married up with my professional interests. I started doing talks internally at my company and then I was asked to write a book. Eventually, some of that work got noticed.

After writing the book, I began to do more public speaking, this time outside of my organization at JUGs and smaller conferences. This progressed to larger conferences and then eventually, I got into the Java Community Process (JCP).

> *"Being a professional evangelist wasn't anything that I sought out."*
>
> —*Reza Rahman*

You can almost map out my progression. The height of that progression was getting hired to be a full-time evangelist, as I mentioned. Being a professional evangelist wasn't anything that I sought out, but once it was offered to me, I realized that it was something that I wanted to do.

In my current job, there is an element of developer advocacy and I think, for the foreseeable future, it will remain with me. Even when I retire from my professional life, I may continue with some things that I'm passionate about, whether that's public speaking, writing a book that has nothing to do with tech, or simply blogging.

**Geertjan Wielenga**: What are some of the disadvantages of this type of work?

**Reza Rahman**: There's not much that I don't like about this work. One problem is that it's difficult to get the right combination in a role. You can get a job that you're passionate about, but it won't necessarily entail much communication or much external communication. On the other hand, you can get a job with a lot of communication, but it might not necessarily be in an area that you're very passionate about.

I've never followed a career trajectory that required me to be a professional developer advocate. If I had chosen that route, there would have been some very serious dilemmas. I see plenty of people job-hopping and going from one professional advocate job to another. I question whether those people are truly passionate about what they're doing. It almost seems like they're more passionate about their role than about the message that they're delivering.

Another downside is that developer advocacy is not clearly defined, as we discussed.

If the company culture is incorrect, developer advocacy can easily be bundled up with sales, marketing, or things of that nature, and that's always difficult. A less enlightened company will want to make a very direct correlation between its revenue and money spent on developer advocates or evangelists.

Those are the two big challenges. Another point is that if you find something that you genuinely care about, even if you're lucky and you manage to align communication with that, navigating ethical dilemmas comes with the territory.

## Facing an ethical dilemma

**Geertjan Wielenga**: One of those ethical dilemmas is that you're an ambassador for a particular company. You may find yourself standing on stage and facing questions about something your company did that's all over the news. Have you encountered that situation?

**Reza Rahman**: Absolutely. Everybody in this role has encountered that situation. It's just like everything else in life: not black or white.

It might be that you need to do some things that you're not comfortable with in the short term because you believe that there's a long-term goal. The situation might work itself out, so you have to weigh that up. Also, you need to weigh up your integrity. There have been situations where it was so bad for me that I had trouble getting out of bed for months on end; my ethical dilemma was so profound. That's a horrible situation to be in as a human being. It's a good indicator that it's time to do something different professionally.

You can talk to those in power and share your views. You need to also think, "Am I overreacting? Is there a silver lining here? Does this make sense from a certain perspective?"

You're serving the customers as a developer advocate; you're not necessarily advocating for the company. That comes in at a very close second. You mentioned the word "ambassador," but that may not be the best metaphor. The job of an ambassador is to serve the interests of the nation they're representing; it's almost the inverse of what developer advocates do.

**Geertjan Wielenga**: A complicating aspect in all of this is that there's not only the company to consider but also the tech community. You have this moral dilemma because abandoning your company might damage that community. What's your view on that?

**Reza Rahman**: You have to make those judgment calls. It's not an easy calculation, but sometimes drastic action is fully justified. No matter how damaging or extreme it might seem, it might be the right thing in the long term.

**Geertjan Wielenga**: Have you always been 100% behind the tech that you've promoted?

**Reza Rahman**: 100% is a bit extreme. That would be more descriptive of an evangelist. I'd say that I've never been so enamored that I didn't see any of the drawbacks. That's religion and that's not what tech is; it has its pros and cons.

What I would say is that I've always believed in the message enough to bother delivering it.

It's never been the case that I've delivered a message that I absolutely had no belief in, at least not in the long term. I've done that for short periods when I made all of those calculations and said, "Okay, this is worth it for now. Maybe there's a light at the end of the tunnel."

**Geertjan Wielenga**: How honest are you when you know that there are bugs in the tech that you're advocating or promoting?

**Reza Rahman**: You should consider the user of the tech when you're doing this job. If you know there's a problem, your first responsibility is to make that clear.

Again, it comes down to all those calculations. If you know something is an issue, you reported that issue back, and you know that it's being solved, there's no benefit in explicitly making things worse by saying, "My product has a problem." That doesn't solve anything.

It's rare that this situation happens anyway. Most developer advocates get a bug fixed in time so that if they're doing a demo, they're not blatantly working around an issue. However, there are some circumstances in which that might occur and the right thing to do is to work around that bug and get the message across that it's a short-term issue that you're dealing with.

> *"The wrong thing to do is play games with the audience and deny that there's an issue."*
>
> —Reza Rahman

If someone does notice something and says, "Hey, you just skirted around that issue," then the wrong thing to do is play games with the audience and deny that there's an issue. That's very damaging to your credibility and the company's credibility. The person is not going to just sit there and think, "Oh, I'm wrong and Reza is right." They're going to think, "What a jerk."

In those situations, you need to acknowledge what's going on, shortly followed by saying, "Check with me later. I'm going to follow up on this."

**Geertjan Wielenga**: Would you say that authenticity is important?

**Reza Rahman**: Yes, if you're not credible then you can't do this job. If nobody believes that you have their best interests in mind, nobody is going to listen to you. They might come to your session for some training or entertainment, but that's where it will end. You wouldn't be able to deliver your fundamental message.

**Geertjan Wielenga**: If you work at one company advocating its products and then you work at another company promoting competing products, can that have an impact on your credibility?

**Reza Rahman**: Not necessarily. Some people think that they need to drink their company's Kool-Aid, but somebody could work for a company and believe in a certain product but realize while working in that space that there's a competing product that's better. You can retain your credibility if you move from one company to another, as long as you're doing it for the right reasons.

If it's obvious that you're only moving companies because of professional reasons and you've been publicly bashing this other company, and then three months later you're working for that very same company saying the opposite, there's not much credibility in that. I would be really frightened of anyone who is even capable of doing that without examining what their belief system is.

**Geertjan Wielenga**: What do you do when you're on stage and someone asks a question that you don't know the answer to? Is how you solve that today different to how you would have solved it years ago?

**Reza Rahman**: I've always simply said, "I don't know." Nobody likes a know-it-all. I hate going to a talk and seeing the person on the podium pretending to know everything about everything, even if they're supposed to be the expert. The reality is that we're all humans and it's physically impossible that anyone will know everything at a given instance in time.

It's also a credibility question. If you don't know an answer but you pretend to, there's a good chance that somebody in the audience will know what you're doing. It's always best to say, "I don't know. Here's my contact information. Could you check back with me in $X$ amount of time? Or if you give me your contact information, I'll find out and send you an email."

**Geertjan Wielenga**: In a way, isn't that kind of interaction potentially more valuable because it provides an opportunity for you to build up a relationship with somebody?

**Reza Rahman**: That's also legitimate. At the end of the day, it's about being true to yourself. It's much easier to be honest than the other way around. There are too many games you have to play if you go down the alternate path.

## The knowledge needed to advocate

**Geertjan Wielenga**: Although you can't know everything, is there a cut-off point for how much you should know to do this job?

**Reza Rahman**: You should know more than 80% of your audience. As long as you know substantially more than most of your audience, you're okay. It depends on your audience too. It's one thing to go and talk about computer science to somebody at school, but if you're talking to some Ph.D. students about a big data topic, you have reason to be concerned about how much you know. It's all relative.

**Geertjan Wielenga**: Doesn't it also depend on what kind of topic you're presenting? If you're presenting your journey into the cloud, for example, that's going to be a very personal story.

**Reza Rahman**: That's also true. You can present a different perspective on just about any topic. It depends on what the value would be to the audience. Nobody wants to hear about the last time you went to Cancún on Spring Break, for example!

**Geertjan Wielenga**: What kind of topics do you find interesting when you go to a conference? Do you decide to go to sessions based on who the speakers are or on the topics?

**Reza Rahman**: It's a bit of both. In general, when I go to conferences, I go to talks that are close to my area of interest, which is relatively narrow. Maybe I'll go to a session on serverless, Kubernetes, or Docker, aside from going to sessions on Java EE, Java, and Spring. Would I attend a talk on how to do business negotiation? Probably not; it's too far removed from my area of expertise. I wouldn't go to a .NET session, to give another example, because that's not something that I will apply anytime soon.

> *"Keynotes are not always substance-driven: sometimes they're personality-driven."*
>
> —*Reza Rahman*

I do occasionally go to listen to particular speakers, but that decision is almost always qualified by the topic that they're presenting on. I don't just say, "Oh, James Gosling is speaking, so I must go there. It doesn't even matter what he's speaking on." I generally don't do that. For that reason, I often avoid keynotes. Keynotes are not always substance-driven: sometimes they're personality-driven. I often find myself not going to those talks because there's just not enough there that catches my interest.

**Geertjan Wielenga**: What are some current developments and trends that you find interesting?

**Reza Rahman**: Right now, obviously I'm following many different things because the Java EE ecosystem is in flux. I'm following MicroProfile and Jakarta Enterprise Edition (EE) very closely.

I think we'll see how things pan out over the next few years. I'm certainly interested in the container space. It's becoming the next server-side; it's not quite there yet, but it's pretty close. Docker, Kubernetes, and Knative are all things I'm following. They're going to become the next operating system/server-side layer.

There's a possibility that Java EE and Jakarta EE might miss the boat altogether on some of those things. People like myself are paying attention to what's going on in those areas to be able to influence them or adapt them. I essentially work for a cloud company these days, so all topics to do with the cloud, such as serverless, are things that I try to stay updated on.

**Geertjan Wielenga**: What's something that you've recently learned that has surprised you?

**Reza Rahman**: I'm doing a Java EE study right now for Escher. I was a little worried because I needed to interview quite a few people for this study; I couldn't just interview 10 people and say I was done. I was worried whether, with all of the uncertainties going on, I'd be able to do that with the Java community.

I was surprised by several things. Reaching those numbers wasn't very difficult in the end. There was almost an abundance of choice. Some people were interested in Azure in particular. That wasn't the objective of my study. I wanted to know what their experience with the cloud was, even if they weren't Azure users. But that interest meant that I can now connect these people to the engineering teams and say, "Go and talk to them about what you need."

The other interesting part is the fact that the Java ecosystem seems to be embracing containerization very heavily and also Platform as a Service (PaaS). I wasn't sure whether the Java ecosystem as a whole is still stuck on on-premise/bare-metal/virtual machines, but, at least from my interviews, that doesn't seem to be the case. In the Java ecosystem, there's a lot of appetite for things like Docker and Kubernetes. Also, the enthusiasm for PaaS was not something that I was expecting.

It goes to show that you can be in a community for almost 20 years and still not know what people are thinking. You might have a few data points here and there from Twitter, but the realities might surprise you.

**Geertjan Wielenga**: Do you use social media to stay up to date, then?

# The problems with social media

**Reza Rahman**: I rely on social media a bit, but it's really difficult in some senses because some people's Twitter feeds are just product marketing or them trying to sell something. An agenda is very obvious from their Twitter streams and it's kind of annoying to follow people like that.

You'll have the same issues if you try to stay up to date with politics through Twitter. To anyone trying to do that, I wish you luck! You can get very one-sided views. It's really difficult to get a clear picture from social media and that's why you need to rely on the free press to some extent. That's true of tech as well.

I do read DZone and InfoQ. I just scan the headlines. If there's something I need to know about, then I set aside some time to go and investigate it. Knative is one of those things. I wasn't aware of it maybe even a few months ago.

I would say that about 20% of my research is on social media, and another 50% is DZone, InfoQ, and other media sites, although DZone is getting a little bit more difficult to follow because it doesn't use a journalistic filter anymore; it just seems to post whatever content comes along. The rest is just my research on specific things. I'll Google a specific topic and read a bunch of people's blogs, or read some product documentation and maybe code something.

**Geertjan Wielenga**: For developer advocates, is there a danger of becoming a jack of all trades, master of none?

**Reza Rahman**: It depends on what you need to master. The reality is that this role and the product management role are very similar; you actually know your domain better than most other people. An engineer might know certain aspects of a subsystem, for example, but for any substantial system, it's impossible to know everything. If that is possible, there's probably something inherently incorrect about that system.

> *"You have a 360-degree view of the entire landscape, which is something that very few other people have."*
>
> —*Reza Rahman*

Who knows a product best? It's probably the developer advocate or evangelist. So, in that sense, you are the master of that domain. Are you the master of a particular skill set? You're probably not the best coder in the house or the best tester in the house, but you tend to know more about the domain that you're working in. You have a 360-degree view of the entire landscape, which is something that very few other people have.

**Geertjan Wielenga**: What are some things that you wish you had known at the start of your career?

**Reza Rahman**: I wish I had known how all-consuming this is. This role is definitely for workaholics. It's an illusion to think, "I'm just going to do this part-time and have a separate life away from it." If you're doing this role for the right reasons, this is your life and what defines you. Everything else happens when you have time to do it, rather than the other way around. Be careful what you wish for.

**Geertjan Wielenga**: What are the early warning signs of burnout?

**Reza Rahman**: Fatigue is a big one. I've managed to avoid it, but I have seen some other people experience it. The body and mind have ways of telling you that you have a system overload.

**Geertjan Wielenga**: You mentioned earlier having a hard time getting out of bed. Was this due to burnout?

**Reza Rahman**: You could classify that as burnout, but that wasn't a very productive period. It had more to do with internal conflict.

**Geertjan Wielenga**: Aside from passion and communication, another key aspect of this role is that you're interacting with people. Typically, people in this role care about people, which is not necessarily what you would expect, because this is a very thing-oriented industry versus people-oriented. Do you agree?

**Reza Rahman**: That's very true; it's ultimately about people and the message. It's about tech, but there's a purpose behind it. I think some people lose sight of that fact and tend to become more focused on things, and that's evident in the way that they carry themselves and the way that they deliver their message. You're right, there is a broader purpose beyond bits and bytes, and some electrons running through some silicon, glass, or copper.

**Geertjan Wielenga**: What is the message that you're communicating with passion?

**Reza's core message**

**Reza Rahman**: The common thread for almost 20 years now has been Java EE, in whatever shape or form, and Jakarta EE going forward. But that's maybe too simple an answer. Why do I care about this Java EE thing in the first place?

My background is not in computer science alone. I have another major in economics and also a minor in math and a minor in philosophy.

When I look at an ecosystem like Java EE, what I see is something beyond technological merit. The real reason that I care about Java EE is that I believe it helps to maintain a healthy competitive ecosystem.

The alternative is an unhealthy monoculture. Coming from an economic standpoint, I don't think that can lead to any good whatsoever.

That's been the core message for me for a while now. We need to be mindful of the long-term competitive health of the ecosystem, and, in fact, of any ecosystem. Is that the only message I'll carry with me for the rest of my career? I'm not sure. Hopefully, I have another 30 or 40 years to go before it's all done for me. Maybe the message will evolve over time, but maybe it won't.

**Geertjan Wielenga**: How do you see your role developing? What is the trajectory for a developer advocate within the industry?

**Reza Rahman**: For a developer advocate, it's tough. There's not much upward mobility, and that's also true for engineering roles. The purely engineering path almost inevitably ends in something like a distinguished engineer, which is the equivalent of a vice president (VP) but without the VP responsibilities. Most of your day is spent writing code.

In a developer advocate or evangelist role, you can be a very important person in the company and have a voice, but I don't know whether it's one of those positions with a career path. If you choose to be a full-time developer advocate, that's basically your role.

There are plenty of examples out there of people who spent their entire career in this role.

It can also be a pathway to a different set of careers. You could move into management or product management, which is slightly different from just pure management.

You could potentially take up a role as a VP of technology too.

In terms of my career, most of my time has been spent as an architect. There's a different path for an architect. My current role in product management is also another role that I'm exploring that's related to an architect but not quite the same. If I did go back to my architect career track, that would lead to a chief information officer (CIO) or chief technology officer (CTO) role. I've flirted with those roles already, but I'm mid-career at this point.

I think I will end up in the executive suite in some shape or form, probably leading some kind of team. Often that is the career path for product managers. They become somebody who provides a higher-level vision for an organization as opposed to a single product.

> *"Career progression has never been my concern."*
>
> —*Reza Rahman*

My concern so far has been asking, "Do I believe in what I'm doing? Does it feel right?" So far, so good. Career progression has never been my concern. My career has progressed without necessarily having to engineer it.

**Geertjan Wielenga**: What would you when you were 20 think of you today?

**Reza Rahman**: That was almost two decades ago now. This morning, I spoke to somebody in Japan and this evening, I'll be talking to my manager in China. I probably wouldn't have expected things to become so global so quickly.

I had grander ambitions back then. My plan was to get on the executive fast-track. Maybe somewhere in the back of my head I still have those ambitions, but it's become more important that I enjoy what I'm doing.

**Geertjan Wielenga**: Thank you, Reza Rahman.

## 30

> *I enjoy working with computers. It's not like I have to spend 12 hours a day working in a coal mine!*

# Adam Bien

# Introducing Adam Bien

Adam Bien is a Java freelancer with a deep admiration of simplicity and lean methodologies, and an astonishing pedigree: a Java Champion, JavaOne Rockstar, NetBeans Dream Team founding member, and 2010 Java Developer of the Year. Adam's been working with Java and its development community since version 1.0. As well as writing books and articles, Adam organizes the "airhacks" Java workshop three times a year in Munich, which he has also turned into a podcast series at `airhacks.fm`. Find Adam on Twitter: `@AdamBien`.

---

**Geertjan Wielenga**: Adam, you're a very well-known public speaker and you have a very specific and well-established methodology in terms of being lean and focused on simplicity. Breaking things down to their absolute basics seems to be your hallmark. Would you agree with that?

## Keeping things simple

**Adam Bien**: Yes, I'm just a developer, so I try to find the simplest possible solutions. I'm not very interested in investigating frameworks just for the sake of it. If you go to a bakery, the bakery isn't playing with five million different tools just because the old flour became too boring after a while.

**Geertjan Wielenga**: Although, to extend that metaphor, could there not be developments in the flour world that mean the baker might want to experiment with the latest things?

**Adam Bien**: Yes, but the baker should just focus on baking better bread and not on evaluating exciting ovens. I have the feeling that we are driven by companies to evaluate frameworks. Netflix, Google, and Facebook have different problems than, I would say, 80 percent of enterprises that most developers are working for. There is a gap there; we shouldn't try to apply nuclear fusion to baking bread!

If you're implementing video streaming, you have different kinds of problems than a company that sells goods. To give another example, Facebook deals with social graphs and a huge number of unique visitors. Only a few companies deal with social graphs as their main business. Also, the scale is unique. A bakery won't sell more bread online just by using Facebook's tech.

At conferences, I usually show a "Hello, World!" version of my daily projects. In recent years, I've just been removing stuff; I can't remember the last time I added a framework or library to an existing project.

**Geertjan Wielenga**: Do you really prefer keeping things as bare as possible, then?

**Adam Bien**: Yes, because I've been doing Java since 1995. I really liked tinkering with frameworks and libraries in my first few years. However, I realized that choosing and evaluating "best-of-breed" techs per project comes with little benefit.

I prefer the opinionated way that Java Platform, Enterprise Edition (Java EE)/MicroProfile vendors operate. They pick, test, and evaluate the API implementation for me and I only have to use it.

If I'm not happy with the choice, I just switch to another application server.

Over time, unmaintained and forgotten dependencies will cause trouble. The fewer external dependencies we use, the less likely it is that something will go wrong. Of course, there should be a balance. There is no need to reinvent the wheel. The added value of libraries such as Apache POI PDF generators is so high that you should just pick them.

Java EE, together with MicroProfile, is getting more and more powerful; therefore, we need fewer and fewer frameworks. The same is true for browsers and web standards. My advice is to take a look at what you already have before you search for fancy stuff. If you can solve problems with plain Java, do it. If plain Java isn't enough, extend to Java EE, then to MicroProfile. Java is the basis of clouds, event stores, and databases; it's hard to escape Java.

**Geertjan Wielenga**: Is the reason that you've focused more on Java EE than on Spring in that debate that you see Java EE as being the basis of Spring?

**Adam Bien**: I've focused on Java EE because of the constant stream of project requests. I've only worked on existing Spring projects and helped with fixing problems and integrations. I noticed that these Spring projects also used Java Persistence API (JPA), Java Message Service (JMS), and Java Database Connectivity (JDBC). I use exactly the same APIs on the application server.

The reason I like Java EE is the out-of-the-box experience. You download the server, regardless of which server it is, then there is no configuration and you can focus on your problem. I like the simplicity.

The assumption in Spring is that before you start, you will try to find a profile or set of libraries. What I observe is that the stock application server setup is already good enough; there is no need for optimization. If I'm asked which server to choose, I tell people to pick the first one and start coding. That way, there is no wasted time in setup; they are productive from the very first second.

Because Java EE is a standardized set of APIs, developers are also constrained; we have to focus on what we have. If we could use any libraries on Earth, I think we would lose a lot of time to evaluation and research. Also, we could quickly lose focus of what we want to build in the first place.

**Geertjan Wielenga**: In addition to the Java world, over the last two or three years you've been looking at JavaScript and HTML in the same lean way. How has that come about?

**Adam Bien**: My Java EE clients asked me for my opinion on the user interface (UI). They were really pleased with the backend but puzzled by the endless possibilities, constant migrations, and bloat in the frontend.

Since 2015 (ES2015/ES5), JavaScript has finally become very similar to Java. I really enjoy the vanilla feel of JavaScript. JavaServer Faces (JSF) is not the ultimate answer. JSF is absolutely great with PrimeFaces as the component provider.

The problem with JSF is that it's not suitable for all kinds of UIs. Sometimes they need a more interactive single-page application or offline applications, and you can't do this efficiently with JSF. For instance, yesterday I showed an enterprise client what you can do without any frameworks, just in the frontend.

The developers couldn't believe how easy it is to develop without any frameworks. Even hardcore backend developers show some interest in the frontend. Hopefully, I will help the company to develop applications with standard frontends and standard backends.

**Geertjan Wielenga**: What is involved in your standard frontend?

**Adam Bien**: A Web Component, ES6, CSS3, and often lit-html. lit-html is an ES6 template implementation from Google's Polymer framework. This library is about 500 lines of code of JavaScript. The dependency is very loose and there are already alternatives on the market.

If Google drops lit-html, we will move to hyperHTML or other libraries with similar functionality. My clients are actually not dependent on any framework, which is important for larger companies. No one likes to migrate just because of the death of an irrelevant framework.

In 2006, everyone claimed Rails would kill Enterprise JavaBeans (EJB) and Java EE. Here we are 13 years later and I'm getting more and more requests about Java EE and MicroProfile.

I worked for a client for the first time in 2005. When I met the team again this year, they said, "Thank you! All these years, we've just made our codebase simpler and simpler with Java EE, without migrations, and now we can remove even more and save a lot of time."

## Being independent

**Geertjan Wielenga**: This whole lean approach is something that you're able to promote because you're working for yourself. You're not promoting a particular tech, framework, or company that has a stack that it wants to get out there in the developer world. You're basically just promoting yourself and your services, right?

**Adam Bien**: Yes, people suspected me of working for Sun Microsystems at one point and they also thought that I was working for Oracle, but I was always independent.

I get hired by product managers and product owners. Actually, for the last project I worked on, a product owner hired me to verify their framework. I said, "You don't need a framework," and this caused an internal escalation, but the developers liked the decision.

> *"Developers own the code; they should be satisfied, not the advocates."*
>
> —*Adam Bien*

You can't be political when working with clients. You should be politically correct but not follow any politics. You should just be honest. Developers own the code; they should be satisfied, not the advocates.

**Geertjan Wielenga**: What is your background? What did you study?

**Adam Bien**: I studied applied computer science. I always liked computers; they were magical machines for me. I really liked C++, then someone said, "Hey, there's a truly object-oriented language called Java."

I found the JavaSoft website with the Java logo. This was pre-JDK 1 and what I really liked was the design and the coffee branding. Back then, if you did C++ for Linux, there was no branding available. Java came with a range of marketing, to the point that I wondered why someone would spend so much promoting a language! I started coding and found that I really liked Java. For many reasons, I knew that it was something special.

**Geertjan Wielenga**: What does your typical day consist of?

**Adam Bien**: It depends. Yesterday I spent eight hours on a flight before running a few workshops and sessions, but what I usually do is work via a virtual private network (VPN) from home.

I could travel and speak all year at conferences, but I don't believe in professional speaking. I'm involved in code reviews, proofs of concept, firefighting, architecture consulting, legacy project migrations, clouds, serverless, and web standards. It never gets boring.

If I just went around speaking at conferences, I would quickly forget about the code. I still need time to code and find problems, so I try to spend as little time as possible at conferences. The only conference I tried to regularly attend was JavaOne.

If I do go to conferences, I will deliver a talk and then return to my actual work as quickly as possible. The reason I attend any conferences at all is that I can present and verify my point of view. If everyone is satisfied with my opinion, or at least not against it, then I'm doing things right.

I was rejected for two conferences recently because they expected the speakers to participate in parties and spend several days at the conferences. I'm not a professional speaker, so I usually don't attend parties. It seems like conferences are developing into being vacations for speakers these days.

**Geertjan Wielenga**: Is your problem with these conferences that they take time away from programming?

**Adam Bien**: Exactly, because I'm expected to spend three days at a conference. If you have 10 conferences a year, that is one month just spent attending parties!

**Geertjan Wielenga**: But are you not learning at these conferences?

**Adam Bien**: Yes, I'm learning, but not when I'm at the parties. At JavaOne, I used to attend all of the talks I could and network as much as I could with other speakers, but the parties were terrible. The music was so loud that you couldn't actually hear anyone.

**Geertjan Wielenga**: By not being employed by a company, you're on your own most of the time. Can you mention any other disadvantages of being a freelancer?

**Adam Bien**: At the beginning, I was afraid that I would become jobless in two weeks because there is no job security, but now I've been working since 1997 as a freelancer. If I don't get a contract, I will go on a real vacation!

**Geertjan Wielenga**: Do you switch everything off when you're on vacation?

**Adam Bien**: No, I still get up early and check emails. My clients can still run into problems, even when I'm on vacation. But I like to be in the middle of nowhere in a nice landscape. I actually wouldn't use computers if I wasn't a programmer; I don't play any computer games.

**Geertjan Wielenga**: How did you get into public speaking in the first place if you prefer to be programming?

## Adam's route to public speaking

**Adam Bien**: I attended the first JavaOne in 2000 and it was full of endless smart people. I couldn't even understand how they had gained such a huge amount of knowledge. I decided it would be great if I could speak at JavaOne, but trying to get a slot didn't work for seven years.

I tried to apply with reasonable topics, like what I was doing in projects, but everything was rejected. Then I submitted a talk on how I hacked my heating. That session got approved, strangely enough. That was just a pet project that I did on the weekends, but off the back of that talk, I became a "JavaOne Rockstar," which only means that the attendees liked my session.

Since then, it has been easier for me to get my talks approved. The heating talk had nothing to do with my work and I would probably not even speak about that topic nowadays because there's no real added value for the audience.

**Geertjan Wielenga**: But these Internet of Things topics are entertaining. It's interesting that a session on how to hack your toothbrush, for example, would be a well-attended session versus some hardcore garbage collection session that would only attract 10 specialists. What kind of sessions do you typically attend?

**Adam Bien**: I attended JavaOne for the talks I couldn't hear anywhere else. What I really appreciated about JavaOne was that I had the unique opportunity to listen to how the engineers were building Java. I don't like listening to other consultants who have prepared a talk and then travel around the world delivering the same session again and again. I can watch a YouTube video for that.

**Geertjan Wielenga**: How do you keep your content fresh?

**Adam Bien**: I want to show something on stage that is usable and I want to ensure that the problems differ from year to year. I get inspiration from projects, code reviews, and my clients. If several clients ask me similar questions, then I use that topic for a talk.

**Geertjan Wielenga**: What are interesting topics for you right now?

**Adam Bien**: From a JavaScript perspective, there are many web APIs, so I'm thinking about what might be interesting for my clients. For JavaScript and Cascading Style Sheets (CSS), the browsers are becoming more and more powerful. In the backend, Jakarta EE, MicroProfile, and GraalVM are super interesting. The problem with Java 8 is that it's already great; it's hard to improve it.

> *"People are amazed at what you can achieve right now without any external libraries."*
>
> *—Adam Bien*

The MicroProfile movement is like an extension of Java EE including Oracle, Payara, TomEE, IBM, and RedHat. All my clients already have various Java EE servers and now they are MicroProfile-capable. Java EE has become so popular in the last few years because people are amazed at what you can achieve right now without any external libraries. Amazingly, you're getting Swagger for free, you're getting Prometheus metrics for free, and you're getting the whole experience without any external dependencies. No dependencies means leaner and faster deployments, and no migrations. Also, all major microservice patterns are just an annotation away.

**Geertjan Wielenga**: Let's talk about the live coding approach that you take. You basically have one slide with your talk's title and then you spend an hour, or however long it is, doing demos and showing code. Are there any pitfalls to this approach?

**Adam Bien**: It's hard to tell how experienced the audience is. You get more and more young developers at conferences, so you have to show the old stuff again. Then, for the more advanced stuff, you might run out of time.

**Geertjan Wielenga**: Have you had any experience with unexpected technical glitches?

**Adam Bien**: One time, at JavaOne, the network was slow, which strangely had a huge impact on the startup time of the GlassFish application server. What usually takes three seconds took five minutes. This had never happened before. I delivered the talk but afterward recorded a screencast on YouTube.

Yesterday, the projector just went dark in my keynote that I actually prepared some slides for. As we've discussed, I'm not a professional speaker, so that means I'm not really prepared. There is no agenda for my talks. I don't have a flow of slides, so I don't get nervous if something unexpected happens.

In the worst possible scenario, I would just pick up another laptop, open Notepad, and write pseudocode. The code wouldn't compile, but at least I would get the message out. If the audience still learns something, no one will complain.

**Geertjan Wielenga**: Do you get a lot of work as a direct result of your conference sessions?

**Getting project requests**

**Adam Bien**: I do get some interesting projects from time to time, but not necessarily just because of my speaking. I have my blog, podcast, online courses, and YouTube channel also.

Sometimes people come to a conference because they saw me on YouTube or listened to the podcast first. Some people go to a session and they suspect thàt I might be a professional speaker. After the session, they ask me whether I actually accept project requests.

**Geertjan Wielenga**: Do you find that there is often a lag to getting a lead and people sometimes contact you years later?

**Adam Bien**: Absolutely, I have clients who saw me speak three years or even five years ago. What you shouldn't do is go to a conference and expect tons of requests. You should deliver your talks without any expectations; often, that will pay off later.

**Geertjan Wielenga**: Why don't you use LinkedIn and Facebook?

**Adam Bien**: I've liked Twitter from the beginning. I can just open my Twitter app, write something, and close it; there are no obligations after that. With Facebook, I procrastinated with the registration, I waited for too long, and now it's pointless. The same is true for LinkedIn. My main strategy is saving time and it's hard to save time with social media.

**Geertjan Wielenga**: Do you read online journals or websites for trends and tips?

**Adam Bien**: I search for topics and try to find as many links as possible, then I bookmark them. If I'm on an airplane, I read everything related to those topics.

**Geertjan Wielenga**: As you travel frequently, do you have any tips around burnout and mental health?

**Adam Bien**: I just focus on the code. If I was learning all the programming languages that come out and die, and all the frameworks that are in development right now, I think it could be really frustrating.

My job is not stressful at all. I can actually drink a good coffee at the airport, on the train, or at the office and enjoy nice views. The Java community is great, my clients are nice, and I enjoy working with computers. It's not like I have to spend 12 hours a day working in a coal mine! Even if I am traveling by train, in Europe they are great. They are warm and dry, and you have power for your laptop.

> *"This is a luxury life from my perspective."*
>
> —Adam Bien

At conferences, everyone is nice. This is a luxury life from my perspective. You have to always remember what lives our predecessors had. This lifestyle would be like a vacation for them!

**Geertjan Wielenga**: Do you have any tips for dealing with jet lag and things like that?

**Adam Bien**: I don't travel that far. I try to focus on conferences that are easy to travel to. For instance, usually, all the conferences that I attend are pretty reachable by airplane directly from Munich. I go by train frequently, so I can work or read. I try to avoid airplanes when I can because that wastes time.

I was in San Francisco for one or two nights recently. I flew in, delivered the talks, and flew back. I couldn't sleep well on the airplane due to jet lag, but I read all the time. After two great nights of sleep at home, I was completely recharged. That was a nice life hack.

My advice is to also travel lean. I take less and less stuff with me, so I can't lose anything. Try to get rid of all the optional stuff. If you forget something, be relaxed about it because you can always buy something at your destination.

**Geertjan Wielenga**: If you're at a party when you're not programming and there are no developers there, how do you describe what you do?

**Adam Bien**: I just say, "I'm a programmer."

**Geertjan Wielenga**: If you were to say you were a programmer 20 years ago, it would be very clear what that meant and people would understand that you were programming the whole day. Now, programming is a social activity. Traditionally, people think that if you're in programming, it means you're this very strange person who can't interact with anyone. How would you describe typical programmers today?

**Adam Bien**: I have found that good programmers, or programmers who like programming, all have a similar mindset. Regardless of which programs we're interacting with, we immediately understand each other and have similar interests.

We're very efficient with our communication, I would say, but we actually have a great sense of humor. I laugh a lot, even at conferences.

We always have fun in sessions or working on projects. Geertjan, do you remember our trip through Poland without a navigation system? We had fun and great conversation in the car about all kinds of topics.

If I have to really focus, I also appreciate working alone. Some quiet days are great.

**Geertjan Wielenga**: If someone hears your story and wants to be in this field for as long as you have been, what kind of qualities would they need to sustain this kind of lifestyle?

**Adam Bien**: You have to be honest with yourself and ask whether you will enjoy being a developer. I like reading and learning; I do it all the time. I try, especially on my travels, to spend every free minute learning. Everything I read is software-related, but I get many ideas from this and it's what I really enjoy.

I think you have to like what you do. If you just want to be a freelancer to earn money, this role won't work. If you like coding and want to improve yourself, this role is for you. I really don't regret anything about the work I've done; I've had a great time.

**Geertjan Wielenga**: Thank you, Adam Bien.

## 31

> *This area will explode in the next few years, simply because the major companies are connecting with developers.*

# Bruno Borges

# Introducing Bruno Borges

A Brazilian and proud immigrant living abroad, Bruno Borges has been a software developer, Java community member, and tech influencer since 2000. He previously built end-to-end business applications as an engineer and team leader. In recent years, he has worked with, or continues to work at, vendors like Oracle and Microsoft in roles related to product management and developer relations strategy. Constantly present at conferences around the world and a contributor to open-source projects, Bruno believes developers are the best source of new business ideas in a digital world, and empowering them with great tech is one of the major goals in his professional life. Find Bruno on Twitter: @brunoborges.

---

**Geertjan Wielenga**: I want to start right in the middle of a topical discussion: on Twitter, you said, "Developer relations isn't simply about traveling around and going to conferences and parties; it's actually part of a strategy of a company." Can you explain more about that?

## Developer relations as a strategy

**Bruno Borges**: When companies decide to build a developer relations team, that becomes a strategy. Developer relations can be something that an individual ends up doing naturally. For example, someone working with open-source foundations in their free time could be described as some sort of developer advocate, but that's more just community engagement.

The formal structure of developer relations within any company is about engaging with the users of a product, service, platform, or API.

For that reason, the company needs to see the discipline of developer relations as having a strategical structure. That structure could be inside the product management team, the engineering team, the marketing team, or even the sales team. Depending on where developer relations is situated, the company's strategy, purpose, goals, and metrics will be influenced.

Not every company can simply go and start up a developer relations team. Sometimes it comes about naturally when different employees sit together and start discussing developer relations as a business strategy.

Generally, companies have the need to position their tech within a developer community, whether that community is an open-source community, a partner community, or a customer developer community. Companies need to start communicating with developers. That is, I think, the ignition for having a developer relations strategy. More and more companies are becoming software companies, so we're seeing developer relations becoming a strategical part of the way companies do business.

**Geertjan Wielenga**: I'm sure for many people who have been involved in this field since the '90s, they accidentally ended up in developer advocacy by being enthusiastic. If you were technical on the one hand but people-oriented on the other hand, you could end up being a developer advocate. It seems like developer relations has a much more formalized structure now. Would you say that being a developer advocate is a far more officially recognized role today?

**Bruno Borges**: Yes, by 2009/2010, we started seeing more formal structures in developer relations.

That's about the time that Google started its developer relations team and IBM started investing in its developerWorks platform, with several engineers creating content specifically for developers. In the last 10 years, we've seen developer relations becoming part of software companies and also non-software companies that rely completely on software, such as banks and retailers.

**Geertjan Wielenga**: Does every company need a developer relations strategy of some kind, then?

**Bruno Borges**: I would say that any company that exposes its software, platform, or services to others, in order for them to build new custom stuff on top of that, does need a developer relations team within the company somewhere. This depends on how the company benefits from software built on top of its own structure externally, of course.

One example is Ford. Ford has a developer relations team that is focused on its partners. Developers work at partner companies to integrate tech with Ford cars. So, a car manufacturer has its own developer relations team, which is interesting.

If a company is a software company, but it only produces software for itself, then that's an example of not needing a developer relations team. But the moment that the company has external developers that need to work directly with its software, whether it's community users, external individuals, partners, independent software vendors (ISVs), or customers themselves, the company would benefit from a developer relations team.

This can help with all the questions, feedback, engagement, and growth that comes from the adoption of software by external developers. That, in essence, is what developer relations can do.

**Geertjan Wielenga**: Apparently, there is so much business now that there are companies out there offering developer relations as a service. Representatives will come in, analyze the situation, and recommend people from their own organization or outside their organization to fulfill developer relations roles. Have you heard about this?

**Bruno Borges**: No, that's amazing to hear and only proves the point that developer advocates are becoming needed by software or software-related companies. Sometimes, the company might not be ready to implement a developer relations strategy right away. It might not have the skills, resources, or people. Having a company that is able to help with navigating through this period is a big signal to the market that this is an important area.

**Geertjan Wielenga**: Developer advocates have had to fight for a place at the table in organizations because there isn't always a direct connection between our work and revenue. Nowadays, there are developer advocacy job positions. You can go to LinkedIn and there are recognized functions within organizations. Would you say that the fight has been won as a result of times changing?

## Winning the fight in companies

**Bruno Borges**: The fight happened in the first place because executive teams were not aware or not educated enough about the benefits of having a developer relations team.

Without that knowledge, they couldn't make a decision about whether it was important to fund developer advocacy within companies.

Now, as we see, developer relations is everywhere. I think it's just a matter of time before executives who previously had doubts catch up with the market. We're going to see developer relations being covered as a formalized extra structure within companies, just like engineering, product management, business operations, and so on.

We're at the bottom of a big hill of adoption of the developer relations discipline within companies. I think this area will explode in the next few years, simply because the major companies are connecting with developers. As I mentioned earlier, even companies that are not traditionally from the IT industry are adopting these strategies. This is a great moment to be involved in this field and for any engineer who would like to do this kind of work, there are fantastic opportunities.

**Geertjan Wielenga**: Has the only change been that many organizations are now doing this and therefore developer relations has become more attractive? Do companies now see value that isn't expressed directly as money?

**Bruno Borges**: It really depends on the company and how the company makes money. It depends also on how a particular product, service, platform, or API generates money. One thing that we can say is that the better the relationship between a company and its customers, the better the customer retention, customer satisfaction, and adoption of growth. I'm not even talking about developers as customers here, just the importance of building customer relationships.

When we consider developers as customers, and we start focusing on that particular set of customers with their specific needs, we can improve that relationship. Soon, it will just be natural to want to better the relationship with developers. This will lead to more satisfaction with products and more adoption of them. New developers will also come to that platform, product, or service.

Customer relationships don't just happen. When we look at account managers, those sales employees work within their accounts and they have one-to-one relationships. Anything that they do keeps those relationships strong and they can easily track that. Account managers are responsible for taking all the actions needed to support a particular customer.

> *"In developer relations, it's hard to track the actions needed to engage with a particular customer."*
>
> —*Bruno Borges*

When we look at the developer relationship, that's often a one-to-many relationship format. You have one developer advocate or you have one program manager in developer relations. You also have one event, one article, or one documentation piece. All of those things are one-to-many relationships and because of that nature, it's difficult to track a direct impact on revenue. In developer relations, it's hard to track the actions needed to engage with a particular customer because you don't have a track ID per customer when it comes to someone coming in to see you, watching a video, reading an article, attending a presentation or workshop, or anything like that.

That said, revenue becomes an indirect metric. Depending on how a developer relations team is structured, it can be possible to track direct revenue. One example is developer relations teams that are focused on the existing customer base of a company and their objective is to help the customers to take advantage of new products and services that the company has recently released. It might be possible to track that because that is a one-to-one engagement. It really depends on how the team is structured, its goals, and how it engages with the developers.

However, the general rule is that developer relations has indirect impact and executives need to understand that. They have to see that there are benefits, but most of that will be indirect, in the same way as brand awareness and customer satisfaction. Those things are measured by analysis on the marketing side. If marketing takes a look at what customers are thinking about the company, that will show the growth opportunity that the company has just based on brand satisfaction. Developer relations is similar to that. It is possible to track developer satisfaction, which might or might not have a direct link to revenue. Tracking will definitely show that there are opportunities for growth.

**Geertjan Wielenga**: What is your own story? How did you end up in this domain?

**Bruno Borges**: Like most developer advocates or developer relations personnel, it was something that just happened. Developer advocacy is not a discipline that is taught at universities; there's no training specifically for this. Most often, somebody will come to realize that what they already do is actually developer relations.

This is a discipline that is a conjunction of several other roles: software engineering, product management, and marketing.

> *"In my view, everyone is always selling something."*
>
> —*Bruno Borges*

Another aspect is sales. Most developers don't like the word "sales," but in my view, everyone is always selling something. Engineers are selling something; they're building software that will be sold somehow, somewhere, to someone. Product managers are helping to manage the development of that product. Marketing is communicating with people about that product. Sales is actually helping people to start using that product by ensuring that they understand the benefits in more detail.

This mix of roles means it's hard for someone to decide to do developer relations just from day one. Coming out of college as a computer scientist and deciding to do this job will not happen anytime soon because, for someone to be able to do developer relations properly, there are so many disciplines that come before that.

In my case, it happened that way. I started as a software engineer and then I became a product manager. As a product manager, I was engaged with marketing divisions and sales divisions directly on a weekly basis. Maybe in some companies, sales, marketing, and product management are pillars that are not needed. I think it might vary. But, in my opinion, those pillars are essential for doing a proper developer relations job. Trying to aim for those pillars is a great foundation.

Just as in computer science, when we go to college for four years, sometimes we don't use some of that background, but it gives us a good foundation.

From outsourcing companies that just build business software for companies, I then went to vendor companies. That's where I landed as a person helping users to take full advantage of the software that they needed to build their own solutions. That process is, ideally, what I see happening to others.

**Geertjan Wielenga**: What kind of personality fits this role best?

**Bruno Borges**: I think any personality fits this role, but I would classify the ideal person as someone who is able to create things without anybody telling them what to do. I think that is crucial.

It's clear that developer relations is a mix of multiple disciplines. Because of that, the kind of person who will be able to do the job is someone who is very proactive in learning and experimenting with things. I know engineers who are great at building things, but only once they are told what to build. That's why we have product managers in most software companies: they are the ones who are able to identify what needs to be built.

It's very important for a developer advocate to know what to build and what the best delivery mechanism for such a creation is. Is it an article? Is it documentation? Is it a video? Is it a presentation? Is it a demonstration? Is it a library? Is it community engagement? That's why you need to be self-sufficient. It's not a requirement to be self-managing, but it's a good idea.

You need to be creative and being able to listen is important too, along with understanding what others are saying but not being biased by a small set of opinions. You need to understand that the world of developers is quite big. We have millions of developers in the world and most of them are not even on Twitter. Most of them are not publicly exposing their opinions about software.

I think the cognitive requirements of a developer advocate are quite demanding: being able to analyze and process all that information to be able to make a decision on what actions to take next. While those qualities are not hard requirements, they will definitely show the potential of an employee to become a developer advocate.

Just as in software engineering, where we have software engineers, architects, and product managers, in the future we might have more content producers, developer relations engineers, product managers, program managers, and so on. That's where you start to see the developer relations team being formed with specific hats or roles. While I was outlining just now the ideal person, that doesn't mean that a team can't be formed by putting together people who have some but not all of those qualities as individuals. You can create value as a team.

**Geertjan Wielenga**: If you see an opportunity for developer relations as an employee, what can you do to make that happen in your company?

## Starting your advocacy work

**Bruno Borges**: Getting started is tough. As you mentioned earlier, sometimes there is an eternal fight to justify that role. That's actually a good way to start, but it's a painful way to start, just because you not only have to do the job, but you have to justify it. I think a good way to begin is simply by performing the expected tasks that a developer relations team would perform without being asked to do that. That would be a side job for sure.

Once you realize that you can actually do this role, that is the moment that you go with a business plan to your company outlining what you have done over a period of time and what the outcome of that was. Maybe the outcome was content, product feedback, customer support, community engagement, or all of that. Most importantly, you need to show what the value was. If you aren't able to convince the company that this work is important, then you should get a full-time job elsewhere.

> *"You have to do developer relations to understand what it's about."*
>
> *—Bruno Borges*

It's also a possibility that you will realize that developer relations is very hard and you don't want to do it again. You may stick to product marketing, product management, or software engineering, and that's okay.

But it's important to go through the exercise of trying to do developer relations in all its forms. Once you do that, you will learn a lot. You have to do developer relations to understand what it's about, and then you can decide whether it's something for you or not. That, in my view, is how you can get started.

**Geertjan Wielenga**: Thank you, Bruno Borges.

## 32

> *Developers have gone from being seen as people with thick-rimmed glasses who build software and sit behind a bunch of managers to being a primary audience that companies want to target.*

# Jono
# Bacon

# Introducing Jono Bacon

Jono Bacon is a community and collaboration strategy consultant, author of *People Powered: How Communities Can Supercharge Your Business, Brand, and Teams* and *The Art of Community*, a columnist for Forbes, and the founder of the Community Leadership Summit. His clients include Deutsche Bank, The Linux Foundation, HackerOne, The Executive Centre, and many others, and he is a regular keynote speaker about community strategy, collaboration, and organizational leadership. Find Jono on Twitter: @jonobacon.

---

**Geertjan Wielenga**: It seems to me that this whole profession has exploded over the last three or four years; would you agree with that?

## The history of developer communities

**Jono Bacon**: I would. A lot of the work has actually been happening for a long time, but we now have a clearer understanding of it and the branding of it has changed. People have been building developer communities for as long as computers have been around. These communities were forged at universities and in local groups before the internet was around, but the internet has provided the ability for this to happen on a much broader scale.

Especially in the earlier days of open source, we saw developer communities forming.

I think what's happened, especially in the last couple of years, is that the value of a developer as a pivotal decision-maker in a company has become better known. Developers have gone from being seen as people with thick-rimmed glasses who build software and sit behind a bunch of managers to being a primary audience that companies want to target. Targeting developers through developer relations has become a thing. I don't think that the patterns have changed massively; it's just that developer relations has now got the attention of more senior decision-makers.

How developer relations is implemented differs very widely. In some companies, you've got developer relations people who are really senior members of staff, while in other companies, they are fairly junior and work in marketing or as individual contributors. We've got a pretty broad scope, but it's still early days.

**Geertjan Wielenga**: In what sense is it still early days?

**Jono Bacon**: When new professions form, in the beginning, companies don't know what to do with them. There isn't a lot of structure and predictability about them.

I'll give an example. Back when I started my career, in the late '90s, I always knew that I wanted to work in communities, but the idea of a community manager wasn't a thing back then in tech. It was around here and there, and there'll always be someone who says they were doing it before anyone else, but as a general role, it wasn't really a thing. I'd never heard of the term "community manager" when I applied for the Ubuntu community manager job at Canonical, for example.

Over the years, community management has become a profession, but at first, nobody knew where it should fit into an organization, where it should report in to, what the value was that you should see from it, what support you needed to give to that person, and so on. Since then, the idea of how a community manager in open source works has become much better understood.

I think we're seeing a similar situation now with developer relations. Developer relations, I would argue, in its current form in most companies, tends to be a bit more of a tech evangelism job. It varies; some people do more in-depth versions of developer relations, such as managing infrastructure and products, but, as a general rule, I think we're still in the early stages for this particular type of job. In the next five years, I predict how the job is managed, who it reports into, what kind of value you expect to see, and so on, will become more solidified.

**Geertjan Wielenga**: In my case, I came from a law background and ended up working as a technical writer. That's the kind of function you had in the late '90s that translates to developer relations today. In fact, on LinkedIn, I changed all of my job roles to "tech evangelist" or "developer advocate." That's what I was really doing; it just wasn't called that back then. Do you agree?

**Jono Bacon**: Yes. We see these patterns forming. As the branding and the market understanding of that role adjusts, you can then look back and say, "Okay, that's what I was doing."

> *"As humans, we need to be able to put things into logical boxes; that's what we're seeing, to a reasonable degree, with developer relations."*
>
> —Jono Bacon

I find developer relations interesting because I see it as a subset of community management. It's always difficult because every company is different, but we're all building engagement with people. Developer relations is about building engagement with a subset of people: developers. As humans, we need to be able to put things into logical boxes; that's what we're seeing, to a reasonable degree, with developer relations.

**Geertjan Wielenga**: If there's one characteristic that is common to all the developer advocates or tech evangelists that I've ever known, it's extreme flexibility. On the one hand, you're coding and on the other hand, you're explaining things. You're actually meeting customers alongside sales and pre-sales people and coming in from a technical angle. You're also engaging with high-level people in your organization to explain what's going on. Would you agree that if you don't enjoy this variety, this may not be a good role for you?

**Jono Bacon**: I would mostly agree with that, except that one of the problems that I see with my clients as a consultant is a lack of consistency in terms of what developer relations people, community managers, and directors of community specifically do.

I think it depends on the company. For example, a developer relations person or community manager joins a company and they start doing the things that they're familiar with, which they believe add value. They start blogging, doing social media, going to meetups, designing swag, and incentivizing and awarding their community members. Executives in the company look at the work that they're doing and say, "That's great, but what this isn't doing is moving the needle that we want to see being moved." This needle may have some relevance to revenue, growth, or market adoption.

What happens is you end up with a really awkward situation where the executives have got a point, because they hired this person with a certain set of expectations, but also, the individual has got a point, because they're doing what they feel that they were hired for. There's a disconnect. Clarity about these roles is important to reduce that disconnect, because, to make a sweeping statement, most people aren't particularly great at setting expectations. This lack of clarity can sometimes generate a bit of angst.

**Geertjan Wielenga**: Mary Thengvall's book, *The Business Value of Developer Advocacy*, is the crux of all these discussions about what the real value-add is and not moving the needle in terms of revenue. Do you think that's valid?

## Making a connection with revenue

**Jono Bacon**: I think it depends. There are some companies that I've worked with, and currently work with, that see community management or developer relations as having a direct connection to revenue. That's a red flag for me.

However, I don't subscribe to the viewpoint that this work shouldn't have any connection to revenue, because I think everything in a business should have a connection to revenue in some form. However, the questions are how direct that connection is, what the expectations that relate to it are, and how it is measured and quantified.

One company that I worked with didn't explicitly say this, but it clearly wanted to see the revenue connection between downloads of its product and customer sales. I said, "You really don't want to connect those two pieces of data; you're going to be ultimately dissatisfied."

Where the company needed to get to was an understanding that if you're focused on building a community, which is about creating awareness and helping people to engage with your product and team, you need to know the value of this work within the context of revenue (such as customer success, enhanced support, and so on).

There needs to be a clear path to overall value for a company or it will struggle to understand why it should fund this work. I don't think it's as simple as saying, "Community managers shouldn't have anything to do with revenue," because other people in the company are going to start questioning why that area is being invested in at all.

The key thing is that value can be either indirect or associative. Sales, for example, has a direct connection to revenue. Marketing people design the funnel that ultimately will have a direct connection to revenue. Community managers and developer relations people, meanwhile, invest in relationships and customer success.

If you build long-lasting, sustainable relationships, what you get is more revenue because people want to refer your product to other people, and that brings more customers in.

> *"Some people have a holier-than-thou attitude that their work should have nothing to do with revenue."*
>
> —*Jono Bacon*

The problem I have is that some people have a holier-than-thou attitude that their work should have nothing to do with revenue. I find that to be a rather unrealistic perspective to take. You need to set the expectations very clearly.

**Geertjan Wielenga**: Could developer relations be seen as an extension of customer support, then?

**Jono Bacon**: Yes. That goes back to my point earlier about the roles and responsibilities, and how most people aren't very good at setting expectations. I think, frankly, we all suck at it. We need to go in and tell people the value that we'll be creating.

**Geertjan Wielenga**: Would you say that burnout can happen if the developer relations person is trying to chase things that they can't possibly achieve?

**Jono Bacon**: Yes, I agree with that. I mentioned earlier that relatively new professions don't come with much security, workflow, method, and so on. We've seen this, for example, with the software development life cycle.

Back in the late '90s, there wasn't really a consistent software development life cycle.

There was a lot of variance in how people built software. Now we have code that lives in repositories, people submit contributions via pull requests, and we've got continuous integration and deployment, rapid release cycles, automated testing, and so on. All of these things are the staples of how good software is made and made consistently. It's taken us years to figure that out with software engineering.

Developer relations and community management don't have that structure: there's no single way of doing it. When I wrote *People Powered* and *The Art of Community*, I wasn't saying that there is only one way of doing it; I was saying, "This is my approach."

Right now, because the profession's relatively young, people who come into it can experience burnout. They try their best to figure out how to offer the most value, but because there isn't a model, sometimes those expectations are not aligned. That can freak people out and create a stressful environment for them. I am confident that this will get better with time.

**Geertjan Wielenga**: One of the key attributes for someone who wants to be involved in this domain is passion. Some people care so much about the specific community that they've been building, or specific tech, that they care more about it than the company for which they're actually doing that work. Have you seen problems occur when the company then pivots in its direction?

**Jono Bacon**: Yes, I have. Where it gets tricky is when you're an ambassador in some ways. You're there to represent the interests of your company and your community.

That can sometimes result in some pretty difficult discussions. Most people in a company, frankly, are not going to understand how communities are built and operate, but many people in the community aren't going to understand the dynamics of how that company operates.

The company always has more information. Even if you are the most developer-friendly community in the world, the company will know its customers better and will also know about certain constraints that it can't talk about publicly. Therefore, to me, the very best people that do this kind of work always look at how they can keep both sides honest and how they can consistently add value to both sides.

Some people will always say, almost as an ethical priority, that the community is their number one focus and the company has to fall in line. If you take that approach, you're going to potentially limit your employment options. I don't think it makes you unethical to say that you need to consistently look at how to build a healthy relationship with both sides of the fence, and frankly, to break the fence down and create an environment where the divisions between company and community are not so strict. At the end of the day, you're getting a paycheck from the company, so you have to provide value to it. But you also need to be in a position where you can go to the company and say that a given decision is a poor one and the team needs to look at it from the perspective of the community that is impacted. This all requires careful balance.

When I meet clients, I often say, "Part of the reason that I'm here is to deliver information that may be uncomfortable to hear, but it will better the relationship between your company and your community."

It has to go both ways. There were times at Canonical when members of the community were just being ridiculous. I'd get on the phone with them and say, "Look, I'm talking to you as a friend and not an employee of Canonical; you're being unnecessarily aggressive right now and not accomplishing what you want to accomplish with this approach."

You've got to put yourself in the position where you can do that and you need trust for that. If the company doesn't believe that you're acting in the interests of both parties, it's very difficult to have those conversations. If your number one priority is always the community, it's very difficult to build that kind of trust with the company, and vice versa.

**Geertjan Wielenga**: Especially if you're working within a large vendor's community, it's very easy to get completely dislocated from that company and be too focused on your community. Would you agree?

**Jono Bacon**: I think it's really hard, particularly in the early stages of your career. You probably have a lot more imposter syndrome and you're nervous about what you're doing. It takes time to have the confidence to go up to your company and say, "We're not doing the right thing." If anyone reading this doesn't feel ready, that's normal. You'll get there.

**Geertjan Wielenga**: Thank you, Jono Bacon.

# Other Books You May Enjoy

If you enjoyed this book, you may be interested in this book by Packt:

**DevOps Paradox**

Viktor Farcic

ISBN: 978-1-78913-363-9

- Introducing DevOps into real-world, chaotic business environments
- Deciding between adopting cutting edge tools or sticking with tried-and-tested methods
- Initiating necessary business change without positional power
- Managing and overcoming fear of change in DevOps implementations
- Anticipating future trends in DevOps and how to prepare for them

- Getting the most from Kubernetes, Docker, Puppet, Chef, and Ansible
- Creating the right incentives for DevOps success across an organization
- The impact of new techniques, such as Lambda, serverless, and schedulers, on DevOps practice

## Architects of Intelligence

Martin Ford

ISBN: 978-1-78913-151-2

- The state of modern AI
- How AI will evolve and the breakthroughs we can expect
- Insights into the minds of AI founders and leaders
- How and when we will achieve human-level AI
- The impact and risks associated with AI and its impact on society and the economy

## Python Interviews

Mike Driscoll

ISBN: 978-1-78839-908-1

- How successful programmers think
- The history of Python
- Insights into the minds of the Python core team
- Trends in Python programming

## Leave a review - let other readers know what you think

Please share your thoughts on this book with others by leaving a review on the site that you bought it from. If you purchased the book from Amazon, please leave us an honest review on this book's Amazon page. This is vital so that other potential readers can see and use your unbiased opinion to make purchasing decisions, we can understand what our customers think about our products, and our authors can see your feedback on the title that they have worked with Packt to create. It will only take a few minutes of your time, but is valuable to other potential customers, our authors, and Packt. Thank you!

# Index

# S

## T

# Index

# Index

## Y

# Pack‹t›

Printed in Poland
by Amazon Fulfillment
Poland Sp. z o.o., Wrocław

59971346R10439